T0230163

Lecture Notes in Computer Science 853

Edited by G. Goos, J. Hartmanis and J. van Leeuwen

Advisory Board: W. Brauer   D. Gries   J. Stoer

Kevin Bolding   Lawrence Snyder (Eds.)

Parallel Computer Routing and Communication

First International Workshop, PCRCW '94
Seattle, Washington, USA, May 16-18, 1994
Proceedings

Springer-Verlag

Berlin Heidelberg New York
London Paris Tokyo
Hong Kong Barcelona
Budapest

Series Editors

Gerhard Goos
Universität Karlsruhe
Postfach 69 80, Vincenz-Priessnitz-Straße 1, D-76131 Karlsruhe, Germany

Juris Hartmanis
Department of Computer Science, Cornell University
4130 Upson Hall, Ithaka, NY 14853, USA

Jan van Leeuwen
Department of Computer Science, Utrecht University
Padualaan 14, 3584 CH Utrecht, The Netherlands

Volume Editors

Kevin Bolding
Lawrence Snyder
Department of Computer Science and Engineering, University of Washington
FR-35, Seattle, WA 98195, USA

CR Subject Classification (1991): C.2, C.1.2, B.4.3, C.4, F.2.2

ISBN 3-540-58429-3 Springer-Verlag Berlin Heidelberg New York

CIP data applied for

© Springer-Verlag Berlin Heidelberg 1994
Printed in Germany

Typesetting: Camera-ready by author
SPIN: 10478946   45/3140-543210 - Printed on acid-free paper

Preface

Due to advances in both hardware and systems design over the last decade, the power of parallel computers has leaped forward dramatically. The backbone of a massively parallel computer is the interconnection network that ties all of the processors together into one coherent machine. Although both interest in networks and routing, as well as the technology itself, has grown very quickly in recent years, there has been little cohesiveness to the routing/interconnection network community. For this reason, the first Parall Computer Routing and Communication Workshop (PCRCW) was formed.

PCRCW '94, held at the University of Washington in Seattle on May 16, 17, and 18, 1994 had three primary goals:

1. To bring researchers from the routing/network community together.
2. To provide a platform for the presentation of the latest work in interconnection networks.
3. To produce a proceedings to disseminate the latest results to the entire research community.

The first goal was accomplished at the workshop, with over 60 attendees, approximately 40% of whom were from industry, with the remaining 60% from academia. The panels, banquet, and forum provided many opportunities for people to meet others in the community. The second goal was satisfied with the invited keynote address by Duncan Lawrie and 23 other talks covering the papers presented in this volume. Finally, the third goal is satisfied with the publication of these proceedings.

This volume includes 23 regular papers, covering areas from details of hardware design to proofs of theoretical issues. There are also many papers dealing with the performance of various adaptive routing schemes, new network topologies, network interfaces and fault-tolerance issues.

We would like to thank the many researchers and attendees who contributed to this successful workshop. The members of the program committee deserve extra thanks for helping in the organization of the workshop and the selection of papers to include. Clifford Lau and the US Office of Naval Research are especially appreciated for their support of this workshop. Finally, we wish to thank Kay Beck for handling the local arrangements and organizational details of the workshop in a nearly glitch-free manner.

Seattle, July 1994

Kevin Bolding
Lawrence Snyder

Program Committee

Lawrence Snyder, Univerity of Washington (chair)

Kevin Bolding, University of Washington
Andrew Chien, University of Illinois
William Dally, Massachusetts Institute of Technology
Smaragda Konstantinidou, IBM T. J. Watson Research Center
Burton Smith, Tera Computer

Contents

Do Faster Routers Imply Faster Communication?

Vijay Karamcheti and Andrew A. Chien

Department of Computer Science
University of Illinois at Urbana-Champaign
1304 W. Springfield Avenue, Urbana, IL 61801
{*vijayk,achien*}*@cs.uiuc.edu*

Abstract. Despite significant improvements in network interfaces and software messaging layers, software communication overhead still dominates the hardware routing cost in most parallel systems. In this study, we identify the sources of this overhead by relating user communication services to particular network hardware features. Based on a detailed analysis of the *active messages* layer on the CM-5, we assign the software messaging cost to specific user communication services and network features. Our study shows that 50–70% of the software cost of messaging can be attributed to providing end-to-end flow control, in-order delivery, and reliable transmission services. This overhead is a direct effect of specific network features – arbitrary delivery order, finite buffering, and limited fault-handling – and is unlikely to be eliminated through improved software implementations. We conclude that reducing this software overhead requires changing the constraints on messaging layers: we propose designing routing networks which replace (or make unnecessary) software to implement user services. Specifically, networks which provide ordering, end-to-end flow control, and hardware-supported fault-tolerance can significantly reduce the end-to-end cost of communication.

1 Introduction

In highly parallel machines, a collection of computing nodes work in concert to solve large application problems. The nodes communicate data and coordinate their efforts by sending and receiving messages through the underlying communication network. Thus, the performance achieved by such machines critically depends on the end-to-end cost of communication mechanisms. There are several contributors to this cost: the routing time, the time to get messages into and out of the network, and software protocol overhead. These times are determined by the design of the routing network and processor-network interface as well as the choice of software protocols.

Recent advances in messaging implementations [25] and improved network interfaces have reduced the software cost of messaging significantly. Despite this progress, software communication overhead still dominates the hardware routing cost. Our study focuses on understanding the relationship between user communication requirements, messaging layer components, and particular hardware features. Messaging layers act as a bridge, enhancing the functionality of the raw hardware to provide higher-level communication abstractions required by user application programs. In this paper, we precisely characterize the software costs in a prototypical messaging layer. This characterization can be viewed as the cost of messaging layer services, or alternately as the cost of particular network hardware features which necessitate software to support those services.

We use the *active messages* layer (CMAM) [25] on the CM-5 [23] for our study. The CMAM message layer is analyzed and extended to expose the cost of communication functionality and network features. We consider several protocols ranging from a base single-packet message send and receive to more sophisticated protocols which provide services such as reliable multi-packet message delivery. These services incur software overhead because they require additional support in the messaging layer for buffer management, in-order delivery, and end-to-end fault tolerance.

Our study shows that this overhead accounts for 50–70% of the total cost and is a direct result of specific network features – arbitrary delivery order, finite buffering, and limited fault-tolerance. Since the CMAM messaging layer is already quite efficient, it is unlikely that this overhead can be reduced any further through improved software implementations. Because user communication requirements are relatively inflexible, we propose designing routing networks which change the constraints on the software layers, facilitating more efficient software (or even eliminating sections of them completely).

The contributions of this paper are:

- A framework which exposes the cost of the messaging layer.
- An assignment of these costs to user services and network hardware features.
- Identification of high level features which, if implemented in hardware, can significantly reduce the software cost of messaging.

The rest of the paper is organized as follows. Section 2 describes the problem context. In Section 3 we list the analysis framework, and justify our approach. Section 4 presents the details of the communication protocols and the corresponding breakdown of costs. Section 5 discusses and generalizes the results. A description of related work appears in Section 6, followed by our conclusions in Section 7.

2 Background

Communication in parallel machines requires both routing hardware and software messaging layers. The hardware provides the basic primitives, and the software layer orchestrates their use to provide application-level communication services. In this section, we discuss typical user communication services, current and likely future routing hardware features, and how a typical messaging layer bridges the two.

2.1 Communication Services

Application programs expect messaging layers to provide a minimal set of communication services. Most messaging layers provide the following services [5, 24, 12]:

- *Message Delivery*
- *Message Ordering*
- *Deadlock/Overflow Safety*
- *Reliable Delivery*

First, the most basic communication service is message delivery. Second, messages between a particular sender and receiver should be delivered in order of transmission. There is some debate about whether this is necessary, but it is both a commonly provided feature and a common programmer's assumption. Third, use of the network should not cause deadlock or the loss of data through some type of buffer overflow, relieving the programmer from explicitly managing the dynamic properties of the parallel system. Finally, messages should be delivered reliably. Most existing parallel machines settle for detecting errors and crashing. Given the expected mean-time-between-failures [15] of such machines, reliable communication is essential to their widespread use. These basic services ease programming concerns about the network for low-level explicit parallel programming (C or FORTRAN and message passing). They also support higher level approaches to programming parallel systems, allowing the compiler to ensure correct program execution without having to explicitly schedule and manage the network resources.

2.2 Routing Hardware Features

Though routing networks in commercial parallel machines (and in research literature) offer varied features, we focus on a few common features which are likely characteristics of future parallel machines and have significant impact on the software messaging layer:

- *Arbitrary Delivery Order*
- *Finite Buffering*
- *Fault-Detection but not Fault Tolerance*

Arbitrary delivery order means that the transmission order of messages between a particular source and destination are not preserved. This may arise because messages pass each other in the network (multipath routing (adaptivity) [9, 20], and virtual channels [7]), or because the network state may be swapped and resumed in a way that does not preserve transmission order (timesharing [10] and process migration). Finite buffering in networks and machines means that flow control is generally necessary for correct execution. Most networks provide deadlock-freedom guarantees based on the assumption that each output eventually absorbs any packets delivered to it, using software to ensure that all node always have enough space to absorb any messages sent to them. Most networks in parallel machines only provide error ' ection, but no error correction capabilities. This means that when a bad packet is detected, the entire computation must be aborted and perhaps the machine will also crash. In the long run, such behavior can incur significant time and computation loss (due to crashes), extra input/output for checkpointing, and poor availability. We believe that future machines will provide reliable message delivery.

2.3 Messaging Layers

Messaging layers bridge the gap between hardware features and communication services. Essentially, the messaging layer uses software protocols to provide any communication services not directly supported in hardware. Figure 1 shows the relationship between elements of a messaging layer, communication services, and network features. Each column in the box shows the messaging layer service needed to support the user requirement above it given the network features below. As can be seen, some of the services require extensive support.

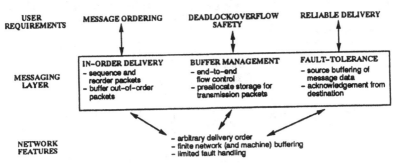

Fig. 1. Messaging layers bridge the gap between user requirements and network features.

Providing message ordering in a network that does not preserve transmission order means that the software must sequence outgoing packets and buffer packets arriving out of order. Ensuring deadlock/overflow safety in networks with finite network and node buffering means that the software must control buffer allocation and message transmission to avoid overcommitment of buffers. Generally this takes the form of preallocating space on the destination prior to transferring the message, ensuring that packets are introduced into the network only when they can be absorbed at the destination. Finally, providing reliable delivery in networks without error correction forces the messaging layer to keep copies of messages in transit. In addition, acknowledgements are also required to release these finite buffer resources.

The next section defines the specific framework used to analyze the costs of the messaging layer features described above.

3   Framework

Despite significant improvements in network interface design and advances in messaging implementations, software overhead of communication still dominates the hardware routing cost. To characterize the reasons for this overhead, we explore costs of communication services in a specific messaging layer, the *active messages* layer [25] on the Thinking Machines CM-5 (Connection Machine Active Messages or CMAM). The CM-5 provides user-level access to the network interface, which is essential for low-cost communication and likely to be a feature of future parallel machines. CMAM is widely recognized an extremely efficient messaging layer; in fact, several commercial vendors are extending their messaging layers to incorporate CMAM features. This efficiency is critical to the study, as our goal is to identify fundamental messaging costs, not that which result from a poor implementation. Further, the availability of the CMAM source code is a pragmatic concern, allowing us to accurately gauge and assign messaging cost, and also to assess the quality of the implementation.

The CM-5 Network To explain how CMAM works, we first describe the CM-5 network interface (NI) and communication mechanisms. The CM-5 NI provides a memory-mapped interface (control registers and network FIFO's) on the processor-memory bus (see Figure 2). A packet is injected into the network by storing the destination node number and data arguments to the NI send buffer. Packets are extracted using LOADs from the receive buffer, while the NI status is queried by loading the control registers.[1]

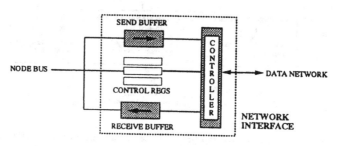

Fig. 2. The CM-5 network interface.

The CM-5 network has a number of features which increase the messaging layer complexity. First, out-of-order delivery requires the messaging layer to sequence and reorder packets. Second, the network interfaces and network have finite buffering, so software buffer management is required. Third, the CM-5 network provides error detection at the packet level, but no error correction, requiring a software protocol to ensure reliable delivery. And finally, the CM-5 network hardware only supports packets with five 32-bit words, so a typical message is broken into many packets, further increasing the software overhead.

CMAM: A Simple Messaging Layer The basic communication primitive provided by CMAM is an active message: a message with an associated small amount of computation (in the form of a handler) at the receiving end. The current CMAM implementation polls the network to accept messages.[2] We use two CMAM interfaces in our study. The first interface provides an active message which carries up to four words of user data and is implemented by the CMAM_4 function at the source, and CMAM_request_poll, CMAM_handle_left, and CMAM_got_left functions at the destination. These functions provide a minimal layer over the raw hardware for injecting and extracting packets from the network. The second interface supports bulk memory-to-memory transfers, and is implemented using CMAM_xfer function which splits up the transfer into a sequence of hardware packets at the source, and CMAM_handle_left_xfer function which reassembles the packets at the destination.

---

[1] While this is not the most efficient type of network interface [13, 8, 4], it has the significant virtue that no changes to the processor are required. Many researchers believe that this type of interface is basically representative of future network interfaces.

[2] The CM-5 NI also supports an interrupt-driven interface for reception; however, the cost is very high for interrupts in the SPARC processor.

4 Analysis of messaging layer

Using CMAM, we examine the costs for implementing typical communication protocols, at each stage relating the measured costs to the network features. To estimate the costs of different portions of the CMAM layer, we use dynamic instruction counts of the CMAM assembly code (some of CMAM is coded in assembly and the rest was generated from the original C code using gcc -O2). Execution paths which minimize the instruction count are chosen, so our measurements are an optimistic estimate of the actual software overhead.

Although actual execution time might be a better metric for characterizing communication cost, we use instruction counts consistently throughout the paper. There are two reasons for this: First, obtaining instruction counts is much simpler than counting actual cycles. This is because the cycle counts depend on details such as write buffers, bus synchronization, memory refresh, and other concerns. Second, the instruction counts represent a more useful and portable characterization of the messaging costs. While the times for each instruction may vary depending on the implementation, it appears likely that the instruction counts will be substantially similar across machines with memory-mapped network interfaces.

We consider the implementation of three communication protocols:

1. **Single-packet delivery** sends and receives a single-packet message.
2. **Finite-sequence multi-packet delivery** sends and receives a fixed-size user message which consists of a several hardware packets.
3. **Indefinite-sequence multi-packet delivery** sends and receives an indefinite sequence of packets, corresponding to an ordered stream of communication.

Single-packet delivery is the cheapest kind of communication possible in the CM-5 – a four word datagram packet. The multi-packet protocols have a base cost based on single packet deliveries but incur additional overhead to support user communication requirements. Finite-sequence multi-packet delivery incurs the costs of buffer management and in-order delivery to support larger messages, preallocating buffers for all injected packets and sequencing and reordering the received packets. Indefinite-sequence multi-packet delivery sees the additional cost of in-order delivery for buffering out-of-order packets at the destination. Both multi-packet protocols also have additional overhead for ensuring reliable transmission.

We now examine these protocols in detail: for each protocol, we first give details of the implementation, and then a breakdown of the measured costs.

4.1 Single-packet delivery

This protocol consists of sending and receiving a message consisting of a single packet. The packet is sent using the CMAM_4 function, and received using a combination of the CMAM_request_poll, CMAM_handle_left, and CMAM_got_left functions. The receiver functions, respectively, check for any outstanding packets, receive waiting packets, and invoke the user handlers for received packets.

Table 1 presents a breakdown of the source and destination costs. Source costs include setting up the network interface (NI), writing user data, and polling a NI

Description	Source	Destination
Call/Return	3	10
NI setup	5	–
Writing to NI	2	–
Reading from NI	–	3
Checking NI status	7	12
Control flow	3	2
	20	27

Table 1. Instruction counts for single-packet delivery.

status register which confirms the send as well as tests for presence of any incoming packets. The destination overhead includes polling the NI to check for any waiting packets, extracting the packet data, vectoring on the hardware message tag, and then invoking the user handler. Thus, single-packet transfer in the CMAM layer is extremely efficient, costing only 47 instructions, of which 34 instructions are dedicated to accessing the network interface. This number is essentially the minimum required to interface with the hardware on a CM-5. However, the single-packet protocol does not meet any of the requirements for communication services – the packets are not ordered, nor are they deadlock/overflow safe, nor are they delivered reliably. Further, communication can only be done in units of four data words.

4.2 Finite-sequence multi-packet delivery

This protocol supports messages of arbitrary size and transfers data from a buffer in the source memory to a buffer at the destination. This protocol is implemented using the CMAM_xfer_N and CMAM_handle_left_xfer functions, and consists of six steps (see Figure 3). The sender first transmits a buffer allocation request to the receiver (Step 1), which allocates a buffer and associates it with a communication segment (Step 2). On receiving the response (Step 3), the sender initiates a sequence of single-packet transfers (Step 4). The receiver node stores the packet data into the allocated segment. On completion of the transfer, the receiver frees the communication segment (Step 5), and sends back an acknowledgement packet (Step 6).

The protocol cost has four components: base single-packet transfers (Step 4), buffer management (Steps 1,2,3 and 5), in-order delivery, and fault-tolerance (Step 6). Single-packet transfers move data from source to destination, contributing a single-packet delivery and reception cost for each transfer. The base cost also reflects the additional LOADs/STOREs required for the memory-to-memory transfer.

Buffer management provides deadlock and overflow safety by preallocating buffer space for messages on their destination nodes. The preallocation cost involves two single-packet deliveries (request and response), and the cost of associating a segment number with the target buffer. The buffer also needs to be deallocated at the end of the transfer (to permit reuse).

In-order delivery ensures that the data gets written at the correct position in the destination's buffer. Its cost arises from the following protocol: each packet carries an offset into the target buffer where its data should be stored. The destination

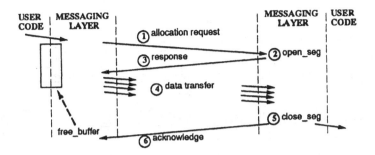

Fig. 3. Protocol for finite-sequence multi-packet delivery.

extracts this offset and updates the communication segment count associated with the transfer. The source overheads include incrementing and storing the offset for each packet, while the receiver overheads include a LOAD to extract the offset and operations to decrement the count. In-order delivery support masks the arbitrary packet delivery order inherent in the CM-5 network.

Fault tolerance ensures that a copy of the data is maintained at the source pending acknowledgement of successful reception. Its costs are that of a single-packet delivery acknowledging successful completion of transfer (source buffering has no cost in our accounting since it can be implemented by not releasing the original message buffer until the acknowledgement is received).

These four components of finite-sequence multi-packet delivery costs are shown on the left in Tables 2 and 3 for two message sizes: small (16 words) and large (1024 words). To obtain the best possible execution path, we assume there is no other communication going on at the source and destination nodes. We observe that buffer management contributes 50% of the total transfer costs for small messages because of the round-trip handshake, but has negligible impact on the communication cost for large messages. Despite this, additional messaging layer costs still account for ~10% of the costs in the latter case. In-order delivery does not contribute as much to the total cost since the requirements on ordering are relaxed: instead of specifying an exact order of arrival, the only user requirement is that the data be placed in the target buffer in order. Knowing the total count of expected packets allows this functionality to be provided cheaply. As we will see in the next section, sequencing can be quite expensive if this information is not available. Fault-tolerance accounts for ~10% of the total cost for the small transfer, but has negligible impact on the costs of the large transfer.

4.3 Indefinite-sequence multi-packet delivery

This protocol supports the sending and receiving of an indefinite length sequence of hardware packets between a pair of nodes. These packets are all part of a larger logical user communication. Such a communication pattern is normally associated with static channels between a pair of user processes (sockets) and is characterized by an indefinite amount of communication through the channels.

Figure 4 shows the protocol steps. The sender first buffers the user message

Message size = 16 words

Finite-sequence multi-packet delivery

Feature	Source	Destination	Total
Base Cost	91	90	181
Buffer Mgmt.	47	101	148
In-order Del.	8	13	21
Fault-toler.	27	20	47
Total	173	224	397

Indefinite-sequence multi-packet delivery

Feature	Source	Destination	Total
Base Cost	80	69	149
Buffer Mgmt.	–	–	–
In-order Del.	20	116	136
Fault-toler.	116	80	196
Total	216	265	481

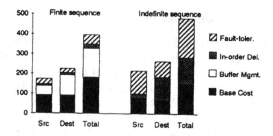

Table 2. Multi-packet delivery: packet size = 4 words, message size = 16 words.

Message size = 1024 words

Finite-sequence multi-packet delivery

Feature	Source	Destination	Total
Base Cost	5635	4626	10261
Buffer Mgmt.	47	101	148
In-order Del.	512	769	1281
Fault-toler.	27	20	47
Total	6221	5516	11737

Indefinite-sequence multi-packet delivery

Feature	Source	Destination	Total
Base Cost	5120	3597	8717
Buffer Mgmt.	–	–	–
In-order Del.	1280	7424	8704
Fault-toler.	7424	5120	12544
Total	13824	16141	29965

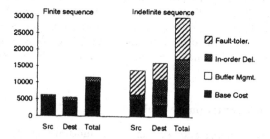

Table 3. Multi-packet delivery: packet size = 4 words, message size = 1024 words.

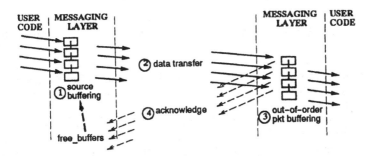

Fig. 4. Indefinite-sequence multi-packet protocol.

(Step 1) (to support retransmission if required), and then sends it using single-packet transfers (Step 2). The receiver node buffers all out-of-order packets (Step 3), initiating the appropriate user handler for each packet arriving in its transmission order. Since the entire transmission may be very large, each packet has its own acknowledgement (Step 4), which allows source storage to be released.

As in Section 4.2, this protocol also has four components contributing to the total cost: base single-packet transfers, buffer management, in-order delivery, and fault-tolerance. The base cost consists of single-packet delivery and reception costs for each transfer.

Buffer management may be required for three reasons: to buffer user messages at the source, to handle out-of-order packets at the receiver, and to store user data into a receiver buffer. We have chosen to account for the source buffering costs as part of the fault-tolerance overheads, and the out-of-order packet buffering as part of the in-order delivery costs. Further, since the user view of register-to-register communication eliminates the need for a separate buffer, buffer management has negligible cost in this protocol[3]

In-order delivery incurs a transmission overhead of sequence numbers and requires the buffering of out-of-order packets at the destination since there is no space allocated for them elsewhere. Note that unlike the finite-sequence multi-packet protocol, one cannot exploit information about the number of expected packets to reduce sequencing costs.

Fault-tolerance costs arise from source buffering and acknowledgement messages. Source buffering contributes additional STOREs to the cost, and supports retransmission in the presence of faults. Each acknowledgement message incurs the cost of a single-packet delivery. For larger (and more predictable) packet sequences, this per-packet cost can be reduced by employing group acknowledgements (at the cost of reserving source buffers for a longer amount of time).

These components of indefinite-sequence multi-packet delivery costs are shown on the right in Tables 3 for the two message sizes of 16 and 1024 words. Message sizes correspond to the total data volume transmitted. To measure in-order delivery costs, we assume that half of the packets arrive out of order. We observe from the

---

[3] Some systems may include buffer management into this protocol to provide overflow safety. This only introduces additional buffer management overhead, but does not affect the cost of the other features.

costs that the in-order delivery functionality accounts for > 50% of the end-to-end costs, and this fraction is independent of the total volume of data transmitted.

The breakdown of costs for the two multi-packet delivery protocols shows that a large fraction of the end-to-end cost is attributable to communication services – in-order delivery, deadlock and overflow safety, and fault-tolerance – and accounts for 50–70% of the total cost in all situations except large finite-sequence multi-packet transfers. Conversely, this functionality can also be viewed as the cost of specific network features – arbitrary delivery order, finite network and node buffering, and limited fault-handling capabilities. This suggests that the end-to-end communication cost can be significantly improved if the underlying network provides more sophisticated functionality, replacing its implementation in software.

5 Discussion

No single study can address all of the issues. In this study, we have chosen to focus on basic delivery, ordering, buffer management, and fault tolerance, while putting aside issues of protection and scheduling. Clearly, any solution which reduces messaging overhead to the level of tens of instructions must deal with these issues.

Studying a particular network, network interface, and messaging layer limits the applicability of our conclusions to a range of similar systems. These concerns can only be mitigated by studying a system that is as representative as possible so the conclusions are broadly applicable. We believe that CMAM on the CM-5 is representative of many future messaging systems. However, in the following paragraphs we consider the effect on our results of modest changes in machine architecture.

Larger packet sizes CMAM on the first version of the CM-5 network interface supports four data words per packet; however, other parallel machines and even the second version of the CM-5 network interface support larger packet sizes. Figure 5 shows the variation in messaging overhead for a message size of 1024 words as the packet size is varied from 4–128 words (assuming that the rest of the network mechanisms remain the same). It is clear that for indefinite-sequence multi-packet delivery, the messaging overhead constitutes a significant fraction over the entire range. For finite-sequence multi-packet deliveries, this overhead is lower, but still significant, accounting for 9–11% of the total cost.

Direct memory access (DMA) hardware One notable shortcoming of the CM-5 network hardware is the lack of any DMA capability. While DMA can reduce the cost of moving large amounts of data, it is unlikely that it would give much benefit for the packet sizes we considered (4–128 words). Further, as with other improvements to the network interface, it would affect only the base cost portions of our instruction counts. If the base cost is reduced, that increases the importance of the costs in the rest of the messaging layer.

Implications for Network Design One important contribution of this study is to concretely establish the cost and benefit of a variety of network features. In many

12

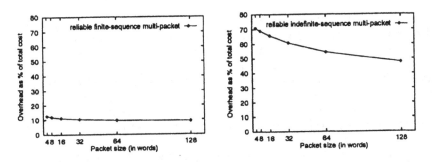

Fig. 5. Messaging layer overhead versus packet size for 1024 words of communication.

cases, there is a tension between optimizing routing performance, and improving end-to-end communication performance. As we have seen in this study, some features which produce improved routing performance may incur unacceptable software costs. For example, a number of designs have proposed out-of-order delivery in order to improve network routing performance (randomization [18, 1] or adaptive routing [20, 7, 9]). Our results show clearly that a significant cost can be incurred for packet sequencing and reordering, so the benefits of out-of-order delivery for the network must be weighed against the software costs of such behavior. Because the software overhead is generally much larger than the hardware routing time, in many cases, the overheads of such features will outweigh their benefits.

Another perspective is that our results point out where "high level" network features can be of most benefit. Such features can eliminate the need for parts of the messaging layer, reducing communication cost. Specifically, if a network could provide in-order delivery, end-to-end flow control, and reliable delivery, it would obviate much of the need for a messaging layer, reducing the messaging cost to the basic data movement cost. Researchers in the routing community are beginning to address such concerns; several recent projects (e.g., Compressionless Routing [17]) provide all three of these features, albeit at some cost.

Communication Cost versus Latency In this study, we have focused on instruction counts as the primary measure of communication cost (performance). Latency is a reasonable alternative performance metric, but is hard to measure in a portable fashion because it depends on a host of low-level system detail as well as software policies such as scheduling. For cases where software overhead dominates, instruction counts are indicative of communication latency.

6 Related Work

A great deal of attention has been focused on the design of interconnection networks, network interfaces, and even fast messaging layers. The main distinction is that our study seeks to implement high level software communication primitives without compromising on performance or functionality.

Research on interconnection networks has focused primarily on optimizing for bandwidth and latency performance metrics [21, 6, 22, 10]. While these are certainly important attributes, much less energy has gone into exploring what impact advanced network features (adaptive routing, virtual channels) have on network interface complexity and software overhead. Our work addresses some of these issues.

Research on network interfaces has focused primarily on reducing message injection (and reception) overhead [13, 8, 19, 4] or offloading the communication onto a coprocessor [14, 16, 3]. Such efforts are complementary to our goal of software protocol overhead reduction. Improvements in network interface can reduce the basic communication cost in our studies. While reducing the basic cost is important, as can be seen from our studies, reducing the software protocol overhead is equally important. Further, reductions in the basic cost will increase the importance of reducing software protocol overhead.

Researchers have explored a variety of approaches for reducing the cost of messaging layers. While substantial progress has been made, much of it has been made at the cost of reducing functionality. For example, techniques for speeding interprocess communication [2, 11, 26] have resorted to lower level (and more risky) communication primitives to achieve high performance. In parallel systems, a number of reduced messaging layers have also been developed. In fact, active messages, the basis for our study, is one such reduced layer. The lowest level primitive – single packet send – is widely used, but is unsafe because no flow control is performed. While reduced functionality layers may be a necessary expedient, a better long term solution would involve full functionality communication primitives and high performance.

7 Conclusions

We have described a study to measure the end-to-end costs of communication by analyzing the costs incurred by a prototypical messaging layer, specifically the CMAM layer running on the CM-5. Since messaging layers must bridge the gap between the hardware and user communication requirements, the costs in a messaging layer often reflect the costs of particular network features. Our study provides a piecewise breakdown of the communication costs and an assignment of that cost the various network features and communication services that incur it.

Our results show that 50–70% of end-to-end messaging cost is attributable to arbitrary order of packet delivery, finite buffering, and limited fault-handling capabilities. And although the CMAM layer is extremely efficient – virtually all of the remaining time is spent copying data to and from the network interfaces – the cost of transmitting a 16-word message is between 285 and 481 instructions with the network features accounting for a major share. While improvements to the CM-5's network interface are possible, paradoxically, such improvements will only exacerbate the situation, causing these features to constitute an even larger percentage of the cost.

There is often a tradeoff between optimizing routing performance and reducing software overhead. As we have seen, some network features may well incur software overheads that outweigh the features' benefits. Because the software overhead is often a dominant contributor, network designers must also consider how their decisions affect the software messaging layers. One possible direction for this work is to broaden the study to a number of parallel systems. Another avenue for future work is to design hardware which provides functionality that eliminates the need for or simplifies the messaging layer.

Acknowledgements

The authors would like to thank Jae-Hoon Kim and John Plevyak for participating in several discussions about the messaging protocols described in the paper.

The research described in this paper was supported in part by National Science Foundation grant CCR-9209336, Office of Naval Research grants N00014-92-J-1961 and N00014-93-1-1086, and National Aeronautics and Space Administration grant NAG 1-613.

References

1. G. Alverson, R. Alverson, D. Callahan, B. Koblenz, A. Porterfield, and B. Smith. Exploiting heterogeneous parallelism on a multithreaded multiprocessor. In *Proceedings of the 6th ACM Interational Conference on Supercomputing*, 1992.

2. B. N. Bershad, T. E. Anderson, E. D. Lazowska, and H. M. Levy. User-level interprocess communication for shared memory multiprocessors. *ACM Transactions on Computer Systems*, 9(2):175–198, May 1991.

3. M. A. Blumrich, Kai Li, Richard Alpert, Cezary Dubnicki, and Edward W. Felten. Virtual memory mapped network interface for the shrimp multicomputer. In *Proceeding of the International Symposium on Computer Architecture*, April 1994.

4. S. Borkar, R. Cohn, G. Cox, S. Gleason, T. Gross, H. T. Kung, M. Lam, B. Moore, C. Peterson, J. Pieper, L. Rankin, P. S. Tseng, J. Sutton, J. Urbanski, and J. Webb. iWarp: An integrated solution to high-speed parallel computing. In *Proceedings of Supercomputing '88*, pages 330–341. IEEE Press, 1988. Orlando, Florida.

5. V. Cerf and R. Kahn. A protocol for packet network interconnection. *IEEE Transactions on Communications*, 1974.

6. W. Dally and C. Seitz. Deadlock-free message routing in multiprocessor interconnection networks. *IEEE Transactions on Computers*, C-36(5), 1987.

7. W. J. Dally and H. Aoki. Deadlock-free adaptive routing in multicomputer networks usin g virtual channels. *IEEE Transactions on Parallel and Distributed Systems*, 4(4):466–74, April 1993.

8. W. J. Dally, A. Chien, S. Fiske, W. Horwat, J. Keen, M. Larivee, R. Lethin, P. Nuth, S. Wills, P. Carrick, and G. Fyler. The J-Machine: A fine-grain concurrent computer. In *Information Processing 89, Proceedings of the IFIP Congress*, pages 1147–1153, August 1989.

9. J. Duato. On the design of deadlock-free adaptive routing algorithms for multicomputers: design methodologies. In *Proceedings of Parallel Architectures and Languages Europe*, 1991.

10. C. Leiserson et al. The network architecture of the Connection Machine CM-5. In *Proceedings of the Symposium on Parallel Algorithms and Architectures*, 1992.

11. Robert Fitzgerald and Richard F. Rashid. The integration of virtual memory management and interprocess communication in accent. *ACM Transactions on Computer Systems*, 4(2):147–77, May 1986.

12. G. Geist and V. Sunderam. The pvm system: Supercomputer level concurrent computation on a heterogeneous network of workstations. In *Proceedings of the Sixth Distributed Memory Computers Conference*, pages 258–61, 1991.

13. D. S. Henry and C. F. Joerg. A tightly-coupled processor-network interface. In *Proceedings of the Fifth International Conference on Architectural Support for Programming Languages an Operating Systems*, pages 111–122, 1992.

14. M. Homewood and M. McLaren. Meiko CS-2 interconnect Elan – Elite design. In *Proceedings of the IEEE Hot Interconnects Symposium*. IEEE TCMM, August 1993.

15. B. Horst. Massively-parallel systems you can trust. In *Proceedings of COMPCON Spring '94*. IEEE Computer Society, IEEE Press, February 1994.

16. Intel Corporation. *Paragon XP/S Product Overview*, 1991.

17. J. Kim, Z. Liu, and A. Chien. Compressionless routing: A framework for adaptive and fault-tolerant routing. In *Proceedings of the International Symposium on Computer Architecture*, April 1994.

18. S. Konstantinidou and L. Snyder. Chaos router: Architecture and performance. In *Proceedings of the International Symposium on Computer Architecture*, pages 212–21, 1991.

19. J. Kubiatowicz and A. Agarwal. Anatomy of a message send in alewife. In *Proceedings of the International Conference on Supercomputing*, 1993.

20. L. Ni and C. Glass. The turn model for adaptive routing. In *Proceedings of the International Symposium on Computer Architecture*, 1992.

21. J. A. Patel. Procesor-memory interconnections for multiprocessors. In *Proceedings of the 6th Annual Symposium on Computer Architecture*, pages 168–177. IEEE Computer Society, IEEE Press, April 1979.

22. C. Seitz and W. Su. A family of routing and communication chips based on the Mosaic. In *Proceedings of the University of Washington Symposium on Integrated Systems*, 1993.

23. Thinking Machines Corporation, Cambridge, Massachusetts. *Connection Machine CM-5, Technical Summary*, November 1992.

24. Thinking Machines Corporation, Cambridge, Massachusetts. *CMMD Reference Manual, V3.0*, May 1993.

25. T. von Eicken, D. Culler, S. Goldstein, and K. Schauser. Active Messages: a mechanism for integrated communication and computation. In *Proceedings of the International Symposium on Computer Architecture*, 1992.

26. M. Young, A. Tevanian, R. Rashid, D. Golub, J. Eppinger, J. Chew, W. Bolosky, D. Black, and R. Baron. The duality of memory and communication in the implementation of a multiprocessor operating system. In *Proceedings of the Eleventh Symposium on Operating Systems Principles*, pages 63–76. ACM, 1987.

Fast Arbitration in Dilated Routers

Matthew E. Becker   Thomas F. Knight, Jr.

Massachusetts Institute of Technology

Abstract. We present a technique, dynamic dilation, which reduces latency in dilated routing components without greatly affecting flexibility. Initially in order to achieve lower latency we limit dilation flexibility, extract parallelism from the arbitration process and pipeline the process into two cycles [ALM90].

For implementation reasons the allocation cycle is required to have some unused latency. Dynamic dilation takes advantage of this latency to allow the dilation of a component to be reconfigured each cycle based on incoming messages. This effectively recovers the flexibility lost by limiting dilation, while retaining extremely low latency.

1 Introduction

The latency and bandwidth of interconnection networks continues to become even more important in the design of parallel computers. As distributed systems get larger and faster, the amount of network traffic increases dramatically. Unless network latency and bandwidth keep pace, overall system performance degrades. However, latency cannot be reduced and bandwidth increased, at the expense of too much flexibility. Examples of desirable flexibility include randomized path selection for fault tolerance or variable dilation for network reconfiguration.

In the case of dilated circuit-switched crossbars, our results from optimizing between latency, bandwidth and flexibility have been promising. The central compromise of flexibility is a limitation on dilation during a single cycle of allocation. This makes path allocation faster, and allows the switch to operate at speeds close to 400 MHz. These results and any that follow come from simulations of a 0.8 micron, 3-metal CMOS process under nominal process corners.

Section 2 of this paper introduces dilated routers and their importance. Section 3 outlines the different styles of dilation. One of these styles, general dilation, is described in detail in section 4 and another, fixed dilation, in section 5. Section 6 reviews the format of messages and the resultant format for pipelining which enables dynamic dilation. In section 7 dynamic dilation is described and compared to the other techniques. Finally the topics and issues presented throughout the paper are reviewed and concluded in Section 8.

2 Role of Dilation in Interconnection Switches

A dilated routing switch is a crossbar routing component used in multistage interconnection networks with the important feature of allowing multiple simultaneous messages to be routed in each logical output direction. An n input switch, for example, having $n/2$ outputs in each logical direction, can route any of the n input messages intended for either logical direction to any of the available $n/2$ physical outputs corresponding to that direction. This switch is said to have a dilation of $n/2$. Normal crossbar components thus have a dilation of 1.

Dilation refers to the number of ports on a particular component which a message can be routed through to get to the *same* place. An important thing to note is that the *same* place could either be a single end point or it could be a set of multiple endpoints which provide the same functionality. An example of multiple endpoints being equivalent logically would be a set of endpoints that provide i/o to the outside world. If a message is willing to pass through any i/o port, then all the i/o endpoints would be the *same*. This distinction of *same* is relevant to the issue of dilation flexibility, because *sameness* can change from message to message.

The use of dilated routing switches is a very effective technique for improving performance of multistage interconnection switches for three important reasons:

- They improve the probability of successful message routing through the switch.
- They enable the construction of multibutterfly networks which further improve statistics and avoid hot spot contention.
- They enable high reliability networks with inherent fault tolerance through source-responsible routing.

2.1 Routing Statistics

Details of the statistical improvements in message routing are more fully analyzed in [KS90], but the key insight can be given here. Imagine a switch with n inputs, where each input is attempting to route to either of $n/2$ outputs. As long as there are less than $n/2$ inputs wanting to route in a given direction, all of the messages will be successfully routed. If more than $n/2$ so desire to route, then any in excess of $n/2$ will fail to route.

Consider now the statistics of the router inputs. It is extremely unlikely that all inputs together wish to route in only one direction. The most probable set of input routings desired is an even split, where half of the inputs route one way while the rest route the other way. The distribution, in fact, is a binomial distribution, with mean $n/2$ and standard deviation $\sqrt{n/2}$. Statistically, almost all messages are successfully routed through such a component, for large n.

Unlike a dilation 1 crossbar component, where the statistics for blocking impose an expected output routing probability of $1 - 1/e$ for a fully loaded set of inputs, a large dilation router can successfully route almost all messages.

The dilation we can use in real routers is limited by the available pin count, and by the necessity, in the final stages of the multistage network, to eventually route to a single final destination or a small set of final destinations – requiring a low dilation router in the final stage.

Statistics further improve dramatically, when compared to other types of networks, for loading even slightly below full loading.

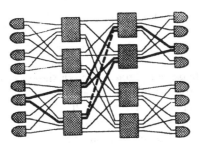

An 8x8 multibutterfly network with a stage of dilation two routers and a stage of dilation one routers. In bold are the equivalent paths from the sixth endpoint to the third endpoint. The dotted line is a blocked connection.

Fig. 1. Multibutterfly with path redundancy

2.2 Multibutterfly Techniques

A significant problem with conventional multistage interconnection networks is the hot spot behavior induced by relatively simple, regular, interconnect patterns such as transpose. In the worst case, the straightforward butterfly network allows only a single message to successfully route due to contention within the switch.

Dilation partially solves this hot spot problem, but the use of the *multibutterfly* interconnection techniques, see Figure 1, essentially eliminates hot spot behavior within the switch. To develop the multibutterfly, we note that in the first stage of an interconnection switch, it makes no difference how we order the outputs which are routed in a logical direction. All of these outputs are logically equivalent. By forming the wiring between the first and second router stages as an expander, we can assure that there are no worst case routing problems. The construction of such multibutterfly networks depends on our ability to construct dilated output routers.

2.3 Fault Tolerance

The availability of multiple router outputs in a single logical direction provides the key idea in construction of wiring and router fault tolerant interconnection networks [LM89] [CED92].

If a particular wire or routing component fails, there is always an alternative path which avoids the wire or components, but arrives at the same destination. By randomly choosing the physical output out of available channels in the specified logical direction, we will route a message on a second attempt through a different path with high probability. Again, the possibility of performing this rerouting relies on the dilation of the switch component [BP74].

2.4 Comparison with Extra Stage Networks

Some designers achieve a portion of the gain associated with dilation through the use of one or more additional stages of routing at the input to a multistage switch. By randomly choosing the path through these extra switch stages, some of the properties associated with dilation can be achieved, primarily a degree of fault tolerance and hot spot avoidance [AS82].

The difficulty with such extra stage approaches is that the extra stage route is usually chosen prior to message routing, providing no opportunity to avoid busy ports in the switch components. By making the decision of physical output port dynamically during the route setup process, we can route around otherwise occupied or faulty output ports in the switch.

2.5 Importance of Dilated Switch Routing

In a dilated switch, then, a portion of the path selection is specified by the logical route carried with the message, and the details of the physical route are decided with a combination of random choice and busy path avoidance in each of the switch components.

The delay associated with route setup in such dilated switch components is an important contributor to end to end latency of interprocessor and cache miss traffic in parallel computer networks.

3 Dilation Strategies

We consider three types of dilated systems: general dilation, fixed dilation and dynamic dilation. General dilation allows each input port to specify its own dilation on any given cycle. This provides a degree of flexibility in terms of reconfigurability. However this generality entails a high latency cost.

Fixed dilation is the most conservative dilation technique with one dilation being statically set for all ports. This technique significantly reduces the complexity and hence latency of arbitration. However because of allocation requirements, the fastest implementation of fixed dilation can be generalized to dynamic dilation without any penalty in latency.

In dynamic dilation, the dilation is configured on each cycle for each chip based on incoming messages. The degree of flexibility for dynamic dilation is the same as the flexibility of general dilation for the most common case.

3.1 Possible Uses of Dilation Flexibility

General and dynamic dilation allow messages to specify dilation, which may be useful for:

- Fault Tolerance - checking a particular path
- Load Balancing - spawning messages to random places

- Research Tool - reconfiguring the network
- Multiple Users - dividing the network
- Explicit Traffic Control - statically controlling traffic patterns

In terms of fault tolerance a message can be forced to route through a specific path by having the message set the dilation to one at each stage. In this way a faulty part of the network could be located at run time. It can similarly be used as a start-up test for the network which can run quickly.

Reconfigurable dilation can be used by a processor that needs to spawn off a new process. In deterministic dilation the initial processor specifies an exact location for the spawned process, which could be in a highly used area of the network. If instead the initial processor sets the dilation as wide as possible, then the spawning process would naturally flow away from highly congested areas. It is also a extremely simple method to provide load balancing.

As a research tool, networks with flexible dilation can be used to test and evaluate many different types of network configurations. All the messages simply must be setup to request a specific dilation at each stage of the network.

In most systems it would be useful to insure that certain users do not affect each other. An example would be regular users and a distributed operating system. Dividing the system usually refers to only processors, with one common network. In order to truly separate the users, the network must also be divided. A simple method of doing this is to give each message access to only a certain set of paths by limiting its dilation. For example specifying a dilation of two would divide the network in half and then one user could use the upper half while the second could only use the lower half.

Run-time flexibility also allows explicit control of path selection. This could be used when a particular application requires a specific traffic pattern to operate efficiently. The application designer could use the control to specify the particular pattern needed.

3.2 Component Format

Before we begin describing the different arbitration techniques in detail, we need to discuss the general format of a component which can be seen in Figure 2. It is made up of four sections:

- The want section interprets allocation requests made by the input ports. It provides information to the allocate arbiter about whether each input port would like to be connected with each output port.
- The priority section stores the availability of the output ports. It updates and passes this information to the allocate arbiter each cycle.
- The dilation section is nonexistent in general and fixed dilation, but in dynamic dilation it arbitrates between input port request for different dilations.
- The allocate arbiter uses the input requests and the output availability to decide on the allocation of new connections. This information combined with previously allocated connections is used for the passing of data through the appropriate ports of the component.

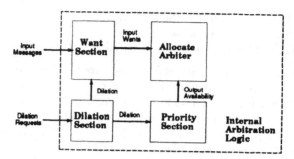

The *want* section interprets the input allocation requests. The *priority* section stores back port availability. The *dilation* section arbitrates between different dilation request in dynamic dilation. The *allocate arbiter* makes the decision on new allocates.

Fig. 2. Internal format for allocator

4 General Dilation: Wave-style arbitration

In general dilation a message on any input port may request any dilation and any set of output ports, which maximizes the probability that it will be connected. The availability of an output port is based on whether the port has been allocated on a previous allocate cycle *and* on whether the output port is allocated to another input port during the same cycle. Similarly, a message's allocate request for an output port depends not only on the original request, but also on whether the request is satisfied by another output port. Consequently the decision about making a connection between a particular input-output port pair requires information about the decision of ports being allocated in the same cycle. This makes allocation in general dilation a sequential process requiring time linear with the total number of ports.

This sequential process is most easily represented by a two-dimensional array of *cross-points* as shown in Figure 3. Each cross-point is associated with an input port on the y-axis and an output port on the x-axis. The allocation begins at the lower left cross-point and proceeds like a wave to the upper right cross-point. A connection is made at a cross-point when the input port wants to connect, the input port request is not previously satisfied, and the output port is available.

In order to prevent starvation and provide fault tolerance, some form of randomness must be added as described in [DCB+94]. Otherwise the lower left input-output port pair has a much higher probability of being connected than the upper right pair. Adding randomness can be accomplished by starting the allocation at a different pair each time and wrapping the previously satisfied and availability information around.

Due to the sequential nature of the process, the fastest general dilation implementation is a factor of five times slower than the fixed and dynamic dilation techniques. The performance figures for general dilation of approximately 14 ns

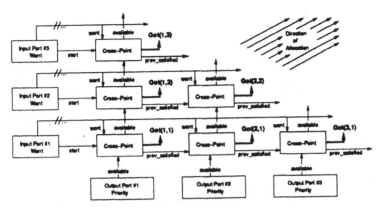

The *want* signals tell each cross-point if its input port wants to be connected to its output port. Intermediary signals, *prev_satisfied* and *available*, contain information on allocates to higher priority cross-points, which prevents multiple allocations to the same port.

Fig. 3. Section of a general dilation allocator

are shown in Table 1. The general dilation techniques and performance figures are very similar to separate work described in [TC93].

5 Limiting Dilation - Fixed Dilation

Fixed dilation schemes produce significantly lower allocation latency, because they restrict the distribution of want signals and the sequential effects of previous allocations. This results from the dilation being configured statically for all input ports. There are two styles of arbitration: wave-style and parallel-style.

In both implementations the available output ports that correspond to equivalent paths are grouped together and are randomly assigned an order of allocation for purposes of fault tolerance [DCB+94]. In the parallel version the input ports are also grouped according to the set of equivalent paths which they request. Within the groups the input ports are randomly assigned an order.

5.1 Fixed Dilation: Wave-Style Arbitration

Similar to the general dilation implementations, fixed dilation wave-style arbitration proceeds like a wave as shown in Figure 4 [MDK91]. However, the signaling propagates along only one axis and therefore passes through half the number of cross-points. At each cross-point an input-output port pair is allocated only if its associated output port is *primary* and the input port is requesting it. Every cross-point above the allocated one receives an unavailable signal on the priority

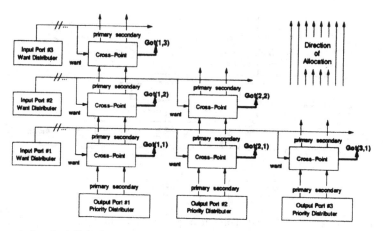

The *want* signals tell each cross-point if its input port wants to be connected to its output port. The *primary* and *secondary* signals contain information on the priority of the output ports. When a secondary port passes a want signal it is promoted to a primary port. When a primary port passes a want signal it creates a connection. Unavailable ports have neither priority line asserted.

Fig. 4. Section of wave-style allocator with a fixed dilation of two

lines. If the priority of an output port is not primary it is promoted to a higher priority whenever it passes a cross-point with a input port request. This method lends itself to a simple pass gate implementation with a low latency of 5.2 ns which is summed up in Table 1.

5.2 Fixed Dilation: Parallel-Style Arbitration

The second implementation of fixed dilation is fully parallelized as shown in Figure 5. As before the allocation cycle begins with grouping and ordering, but this time of both input and output ports. The cross-point receives the randomized order in which its associated ports are to be allocated. The priorities at each cross point are then summed up and if these numbers match, the pair is connected. For example if a cross-point has a second priority input port and the output port is the second to be allocated then a connection is made. Because the decision of each cross-point can be completed in parallel, the allocation process provides extremely low latency.

The fixed dilation scheme implemented with parallel techniques minimizes single cycle latency as shown in Table 1. The figure of 4.3 ns includes four gate delays for the want section, six gate delays for the allocation process, and four gate delays for data propagation. In a 0.8-micron technology, a gate delay translates to a little over 0.3 ns.

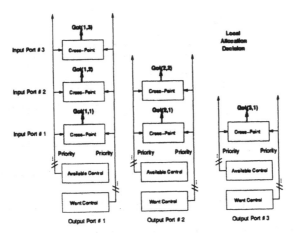

The *availablepriority* signals tell each cross-point which order the back ports will be allocated. The *wantpriority* signals of the input ports for a specific output port inform the cross-points of the input port ordering. The cross-point allocates when the output priority matches the input priority.

Fig. 5. Section of parallel-style allocator

6 Message Format and Pipelining

Messages begin with routing words followed by data words. The routing words which set up new paths, require more processing than the data words. For this reason the allocation logic can be pipelined to increase network performance.

The routing words contain destination information, which allows a message to route through a stage of the network. Because of extra word width, often a routing word can be used to traverse more than one stage. However in large multi-stage networks it often cannot be used to cross the entire network, and must be *swallowed* at some point. During a swallow the original routing word is discarded and a new routing word with information for subsequent stages propagates to the front of the message as shown in Figure 6.

Because arbitration latency is high, the allocation of initial routing words limits the clock frequency of the network. The latency of a single cycle allocate which allows a routing word to be used for multiple stages requires the full 4.3 ns. The case of a small message, containing only eight data words, requires 25.8 ns to make a initial connection through the network seen in Figure 6. For the entire message to completely traverse this network requires 55.9 ns.

Compared to routing words, data words require much less processing time, only about 1.8 ns. One obvious way to improve network performance is to pipeline the initial allocation process into two cycles of 9 gate delays or 2.7 ns. This cycle time is limited by a feedback path associated with port availability,

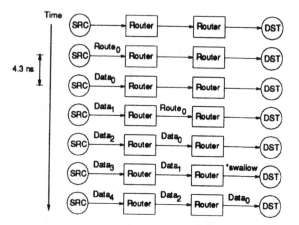

The network is idle when SRC starts to input a message to be routed to DST. The message requires one cycle to cross every wire and go through a component. Because of the limited width of the routing words, in the last stage the routing word has been used up and is *swallowed*. In the fastest single cycle implementation each cycle lasts for 4.3 ns.

Fig. 6. Message Routed Through a Network with Single-Cycle Allocate

which will be described later. From the system viewpoint the network appears to be swallowing a routing word at each stage.

For the example network shown in Figure 7, this double-cycle allocate increases the number of routing words from one to two, and the total message length to ten words when compared to the single-cycle allocate. However, the increased clock frequency on all words offsets the cost of requiring a new routing word for each network stage. An initial connection requires only 18.9 ns and the total transit time reduces to 35.1 ns. When compared to similar single-cycle allocate, the pipelining increases bandwidth, decreases total latency, and actually *decreases* initial connection latency.

7 Dynamic Dilation

By reducing flexibility given to input port requests, we were able to increase bandwidth and reduce latency. This is the move from general dilation to fixed dilation. Fixed dilation does not allow a message to decide its dilation. Instead, this is statically set at design time. In the process of *reducing* allocation latency we pipelined the allocation decision into two unequal cycles. The reason for this is explained in Section 7.1. Dynamic dilation uses the extra time in one cycle to recover the lost dilation flexibility. As with fixed dilation, the entire chip operates in one dilation during each allocate cycle. But, similar to general dilation, dilation is chosen based on the input port allocate requests at the beginning of each cycle.

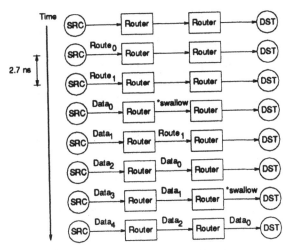

In this case the allocation process occurs over two cycles which forces a routing words to be swallowed at each stage. The data words of the message still requires only one cycle to cross every wire and go through each component. Each cycle lasts for only 2.7 ns.

Fig. 7. Message Routed Through a Network with Double-Cycle Allocate

Because the component must handle multiple requests for allocation in a single cycle, two input ports might request different dilations. This requires some mediation to chose a single dilation to be used for all the ports. To insure that an input port is not forced to take a port it does not consider equivalent, the lowest dilation must always be chosen.

A simple example would be if two input ports simultaneously requested dilation two and dilation four. If the chip dilation were incorrectly set to four then the input port requesting dilation two could be connected to any of four output ports even though it considers two ports to not be equivalent to the ones it is requesting. However if dilation two is chosen then the input port requesting dilation four is only forced to take a subset of the requested ports, but each one is still acceptable.

7.1 Timing Issues

The breakdown of delay in the final version of the dynamic dilation allocator is shown in Figure 8. The most important part of the diagram is the feedback path in which the new allocates of one cycle are fed back into the availability paths of the next cycle. This must occur on a cycle by cycle basis or it would allow an allocation of an output port on one cycle and then another allocation of the same port on the next cycle. The feedback path which fills the second allocate stage limits the cycle time to 2.7 ns.

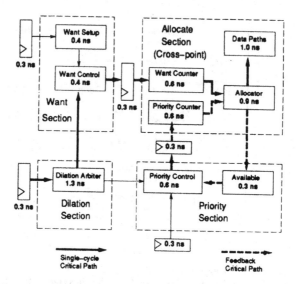

This diagram includes all the major functional units of the allocate logic with their associated delays. Included are the pipeline stages used to reduce overall network latency. The dotted bold path shows the feedback loop which limits cycle time to 2.7 ns. The plain bold path marks the critical path of an unpipelined version of the allocator which requires 4.8 ns.

Fig. 8. Timing/Circuit Diagram of Dynamic Dilation

The latency of the first cycle turns out to be only 2.2 ns, even with the added logic to support dynamic dilation. Therefore the addition of dynamic dilation comes at simply the cost of filling up the unused part of the first cycle. Since more time is available it may be possible to add other options, such as message buffering, at similarly no cost to cycle time.

7.2 Logic Description of Allocation in Dynamic Dilation

Dynamic dilation requires very low latency because it solves a simple problem. In dynamic dilation a decision still requires information about other allocates, but this information is part of the input and output priority information distributed to each cross-point.

The cross-point sums the priority of input ports that are requesting a connection with the associated output port. The summation is implemented with a logarithmic tree of counters, where each stage of the tree combines the requests hence reducing the number of input requests as shown in Figure 9. On the output side a similar summation occurs. Each cross-point then simply compares the summer output lines to find two that are asserted with the same sum. This

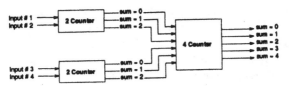

The 4 wide summer operates on the priority and want signal passed to the cross-point at a speed within only 2 gate delays or 0.6 ns. This summer has very low latency in the four input case and scales logarithmically.

Fig. 9. Logarithmic Summer

allocate information is passed to the data paths and back to the priority section as part of the availability feedback loop.

7.3 Flexibility Comparison to General Dilation

Dynamic dilation provides as much flexibility as general dilation in all instances except for multiple allocations requesting different dilations in one cycle. Normally when there is only one requesting port, the port would get whichever dilation it requested. Because there is only one allowed dilation each cycle, if two ports request different dilation then one will be forced to take a dilation it did not request.

However, the likelihood of such an event is rare. $t_{network}$ represents the average number of cycles a message ties up a given routing component. If one assumes peak network load, then every $t_{network}$ a new message is begun. Therefore, the reciprocal of $t_{network}$ becomes the frequency at which a new route will begin in that routing component or the probability that a route will start on a given cycle. From this, $P_{2messages}$, the probability that two messages arrive on a given cycle, where N_{ports} is the number of ports, can be calculated:

$$P_{2messages} = \binom{N_{ports}}{2} * \left[\frac{1}{t_{network}}\right]^2 * \left[1 - \frac{1}{t_{network}}\right]^{N_{ports}-2} \quad (1)$$

The first term in the above equation is the number of combinations of getting exactly two incoming messages. The other two terms are the probabilities of getting two incoming messages and $(N_{ports} - 2)$ non-requesting ports.

The probability of getting a collision between two ports requesting *different* dilations, $P_{collision}$, relies on the distribution of dilation requests. If one assumes an even distribution of these probabilities, $P_{different}$, then $P_{collision}$ follows easily:

$$P_{collision} = [1 - P_{different}] * P_{2messages} \quad (2)$$

The first term is equal to the probability of the second message not being the same dilation as the first. In an example network with four input ports per component ($N_{ports} = 4$), there would be 3 different dilations which makes $P_{different} = \frac{1}{3}$. Assuming $t_{network} = 25$ cycles, a conservative estimate, $P_{2messages}$ would be about 0.6%. $P_{collision}$ comes out to about 0.4%.

These back-of-the-envelope calculations do not include the second order effect of more than two messages coming in at the same time. The probability of getting three messages at once is small compared to the probability of getting two, by a factor of 25.

Once the secondary effects are ignored, one realizes that these calculations are extremely conservative. First we assumed a message is being injected as soon as a reply returns from the previous message. Usually the processor will not be able to sustain this speed, because it needs to process one message before sending out the next. Also in the example, the amount of time that a message spent in the network was assumed to be very small. Often a message will travel to its destination and wait some time before a reply. Also the message length is probable longer than that assumed in the example. Finally the distribution of message dilations is assumed to be as wide as possible. It is more likely that most messages will be of the same dilation at a particular stage. In this light the result of less than 1% is quite impressive.

7.4 Comparison with other techniques

Table 1 summarizes the performance of various implementations of the three different dilation schemes. General dilation is by a factor of five the slowest scheme, but provides the highest probability of getting a connection. The wave-style and parallel-style implementations of fixed dilation greatly reduce latency, but severely limit dilation flexibility. The pipelined versions of dynamic and fixed dilation provide the lowest network latencies of every other technique. In addition the pipelined version of dynamic dilation allows almost as much flexibility as the general dilation scheme.

8 Conclusions

Dilated self-routing crossbars can serve as a building block for multi-path interconnection networks. They provide fault tolerance and contention control with extremely low latency. Fixed dilation minimizes the allocation latency of a single routing component. However, cross network latency can be further reduced by pipelining the allocate process into two cycles. The pipelining gives us the opportunity to regain some flexibility which was lost in the single cycle fixed dilation schemes. Pipelined dynamic dilation routing components therefore provides routing flexibility as well as very low latency.

Type	Allocate Latency (ns)	Initial Connection Latency (ns)	Total Connection Latency (ns)
general	14	84	182
fixed wave	5.2	31.2	67.6
fixed parallel	4.3	25.8	55.9
piped fixed	2.7 (x2)	18.9	35.1
piped dynamic	2.7 (x2)	18.9	35.1

These results are for an 8 word message traveling the network shown in Figure 7. The *allocate latency* sets the system clock. The *initial connection latency* is for one hop across the network, while the *total connection latency* is for the entire message.

Table 1. Dilation Performance Results

References

[ALM90] S. Arora, T. Leighton, and B. Maggs. On-line algorithms for path selection in a non-blocking network. In *Proceedings of the 22nd Annual ACM Symposium on Theory of Computing*, pages 149–158, May 1990.

[AS82]   George Adams and Howard Siegel. The Extra Stage Cube: A Fault-Tolerant Interconnection Network for Supersystems. In *Trans. on Computers, vol. c-31, no. 5*, pages 443–454, West Lafayette, Indiana, May 1982. IEEE.

[BP74]   L. A. Bassalygo and M. S. Pinsker. Complexity of optimum nonblocking switching networks without reconnections. *Problems of Information Transmission*, 9:64–66, 1974.

[CED92] Frederic Chong, Eran Egozy, and André DeHon. Fault Tolerance and Performance of Multipath Multistage Interconnection Networks. In Thomas F. Knight Jr. and John Savage, editors, *Advanced Research in VLSI and Parallel Systems 1992*, pages 227–242. MIT Press, March 1992.

[DCB+94] André DeHon, Frederic Chong, Matthew Becker, Eran Egozy, Henry Minsky, Samuel Peretz, and Thomas F. Knight, Jr. METRO: A Router Architecture for High-Performance, Short-Haul Routing Networks. In *Proceedings of the International Symposium on Computer Architecture*, pages 266–277, May 1994.

[KS90]   Thomas F. Knight Jr. and Patrick G. Sobalvarro. Routing Statistics for Unqueued Banyan Networks. AI memo 1101, MIT Artificial Intelligence Laboratory, September 1990.

[LM89]   Tom Leighton and Bruce Maggs. Expanders Might Be Practical: Fast Algorithms for Routing Around Faults on Multibutterflies. In *IEEE 30th Annual Symposium on Foundations of Computer Science*, 1989.

[MDK91] Henry Minsky, André DeHon, and Thomas F. Knight Jr. RN1: Low-Latency, Dilated, Crossbar Router. In *Hot Chips Symposium III*, 1991.

[TC93]   Y. Tamir and H.C Chi. Symmetric Crossbar Arbiter for VLSI Communication Switch. In *Trans. on Parallel and Distributed Systems, vol. 4, no. 1*, pages 13–27, UCLA, California, January 1993. IEEE.

Performance Analysis of a Minimal Adaptive Router

Thu Duc Nguyen and Lawrence Snyder

Department of Computer Science and Engineering
University of Washington, Seattle, WA 98195

Abstract. Two classes of adaptive routers, minimal and non-minimal, are emerging as possible replacements for the oblivious routers used in current multicomputer networks. In this paper, we compare the simulated performance of three routers, an oblivious, a minimal, and a non-minimal adaptive router, in a two-dimensional packet switching torus network. The non-minimal adaptive router is shown to give the best performance and the oblivious router the worst. Significantly, however, for many traffic patterns, the minimal adaptive router's performance degrades sharply as the network saturates. Based on an analysis made using several visualization tools, we argue that this performance drop results from non-uniformities introduced for deadlock prevention. Furthermore, this analysis has led us to believe that *network balance* is an important performance characteristic that has been largely overlooked by designers of adaptive routing algorithms.

1 Introduction

As processors and network interfaces become faster, many researchers have speculated that these components may soon outpace the oblivious routers used in today's multicomputer networks. Thus, researchers have proposed numerous adaptive routing algorithms, arguing that adaptive routers can outperform oblivious routers because they are more flexible. Adaptive routing can be partitioned into two classes, minimal and non-minimal. To date, the question of *"how much adaptivity?"* seems to present a classic complexity vs. flexibility/performance tradeoff.

Simulation studies have shown that non-minimal adaptive routers can significantly outperform oblivious routers in hypercube and torus topologies [11, 3, 9, 12, 7]. Boppana and Chalasani [4] and Berman et al. [1] have shown that several minimal adaptive routing algorithms outperform oblivious routing for wormhole routing networks. Comparatively little is known, however, about the performance of minimal adaptive routers in virtual cut-through packet switching networks. Two differences make packet switching networks interesting: (1) Packet switching routers have larger buffers than typically assumed for wormhole routers; (2) Stalled packets are completely buffered in routers, releasing physical channels to be used by other packets. These differences can cause routing algorithms' behavior to differ significantly.

In this paper, we compare the simulated performance of three routers, an oblivious, a minimal, and a non-minimal adaptive router, in a two-dimensional virtual cut-through packet switching torus network. We base our minimal adaptive router on a routing algorithm designed by Cypher and Gravano [5]. This algorithm is particularly attractive because it:

- provides *fully* minimal adaptive routing (that is, a packet may be routed along all minimal paths between the source and destination),
- is deadlock and livelock free, and
- requires a provably minimal amount of buffer space (i.e. virtual channels) for deadlock-prevention.

We compare the performance of this minimal adaptive router against simulation results previously documented by Fulgham and Snyder [9] for a state-of-the-art oblivious and a non-minimal adaptive router (Chaos router [11, 3, 2]).

Typically, it is difficult to compare simulation results because different simulation systems encompass different router designs and different timing assumptions (e.g. clock cycle length). In our study, however, performance results for all three routers have been obtained using the same simulator, allowing "apples-to-apples" comparisons. Furthermore, this simulator was designed and implemented at the University of Washington to mimic the behavior of UW chip designs at the system clock level. Router designs for components that are independent of the routing algorithms, e.g., channel arbitration, derive from a chip implementation and so are the same for all three routers. On the other hand, algorithm specific factors, e.g., the latency of a routing decision, are modeled using variable parameters of the simulator. Reported behavior of the simulated oblivious and Chaos routers match actual physical implementations.

Our simulation results show that the minimal adaptive router outperforms the oblivious router but is outperformed by the non-minimal adaptive router. Significantly, for many traffic patterns, the minimal adaptive router's performance degrades sharply as the network saturates. Based on an analysis made using several visualization tools, we argue that this performance drop results from non-uniformities introduced for deadlock prevention. Furthermore, this analysis has led us to believe that *network balance* is an important performance characteristic that has been largely overlooked by designers of adaptive routing algorithms.

This paper is organized as follows. Section 2 describes the three routers. Section 3 describes the simulation methodology. Section 4 presents our simulation results and compares the minimal adaptive router to the Chaos and oblivious routers. Section 5 discusses related work and other minimal adaptive routing algorithms. Section 6 presents our conclusions.

2   Router Descriptions

In this section, we first describe the simulated network and briefly review the oblivious and Chaos routers. We then describe in slightly more detail the minimal adaptive routing algorithm and our simulation models.

In this study, we focus on virtual cut-through packet switching in a two-dimensional torus network with 256 routing nodes. We shall refer to the two dimensions of the torus as the x and y dimensions. Each router is labeled by a pair of coordinates (x, y) given by its position with respect to some router designated to have coordinate $(0, 0)$.

Each router has five bi-directional channels, with four channels connecting the router to its neighbors and one connecting the router to its processor. Each channel is connected to two sets of buffers at a router, the *input frames* and the *output frames*.[1] Each channel can only transmit in one direction at a time. Note that because all routers in the network are attached to processors, traffic can be and is introduced into the network from all nodes.

Each packet is composed of 20 flits (flow control units), with the first flit being large enough to hold the destination address. This implies that each flit must contain at least 8 bits, since our network has 256 nodes. All three routers can send or receive one flit over each of its five channels in one routing time unit (cycle). All three routers are virtual cut-through routers [10] – that is, once the header flit of a packet has been received and decoded, the router can direct that packet to a free channel before the packet has entirely arrived at that node. Input frames are connected to output frames via a full crossbar, allowing multiple packets to be in transit across a router concurrently.

2.1 Oblivious Router

The oblivious router uses dimension order routing; each packet is first routed in the x dimension until it reaches a router with the same x coordinate as the destination, then routed along the y dimension until it reaches the destination. This means that, at any time, each packet has only one permissible path through a router that it has reached. If the needed out channel is busy, the packet must wait. Deadlock is avoided using virtual channels as described by Dally and Seitz [6].

In the simulated model, the oblivious router requires two cycles to process a header flit and one cycle to route a packet across the wires of the appropriate channel, resulting in a minimum routing latency of three cycles. Headers of incoming packets are processed concurrently but only one routing decision can be made per cycle. That is, only one input to output frame setup can be done per cycle. To route packets, the oblivious router services its outframes in a round-robin fashion, moving to the next *interesting* output frame on each cycle. An output frame is interesting if it is available for use and is desired by some packet. If more than one packet wants a particular output frame, then one is chosen at random.

2.2 Chaos Router

Under normal routing conditions, the Chaos router routes packets from its input frames to its output frames similar to a minimal adaptive router. The Chaos router has a central multiqueue used to avoid head-of-line blocking and for deadlock prevention. A packet is moved into the multiqueue if it is potentially in a deadlock loop or if it has stalled at an input frame. When an output frame becomes available, packets in the multiqueue desiring that output frame have priority over packets in input frames. If more than one packet in the multiqueue desires the channel, the output frame is allocated using FIFO ordering. If a packet must be moved into the multiqueue when it is full, a packet in the

---

[1] For the oblivious and minimal adaptive routers, each end of a channel is connected to two sets of buffers rather than just two buffers because of the use of virtual channels for deadlock-prevention. For the Chaos router, each end of the channel is connected to just one input frame and one output frame.

queue is chosen at random and is *derouted* to the next available output frame; such a deroute may take the packet further away from its destination. Derouting is the only mechanism that can cause packets to be routed along non-minimal paths.

Like the oblivious router, the Chaos router services its channels using a round-robin policy. Because of its relative complexity, the Chaos router is charged with three cycles to process a header flit, resulting in a minimum routing latency of four cycles. Furthermore, implementation considerations [2] specify that a cut-through of a packet from the multiqueue to an output frame stalls the router's cut-through function for two cycles. In our simulation, the multiqueue can hold up to five packets and has crossbar connections to the input and output frames, allowing multiple packets to be transmitted into and out of the multiqueue. Like the oblivious router, however, the Chaos router can only process one packet header at a time.

2.3 Minimal Adaptive Router

The minimal adaptive routing algorithm specified by Cypher and Gravano [5] works as follows. Each router consists of three central FIFO queues, called the A, B, and C queues, representing three virtual channels. Each incoming channel is connected to all three queues. Similarly, each queue is connected to all outgoing channels. Packets are initially injected into the A queue. When a packet is in the A queue, the router examines the set of all possible minimal paths. If the packet can be routed in the positive direction using an internal edge, it is moved to the A queue of any neighbor which lies on a minimal path. Otherwise, the packet is moved into the B queue. For a packet in the B queue, the router likewise examines the set of all possible minimal paths. If the packet can be routed along a minimal path in the negative direction using an internal edge or in the positive direction using a wrap edge, then it is moved to the B queue of any neighbor which lies on a minimal path. Otherwise, the packet is moved into the C queue. For a packet in the C queue, the router checks to see whether it is the packet's destination. If so, it delivers the packet to the attached node. If not, then the packet is moved to the C queue of any neighbor which lies on a minimal path.

For our simulation, we have adapted the above algorithm to two simulation models. Figure 1 depicts a possible minimal adaptive router design that emphasizes simplicity, differing from the oblivious router only in that it routes packets adaptively. Figure 2 depicts a second possible minimal adaptive router that leverages the design of the Chaos router's central multiqueue to prevent stalled packets from holding on to valuable channel resources. We shall refer to these two simulation models as MA and MA-Q, respectively.

In the first model (Figure 1), each set of input and output frames connected to a channel consists of three buffers, one for each of the three virtual channels, A, B, and C. Each buffer is capable of storing one packet. Movements between queues as described above (e.g. from A to B) happen during the cut-through. Each router in the network maintains a bit-mask that describes whether the router's coordinate is 0, K,[2] or neither in each dimension. Using this mask and packets' headers containing the number of hops that the packet must still traverse in each direction, the above conditions can be tested

---

[2] In a k-ary n-cube network, $K = k - 1$. For a 256 node torus, $K = 15$.

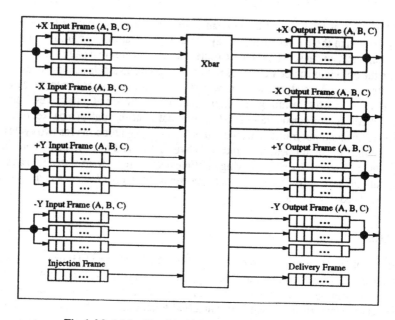

Fig. 1. Model for Simulated Minimal Adaptive Router (MA)

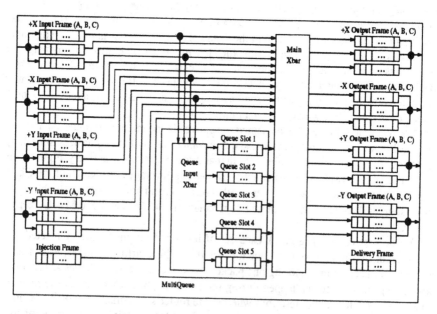

Fig. 2. Model for Simulated Minimal Adaptive Router With Central Queue (MA-Q)

efficiently. Suppose a packet is to be moved from the A queue to the B queue, when the router directs the packet from an input frame to an output frame, it simply directs the packet from the A buffer of the inframe to the B buffer of the outframe.

In the second model (Figure 2), in addition to the input and output frames, each router has a multiqueue as in the Chaos router. Each buffer in this model can hold exactly one packet and the multiqueue can hold five packets. As will be discussed below, early simulations show that performance limiting congestion occurs only in the A virtual channels. Thus, all buffer space in the central queue is reserved for packets traversing A virtual channels. When a packet traversing an A virtual channel stalls, it is moved into the multiqueue.

Both minimal adaptive routers are charged with three cycles for processing the header of a packet, resulting in a minimum routing latency of four cycles. Usage of the central queue incurs exactly the same penalty as for the Chaos router; that is, the routing of a packet from the multiqueue to an output frame stalls the router's cut-through function for two cycles. Output frames are serviced using a round-robin policy similar to the oblivious and Chaos routers. Only one packet header can be processed per cycle.

3 Methodology

All simulation experiments were performed using the Chaos project simulator. This simulator was designed and implemented to mimic the behavior of router chip designs at the system clock level. Simulated traffic is generated as follows. Each node generates packets independently. Packets are generated according to a Poisson distribution, with the mean arrival rate specified by the presented load. Furthermore, packets' destinations are chosen according to the following traffic patterns. To describe the patterns, let each node (x, y) also be labeled with a number xy, where xy is the value resulting from the concatenation of x and y. xy's binary representation is $a_{n-1}a_{n-2}...a_0$.

- *Random:* Destinations are chosen at random with equal probability.
- *Transpose:* Each node sends only to the destination given by $a_{(n/2)-1}a_{(n/2)-2}...a_0a_{n-1}a_{n-2}...a_{n/2}$.
- *Bit Reversal:* Each node sends only to the destination given by $a_0a_1...a_{n-1}$.
- *4X Hot Spots:* Ten randomly chosen nodes are distinguished. Destinations are chosen at random with the probability of choosing a distinguished node being 4 times the probability of choosing a normal node.

Various quantities such as throughput, source queueing time, latency, delay, number of hops, etc., can be measured using our simulator. Results are presented in terms of loads normalized to the bisection bandwidth. That is, loads are normalized with respect to the maximum theoretical load for uniform random traffic, where network bisection saturates. For a torus network with 256 nodes, the maximum injection rate, corresponding to a load of 100%, is one message every 80 cycles.

4 Simulation Results

Typically, router performance is assessed by two quantitative parameters, throughput and latency. Aside from throughput and latency, however, we believe that qualitative

Table 1. Minimum normalized load when saturation is detected (5% increments)

Traffic Pattern	Saturation			
	Obliv	Chaos	MA	MA-Q
Random	65	95	80	80
Hot Spot	50	90	70	70
Bit Reversal	40	85	65	65
Transpose	55	55	55	55

characteristics such as whether bandwidth and latency are location dependent may be important as well. In this section, we first discuss the throughput and latency characteristics of the minimal adaptive router and compare them with those of the Chaos and oblivious routers. We then discuss more qualitative characteristics of the minimal adaptive router observed using visualization tools.

4.1 Throughput

Throughput is defined as the sustained data delivery rate given some applied load. Two important throughput characteristics are saturation loads and sustained delivery rates after saturation. Saturation is defined as the first applied load when the network throughput is lower than the aggregate packet creation rate at source nodes. Note that throughput before saturation is not particularly interesting. By definition, before saturation, the throughput is simply equal to the applied load because all created packets are successfully injected into, routed, and delivered by the network.

In practical situations, one does not expect a network to operate close to or above saturation for extended periods of time. Network traffic, however, is known to be bursty, and peak transmission periods can often cause network saturation. Thus, saturation and throughput after saturation are important parameters that determine how often a network might reach saturation and whether it can recover once saturation has been reached.

Saturation. Table 1 gives the saturation loads for the simulated routers. Results are given for only one representative Hot-Spots configuration although we simulated six different configurations.

We observe the following:

- The MA router saturates at the same or higher load than the oblivious router in all cases.
- The Chaos router saturates at the same or higher load than the MA router in all cases.
- The MA-Q router saturates at the same load as the MA router in all cases.

For Random, Bit Reversal, and Hot Spots traffic, the minimal adaptive routers saturate at loads that are 15 to 25% higher than the oblivious router, while saturating at loads 15 to 20% lower than the Chaos router.

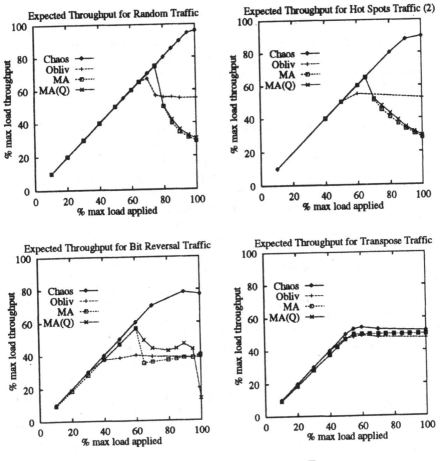

Fig. 3. Expected Throughput on a 256 Node Torus.

The Transpose traffic pattern seems to be universally hard, causing all routers to saturate at a normalized load of 55%. This is because under the transpose pattern on the torus, the destination of each packet is a reflection of the source about the line $y = -x$, forcing all packets to go through the center of the network [9]. This results in a continuous area of congestion along this diagonal for all routers.

Post-Saturation. Figure 3 gives the throughput vs. normalized load plots for the simulated routers. We observe the following post-saturation characteristics:

- The Chaos router either maintains the throughput reached at saturation or experiences only slight throughput degradation in all cases.
- The oblivious router's throughput degrades significantly for Random traffic after saturation. Bolding and Snyder postulate that this throughput degradation results

from network asymmetries introduced by the use of virtual channels for deadlock prevention [3].

- The MA router's throughput degrades significantly for Random, Hot Spots, and Bit Reversal traffic after saturation. We believe that this also results from network asymmetries introduced for deadlock prevention. We explain this behavior below.
- The MA-Q router's throughput does not degrade as badly as the MA router for Bit Reversal.

Two visualization tools developed in conjunction with the simulator assist in explaining the minimal adaptive router's post-saturation behavior. The first visualizer displays graphically the packet population at each node for A, B, and C buffers during the simulation. This visualizer shows that, as the applied load increases, heavy congestion develops in the A virtual channels at the center of the network[3]. Contention for B and C virtual channels is relatively light at all loads. To understand this phenomenon, we note that in general, packets can move in four directions, $++$, $+-$, $-+$, and $--$. Furthermore, recall that packets traveling in the $++$, $+-$, and $-+$ must be routed using A virtual channels until all positive moves have been exhausted. Intuitively, one can see that, at the center of the network, a majority of packets are injected in A buffers and must initially be routed using A virtual channels.

The second visualizer allows us to observe routing decisions and packet movements within a router during a simulation run. This visualizer shows that, at network saturation, packets that can be routed immediately using B channels are routed and delivered with minimal delay once they have been injected. Also, there is greater contention for A virtual channels leading in positive directions than for A virtual channels leading in negative directions. This is consistent with the routing algorithm because all packets moving in $++$, $+-$, and $-+$ directions have positive moves but not all have negative moves. Thus, this nonuniformity seems to cause negative moves to often be used first in routing a packet that have both positive and negative moves. This forces packets that could have been partly routed using B virtual channels to be entirely routed using A virtual channels.

The above observations lead us to believe that the following takes place at network saturation. The bottom right corner of the network (the white nodes in Figure 4(a)) remains clear of congestion and act as a "drain" area for the network. Congestion does not develop in this area because all injected packets quickly become routable using B virtual channels. As the applied load increases, congestion first develops at the center of the network. Packets with positive moves injected by nodes far away from the drain area (the gray nodes in Figure 4(a)) must enter or pass through the congested middle before they can be delivered. In fact, congestion becomes so bad that once a gray node injects a packet with a positive move, this packet stalls in the injection frame, preventing the node from further traffic injection. Thus, a buffer waiting pattern develops as shown in Figure 4(a) where all packets at gray-shaded nodes can only be routed using A virtual channels in the directions shown. When this waiting pattern develops, the sustained throughput of all gray nodes is effective determined by the throughput of the black nodes in Figure 4(a).

---

[3] Locations within the network (e.g. center or bottom right hand corner) are interpreted with respect to a flattened torus with origin (0, 0), looking like a mesh with long wrap edges.

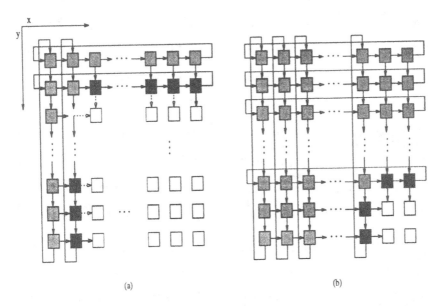

Fig. 4. Interlocking Buffer Waiting Pattern at High Loads: (a) shows interlocking buffer waiting forming at high loads causing black nodes to be the throughput bottleneck; (b) shows interlocking buffer waiting spreads as load increases, causing the congested area to have an even smaller bottleneck.

As the applied load increases beyond the saturation load, the "stalled" area shown in Figure 4(a) spreads to a larger portion of the network, further decreasing the number of nodes at the edge of the congested area as shown in Figure 4(b), causing throughput to degrade further. To validate this theory, we modified the simulator to stop generating traffic after network saturation. We then watched the network as it drained. This draining process can be observed to be the exact inverse of Figures 4(a) and 4(b).

4.2 Latency

Latency is defined as the average delay that a packet will experience in the network once it has been successfully injected by the source. Successful injection of a packet is defined as the successful transmission of that packet from the processor into the injection input frame at the router. Thus, latency does not include the time that processors must wait for input frames to become free but does include any stalling time at the injection input frame. Latency is defined in this manner so that saturated and supersaturated loads can be studied. Under saturated and supersaturated loads, the average delay time between packet creation and delivery rises to infinity and becomes a meaningless parameter.

Figure 5 shows that, before saturation, the latencies of all three routers are comparable. At low loads, latency is slightly lower for the oblivious router than the Chaos and minimal adaptive routers. This is as expected given that the oblivious router has a lower minimum cross-chip latency (3 vs. 4 cycles). For all traffic patterns, however, the

41

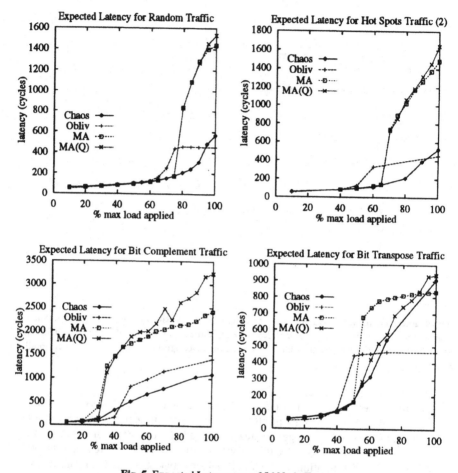

Fig. 5. Expected Latency on a 256 Node Torus.

oblivious router's latency soon matches that of the other three routers (at most by loads of 40%).

For all traffic patterns, latency for the oblivious and MA routers jumps sharply at network saturation. Note that, except for the Transpose traffic pattern,[4] this is also true for the MA-Q router. This is consistent with the sudden change of slope in these routers' throughput curves. Under Random and Hot Spots traffic, the minimal adaptive routers' latencies continue to rise sharply after saturation. This is consistent with the throughput degradations shown by these routers' throughput curves.

For all traffic patterns, latency for the Chaos router starts to rise somewhat before saturation and continues to rise after saturation. The rise in latency corresponds to der-outes that begin to happen as the network becomes congested. In all but one case, the

---

[4] Interestingly, this is the only pattern where the MA-Q router's behavior differs significantly from that of the MA router.

Chaos router's latency eventually rises above that of the oblivious router. In only one case does the Chaos router's latency rise above that of the minimal adaptive router — > 90% load under the Transpose traffic pattern.

4.3 Routing Imbalances

We have already noted that significant non-uniformities are introduced by the Cypher-Gravano algorithm. Simulation results and visualization tools have shown that such non-uniformities limit achievable throughput. Aside from this throughput limitation, however, these non-uniformities are further undersirable because they cause perceived bandwidth and latency to differ depending on nodes' locations in the network. For Random traffic, even before network saturation, packets originating from the bottom right hand corner of the torus can be expected to have lower latency than packets originating elsewhere in the network. Furthermore, even at extreme network saturation, packets injected at nodes at the bottom right hand corner of the network experience little or no network contention. This is because these packets typically require very little routing using A buffers. On the other hand, as the network approaches saturation, congestion is acute for nodes at the upper left hand corner and along the top and left edge of the network, throttling traffic injection at these nodes. As noted, at network saturation, we have observed packets stalling in injection frames for tens of thousands of cycles. One unrealistic assumption built into our simulator is the assumption that traffic injection at each node is independent of traffic injections at other nodes. In practice, processors in a multicomputer are cooperating in running parallel applications such that the above assumption of injection independence cannot hold true. In fact, unless sophisticated load-balancing techniques are applied (and perhaps even if they are applied) the progress of a parallel computation will be limited by the throughput of the congested area, suggesting that achievable throughput may be much lower the simulation results given above.

5 Related Work

Felperin et al. have reported results for a minimal adaptive routing algorithm in packet switching mesh networks [8]. In fact, the algorithm is similar to the algorithm studied here but only works for mesh and hypercube networks. Simulation results show that this algorithm achieves throughput of 75% for Random traffic and 35% for Transpose traffic before network saturation. Unfortunately, this study makes two unrealistic assumptions: delivery queues are infinitely large and cross-node latency is only one cycle. This makes it difficult to compare the results of this study to other simulation studies of adaptive routing algorithms.

In their paper, Felperin et al. also describes a fully-adaptive minimal routing algorithm, "4-classes", for torus networks. This algorithm is interesting because it requires one more virtual channel than the Cypher-Gravano algorithm but, for Random traffic, divides packets uniformly into four classes, those with only positive moves, only negative moves, positive moves in the x dimension and negative moves in the y dimension, negative moves in the x dimension and positive moves in the y dimension (i.e. x^+y^+,

x^-y^-, x^+y^-, and x^-y^+). Unfortunately, Felperin et al. did not report any simulation results for this algorithm.

A number of other researchers have reported simulation results for minimal adaptive routing algorithms in wormhole routing networks [4, 1]. Unfortunately, no meaningful comparisons can be made because buffer availability and resource consumption, especially in the presence of network congestion, is so different for wormhole routing than for virtual cut-through packet-switching routing.

6 Conclusions

Although many minimal adaptive routing algorithms have been published in the last several years, relatively little is known about their performance in virtual cut-through packet-switching networks. Furthermore, because of differences in simulation assumptions, it has been difficult to compare reported performance of minimal and non-minimal adaptive routing algorithms. In this study, we have presented simulated performance results for a minimal adaptive router in a virtual cut-through packet-switching torus network and compared these results to performance data previously reported for the oblivious and Chaos routers. More importantly, all performance data cited here for the three routers were obtained using a single simulator that was designed and implemented to reflect practical router implementations.

Our data show that a minimal adaptive router based on the Cypher-Gravano algorithm outperforms the oblivious router but falls short of the Chaos router. In some cases, the minimal adaptive router saturates before the Chaos router because of its inability to make use of non-minimal paths to avoid local congestion. In other cases, our visualization tools show that, the minimal adaptive router saturates before the Chaos router because the Cypher-Gravano routing algorithm introduces significant non-uniformities in buffer usage.

We also believe that system throughput and average latency do not offer the full story about routers' performance. Our visualization efforts show that the Cypher-Gravano algorithm causes significant network imbalances. Such imbalances are undesirable in the design and implementation of real multicomputer systems. We believe that designers of adaptive routing algorithms should pay careful attention to asymmetries introduced by their algorithm. Efforts to reduce asymmetric use of network resources can pay off with higher performance and better applicability.

7 Acknowledgements

We would like to thank Kevin Bolding and Melanie Fulgham for their generous help in all phases of the project. We would also like to thank the Chaos group for helpful discussions and review. Donald Chinn first advanced the idea for our X-based visualization tools. Sung-Eun Choi made the first visualization tool a reality and setup the framework for further visualization work.

References

1. P. Berman, L. Gravano, G. Pifarré, and J. Sanz. Adaptive deadlock- and livelock-free routing with all minimal paths in torus networks. In *Proceedings of the Symposium on Parallel Algorithms and Architectures*, 1992.
2. K. Bolding, S.-C. Cheung, S.-E. Choi, C. Ebeling, S. Hassoun, T. A. Ngo, and R. Wille. The chaos router chip: Design and implementation of an adaptive router. In *Proceedings of VLSI '93*, Sept. 1993.
3. K. Bolding and L. Snyder. Mesh and torus chaotic routing. In *Proceedings of the Advanced Research in VLSI and Parallel Systems Conference*, Mar. 1992.
4. R. V. Boppana and S. Chalasani. A comparison of adaptive wormhole routing algorithms. In *Proceedings of the International Symposium on Computer Architecture*, May 1993.
5. R. Cypher and L. Gravano. Adaptive, deadlock-free packet routing in torus networks with minimal storage. In *International Conference on Parallel Processing*, 1992.
6. W. Dally and C. Seitz. Deadlock-free message routing in multiprocessor interconnection networks. *IEEE Transactions on Computers*, C-36(5):547–553, May 1987.
7. W. J. Dally and H. Aoki. Deadlock-free adaptive routing in multicomputer networks using virtual channels. *IEEE Transactions on Parallel and Distributed Systems*, 1992.
8. S. A. Felperin, L. Gravano, G. D. Pifarré, and J. L. C. Sanz. Fully-adaptive routing: Packet switching performance and wormhole algorithms. In *Supercomputing '91 Proceedings*, Nov. 1991.
9. M. L. Fulgham and L. Snyder. Performance of chaos and oblivious routers under non-uniform traffic. Technical Report 93-06-01, Department of Computer Science and Engineering, University of Washington, June 1993.
10. P. Kermani and L. Kleinrock. Virtual cut-through: A new computer communication switching technique. *Computer Networks*, 3:267–286, 1979.
11. S. Konstantinidou and L. Snyder. Chaos router: Architecture and performance. In *Proceedings of the 18th International Symposium on Computer Architecture*, pages 212–221, May 1991.
12. J. Y. Ngai and C. L. Seitz. A framework for adaptive routing in multicomputer networks. In *Proceedings of the Symposium on Parallel Algorithms and Architechtures*, pages 1–9, 1989.

Performance Evaluation of Adaptive Routing Algorithms for k-ary n-cubes

José Duato   Pedro López

Facultad de Informática
Universidad Politécnica de Valencia
P.O.B. 22012. 46071 - Valencia, SPAIN
E-mail: {jduato,plopez}@aii.upv.es

Abstract.   Deadlock avoidance is a key issue in wormhole networks. A first approach [9] consists in removing the cyclic dependencies between channels. Although the absence of cyclic dependencies is a necessary and sufficient condition for deadlock-free deterministic routing, it is only a sufficient condition for deadlock-free adaptive routing. A more powerful approach [12] only requires the absence of cyclic dependencies on a connected channel subset. Moreover, we proposed a necessary and sufficient condition for deadlock-free adaptive routing [15].

In this paper, we design adaptive routing algorithms for k-ary n-cubes. In particular, we propose partially adaptive and fully adaptive routing algorithms which considerably increase the throughput achieved by the deterministic routing algorithm. Also, we evaluate the performance of the new routing algorithms under both, uniform and non-uniform distribution of message destinations.

1 Introduction

A lot of research effort has been dedicated during the last decade to improve the performance of multicomputers [2]. A key architectural issue is the interconnection network. In first generation multicomputers, a store-and-forward flow-control mechanism has been used. Each time a message reaches a node, it is buffered in local memory. However, second generation multicomputers use wormhole routing flow-control [9]. Each message is serialized into a sequence of parallel data units, referred to as flow control units, or flits [8]. The flit at the head of a message determines the route. As the header flit is routed, the remaining flits follow it in a pipeline fashion. When the header is routed, the router can offer one or more alternative paths, depending on whether the routing algorithm is deterministic or adaptive. If all the channels offered by the router are busy, the header is blocked until one of those channels is freed; the flow control within the network blocks the trailing flits. Virtual cut-through [22] is very

---

This work was supported by the Spanish CICYT under Grant TIC91-1157-C03-03

similar to wormhole. However, when a header becomes blocked, the message is stored, removing it from the network. As a consequence, virtual cut-through usually requires a fixed packet size and a larger amount of buffer storage [24].

Wormhole flow-control has two important advantages over the store-and-forward flow-control. Firstly, it avoids using storage bandwidth in the nodes through which messages are routed. Secondly, this technique makes the message latency largely insensitive to the distance in the message-passing network.

Deadlocks may appear if the routing algorithms are not carefully designed. A deadlock in the interconnection network of a multicomputer occurs when no message can advance toward its destination because the queues of the message system are full. Many deadlock-free routing algorithms have been developed for store-and-forward computer networks [17, 20, 32]. These algorithms are based on a structured buffer pool. However, with wormhole routing, buffer allocation cannot be restricted, because flits have no routing information. Once the header of a message has been accepted by a channel, the remaining flits must be accepted before the flits of any other message can be accepted. So, routing must be restricted to avoid deadlock. Dally [9] proposed the necessary and sufficient condition for a deterministic routing algorithm to be deadlock-free. Based on this condition, he defined a channel dependency graph and established a total order among channels. Routing is restricted to visit channels in decreasing order to eliminate cycles in the channel dependency graph. If the routing restrictions disconnect the network, physical channels are split into virtual channels to connect the network again. This technique has been applied to the design of routing chips for multicomputers [8], multicomputer nodes with integrated communication support [5] and systolic communication [25, 5]. Also, the use of virtual channels can increase throughput considerably [10].

Although Dally's theorem was proposed for deterministic routing, it has been applied to adaptive routing [21, 29, 6, 18]. Also, it has been applied to multicast routing [26]. In these cases, Dally's theorem becomes a sufficient condition for deadlock-freedom. An innovative view of the conditions for deadlock-free adaptive routing is the turn model [18]. In this model, a message produces a turn when it changes direction, usually changing from one dimension to another. Turns are combined into cycles. Prohibiting just enough turns to break all the cycles prevents deadlock. However, the turn model is also based on Dally's theorem, requiring the absence of cycles in the channel dependency graph. This approach is too restrictive, limiting the number of alternative paths that can be used.

A different approach consists of allowing the existence of cyclic dependencies between channels, providing fully adaptive routing with a modest number of virtual channels. The *-channels algorithm [3] prevents deadlock by dynamically disallowing paths based on occupancy of buffers in neighboring nodes.

The theory proposed by us [12, 14] is not restricted to a particular topology or routing algorithm. Cyclic dependencies between channels are allowed, provided that there exists a connected channel subset free of cyclic dependencies. To simplify the application of this theory, we proposed two design methodologies. The resulting routing algorithms achieve good performance because the channels belonging to the cyclic subset can be used almost without restrictions. Several authors have proposed and evaluated routing algorithms based on our theory [13, 14, 16, 28, 30]. Recently, Lin et al. [27] have proposed the message flow model which also allows the existence of cyclic dependencies between channels. The authors also propose fully adaptive routing algorithms for meshes and hypercubes.

More recently, we proposed a necessary and sufficient condition for deadlock-free adaptive routing [15]. Recent studies [7] have shown that virtual channels are expensive, increasing node delay considerably. Thus, there is a growing interest on the design of fully adaptive routing algorithms with minimum routing restrictions and as few virtual channels per physical channel as possible [19]. The theorem proposed in [15] is the key for the design of those routing algorithms.

In this paper, we propose partially adaptive and fully adaptive routing algorithms for k-ary n-cubes which considerably increase the throughput achieved by the deterministic routing algorithm. Also, we evaluate the performance of the new routing algorithms under both, uniform and non-uniform distribution of message destinations. In section 2, we present a routing algorithm for ring interconnection networks. Then, in section 3, we design adaptive routing algorithms for k-ary n-cubes. The resulting algorithms are evaluated by simulation in section 4. In particular, we show that it is possible to double the throughput achieved by the deterministic routing algorithm proposed in [9] without increasing the hardware complexity significantly. Finally, some conclusions are drawn.

2 Routing algorithm for rings

Consider a unidirectional ring with four nodes denoted $n_i, i = \{0, 1, 2, 3\}$ and two channels connecting each pair of adjacent nodes, except nodes n_3 and n_0 which are linked by a single channel. Let $c_{Ai}, i = \{0, 1, 2, 3\}$ and $c_{Hi}, i = \{0, 1, 2\}$ be the outgoing channels from node n_i. The routing algorithm can be stated as follows: If the current node n_i is equal to the destination node n_j, store the message. Otherwise, use either $c_{Ai}, \forall j \neq i$ or $c_{Hi}, \forall j > i$. In other words, c_{Ai} channels can be used to forward messages to all the destinations. However, c_{Hi} channels can only be used if the destination is higher than the current node. For messages that are allowed to use both channels, a higher priority has been assigned to c_{Hi} channels in order to favour messages with a single routing choice. Figure 1 shows the network.

This routing algorithm is deadlock-free, as shown in [15]. It must be noticed that, after accepting a tail flit, a queue must be emptied before accepting another header flit. Thus, when a message is blocked, its header flit will always occupy the head of a queue.

The routing algorithm remains deadlock-free if an additional channel c_{W3} is added in parallel with c_{A3} with the same routing capability as c_{A3}. This extension is useful to have the same number of channels connecting each pair of nodes.

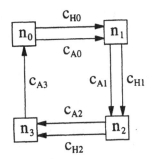

Fig. 1. Network for the example

3 Adaptive routing on k-ary n-cubes

In this section, we propose two adaptive routing algorithms for k-ary n-cubes: partially adaptive and fully adaptive. They are based on the extension of the algorithm for unidirectional rings proposed in section 2. First, we will extend this routing algorithm for bidirectional rings. As channels are bidirectional, they can be split into two unidirectional channels. Thus, both versions of the routing algorithm (with c_{Hi} and c_{Li} channels) are used, always forwarding messages through a minimal path. As messages follow a minimal path, once a message starts crossing channels in one direction, it cannot turn and continue in the opposite direction. Thus, the use of bidirectional channels does not introduce any additional channel dependency and the routing algorithm is deadlock-free.

The partially adaptive routing algorithm for k-ary n-cubes uses the algorithm for bidirectional rings (with c_{Wi} channels) inside each dimension. Channels can only be used crossing dimensions in ascending order. As stated above, a higher priority has been assigned to c_{Hi} (c_{Li}) channels in order to favour messages with less routing choices. The result is a partially adaptive minimal routing algorithm which only requires two virtual channels per physical channel. As dimensions are crossed in ascending order, adding dimensions does not introduce any additional cyclic dependency and the routing algorithm is still deadlock-free.

To design a fully adaptive routing algorithm based on the new theory we use the first design methodology proposed in [12, 14]. This methodology starts from a basic routing algorithm, adding virtual channels in a regular way. In this case, we start from the partially adaptive routing algorithm. Then, we add a third virtual channel to each physical channel. The third virtual channel is used for fully adaptive routing, crossing dimensions in any order following a minimal path. Obviously, the first and second virtual channels are used exactly in the same way as in the partially adaptive algorithm. The selection function [14] assigns priorities cyclically among the virtual channels crossing different dimensions, thus minimizing channel multiplexing. Also, inside each dimension, the fully adaptive virtual channel has higher priority than the original ones. The result is a fully adaptive minimal routing algorithm with three virtual channels per physical channel. Similarly to the example proposed in [14], it is easy to prove deadlock-freedom.

4 Performance evaluation

We have evaluated the behavior of the new adaptive algorithms by simulation. The evaluation methodology used is based on the one proposed in [14]. The most important performance measures are latency (time required to deliver a message) and throughput (maximum traffic accepted by the network). Traffic is the flit reception rate. Latency is measured in nanoseconds. Traffic is measured in flits per node per microsecond. Notice that we have used absolute measurement units because we are going to compare routing algorithms that involve different implementations, and consequently, different clock frequencies.

Taking into account the sizes of current multicomputers and the studies about the optimal number of dimensions [1], we have evaluated the performance of the new algorithms on a 8-ary 3-cube network (512 nodes). In addition, the deterministic algorithm proposed in [9] for the k-ary n-cube, modified so that it uses bidirectional channels, has been evaluated for comparison purposes. It uses two virtual channels per physical channel as the partially adaptive algorithm.

4.1 Multicomputer model

Our simulator models the network at the flit level. Each node of the network consists of a processor, its local memory, a router, a switch, and several channels. A two-port architecture [31] is considered. However, in order to analyze the network bandwidth more accurately, we do not consider contention in the delivery buffers.

The router decides the output channel for a message as a function of its destination node, the current node and the output channel status. The router can only process one message header at a time. It is assigned to waiting messages in a demand-slotted round-robin fashion (including those messages generated in the local processor). When a message gets the router but it can not be routed because all the alternative output channels are busy, it must wait in the input buffer until its next turn.

The switch is a crossbar. So, it allows multiple messages traversing it simultaneously without interference. It is configured by the router each time a successful routing is made.

Physical channels can be split into several virtual channels. Virtual channels are assigned to the physical link using a demand-slotted round-robin arbitration scheme. Each virtual channel has an associated buffer. This buffer is divided into two halves, one associated with the output port of the switch, and another one associated with the input to the next node's switch. The size of these buffers affects algorithm performance. We have used the criterion of keeping constant and equal to 12 flits the total buffer capacity associated to each physical channel, regardless of the number of virtual channels.

We assume that all operations inside each node are synchronized by its local clock signal. To compute the clock frequency of each node, we will use the delay model proposed in [7]. It assumes 0.8 micron CMOS gate array technology for the implementation.

- Router. Routing a message involves the following operations: Address decoding, routing decision, and header selection.

  The first operation extracts the message header and generates requests of acceptable outputs based on the routing algorithm. In other words, the address decoder implements what we have called routing function [14]. According to [7], the address decoder delay is constant and equal to 2.7 nanoseconds.

  The routing decision logic takes as inputs the possible output channels generated by the address decoder, and the status of the output channels. In other words, this logic implements what we have called selection function [14]. This circuit has a delay that grows logarithmically with the number of alternatives, or degree of freedom, offered by the routing algorithm. Representing by F the degree of freedom, this circuit has a delay value given by $0.6 + 0.6 \log F$ ns.

  Finally, the router must compute the new header, depending on the output channel selected. While new headers can be calculated in parallel with the routing decision, it is necessary to select the appropriate one when this decision is made. This operation has a delay that grows logarithmically with the degree of freedom. Thus, this delay will be $1.4 + 0.6 \log F$ ns.

  Therefore, total routing time will be the sum of all delays, yielding:

  $$T_r = 2.7 + 0.6 + 0.6 \log F + 1.4 + 0.6 \log F = 4.7 + 1.2 \log F \text{ ns.}$$

  Notice that the header flit is not transferred to the output channel during the routing operation. This transfer will be performed later by the switch.

- Switch. The time required to transfer a flit from one input channel to the corresponding output channel is the sum of the delay involved in the internal flow control unit, the delay of the crossbar, and the set-up time of the output channel latch.

  The flow control unit manages the buffers, preventing overflow and underflow. It has a constant delay equal to 2.2 ns.

  The crossbar is usually implemented using a tree of selectors for each output. Thus, its delay grows logarithmically with the number of ports. Assuming that P is the number of ports of the crossbar, its delay is given by $0.4 + 0.6 \log P$ ns.

  Finally, the set-up time of a latch is 0.8 ns.

  Therefore, switch time is:

  $$T_s = 2.2 + 0.4 + 0.6 \log P + 0.8 = 3.4 + 0.6 \log P \text{ ns.}$$

- Channels. The time required to transfer a flit across a physical channel includes the off-chip delay across the wires, and the time required to latch it onto the destination. This time is the sum of the output buffer, input buffer, input latch and synchronizer delays. Typical values for the technology used are 2.5 (with 25 pF load), 0.6, 0.8, and 1.0 ns, respectively, yielding 4.9 ns per flit. Notice that we assume that all the channels have the same off-chip delay across the wires. These could be accomplished by assembling the network in three dimensions.

If virtual channels are used, the time required to arbitrate and select one of the ready flits must be added. The virtual channel controller has a delay logarithmic in the number of virtual channels per physical channel. Notice that we do not include any additional delay to decode the virtual channel number at the input of the next node, because virtual channels are usually identified using one signal for each one [8]. If V is the number of virtual channels per physical channel, virtual channel controller delay is $1.24 + 0.6 \log V$ ns.

Then, total channel delay yields:

$T_c = 4.9 + 1.24 + 0.6 \log V = 6.14 + 0.6 \log V$ ns.

Next, we will instantiate these times for every routing algorithm evaluated:

1. Deterministic routing. This routing algorithm has a single routing choice. The switch is usually made by cascading several low size crossbars, one per dimension. Each of them switches messages going in the positive or negative direction of the same dimension, or crossing to the next dimension. As there are two virtual channels per physical channel, each crossbar has 5 ports. Taking into account that dimensions are crossed in order, most messages will continue in the same dimension. Thus, the number of crossbars traversed will be one most of the times. Then, for the deterministic routing algorithm, we have $F = 1$, $P = 5$, and $V = 2$, obtaining the following delays for router, switch and channel, respectively:

$T_r = 4.7 + 1.2 \log 1 = 4.7$ ns.

$T_s = 3.4 + 0.6 \log 5 = 4.8$ ns.

$T_c = 6.14 + 0.6 \log 2 = 6.8$ ns.

2. Partially adaptive routing. The number of routing choices is equal to two, because there are two virtual channels per physical channel that can be used in most cases, but dimensions are crossed in order. Because dimensions are crossed in order, the switch can be the same as for the deterministic algorithm. Substituting $F = 2$, $P = 5$, and $V = 2$:

$T_r = 4.7 + 1.2 \log 2 = 5.9$ ns.

$T_s = 3.4 + 0.6 \log 5 = 4.8$ ns.

$T_c = 6.14 + 0.6 \log 2 = 6.8$ ns.

3. Fully adaptive routing. In this case, the number of routing choices is 5, because we have one virtual channel in each dimension that can be used to cross the dimensions in any order, and also the two channels provided by the partially adaptive algorithm. As there are two channels per dimension, with three virtual channels per physical channel, plus two memory channels, the switch is a 20 port crossbar. Thus, we have $F = 5$, $P = 20$, and $V = 3$. Substituting:

$T_r = 4.7 + 1.2 \log 5 = 7.5$ ns.

$T_s = 3.4 + 0.6 \log 20 = 6$ ns.

$T_c = 6.14 + 0.6 \log 3 = 7.1$ ns.

Assuming that the three operations must be performed in one clock cycle, the clock period is determined by the slowest operation. Hence:

1. $T_{\text{Deterministic}} = \max(T_r, T_s, T_c) = \max(4.7, 4.8, 6.8) = 6.8$ ns.

2. $T_{\text{Partially adaptive}} = \max(T_r, T_s, T_c) = \max(5.9, 4.8, 6.8) = 6.8$ ns.

3. $T_{\text{Fully adaptive}} = \max(T_r, T_s, T_c) = \max(7.5, 6, 7.1) = 7.5$ ns.

That is, the deterministic or the partially adaptive routing algorithm require the same clock period of 6.8 ns. Notice that routing time is greater in the latter case, but channel time dominates in both cases, thus being the bottleneck. For the adaptive algorithm, we must slow down the clock frequency by 10 %, increasing clock period up to 7.5 ns.

4.2 Message generation

Message traffic and message length depend on applications and operating system. For each simulation run, we have considered that message generation rate is constant and the same for all the nodes. Once the network has reached a steady state, the flit generation rate is equal to the flit reception rate (traffic). We have evaluated the full range of traffic, from low load to saturation. On the other hand, we have considered three kinds of message distribution: uniform, with locality, and specific.

In the first case, message destination is randomly chosen among all the nodes. This pattern has been widely used in other performance evaluation studies [10, 6, 4]. For the message distribution with locality, the destination node is uniformly distributed inside a cube centered at the source node. We have considered two values for the side of this cube: 2 and 4 channels, modeling short and medium distance traffic, respectively. Finally, we have considered specific communication patterns between pairs of nodes. These patterns have been selected taking into account the permutations that are usually performed in parallel numerical algorithms [33, 23]:

- Bit-reversal. The node with binary coordinates $a_{n-1}, a_{n-2}, ..., a_1, a_0$ communicates with the node $a_0, a_1, ..., a_{n-2}, a_{n-1}$.

- Perfect-shuffle. The node with binary coordinates $a_{n-1}, a_{n-2}, ..., a_1, a_0$ communicates with the node $a_{n-2}, a_{n-3}, ..., a_0, a_{n-1}$ (rotate left one bit).

In this case, the destination node for the messages generated by a given node is always the same. Thus, the utilization factor of all the network links is not uniform.

For message length, 16-flit and 64-flit messages were considered. Nevertheless, we have found that message length does not affect very much the relative performance of the algorithms. Thus, we will only show the results for short messages.

For the fully adaptive algorithm, we have used the injection limitation mechanism proposed in [30], in order to prevent performance degradation when the traffic is near saturation. Basically, we estimate the amount of traffic in the network by considering the total number of free virtual channels at each node. If this number is lower than an empirically obtained threshold, the message is buffered until this situation change. Additionally, in order to guarantee the absence of livelock, this limitation mechanism is combined with a timeout mechanism, injecting messages when the time they have been waiting is greater than another threshold. For the partially adaptive routing algorithm, we have found that the injection limitation mechanism is not needed.

4.3 Simulation results

Figure 2 shows the average message latency versus traffic when using a uniform distribution for message destination. Figure 3 compares the same routing algorithms on the same network when messages are sent locally. In this case, message destinations are uniformly distributed inside a cube centered at the source node with side equal to four channels.

As can be seen, both adaptive algorithms considerably increase performance over the deterministic one. The partially adaptive algorithm increases throughput by 67 % for the uniform distribution and it almost doubles throughput when messages are sent locally. Taking into account that our algorithm allows most messages to choose between two virtual channels instead of one, this improvement is due to the ability of using alternative channels without adding more virtual channels. The advantages of virtual-channel flow control were properly highlighted in [10]. These results are improved for the uniform distribution by the fully adaptive algorithm, which increases throughput over the deterministic one by a factor of 2.4. The higher performance achieved by the fully adaptive algorithm is mainly due to the additional freedom to cross dimensions in any order. The fully adaptive algorithm also achieves a reduction in message latency with respect to the deterministic and the partially adaptive ones if traffic is greater than 14 flits/node/μs and 34 flits/node/μs, respectively, and for uniform traffic. Notice that for low values of traffic, the simpler routing algorithms achieve better performance, due to the lower clock frequency of the adaptive algorithm.

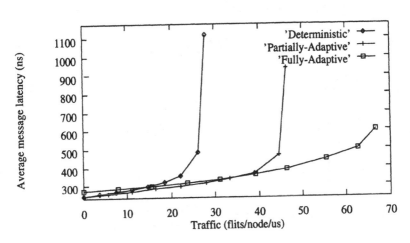

Fig. 2. Average message latency versus traffic for uniform distribution of message destinations

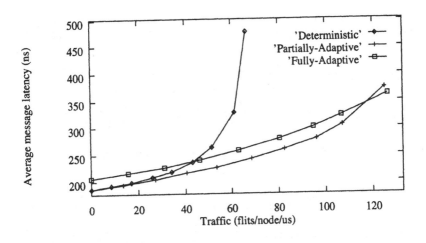

Fig. 3. Average message latency versus traffic for local traffic

Figure 4 shows the results achieved by the algorithms when traffic is very local. Message destination is randomly chosen inside a cube centered at the source node with side equal to 2 channels. As can be expected, the use of the adaptive algorithms is not as advantageous as above, because the average distance traversed by messages is very short. In particular, the fully adaptive algorithm only achieves a 6 % more throughput than the deterministic one, and a lower throughput than the partially adaptive one. Despite its limited adaptivity, the partially adaptive algorithm increases throughput by 23 % over the deterministic

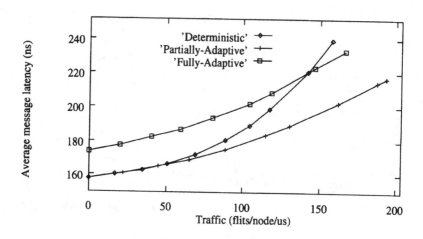

Fig. 4. Average message latency versus traffic for very local traffic

one. Message latency is lower for the partially adaptive algorithm for the whole range of traffic. However, the fully adaptive algorithm only has a lower message latency than the deterministic one for values of traffic greater than 90 % of its throughput.

As stated in [11], adaptive routing is required for many non-uniform traffic patterns. Figures 5 and 6 compare the routing algorithms considering the specific communication patterns described above (bit-reversal and perfect-shuffle). In both cases, the deterministic algorithm achieves very poor performance. In these situations is when an adaptive routing algorithm is required.

The fully adaptive algorithm increases throughput over the deterministic algorithm by a factor of 2 for the perfect-shuffle communication pattern, and by a factor of more than 6 when using the bit-reversal communication pattern. In addition, it must be noticed that message latency grows very fast when the deterministic algorithm is used. The worst case is the bit-reversal distribution. However, the fully adaptive algorithm keeps a very low latency for the range of usable traffic. For the bit-reversal pattern, the partially adaptive algorithm only achieves a little more throughput (about 23 % more) over the deterministic one. For the perfect-shuffle distribution, the partially adaptive algorithm behaves better, increasing throughput by 56 % over the deterministic one.

Finally, it must be noticed that more virtual channels can be used in all the routing algorithms. But delays will increase accordingly. For instance, the partially adaptive algorithm with 3 virtual channels (two c_{Ai} and one c_{Hi} or c_{Li}) increases average latency by up to a 15 % for a uniform distribution of destinations, whereas throughput is only improved by 7 %. Thus, it is not interesting.

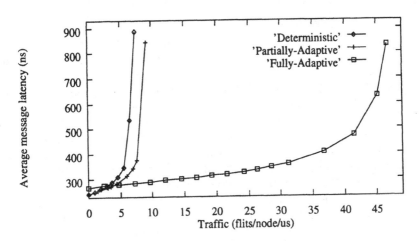

Fig. 5. Average message latency versus traffic for bit-reversal traffic pattern

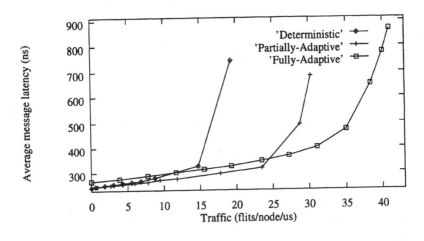

Fig. 6. Average message latency versus traffic for perfect-shuffle traffic pattern

5 Conclusions

In this paper, we have designed two routing algorithms for k-ary n-cubes, based on the theory proposed in [15]. The first algorithm is partially adaptive and it only requires two virtual channels per physical channel. The second algorithm is fully adaptive. It requires three virtual channels per physical channel.

The performance of these algorithms has been analyzed by simulation, and compared with the deterministic routing algorithm proposed in [9]. Uniform, local, and non-uniform communication patterns have been considered in the evaluation of the algorithms.

To make a fair comparison, we have taken into account the delays of the main components of the communication controller for each routing algorithm considered, according to the delay model proposed in [7]. The implementation of our partially adaptive algorithm is almost as simple as the deterministic one. Both of them use the same number of virtual channels, and a very similar crossbar. The only additional cost is produced by considering the status of the output virtual channels in the current dimension. However, the additional circuits do not require a lower clock frequency. This low extra implementation cost is unusual in adaptive algorithms [7], making our proposal very attractive from the practical point of view. On the other hand, the fully adaptive routing algorithm requires at least one additional virtual channel per physical channel and a more complex switch and router. As a consequence, clock period increases by 10 %.

The simulation results show that the partially adaptive algorithm behaves better than the deterministic one for all the communication patterns considered. The fully adaptive routing algorithm achieves a great improvement over the other ones when non-uniform communication patterns or uniform communication patterns without locality are used. However, if messages are sent locally, the improvement of the adaptive algorithm over the partially adaptive one is small.

References

1. A. Agarwal, "Limits on interconnection network performance", *IEEE Trans. Parallel Distributed Syst.*, vol. 2, no. 4, pp. 398–412, Oct. 1991.

2. W.C. Athas and C.L. Seitz, "Multicomputers: Message-passing concurrent computers," *IEEE Comput. Mag.*, vol. 21, no. 8, pp. 9–24, Aug. 1988.

3. P.E. Berman, L. Gravano, G.D. Pifarré and J.L.C. Sanz, "Adaptive deadlock- and livelock-free routing with all minimal paths in torus networks," in *Proc. 4th ACM Symp. Parallel Algorithms Architectures*, June 1992.

4. R.V. Bopana, and S. Chalasani, "A comparison of adaptive wormhole routing algorithms," in *Proc. 20th Annu. Int. Symp. Comput. Architecture*, May 1993.

5. S. Borkar et al., "iWarp: An integrated solution to high-speed parallel computing," in *Proc. Supercomputing'88*, Nov. 1988.

6. A.A. Chien and J.H. Kim, "Planar-adaptive routing: Low-cost adaptive networks for multiprocessors," in *Proc. 19th Annu. Int. Symp. Comput. Architecture*, May 1992.

7. A.A. Chien, "A cost and speed model for k-ary n-cube wormhole routers," in *Proc. Hot Interconnects'93*, Aug. 1993.

58

8. W.J. Dally and C.L. Seitz, "The torus routing chip," *Distributed Comput.*, vol. 1, no. 3, pp. 187–196, Oct. 1986.

9. W.J. Dally and C.L. Seitz, "Deadlock-free message routing in multiprocessor interconnection networks," *IEEE Trans. Comput.*, vol. C-36, no. 5, pp. 547–553, May 1987.

10. W.J. Dally, "Virtual-channel flow control," *IEEE Trans. Parallel Distributed Syst.*, vol. 3, no. 2, pp. 194–205, Mar. 1992.

11. W.J. Dally and H. Aoki, "Deadlock-free adaptive routing in multicomputer networks using virtual channels," *IEEE Trans. Parallel Distributed Syst.*, vol. 4, no. 4, pp. 466–475, April 1993.

12. J. Duato, "On the design of deadlock-free adaptive routing algorithms for multicomputers: design methodologies," in *Proc. Parallel Architectures Languages Europe 91*, June 1991.

13. J. Duato, "Deadlock-free adaptive routing algorithms for multicomputers: evaluation of a new algorithm," in *Proc. 3rd IEEE Int. Symp. Parallel Distributed Processing*, Dec. 1991.

14. J. Duato, "A new theory of deadlock-free adaptive routing in wormhole networks," *IEEE Trans. Parallel Distributed Syst.*, vol. 4, no. 12, pp. 1320–1331, Dec. 1993.

15. J. Duato, "A necessary and sufficient condition for deadlock-free adaptive routing in wormhole networks," in *Proc. Int. Conf. Parallel Processing*, Aug. 1994.

16. P.T. Gaughan and S. Yalamanchili, "Adaptive routing protocols for hypercube interconnection networks," *IEEE Comput. Mag.*, vol. 26, no. 5, pp. 12–23, May 1993.

17. D. Gelernter, "A DAG-based algorithm for prevention of store-and-forward deadlock in packet networks," *IEEE Trans. Comput.*, vol. C-30, pp. 709–715, Oct. 1981.

18. C.J. Glass and L.M. Ni, "The turn model for adaptive routing," in *Proc. 19th Annu. Int. Symp. Comput. Architecture*, May 1992.

19. C.J. Glass and L.M. Ni, "Maximally fully adaptive routing in 2D meshes," in *Proc. Int. Conf. Parallel Processing*, Aug. 1992.

20. K.D. Gunther, "Prevention of deadlocks in packet-switched data transport systems," *IEEE Trans. Commun.*, vol. COM-29, pp. 512–524, Apr. 1981.

21. C.R. Jesshope, P.R. Miller, and J.T. Yantchev, "High performance communications in processor networks," in *Proc. 16th Annu. Int. Symp. Comput. Architecture*, May–June 1989.

22. P. Kermani and L. Kleinrock, "Virtual cut-through: a new computer communication switching technique," *Comput. Networks*, vol. 3, pp. 267–286, 1979.

23. J. Kim, A.Chien, "An evaluation of the planar/adaptive routing," in *Proc. 4th IEEE Int. Symp. Parallel Distributed Processing*, 1992.

24. S. Konstantinidou, L. Snyder, "Chaos router: Architecture and performance," in *Proc. 18th Annu. Int. Symp. Comput. Architecture*, May 1991.

25. H.T. Kung, "Deadlock avoidance for systolic communication," in *Proc. 15th Annu. Int. Symp. Comput. Architecture*, May–June 1988.

26. X. Lin and L.M. Ni, "Deadlock-free multicast wormhole routing in multicomputer networks," in *Proc. 18th Annu. Int. Symp. Comput. Architecture*, May 1991.

27. X. Lin, P.K. McKinley and L.M. Ni, "The message flow model for routing in wormhole-routed networks," in *Proc. 1993 Int. Conf. Parallel Processing*, Aug. 1993.

28. Z. Liu, J. Duato and L.-E. Thorelli, "Grouping virtual channels for deadlock-free adaptive wormhole routing," in *Proc. Parallel Architectures Languages Europe 93*, June 1993.

29. D.H. Linder and J.C. Harden, "An adaptive and fault tolerant wormhole routing strategy for k-ary n-cubes," *IEEE Trans. Comput.*, vol. C-40, no. 1, pp. 2–12, Jan. 1991.

30. P. López and J. Duato, "Deadlock-free adaptive routing algorithms for the 3D-torus: limitations and solutions," in *Proc. Parallel Architectures Languages Europe 93*, June 1993.

31. P.K. McKinley, H. Xu, A. Esfahanian and L.M. Ni, "Unicast-based multicast communication in wormhole-routed networks," in *Proc. 1992 Int. Conf. Parallel Processing*, Aug. 1992.

32. P.M. Merlin and P.J. Schweitzer, "Deadlock avoidance in store-and-forward networks – I: Store-and-forward deadlock," *IEEE Trans. Commun.*, vol. COM-28, pp. 345–354, Mar. 1980.

33. P.R. Miller, "Efficient communications for fine-grain distributed computers," Ph.D Thesis, Southamptom University, 1991.

The Performance of Adaptive Routers on Worst Case Permutations

Donald D. Chinn *

Department of Computer Science and Engineering
University of Washington
Seattle, WA 98195 USA

Abstract. Chaotic routing [4, 13, 14] is a randomized, nonminimal adaptive routing algorithm for multicomputers. An adaptive routing algorithm is one in which the path a packet takes from its source to its destination may depend on other packets it encounters. Such algorithms potentially avoid network bottlenecks by routing packets around "hot spots." Minimal adaptive routing algorithms have the additional advantage that the path each packet takes is a shortest one.

Chinn, Leighton, and Tompa [6] provide a lower bound for permutation routing problems on the $n \times n$ mesh for a large class of deterministic minimal adaptive algorithms. Specifically, they prove that for any such routing algorithm, there exists a permutation that requires $\Omega(n^2/k^2)$ steps to route all the packets in the permutation, where k is the number of packets a node can contain.

We present experimental results showing the performance of the Chaos router on permutations for which a deterministic minimal adaptive version of the Chaos router performs poorly. The results show that on these worst case permutations, the time the Chaos router takes to deliver all packets in the permutation closely fits a polynomial in n whose degree is $3/2$. From these experiments, we conjecture that no practical router for the $n \times n$ mesh can route arbitrary permutations in time proportional to n, even though the mesh topology has the bandwidth to do so.

1. Introduction

Routers in almost all state-of-the-art machines use *oblivious* algorithms, where a message's path depends only on the source and destination addresses of the packet. The simplest of these algorithms is the *dimension order* algorithm: a packet moves along its row until it reaches its destination column, and then moves along that column until it reaches its destination. The logic to implement the routing decisions and guarantee deadlock-freedom is relatively simple in this

---

* dci@cs.washington.edu; This material is based upon work supported in part by the National Science Foundation under Grant MIP-9213469.

approach. However, oblivious routing performance degrades quickly in the presence of congestion and/or faults, because the algorithm is not flexible enough to use the available bandwidth effectively. Machines that use oblivious algorithms include the Intel Touchstone [11] and Paragon, the MIT J-machine [18], and the Mosaic from Cal Tech [19].

Adaptive routing is an alternative to oblivious routing. In adaptive algorithms, the path a message takes from its source to its destination may depend on packets it encounters. Intuitively, adaptive routers potentially can use the available bandwidth to relieve the congestion or to route around faults. In *minimal* adaptive routing, the path a packet takes is a shortest one. An example of a minimal adaptive algorithm is the one of Cypher and Gravano [7] or of Chien and Kim [5]. In *nonminimal* adaptive routing, a packet may take any path between its source and its destination, possibly making moves in the network that place it farther from its destination than before the move. When a packet makes such a move, the packet is said to have been *derouted*. Nonminimal routing allows the most flexibility in packet paths, but at a cost of more complex logic to avoid *livelock*, the situation in which a packet never reaches its destination because it is derouted frequently. Examples of adaptive routers include the Chaos router [4, 13, 14] and the Ngai and Seitz router [16, 17].

One of the simplest benchmarks for a router's performance is how it performs in the worst case on static *one-to-one* (or *partial permutation*) routing problems, where each processor sends at most one message and receives at most one message. The motivation behind this metric of performance is that the traffic generated by a static permutation does not contain any "hot spots", where one node is the destination of many packets. When there are hot spots, performance can be limited by delivery bandwidth. Another reason for interest in permutations is that those that arise in practice, such as the transpose permutation, cause poor performance on some networks. This fact immediately raises the question of whether there is a permutation, for any given network, that causes poor performance. On the $n \times n$ mesh, there theoretically is enough bandwidth to deliver all packets in any permutation in time proportional to n. At the very least, a good routing algorithm should be able to route permutations efficiently (i.e., in $O(n)$ time).

Chinn, Leighton, and Tompa [6] (hereafter referred to as CLT) show that for any algorithm in a large class of deterministic minimal adaptive algorithms for the $n \times n$ mesh, there exists a permutation for that algorithm such that it takes $\Omega(n^2/k^2)$ steps to route all packets in the permutation, where k is the number of packets a node can hold at one time. The class of algorithms for which the lower bound applies is the set of algorithms such that the routing decisions of a node are based only on local information and the only parts of the destination addresses used to make routing decisions are the directions packets in the node can move profitably (i.e., directions that a packet can take to move closer to its destination). In particular, the dimension order algorithm with first-in-first-out (FIFO) queues is in this class. The permutation that yields the lower bound, loosely speaking, is constructed by running the minimal adaptive algorithm and altering the destinations of packets as necessary to make them restricted packets (i.e., packets that have only one profitable direction), causing one large hotspot at the intersection of the paths of these restricted packets. (See Figure 2 in Section 3.)

The key fact about the CLT lower bound is that it is constructive: given an algorithm in the class for which the lower bound applies, one can build a permutation that requires the algorithm $\Omega(n^2/k^2)$ time to route. We can now explore the difference between minimal adaptive algorithms and nonminimal adaptive algorithms by running the permutation constructed in the lower bound (hereafter called the *CLT permutation*) on a nonminimal adaptive algorithm.

Chaotic routing [4, 13, 14] is a randomized, nonminimal adaptive algorithm that is competitive with state-of-the-art oblivious routers. In the Chaos algorithm, a node deroutes packets when it becomes congested, randomly picking which packet to deroute among the packets it contains. Thus, areas of local congestion dissipate via this diffusion mechanism. More details about the algorithm will be given in Section 2.

The question we wish to answer is: How well does Chaos perform on a worst case permutation. Our method was as follows. We first removed all of the derouting logic from the Chaos simulator, which also removed all sources of randomness in the algorithm. Call the resulting routing algorithm *minimal Chaos*. Minimal Chaos falls into the class of algorithms described by CLT. We constructed the CLT permutation for that algorithm and then ran Chaos on that permutation. The difference in running times of the two algorithms is a measure of how effective the derouting mechanism is in Chaos. By running the experiments over a range of mesh sizes, we observed that the behavior of Chaos on the CLT permutation on the $n \times n$ mesh is approximated closely by a polynomial of degree $3/2$.

The remainder of the paper is organized as follows. Section 2 briefly describes the Chaos algorithm. Section 3 describes and gives the results of two experiments that follow the above method. Section 4 gives conclusions.

2. The Chaos Router

Figure 1 shows the block diagram of a node of the Chaos router. A more detailed description of its operation can be found elsewhere [3, 13], but we briefly describe it here.

A node consists of four *input frames* and four *output frames*, one for each of the four neighbors of a node. Each frame can hold exactly as many flits as there are in one packet. A *flit* can be defined as the amount of data that can be transmitted between two nodes in one cycle. In addition to its four pairs of input and output frames, each node has a *central queue* (also called the *multiqueue*)

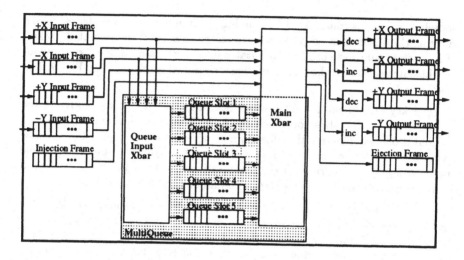

Fig. 1. A Chaos router node.

that can hold up to five packets. There is also a mechanism to inject packets into a node and to deliver packets whose destination is that node.

The Chaos algorithm works as follows. Each of the four directions is examined continuously in turn. If the output frame of the current direction is occupied by a packet, then the next direction is considered. Otherwise, since the output frame is empty, the node tries to find a packet that can profitably use the output frame (i.e., a packet that can move closer to its destination by crossing the associated wire) in its central queue or one of its input frames. If such a packet exists, then one of them is moved into the output frame.

A packet in an input frame with an empty output frame in the same direction must be moved from the input frame if a packet is moved into the output frame. This requirement is necessary to prevent deadlock. If a packet is in an input frame and there is free space in the central queue, then it is moved to the central queue. If, however, there is no space in the central queue (which can happen at this point only if none of the packets in the queue could profitably use the output frame), then a packet is chosen randomly among the five packets in the central queue and moved into the output frame, freeing space in the central queue for the packet in the input frame.

The packet that is chosen randomly is derouted, since it could not profitably use the output frame. There is nothing to prevent a packet from being derouted frequently, resulting in a livelock situation. However, the Chaos algorithm is *probabilistically livelock-free*: the probability that a packet has not been delivered after T time tends to zero as T tends to infinity. (A proof of this can be found in [13] for the hypercube; the proof for the mesh is almost identical [3].)

The Chaos router has a mechanism called *virtual cut-through*, which allows the head of a packet to move from frame to frame (either the input frames, the output frames, or the central queue) without waiting for the tail to arrive in the same buffer space. The router also has a mechanism called *multiqueue bypass*, which allows a packet in an input frame to move directly to an output frame if no packet in the central queue can profitably use the output frame.

In a lightly loaded situation, a packet can take advantage of both virtual cut-through and multiqueue bypass. The header of a packet that enters an input frame at the beginning of cycle t can be in an output frame as early as the beginning of cycle $t + 3$. Since it takes one more cycle for the header to be transmitted to the next node, a header can reside in a node for as few as four cycles.

In a heavily loaded situation, a packet typically moves from an input frame to the central queue, and then from the central queue to an output frame. After the first flit of a packet in an output frame is transmitted to the next node, it takes three cycles to decide which packet to move from the central queue to the output frame. Therefore, in heavily loaded situations, packets can enter an output frame at a rate of one every $s + 3$ cycles, where s is the size of a packet in flits.

In the experiments we describe in Section 3, all packets consisted of 10 flits. Thus, a wire will transmit a packet every 13 cycles in heavily loaded situations, and a packet header can advance one node every four cycles in lightly loaded situations.

The minimal Chaos router works exactly as the Chaos router does, except that the derouting mechanism (and hence all sources of randomness in the algorithm) is disabled. If a packet is in an input frame, its associated output frame is empty, and the central queue is full, then no packet is derouted to make space. The incoming packet must wait until space is free in the central queue as packets are moved profitably through the output frames. It is not hard to see that minimal Chaos is in fact a deterministic minimal adaptive algorithm.

In a general routing situation, minimal Chaos would not be deadlock-free, but in the experiments we performed, all packets have destinations south and/or east of their starting node (and hence no packet needs to move north or west). Thus, no cyclic dependencies for resources can exist, and so the network never gets into a deadlocked situation.

Minimal Chaos is, in a sense, an ideal minimal adaptive algorithm, since it has no mechanism to prevent deadlock. Mechanisms to prevent deadlock, such as virtual channels [8] or that of Cypher and Gravano [7], complicate the logic needed to implement the algorithm.

3. The Experiments

We now describe the experiments we performed on the minimal Chaos and Chaos routers. Table 1 in the Appendix gives all of the data of the experiments.

3.1. Experiment 1

Minimal Chaos falls into the class of algorithms in the CLT lower bound: it is deterministic and minimal adaptive, routing decisions are based only on local information, and the only parts of the destinations of packets used to make routing decisions are their profitable directions. In our first experiment, we built the CLT permutation for minimal Chaos. This permutation is constructed by injecting one packet into each of the nodes in a $cn \times cn$ corner of the mesh (where c is a constant, about $1/17$); these packets have destinations in one of several rows or columns just outside the corner (see Figure 2). A hot spot develops at the intersection of the destinations, since all packets in the permutation pass through that area.

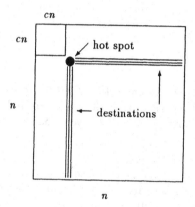

Fig. 2. Generating the CLT permutation.

The time it takes the last packet to reach its destination conceptually can be thought of as the sum of two components: the time it takes for the packet to escape the congestion at the hot spot and the time it takes the packet to reach its destination once it has escaped the hot spot. In the CLT result, the *congestion component* on the $n \times n$ mesh grows quadratically with n. The other component, what we will call the *distance component*, grows linearly with n.

In order to isolate the congestion component, we altered the CLT permutation so that the last twelve packets to be delivered were ones whose destinations were at the outer edge of the mesh. Running the altered permutation on minimal Chaos confirmed that the last packets to be delivered were near the edge of the mesh. Thus, we were able to ensure that the distance component grew linearly (the distance component is roughly $4 \cdot (n - cn)$), allowing us to observe how the congestion component grew.

We then ran the Chaos algorithm on this permutation. The division between the congestion component and the distance component was not as clear in the

Chaos case because there was no guarantee that the last packets to be delivered in the Chaos experiments were near the edge of the mesh. However, we discovered empirically that in fact, of the last packets to be delivered, one of them always had a destination near the edge of the mesh.

The results of the experiment are shown in Figure 3. The top curve represents the performance of minimal Chaos on the altered permutation, and the bottom curve represents the performance of Chaos on the same permutation.

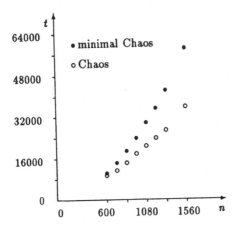

Fig. 3. Results of Experiment 1. The top curve represents minimal Chaos, and the bottom curve represents Chaos.

As predicted by the CLT result, the congestion component of minimal Chaos grows quadratically with n and dominates the distance component. The results for Chaos, however, are inconclusive: it is difficult to estimate what the asymptotic behavior of the bottom curve of Figure 3 is.

The experiment described above began with each node examining the south direction. In an asynchronous environment, the directions nodes are examining when packets are injected are unpredictable. We ran the Chaos algorithm on the CLT permutation with each node initially examining a random direction in order to isolate the effect of the initial state of the nodes. Chaos delivered the packets faster in the random initial state experiments than in the "all examining south" experiments, which is to be expected, since the constructed permutation was built assuming the "all examining south" initial state. However, in all of the five problem sizes for which we did this "random" experiment, Chaos performed no better than 4% better than the results in Figure 3.

The Chaos simulator has an animation package that allows us to observe the behavior of the algorithms by coloring nodes according to how many packets there are in them (see Figure 4). Using the animations, we observed that beyond some distance from the hot spot, packets advance virtually uninterrupted (i.e., at roughly one node every four cycles). This provided the motivation for Experiment 2, which concentrated on the congestion component of delivery time.

3.2. Experiment 2

From the animations of Experiment 1, we discovered not only that packets advance virtually uninterrupted after they escape the hot spot, but also that packets destined for the same row or column "fall into line," so that, informally speaking, nothing interesting happens beyond the hot spot. This fact allowed us to simulate just a small portion of the mesh (i.e., the relevant corner of the mesh) and still observe the same behavior.

Figure 4 shows a typical state of the network in the 150 × 150 corner of the 1560 × 1560 mesh running the CLT permutation on Chaos.

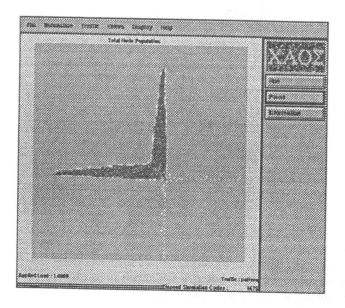

Fig. 4. A snapshot of the 150 × 150 corner of the 1560 × 1560 mesh. The snapshot is of the CLT permutation running on Chaos. Dark areas are heavily congested, whereas white nodes have just one packet in them.

Experiment 2, then, is identical to Experiment 1, except that only a $2cn \times 2cn$ part of the mesh was simulated. When a packet reaches the edge of the submesh, it immediately is removed from the network. Everything else about the experiment is the same: we built the CLT permutation on minimal Chaos with southward initial states and then ran the permutation on Chaos.

Since we were simulating a much smaller part of the mesh, we had enough memory in our machines to simulate much larger meshes in Experiment 2 than in

Experiment 1. Figure 5 shows the results of Experiment 2, which were consistent with the results in Experiment 1.

The curve for Chaos closely fits the curve defined by $4cn + 0.476n^{3/2}$, also plotted in Figure 5. We arrived at this function by first subtracting an estimate of the distance component, $4 \cdot cn$, from the observed data. The congestion component was estimated to be the number of cycles observed minus this estimate of the distance component. If the congestion component grows proportionally to n^x, then the ratio of the congestion components for two different problem sizes is related to the ratio of the problem sizes as follows:

$$\frac{\text{congestion component on the } m \times m \text{ mesh}}{\text{congestion component on the } n \times n \text{ mesh}} = \left(\frac{m}{n}\right)^x \qquad (1)$$

For any two problem sizes, we can compute x by taking the logarithm of both sizes of Equation (1) and solving for x. We computed x for each pair of problem sizes and observed that the computed values were near 1.5 for almost all pairs. In particular, for pairs of problem sizes that differed by 480 or more, the computed value of x is always between 1.4 and 1.7. The coefficient of our $n^{3/2}$ term was calculated using a curve-fitting algorithm on the observed data minus the assumed distance component of $4cn$.

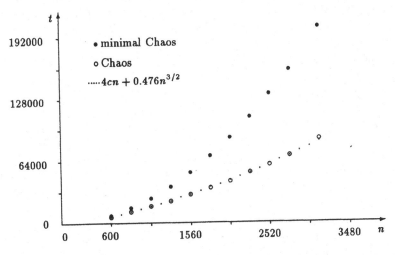

Fig. 5. Results of Experiment 2. The top curve represents minimal Chaos, and the bottom curve represents Chaos.

As in Experiment 1, we ran Chaos on the CLT permutation with each node in a random initial state. For all of the six mesh sizes on which we did the experiment with random initial states, Chaos performed no better than 10% better than the results in Figure 5. It is not surprising that the percentage difference is greater than in Experiment 1, since the distance component, which is not affected by random initial state, is much greater in Experiment 1 than in Experiment 2.

The CLT permutation arranges packets so that in minimal Chaos, packets destined for, say, the fourth row south of the hot spot are delayed by packets destined for the third, second, and first rows south of the hot spot. Similarly, packets destined for the fifth row are delayed by the fourth, third, etc. However, when we run Chaos on these permutations, the packets destined for the first row south of the hot spot are delayed by the second, third, etc. rows of packets. That is, although the worst case permutation for minimal Chaos causes poor behavior in Chaos, it does not do so in the same way as in the CLT lower bound.

4. Conclusions

Our experiments have examined the performance of the Chaos router on worst case permutation routing instances. We conclude from the results that a polynomial in n of degree $3/2$ approximates the performance of Chaos on worst case permutations constructed for a deterministic minimal adaptive version of it. The experiments presented here do not preclude the existence of permutations that cause quadratic behavior for Chaos, although this seems unlikely to us after observing the way Chaos routes packets. Note that for state-of-the-art dimension order routers, the CLT result shows that there exist permutations that cause quadratic behavior.

The results suggest that for practical routers, there is a connection between the worst case permutations for minimal adaptive algorithms and nonminimal adaptive algorithms. We emphasize "practical" because the algorithms must be simple, so that they can be built with a small amount of hardware. In particular, these algorithms will have to make local decisions. In lightly-loaded situations, a practical nonminimal adaptive algorithm will behave like a minimal adaptive algorithm, because in such situations there is no reason to deroute. Given that assumption, then only when congestion is heavy can a nonminimal algorithm behave differently from a minimal algorithm. But by then, it perhaps is too late to try to relieve the congestion.

I^r t potato or *deflection* routing [1, 2, 9, 10, 12], where a node must send on the next step any packets it receives in the current step, offers the possibility of simple logic and simple algorithms. Because nodes in hot potato routing do not use extra buffer space, congestion does not have a chance to build as it does in networks where nodes do have extra buffer space. *Greedy* hot potato routing [2], where packets use profitable outlinks whenever they are available, might be a nonminimal adaptive solution to route arbitrary permutations in time linear in n on the $n \times n$ mesh. Makedon and Symvonis [15] give an algorithm that is based on odd-even transposition and behaves much like a hot potato algorithm. Their algorithm uses a small amount of buffer space and is simple.

Future work includes examining and comparing the behavior of other minimal and nonminimal algorithms on worst case permutations. Open problems include showing, either empirically or theoretically, that there is no practical algorithm, where "practical" is appropriately defined, that can route all permutations on the $n \times n$ mesh in time proportional to n. The observation that Chaos does not use all of the bandwidth available to it in worst case situations — that it appears to run in time proportional to $n^{3/2}$ on worst case permutations — suggests that this conjecture might be true.

Acknowledgement

The author is grateful to Kevin Bolding, Jeff Dean, Larry Snyder, and Martin Tompa for helpful discussions.

Appendix

Table 1. Data for Experiments 1 and 2.

n	cn	Experiment 1		Experiment 2	
		min. Chaos	Chaos	min. Chaos	Chaos
600	35	10529	9382	8318	7075
720	42	14382	11699		
840	49	18815	14423	15765	11588
960	56	24091	17786		
1080	63	29792	21015	25505	17112
1200	70	35740	24227		
1320	77	42554	27152	37626	22529
1560	91	58262	36068	52430	29815
1800	105			68696	36051
2040	119			88162	43260
2280	133			109210	51428
2520	147			133277	60357
2760	161			158961	69456
3120	182			202982	86537

The difference in the observed data from Experiment 1 and Experiment 2 on the same problem sizes is due to the difference in the distance components of the two experiments. It is approximately $4(n - cn)$ cycles in Experiment 1, whereas it is approximately $4cn$ cycles in Experiment 2.

References

1. A. Bar-Noy, P. Raghavan, B. Schieber, and H. Tamaki. Fast deflection routing for packets and worms. In *Proceedings of the Twelfth Annual ACM Symposium on Principles of Distributed Computing*, pages 75–86, 1993.

2. A. Ben-Dor, S. Halevi, and A. Schuster. On greedy hot-potatoe routing. Technical Report PCL Report #9204, CS Department, Technion, Jan. 1993.

3. K. Bolding. *Chaotic Routing: Design and Implementation of an Adaptive Multicomputer Network Router*. PhD thesis, University of Washington, Seattle, WA, July 1993.

4. K. Bolding, M. Fulgham, and L. Snyder. The case for chaotic adaptive routing. Technical Report TR 94-02-04, University of Washington Department of Computer Science and Engineering, Mar. 1994.

5. A. Chien and J. H. Kim. Planar-adaptive routing: Low-cost adaptive networks for multiprocessors. In *Proceedings of the 19th International Symposium on Computer Architecture*, pages 268–277, 1992.

6. D. D. Chinn, T. Leighton, and M. Tompa. Minimal adaptive routing on the mesh with bounded queue size. In *Proceedings of the 1994 ACM Symposium on Parallel Algorithms and Architectures*, Cape May, NJ, June 1994.

7. R. Cypher and L. Gravano. Adaptive, deadlock-free packet routing in torus networks with minimal storage. In *1992 International Conference on Parallel Processing*, pages 204–211, 1992.

8. W. Dally and H. Aoki. Deadlock-free adaptive routing in multicomputer networks using virtual channels. *IEEE Transactions on Parallel and Distributed Systems*, 4(4):466–75, Apr. 1993.

9. U. Feige and P. Raghavan. Exact analysis of hot-potato routing. In *Proceedings 33rd Annual Symposium on Foundations of Computer Science*, pages 553–562, Pittsburgh, PA, Oct. 1992.

10. B. Hajek. Bounds for evacuation time for deflection routing. *Distributed Computing*, 5:1–6, 1991.

11. Intel. A Touchstone DELTA system description. Technical report, Intel, Portland, OR, 1991.

12. C. Kaklamanis, D. Krizanc, and S. Rao. Hot-potato routing on processor arrays. In *Proceedings of the 1993 ACM Symposium on Parallel Algorithms and Architectures*, pages 273–282, June 1993.

13. S. Konstantinidou and L. Snyder. The chaos router: A practical application of randomization in network routing. In *Proceedings of the 1990 ACM Symposium on Parallel Algorithms and Architectures*, pages 21–30, June 1990.

14. S. Konstantinidou and L. Snyder. Chaos router: Architecture and performance. In *Proceedings of the 18th International Symposium on Computer Architecture*, pages 212–221, May 1991.

15. F. Makedon and A. Symvonis. An efficient hueristic for permutation on meshes with low buffer requirements. *IEEE Transactions on Parallel and Distributed Systems*, 4(3):270–6, Mar. 1993.

16. J. Y. Ngai and C. L. Seitz. A framework for adaptive routing in multicomputer networks. In *Proceedings of the Symposium of Parallel Algorithms and Architectures*, pages 1–9. ACM, 1989.

17. J. Y. Ngai and C. L. Seitz. A framework for adaptive routing in multicomputer networks. *Computer Architecture News*, 19(1):6–14, Mar. 1991.

18. M. Noakes and W. Dally. System design of the J-Machine. In *Proceedings of the 6th MIT Conference on Advanced Research in VLSI*, pages 179–194, 1990.

19. C. Sietz, N. Boden, J. Seizovic, and W. Su. The design of the Caltech Mosaic C multicomputer. In *Proceedings of the Symposium on Integrated Systems*, pages 1–22, 1993.

On the Effect of Queue Sizes and Channel Scheduling Policies in the Segment Router

S. Konstantinidou

IBM T.J. Watson Research Center
Route 134
Yorktown Heights, NY 10598
konstant@watson.ibm.com

Abstract. In this paper, we consider the effect of queue size and channel allocation policy on the performance of the Segment router [10]. The design decisions of the Segment router are motivated by the need to improve the network performance when the traffic consists of messages with widely different lengths. The Segment router provides separate buffer pools and implements different queueing policies for short and long messages. Furthermore it time-multiplexes the physical channels of the network fairly among the classes, possibly giving them different quantums of service.

Our experimental results show that increasing the size of the buffer pool in the Segment router improves the performance of small messages whereas increasing the segment size improves the performance of long messages.

1 Introduction

In massively parallel architectures the interconnection network remains one of the most critical components, as it provides the means through which processors, memories and I/O devices communicate and synchronize with each other. The characteristics of traffic in the interconnection networks of current massively parallel architectures are not well understood. Information, such as message length distribution, burstiness of traffic and frequency of hot-spots, is essential in designing networks that support efficiently parallel applications. This issue is of increasing importance and it has become the focus of recent studies [6, 2].

An early result of such studies is that the traffic generated by parallel applications consists of a large number of small messages but also a non-negligible amount of long messages. As an example, in a study of eight complete scientific applications [2], we found that approximately 48% of all data-carrying messages were at most 16 bytes long. On the other hand, over 80% of the communicated data were sent in messages 8KB and longer.

In general, short messages are used for data exchanges and, more importantly, as control messages by the operating system and the communication protocols of the parallel machine; such messages for example include acknowledgements and requests to send. Long messages are used for data and code distribution, either among the processors or between the processors and the I/O devices.

It is well known that the latency a short message can experience in the network if it faces contention for resources by a long message, can be unacceptably high. Two distinct components contribute to this latency: First, if a long message becomes blocked it is possible that it cannot be completely stored in the routing node where its header became blocked. Then such a long message can retain, and keep idle, multiple channels in the network. Second, if a long message is currently being transmitted over a network channel, a short message must wait at least as many cycles as it takes for the channel to complete servicing the long message; this time is proportional to the length of the long message.

Two techniques have been suggested previously that address the problems of throughput degradation and increased latency for small messages in the presence of bimodal traffic, *multi-packet messages* and *byte-streaming* [13]. In architectures that support multi-packet messages [15, 18], a logically single, long message is divided into a number of packets of fixed length. Multi-packet messages require replication of the packet header information, the information that allows the network to correctly route a message from its source to its destination. They also require that each packet carries information regarding its order within the whole message, so that the message can be reconstructed from its packets at the destination node. This replication of information consumes a non-negligible fraction of the network bandwidth. Furthermore, as the packets of a single, long message arrive at the destination interleaved with packets from other messages, they must be processed thus increasing the complexity of the processor-to-network interface.

The second solution, byte-streaming, time-multiplexes the physical channels of the network among multiple contending messages at the granularity of a byte. The concept of time-multiplexing the physical channels of the network among multiple logical channels, or *lanes*, was used in the routing elements of the iWARP architecture [1] and it was studied as a method to improve the performance of wormhole routers in [5]. Recently, the use of lanes as a method to improve the performance of adaptive, wormhole routers in the presence of bimodal traffic was considered in [8, 9].

A known inefficiency of this technique is the increase in the handshaking required for each input lane of a routing element to notify the corresponding output lane of a neighboring element that it is not blocked [5]. Clearly, increasing the number of lanes per physical channel as suggested in [5, 1], further increases this inefficiency. Furthermore, as the number of lanes per physical channel increases, the logic that interfaces the processing nodes to the network becomes significantly more complicated. In this case multiple messages can be injected from one processing node to the network simultaneously and multiple messages may be delivered simultaneously. Thus keeping the number of lanes per physical channel small is clearly desirable.

In [10] we presented the Segment router, a novel router design that addresses the problem of performance degradation in the presence of bimodal traffic but tries to avoid the disadvantages of previously known solutions. The Segment router divides messages into two classes based on their length. Each router uses different queueing policies and buffer pools for short and long messages; the network channels are fairly multiplexed between the two classes although the quantum of service given to each class of messages may vary.

It is important to note that the Segment router does not give complete priority to either class of messages nor does it support deadline routing. Priority routing has been considered extensively in the area of communication networks [3, 12, 13] and it is essential in networks with hard real-time traffic [14]. Nevertheless it is prone to starvation, it is difficult to implement and it does not necessarily optimize performance in the context of parallel computing. In particular, as observed in [2], it is possible that it is the same application that sends both short and long messages; in this case clearly the performance of both classes of messages is of importance, which argues against priority routing. It is also possible that messages of different classes belong to different applications that are executing simultaneously on different partitions of the same architecture. Once again, the performance of both classes of messages is important. The design decisions of the Segment router have two performance objectives: to improve the maximum sustained throughput of the network in the presence of bimodal traffic and to reduce the disproportional performance degradation suffered by small messages in this type of traffic.

In the following we present the architecture of a Segment router node and then we consider the effect of queue sizes and channel scheduling policies on its performance.

2 Description of the Segment router

The Segment router [10] was designed to specifically address the performance degradation in networks in the presence of bimodal traffic. The Segment router avoids the need for a large number of lanes through the use of buffering. In particular, each Segment router has a centralized, dynamically allocated buffer pool, conceptually similar to the *multiqueue* design proposed in [16, 17]. The centralized buffer pool is used only by the short messages. Very limited buffering is provided for long messages, in the form of small FIFO buffers associated with the ports of each routing element. This design decision has two advantages: First, it is impossible for a single, long message to retain all the buffers of a routing element, preventing short messages from making progress and thus creating hotspots. Second, the centralized buffer pool can be assigned at the granularity of a short packet size. This guarantees that no channel can be idle while being retained by a blocked short message.

As it is still possible that a channel can be idle due to a blocked, long message, the physical channels of the network are multiplexed between the long and short messages at the granularity of a *segment*, a logical subdivision of a long message. Intuitively, the channel allocation policy considers long messages as consisting of a number of *segments* of length S bytes. If a channel is assigned to a long message, after the transmission of each segment it checks for the existence of waiting short messages. If such a message exists, it is transmitted over the

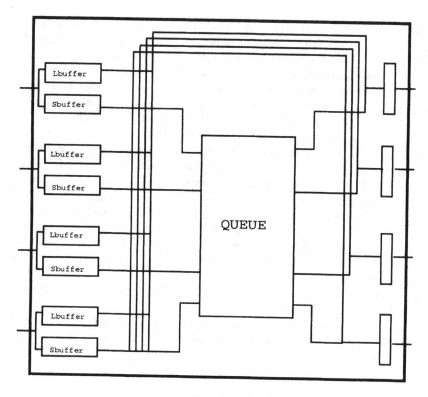

Fig. 1. Block diagram of a Segment routing node.

channel followed by the next segment of the long message. The segments of a long message do not carry header information and are routed in order following the same path, although interspersed with complete short messages. Thus the Segment router avoids the inefficiencies of multi-packet messages. A block diagram of the architecture of a Segment router is shown in Figure 1.

An important observation regarding the channel assignment rules described is that the channel is only multiplexed between one long and (possibly) many short messages. It is never multiplexed between two long messages. A second important observation is that no class of messages has absolute priority in accessing the channel, thus making starvation impossible. Finally, once the transmission of a packet or segment starts over a channel, it is guaranteed to complete; that is there is always sufficient storage for the whole body of a packet or a segment. Thus, for short messages the network implements virtual cut-through routing [7]. For long messages, the network implements a form of buffered, wormhole routing.

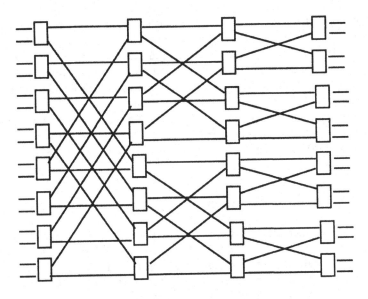

Fig. 2. A 16-node regular butterfly.

3 On the performance of the Segment router

In this section we use simulations to help us understand the performance of the
Segment router and methods to improve it. For all the following experiments we
assume a butterfly network with the processors attached to the input and output
ports of the network. An example of a 16-node butterfly is shown in Figure 2.
It should be noted though that our scheme is a combination of queueing and
channel allocation policies that is applicable to any network.

The simulator models the routing elements of the network at the register-
transfer level; time is measured in simulation *cycles*. The operations that take
place at each cycle can be classified as either decision making or byte propaga-
tions. Assuming routing elements with degree d, decisions that can complete in
one cycle are:

- The assignment of as many as d messages from input buffers and the central
  Queue to output channels, assuming no conflicts.
- The assignment of as many as d messages from input buffers to the queue.

Once any of these decisions has been made it effectively establishes a transmission between a *source* and a *receiver* buffer. For any such established transmission, a byte of data is transferred per cycle.

In the following experiments, an *open model* [11] is used for the traffic generation. Each processor generates messages at a fixed rate $\lambda, 0 < \lambda \leq 1$. When
λ equals 1, each node generates one byte at every simulation cycle. For all the
following experiments we assume uniform message destination generation. Although such a model may not accurately reflect the traffic on the interconnec-

tion network of a parallel architecture, it is useful in that it provides bounds on the sustained network throughput. In particular, under these conditions, it is expected that the network latency should increase as the applied load increases until the network reaches *saturation*. In all the following experiments we measure latency in simulation cycles; both the network service time and the source queueing time is included in the reported latency.

All the experiments are on networks with $N=1024$ processors, using switches of degree 4; thus in all networks there are 5 stages of 256 switches. In all simulated networks, messages experience at least two cycles of latency at every stage of the network.

4 The effect of queue size

In [10], we considered the performance of the Segment router and we compared it to the performance of three other networks: a regular butterfly with no support for bimodal traffic, a network that packetizes long messages and byte-streamed networks with different number of lanes. The storage and bandwidth characteristics of the simulated networks are as follows:

- Segment router. All the network channels are byte-wide. The size of the Lbuffers and Sbuffers is 20 bytes. The capacity o f the dynamically allocated queue is four 20-byte packets. Thus each switch has total buffering capacity of 240 bytes. For fair comparisons , we will provide the same per switch buffering capacity to all modeled switches although the queueing policies and the buffer allocation policies could be different. Each processor is modeled as a source of traffic by two queues of infinite capacity: one queue for short messages and one queue for long messages. Messages, generated by a pseudo-random process, are appended at the end of the appropriate queue. The channel connecting the processor-source to a switch is scheduled by exactly the same algorithm as the network channels. The processors, as message destinations, continuously consume bytes; no latency is introduced at the destination.
- Regular butterfly. There is a 20-byte buffer associated with each input port and a central dynamically allocated queue with capacity 160 bytes. The unit of storage allocation in the queue is a byte. In the case of traffic consisting of both short and long messages, routing makes no distinction between the two. Each processor is modeled as a source of traffic by a queue of infinite capacity. Messages, generated by a pseudo-random process, are appended to the end of the queue and are injected into the network in a FIFO order. The processors, as message destinations, continuously consume bytes; no latency is introduced at the destination.
- Packetizing butterfly. Long messages are divided into 20-byte packets. For the packetization a two-byte header overhead is added to each packet. The modeled switch is identical to the previous one; a 20-byte buffer is associated with each input port and there is a central, dynamically allocated queue with capacity 160 bytes.

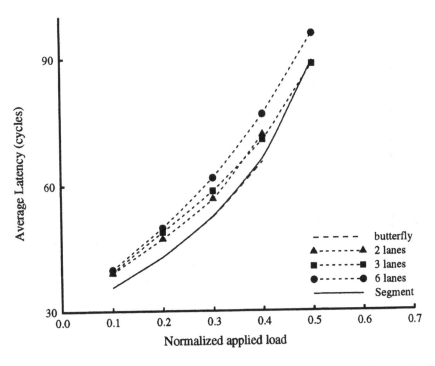

Fig. 3. Average message latency of a regular butterfly, a byte-streamed network with 2, 3 and 6 lanes per channel and the Segment router. Random traffic of 20-byte long messages.

Each processor is modeled as a source of traffic by a queue of infinite capacity. Messages, generated by a pseudo-random process, are appended to the end of the queue: short messages as one 20-byte packet and long messages as a stream of 20-byte packets. The processors, as message destinations, continuously consume bytes; no latency is introduced at the destination.

– Byte-streamed butterfly. For this network k lanes are associated with each input and output channel. In order to equalize the capacity of this network to the buffering capacity of the other alternatives, a FIFO buffer of p bytes is associated with each lane at the output ports, such that $kdp = 240$ bytes, where d is the degree of the switch and k is the number of lanes per channel. The physical channels of the network are multiplexed among their associated lanes as follows: at every simulation cycle, the "least recently served" lane that can transmit a byte, is assigned the channel. This lane then becomes the most recently served. A lane can transmit a byte if there is a byte waiting to be transmitted and the input lane at the receiver end of the channel is not blocked.

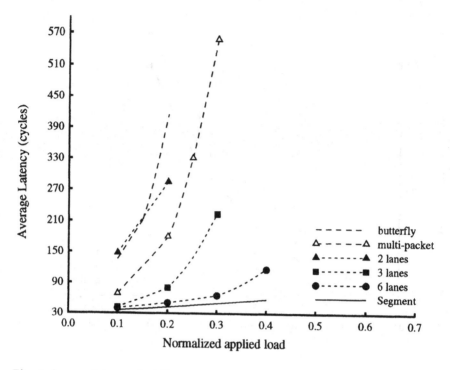

Fig. 4. Average latency of small messages for traffic consisting of 99% 20-byte messages and 1% 1000-byte messages

Each processor is modeled as a source of traffic by one queue of infinite capacity plus k lanes. When a message is generated by a pseudo-random process, if there is an empty lan e, it is assigned the lane, otherwise it is appended to the end of the queue. When a source lane becomes empty, it checks the source queue for messages and retrieves the first, in a FIFO order, if such a message exists. The processors, as message destinations, continuously consume bytes; no latency is introduced at the destination.

In Figure 3 we show the average message latency with random traffic and messages of size 20 bytes. In Figure 4 we show the average latency of short messages, for traffic consisting of 99% 20-byte messages and 1% 1000 byte messages. Under bimodal traffic, the maximum sustained throughput of the regular network dropped by 60% and the latency of small messages increased dramatically. All networks with support for bimodal traffic improved both on the throughput and the latency of small messages with the Segment router being the best.

In the following we consider methods to further improve the performance of the Segment router, starting with the obvious choice of increasing the size of the buffer pool. Elementary network theory tells us that the network population, in number of messages, is directly proportional to the throughput but inversely

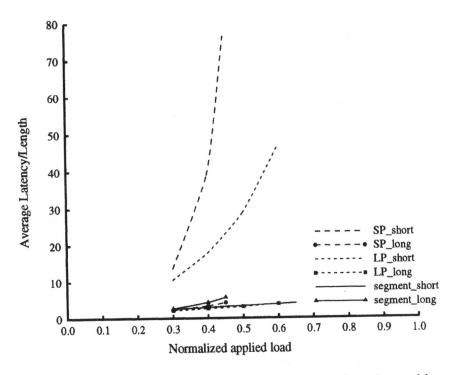

Fig. 5. Latency increase, measured as *(Average latency/Length)*, for short and long messages, in a packetizing router with a small queue (SP), a packetizing router with a large queue (LP) and the Segment router.

proportional to latency. Therefore in the following we will focus on both the maximum sustained throughput by the different networks we compare as well as the latency the classes of messages experience. In byte-streamed networks it is known that an increase in the number of lanes is much more beneficial to network performance than an increase in buffer pools [5]. Therefore in the following we will concentrate on comparisons between the Segment router and a network that packetizes long messages.

In Figure 5 we show the increase in latency for both small and long messages for the packetizing router with a small central queue (400 bytes) and a large queue (4096 bytes). In comparison, the latency increase for the two classes of messages in the Segment router is shown. For this experiment, the Segment router has the same per node buffer capacity as the packetizing router with a small queue. These results show that in the packetizing router, where long messages are divided in a sequence of small packets, increasing the queue size increases the maximum sustained throughput (MST). In particular by increasing the queue size by a factor of 4 the MST increased to 0.45 and by increasing the queue size by a factor of 100 increased the MST to 0.65. The problem with the method is that it increased dramatically the latency of small messages, by as much as a factor of 76, whereas the latency of long messages remained relatively low.

We tested the Segment router by increasing its central queue. Since the central queue is only used by small messages we expected to see the performance improvement only in the throughput of small messages. The results validated our intuition: the two classes of messages exhibited different maximum sustained throughputs. As shown in Figure 5, with a queue size of 16 packets, the traffic consisting of long messages saturated at approximately MST 0.4 whereas the MST of small messages was 0.65. The latency of both small and long messages remained small.

The results of this comparison are very important. What they tell us is that an increase in the size of the buffer pool increases the maximum sustained throughput by the network in both the packetizing network and in the Segment router. The difference in the performance of these two solutions is qualitative: in the packetizing network, small messages still face disproportionately large latencies whereas in the Segment router the latency of small messages increases at the same rate as the latency of large messages. Therefore, packetizing long messages solves only one of the problems created by bimodal traffic, namely throughput degradation, but does not improve the performance of small messages.

5 Channel Scheduling policies

In the following we will concentrate on the performance of the Segment router and consider the effect that the channel allocation policy and segment size have on the network throughput and message latency. We consider four different scheduling policies:

Scheduling for maximum channel utilization. In [10] we considered a simple channel assignment protocol for the Segment router. Briefly, if the channel is free it is assigned to a waiting long message, otherwise it is assigned to a waiting short message. Once transmission of a segment of a long message completes, the channel services one waiting short message, and then services the next segment of the long message to which it is dedicated. Given this protocol, it is possible that channels assigned to long messages remain idle due to a lack of both a waiting small message and a buffered segment in the routing node. We will call this effect a bubble in the path of a long message. It is possible to eliminate such bubbles by changing the channel allocation policy as follows: If the channel is assigned to a long message, it will continue propagating segments of the long message as long as the receiving input buffer does not contain the first byte of a segment. The channel is relinquished to a waiting small message at the end of the transmission of a long message and in between segments iff a segment is already buffered in the routing node. It is easy to see that in this case, no bubbles can appear in the path of a long message. At the destination, the channel is allocated as in the pure Segment router, that is alternating between segments of the same long message and short messages. The motivation behind

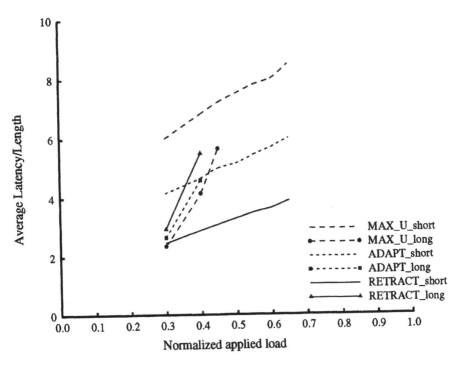

Fig. 6. Normalized average latency of short and long messages. Curves show the relative performance of three different scheduling policies: scheduling for maximum channel utilization (MAX_U), adaptive scheduling (ADAPT) and conditional retracting of blocked long messages (RETRACT).

this scheduling policy us that it guarantees that a channel assigned to a long message will never be kept idle.

Adaptive scheduling. In this case, as in the previous one, the channel scheduler once again tries to avoid bubbles unless there are more that 3 short messages waiting for the channel, in which case the channel is given to one short message.

Conditional retracting of long messages. An alternate attempt to improve the performance of long messages in the Segment router is by emulating circuit-switching. Since long messages can block each other, they can unnecessarily keep channels from being used by other long messages (of course the channels are being used by short messages). In this case we assume that if a long message becomes blocked, it retracts to its source node relinquishing the channels it has acquired. In order to guarantee freedom from starvation, we allow no more than 3 retractions per message. After three tries the long message must stay in the network until it can reach its destination.

83

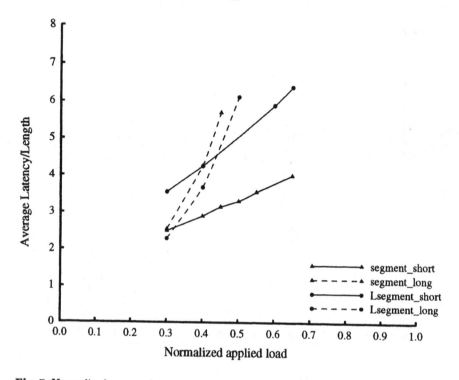

Fig. 7. Normalized average latency of short and long messages. Curves show the relative performance of the basic Segment router and a Segment router with a large queue and 80-byte segment size.

Increasing the segment size. In this final scheduling policy considered, we allow for the static channel allocation but vary the segment size, that is the quantum of service provided by the channel to the two classes.

In Figure 6, we show the increase in latency for the two classes of messages under three different scheduling policies: scheduling for maximum channel utilization (MAX_U), adaptive scheduling (ADAPT) and conditional retracting of blocked long messages (RETRACT). The first policy, MAX_U, increases significantly the latency of small messages. The reason for this is that long messages rarely end up relinquishing the channels to short messages; it only happens if a long and short message are contending at the destination.

The second policy, ADAPT, resulted in improved performance in terms of latency for short messages, and a decrease in the MST of long messages.

Finally, the third policy, RETRACT, not only does not improve latency but it actually results in worse maximum sustained throughput, as long messages temporarily acquire resources and then release them. That is, as the applied load increases, this solution results in *throttling* of the network.

In Figure 7, we show the increase in latency for the basic Segment router and a Segment router with a large queue and a segment size of 80 bytes. As expected increasing the segment size, improves the maximum sustained throughput of long messages while the latency experienced by small messages remains small. This provides us with a valve to balance the performance of the Segment router; whereas increasing the queue size improves the performance of small messages, increasing the segment size improves the performance of long messages. A combination of these two techniques can improve the overall network performance.

6   Conclusions

In this paper we considered the effect of increasing the buffer pool size and channel allocation policies in networks with bimodal traffic. Under such traffic characteristics two important performance metrics deteriorate: one is the maximum sustained throughput and the other is the latency of small messages. A common solution to these problems requires that long messages be divided into short packets. In comparison, the Segment router provides separate buffer pools and implements different queueing policies for short and long messages. Furthermore it time-multiplexes the physical channels of the network fairly among the classes.

We found that packetizing long messages, a common solution in parallel architectures, can benefit from increasing buffer pool sizes but only with respect to the network throughput. The latency of small messages remains disproportionately and unacceptably high. The reason for this is that the packets of a long message enter the network in a burst, occupying resources in the buffer pools and forcing small messages to wait for resources. In comparison, the Segment router improves the network throughput while at the same time providing enough support for small messages to keep their latencies small and proportional to the latencies experienced by long messages.

In this paper we also considered methods to improve the performance of the Segment router. In particular we considered a number of channel allocation policies, both static and adaptive to network traffic. We found that with a simple static channel allocation policy, increasing the segment size improves the performance of long messages. In combination with the fact that an increase in the buffer pool size can improve the performance of small messages, these two parameters can help us determine the optimal design of the Segment routing nodes for a variety of traffic loads.

References

1. S. Borkar, R. Cohn, G. Cox, H.T. Kung, M. Lam, M. Levine, B. Moore, W. Moore, C. Peterson, J. Susman, J. Sutton, J. Urbanski, and J. Webb. Supporting systolic and memory communication in iWARP. In *Proc. 17 Annual International Symposium on Computer Architecture*, pages 70–81, 1990.
2. R. Cypher, A. Ho, S. Konstantinidou, and P. Messina. Architectural requirements of parallel scientific applications with explicit communication. In *International Symposium on Computer Architecture*, pages 2-13, 1993.

3. J.N. Daigle. Message delays with prioritized HOLP and round-robin packet servicing. *IEEE Transactions on Communications*, 35:609–619, 1987.

4. W.J. Dally. Wire-efficient VLSI multiprocessor communication networks. In *Proc. Stanford Conference on Advanced Research in VLSI*, pages 391–415, 1987.

5. W.J. Dally. Virtual-channel flow control. In *Proc. 17th Annual International Symposium on Computer Architecture*, pages 60–68, 1990.

6. J.-M. Hsu and P. Banerjee. Performance measurement and trace driven simulation of parallel cad and numeric applications on a hypercube multicomputer. In *Proc. 17th Annual International Symposium on Computer Architecture*, pages 260–269, 1990.

7. P. Kermani and L. Kleinrock. Virtual cut-through: A new computer communication switching technique. *Computer Networks*, pages 267–286, September 1979.

8. J.H. Kim and A.A. Chien. Evaluation of wormhole routed networks under hybrid traffic loads. In *Proceedings of the Hawaii International Conference on System Sciences*, 1993.

9. J.H. Kim and A.A. Chien. The impact of packetization in wormhole-routed networks. In *Proceedings of PARLE*, June 1993.

10. S. Konstantinidou. The Segment router: a novel router design for parallel computers. In *Proc. ACM Symposium on Parallel Algorithms and Architectures*, 1994 (to appear).

11. E.D. Lazowska, J. Zahorjan, G.S. Graham, and K.C. Sevcik. *Quantitative System Performance*. Prentice Hall, 1984.

12. C.Y. Lo. Performance analysis and application of a two-priority queue. *AT&T Technical Journal*, vol. 66:82–96, 1987.

13. S.P. Morgan. Queueing disciplines and passive congestion control in byte-stream networks. *IEEE Transactions on Communications*, 39:1097–1106, 1991.

14. J. Rexford and K. G. Shin Support for Multiple Classes of Traffic in Multicomputer Routers. In *Proc. Parallel Computer Routing and Communication Workshop*, May 1994.

15. C.L. Seitz, W.C. Athas, C.M. Flaig, A.J. Martin, J. Seizovic, C.S. Steele, and W.K. Sun. The architecture and programming of the Ametek series 2010 multicomputer. In *Third Conference on Hypercube Computers*, pages pp. 33–36, 1988.

16. Y. Tamir and G.L. Frazier. High-performance multi-queue buffers for VLSI communication switches. In *Proc. 15th Annual International Symposium on Computer Architecture*, pages 343–354, 1988.

17. Y. Tamir and G.L. Frazier. The design and implementation of a multi-queue buffer for VLSI communication switches. In *International Conference on Computer Design*, pages 466–471, 1989.

18. Thinking Machines Corporation. *The Connection Machine CM5 Technical Summary*. October 1991.

The Offset Cube:
An Optoelectronic Interconnection Network

D. Scott Wills, W. Stephen Lacy, and Jose Cruz-Rivera

School of Electrical and Computer Engineering
Georgia Institute of Technology
Atlanta, Georgia 30332-0250

Abstract. This paper introduces a new network topology, the *offset-cube*, for three-dimensional image processing systems. It provides general node-to-node communications for random message traffic with an average latency that is comparable to a k-ary 3-cube. It is well suited for communication patterns common in image processing applications (e.g., image scaling, overlapping segmentation). The offset-cube topology provides an extremely compact, through-wafer implementation employing integrated optoelectronic devices. This paper describes work in progress towards the examination of this new topology and its implementation including architectural issues (e.g, oblivious and adaptive minimal routing algorithms, performance analysis with random traffic and trace-driven workloads, comparison with k-ary 3-cubes), plus implementation issues in building a scalable system.

1 Introduction and Motivation

Fine-grain parallel architectures offer high performance for high-throughput applications such as image processing (e.g., filtering, edge detection, convolution), object recognition, and image compression. Existing scan-line array processors (SLAPs) and two-dimensional array processors provide high performance solutions for this class of applications. However, when handling continuous image streams, the processing time of one image is limited by the image rate. Intra-image communication and synchronization overhead further reduce the amount of processing that can be performed on each image. These systems are not well suited to applications that require several levels of processing since it is difficult to scale the number of processors beyond the image resolution.

Three-dimensional processing geometries overcome these limitations by allowing image sequences to be passed continuously through multiple layers of processing. Images collected by a focal plane array of detectors can be passed downward through multiple processing layers. Each layer contains an array of fine-grain parallel processing elements executing a different image transformation. Strong spatial reference locality exhibited by most image processing operations prevents communications bottlenecks at the center of processing layers. Bi-directional communication between layers allows iterative processing algorithms.

For general purpose parallel processing, a k-ary 3-cube (three-dimensional mesh) network topology is commonly used [6, 17]. Each symmetric dimension offers an identical communication bandwidth. When processing images, the vertical communication channels transport image data between processing layers while horizontal channels distribute data within a layer. However, load imbalances between these orthogonal dimensions often result in wasted capacity.

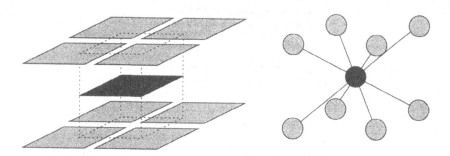

Fig. 1. The connections of a node (in black) in an offset cube

This paper introduces a new topology, the *offset-cube*, designed specifically for image processing communication patterns [20, 21]. It is formed by offsetting alternate processing layers so that each processing element communicates with four neighbors above and four neighbors below, as illustrated in Figure 1. This topology eliminates most of the intra-layer communication by allowing image data to be copied during the inter-layer communication.

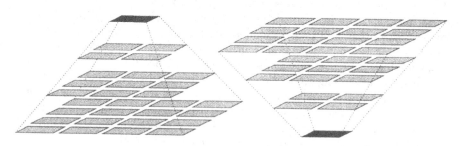

Fig. 2. Image Broadcast and Concentration

Figure 2 shows how a part of an image is broadcast to increasing larger regions of processing elements on subsequent layers. Alternatively, a large segment of the image can be concentrated at a single processing node. Because all communication channels are vertical (and symmetric), image processing communication patterns produce more uniform loading. Yet general node-to-node communication is supported by this topology.

This paper describes the offset-cube topology, including a formal definition, naming scheme, and a minimal oblivious and adaptive routing algorithm. It includes early simulation results comparing its performance to a k-ary, 3-cube for both random and trace-driven traffic. It also presents a novel approach for implementation using a new optoelectronic interconnect technology which supports extremely dense, manufacturable systems. Finally, the status the project and future work is described.

2   Topology

The offset-cube topology is easily created using several identical processing planes containing two-dimensional arrays of processing elements. Alternating planes are staggered by half the width of a processing element in each of the horizontal dimensions. With this positioning, a processing element is adjacent to a quadrant of four processing elements in the plane above it and four in the plane below it. An integrated router within each processing element allows it to send or receive data to or from any of the eight channels. Data can also be routed from any input channel to any output channel to support general node-to-node communication.

The topology is formally defined as follows. Consider a set of k^2L vertices (representing processing elements) where k is the length of each side of a square vertex array on each layer and L is the number of layers. The vertices are named by triples $< x, y, l >$ where l is the layer number between 0 and $(L-1)$ inclusive. For even values of l, $x = 2i$ and $y = 2j$ where i and j are the vertex's coordinates within a layer assuming values between 0 and $k-1$. For odd values of l, $x = 2i+1$ and $y = 2j + 1$ for i and j between 0 and $(L - 1)$ inclusive. The offset cube topology is defined by the edges connecting each vertex $< x, y, l >$ with its neighbors $< x \pm 1, y \pm 1, l \pm 1 >$.

Boundary vertices have less than eight edges, and are defined in six overlapping sets.

1. vertices $< 0, y, l >$ are connected with its neighbors $< 1, y \pm 1, l \pm 1 >$
2. vertices $< 2k-1, y, l >$ are connected with its neighbors $< 2k-2, y \pm 1, l \pm 1 >$
3. vertices $< x, 0, l >$ are connected with its neighbors $< x \pm 1, 1, l \pm 1 >$
4. vertices $< x, 2k-1, l >$ are connected with its neighbors $< x \pm 1, 2k-2, l \pm 1 >$
5. vertices $< x, y, 0 >$ are connected with its neighbors $< x \pm 1, y \pm 1, 1 >$
6. vertices $< x, y, L >$ are connected with its neighbors $< x \pm 1, y \pm 1, L - 1 >$

For a symmetric cube, $L = 2k + 1$ creating a *k-ary offset cube*. The offset cube topology is isotropic, and is illustrated in Figure 3.

In a k-ary 3-cube, a shortest path routing algorithm uses channel routes to reduce the difference in coordinates of the source and destination vertices. Dimension order routing is a well-performing deterministic shortest path algorithm that reduces the coordinate differences one at a time (i.e., x, then y, then z).

A shortest path routing algorithm for an offset cube is more complicated since each channel hop changes all three coordinates. If one coordinate difference

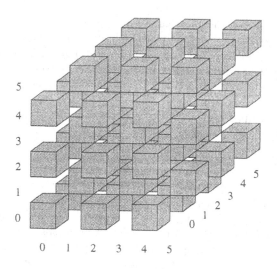

Fig. 3. A 3-ary Offset Cube Topology

reaches zero, it must be increased in the next hop to reduce differences in other dimensions. This creates "bouncing" routes where a message alternates between neighboring planes as it moves through one dimension.

The minimum path cost of routing a message between vertices A and B on an offset cube is:

$$hops_{min} = \max(|X_B - X_A|, |Y_B - Y_A|, |Z_B - Z_A|) \tag{1}$$

An initial implementation of minimal oblivious and adaptive routing algorithms have been developed and analyzed. A more complete, deadlock-free algorithm is being developed based on techniques [8]. In these oblivious and adaptive algorithms, a single positive and negative adjustment in each diagonal dimension are affected in defined order (like dimension ordering in a k-ary 3-cube). Virtual channels are used to break potential cycle when network boundaries demand premature adjustments. These new routing algorithms will be presented and analyzed in future publications.

3   Network Performance

This section compares the performance of the offset cube topology and a k-ary 3-cube. The complete details will be available in [13]. To compare these topologies, a simulator which measures network performance under similar conditions and loads has been built. Both a random traffic and trace-driven workload is used for the analysis.

3.1   Random Traffic

In these experiments, randomly generated traffic at different loading levels is injected into a 216 k-ary 3-cube and a 225 node offset cube. The simulator uses flit-level, time-stepped execution. The simulations were performed using the following parameters and assumptions:

1. Wormhole flow control is used.
2. Eight virtual channels are associated with each physical channel in the network. However, physical channels connecting source/sink nodes to the network have only one virtual channel associated with them.
3. A virtual channel buffer can hold 2 message flits.
4. Each bidirectional network link is full duplex.
5. Source queueing is used at the inputs to the network. The size of each source queue is limited to 100 messages. Injected messages arriving at a full queue are dropped.
6. Arbitration between virtual channels requesting permission to transmit is performed using a FIFO discipline.
7. Message latency is measured as the number of network cycles from the time a message is added to the appropriate source queue until the time the last flit of the message is received at its destination node.
8. Throughput is measured as the average number of flits arriving per destination node per cycle after the network has reached steady-state.
9. For k-ary 3-cube simulations, a 6-ary 3-cube (216 nodes) was used.
10. For offset cube simulations, an offset cube with k = 5 and L = 10 (225 nodes) was used.
11. Each source node generates messages with exponentially distributed inter-arrival times and with uniformly distributed destination nodes. A constant message length of 20 flits is used for all random-traffic simulations.
12. Each datapoint is obtained by collecting statistics over 20,000 network cycles after a 10,000 cycle warm-up period.

Figure 4 compares the performance of dimension-order routing on the 6-ary 3-cube to that of oblivious diagonal shortest-path routing on the offset cube. Although the 6-ary 3-cube performs best, the difference in saturation throughput is small: 0.2 flits/node/cycle for offset cube and 0.25 flits/node/cycle for the 3-cube.

The capacity loss is due to loading in the center of the network. For random traffic, deterministic routing on a 3-cube does a reasonable job of distributing traffic across the entire network. The offset cube's diagonal routing creates much higher traffic in the center of the network. This has been verified by comparing cross-sectional loading profiles for a 3-cube with dimension order and diagonal routing algorithms.

To better utilize the capacity of the offset cube network, a simple adaptive routing algorithm is employed. Local information (the number of virtual channels in use) is used to select between shortest path outputs at each node. A similar adaptive routing technique was developed for k-ary 3-cubes. In the latter, lower dimensions are given priority so that the technique defaults to dimension-order routing in the absence of contention. Figure 4 also compares the performance of the two adaptive algorithms. The adaptive offset-cube algorithm creates a more uniform distribution of traffic across the network, alleviating the hot-spot effect encountered in the center of the cube.

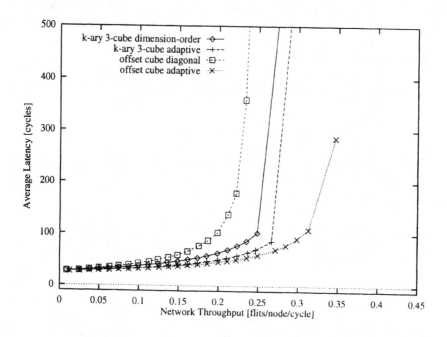

Fig. 4. Performance of Offset Cube, 3-Cube

3.2 Trace-Driven Traffic

In order to evaluate the effectiveness of an offset-cube network for specific applications, a more realistic network traffic workload is needed. A fine-grain, message passing architecture optimized for high throughput, low memory operation has been specified. This architecture, named Pica [22], is based on earlier work by the author on the J-Machine architecture at MIT [7]. An assembler and instrumented instruction-level simulator for this architecture have been implemented. Using these tools, several applications and kernels have been implemented, including convolution, relaxation, FFT, edge detection, JPEG compression, and matrix manipulation [19]. Using the instruction-level simulator, message traces from these applications are being collected and used by the network simulator.

In this section, traces from two parallel kernels (thermal relaxation and matrix multiplication) and two full-scale applications (an instance of a Joint Photographic Experts Group (JPEG) image compression algorithm and a positron emission tomography (PET) image reconstruction algorithm) are used to compare similarly sized offset cubes and k-ary 3-cubes. These applications exhibit a variety of logical communication patterns, including nearest-neighbor, bounded local neighborhoods, and angular rotations that are useful in evaluating the capabilities of these networks. The communication characteristics of the kernels and applications are described by the metrics presented in Table 1.

Table 1. Summary of Workload Applications

	Therm Relax	Matrix Mult	JPEG	PET
Number of Nodes	1024	625	288	192
Number of Messages Generated	84,549	189,400	177,439	132,988
Total Execution Cycles	2,860	64,206	124,287	67,672
Avg. Message Length (words)	1.99	8.23	2.07	2.61
Injected Messages/Cycle/Node	0.00289	0.00472	0.00496	0.010235
I/O Rate (words/instruction)	0.08573	0.044252	0.05139	0.04877

The trace-driven network simulations were performed by varying the number of virtual channels, the routing algorithm, and the network topology. For discussion purposes, the results obtained for the case of four virtual channels and adaptive routing will be used as a baseline in comparing the offset-cube to the k-ary 3-cube. This combination of parameters is chosen since simulations reveal that the applications require a minimum of four virtual channels to avoid deadlock conditions and that the use of adaptive routing provides performance levels that are at least comparable to, if not better than, those obtained via deterministic routing. Furthermore, increasing the number of virtual channels beyond 4 does not provide significant performance enhancements for the workloads, except for JPEG, and then only for the deterministic routing case. The baseline results for all workloads are presented in Table 2. These simulations assume four virtual channels and an adaptive routing algorithm. *Latency* includes source queuing delays, while *Network Latency* corresponds to delivery latency once the message has entered the network. Latency is given in cycles and *Norm.* refers to latency normalized to the no-load latency.

Thermal Relaxation: The first message trace to be considered is that of the thermal relaxation kernel. This kernel solves Laplace's equation ($\nabla^2 u = 0$) using the Gauss-Jacobi method over an $N x N$ grid. The resulting communication patterns are static in nature and correspond to a logical nearest-neighbor type access ($P_{i,j} \rightarrow P_{i\pm1,j\pm1}, i, j \in \{0 : N - 1\}$), where each logical processor must communicate with it's north, east, west, and south neighbors during each iteration (assuming a one-to-one mapping between processors and grid data points).

Table 2. Baseline Results for Trace-Driven Network Simulations

	Therm Relax		Matrix Mult		JPEG		PET	
	11-ary	Offset	9-ary	Offset	8-ary	Offset	6-ary	Offset
Latency	19.19	23.24	88.26	89.18	43.64	41.86	18.36	18.84
Norm. Latency	1.86	1.83	3.42	3.24	4.40	4.14	1.26	1.27
Network Latency	12.19	16.25	23.67	25.05	18.46	19.22	14.34	15.08
Norm. Net. Latency	1.19	1.25	1.07	1.06	1.54	1.49	1.10	1.10
Source Queuing (%)	36.48	30.08	73.18	71.91	57.70	54.06	11.90	20.00

The particular implementation of the algorithm from which the message trace was obtained, however, corresponds to 10 iterations over a data grid of 64x64 elements, employing 1,024 processing nodes. Thus, each processor is allocated with four grid data elements, reducing in this manner the number of data exchanges per iteration per node to two. Nevertheless, of all the applications discussed herein, thermal relaxation required the highest I/O rate based on the effective number of words/instruction (0.08573) required during execution.

The network configurations used for the thermal relaxation workload evaluation consisted of a $10x11x10$ offset-cube and an 11-ary 3-cube. Simulation results revealed that adaptive routing outperforms deterministic routing for all virtual channel number and network topology combinations. The overall latency difference between adaptive and deterministic routing for the baseline case of 4 virtual channels being 8.19% and 19.83% for the 11-ary and offset-cube, respectively. Direct comparison between topologies reveals that the 11-ary is superior to the offset-cube in terms of overall latency by 17.41% and in terms of network latency by 24.97%. Source queuing constituting 36.48% and 30.08% of the overall latency for the 11-ary and offset cube, respectively. Similar trends are evidenced for the deterministic routing case.

While thermal relaxation exhibits the most structured of the communication patterns studied, the low number of injected messages/cycle/node and relatively low burstiness of traffic allowed it to achieve the second lowest source queuing delay. This translated into a low normalized latency for both the 11-ary and offset-cube topologies. The superiority of the 11-ary over the offset-cube network is expected, due to the lack of node placement optimization for the offset-cube implementation. A placement analysis reveals that the linear mapping of nodes employed converts the logical nearest-neighbor communication patterns of thermal relaxation to communication between physical nodes an average distance of 5 and 6.2 hops away on the 11-ary and offset-cube, respectively.

Matrix Multiplication: The second message trace to be considered is that of NxN matrix multiplication. The algorithmic implementation is based on the sub-block decomposition method [9]. The communication patterns of this algorithm are either logical nearest-neighbor ($P_{i,j} \rightarrow P_{i,j+1}, i, j \in \{0 : N-1\}$) during the *columnroll* stage or logical local neighborhood ($P_{i,(i+k)modN} \rightarrow P_{i,j}, i, j, k \in \{0 : N-1\}$), during the *rowbroadcast* stage [19]. The message trace obtained corresponds to the multiplication of two 150x150 matrices, employing 625 processing nodes. With each processing node being in charge of a 6x6 sub-block computation.

The network configurations used for the thermal relaxation workload evaluation consisted of a 9x9x8 offset-cube and a 9-ary 3-cube. Simulation results revealed that adaptive routing outperforms deterministic routing for all virtual channel number and network topology combinations. The overall latency difference between adaptive and deterministic routing for the baseline case of 4 virtual channels being 2.77% and 7.53% for the 9-ary and offset-cube, respectively. Direct comparison between topologies reveals that the 9-ary is superior to the offset cube in terms of overall latency by 1.07% and in terms of network latency by 5.52%. Source queuing constituting 73.18% and 71.91% of the overall latency for the 9-ary and offset-cube, respectively. The same trends are present for the deterministic routing case.

Although the matrix multiplication trace exhibits a relatively low message injection rate, it has the highest source queuing delays. This can be attributed to the long messages exchanged between processors and the burstiness of the resulting traffic. The high source queuing delay is in turn responsible for the high latency values obtained.

JPEG: The third message trace under study corresponds to an implementation of the Discrete Cosine Transform (DCT) -based JPEG image compression algorithm [18]. The logical communication patterns present in this application correspond to localized neighborhoods where a given logical processor is expected to communicate with other processors a bounded distance away. The message trace obtained corresponds to the compression of a 256x256 image using a total of 288 processing nodes.

The network configurations used for the JPEG image compression workload evaluation consisted of a 16x8x3 offset-cube and an 8-ary 3-cube. Simulation results revealed that adaptive routing outperforms deterministic routing for all virtual channel number and network topology combinations. The overall latency difference between adaptive and deterministic routing for the baseline case of 4 virtual channels being 22.87% and 25.57% for the 8-ary and offset-cube, respectively. Direct comparison between topologies reveals that the offset-cube is superior to the 8-ary in terms of overall latency by 4.08%, while the 8-ary is superior to the offset-cube in terms of network latency by 4.00%. Source queuing constituting 57.70% and 54.06% of the overall latency for the 8-ary and offset-cube, respectively. Similar trends are present for the deterministic routing case. Contrary to the other applications, a significant benefit is seen in increasing the number of virtual channels from 2 to 8 in the deterministic routing case. A decrease in overall latency of 38.38% is present, as opposed to a decrease of only 4.34% in the adaptive routing case.

The high level of burstiness exhibited by the JPEG traffic profile contributes to this trace having the highest latency values. The low average distance between logical communicating nodes and the three-plane node-placement strategy that results in a *pipelined* implementation of the JPEG algorithm contribute to the offset-cube's superior performance over the 8-ary 3-cube it is compared against.

PET: The final application studied is a maximum likelihood-expectation maximization (ML-EM)algorithm for the reconstruction of $N x N$ PET images [5]. PET image reconstruction is a member of the family of problems based on reconstructions from angular projections. The message trace used corresponds to the reconstruction of a 64x64 image (with projections taken over 4 angles) using 192 processing nodes. The dominant communication pattern is that of angular rotations ($P_i \rightarrow P_{i \cos \theta + j \sin \theta}, i, j \in \{0 : N - 1\}$).

The network configurations used for the PET image reconstruction workload evaluation consisted of a 8x8x3 offset-cube and a 6-ary 3-cube. Simulation results revealed that adaptive routing outperforms deterministic routing for all virtual channel numbers for the offset-cube, while the opposite is true for the 6-ary (albeit by a negligible margin). The overall latency difference between adaptive and deterministic routing for the baseline case of 4 virtual channels being 1.07% and 15.94% for the 6-ary and offset-cube, respectively. Direct comparison between topologies reveals that the 6-ary is superior to the offset-cube in terms of overall latency by 2.56% and in terms of network latency by 4.89%. Source queuing constituting 11.90% and 20.00% of the overall latency for the 6-ary and offset-cube, respectively. The same trends are present for the deterministic routing case.

While the PET trace exhibits the highest injected massage rate of all the traces, the fact that it presents the highest uniformity in the distribution of source-destination pairs and that its message traffic profile does not exhibit a high degree of burstiness, enables it to have the lowest source queuing delay. The distribution of source-destination pairs being a consequence of task allocation, where two processing nodes are assigned to operate over a single row of the image being reconstructed. Thus, these two nodes communicate with virtually all other nodes as the column variable j is varied.

Summary: The applications studied here indicate the desirability of an offset-cube topology employing 4 virtual channels and using an adaptive routing algorithm. Source queuing delays for all workload traces correlated well with the level of burstiness exhibited by the corresponding traffic profiles and with the uniformity with which the source-destination pairs were distributed. The trace-driven network simulation results presented show that the offset-cube is comparable in performance to k-ary 3-cubes. Performance differences being attributed to how well the node placement strategy used for simulations correlated with the static communication patterns inherent in the algorithms. Hence, the development of heuristics that would optimize the process of mapping nodes to physical locations within the offset-cube, such that traffic is directed more to the vertical links, can provide significant improvements for the communication patterns studied. Even though the communication patterns exhibited by the workloads presented are not the patterns the offset-cube is expected to do better with (traffic mostly along vertical direction), we conclude that even under these circumstances the offset-cube is competitive and potentially favored in those instances where high throughput, high-density considerations point to opto-electronic technology network implementations. Furthermore, applications such as JPEG and PET image reconstruction lend themselves to stream processing, a situation where the optical I/O advantage of the offset-cube is significant. Future work will consider optimal node-placement strategies for the offset-cube topology.

4 An Optoelectronic Network Implementation

These are several approaches to implementing an offset-cube topology depending on the network size, system density, and node bandwidth requirements. For low to moderate throughput (1 – 10 GBits/sec I/O bandwidth), low density systems (10,000 – 100,000 in^3), a three-dimensional wire approach similar to that employed in the MIP J-machine is appropriate [16]. Image processing systems often demand high network throughput (10 – 200 GBits/second I/O bandwidth) in a high density system ($< 100in^3$). Wire interconnect technologies for these systems have been demonstrated as research projects (e.g., thermomigrated feedthroughs and microbridge interconnects [14, 10]). However, the reliability and manufacturability costs of these technologies are a concern even if they are widely used.

Several optoelectronic interconnect technologies are currently being developed including both guided-wave [3, 15], and free-space [1, 4, 11] interconnects. Guided-wave approaches are most applicable to planar interconnect applications (e.g., MCMs), and are not well suited to three-dimensional interconnects. Free-space approaches can be used for three-dimensional connections. Often, microlenses and holograms are used to establish fixed or varied interconnection patterns between processing planes. Yet the alignment sensitivity, size, and complexity of these systems present serious obstacles to their application in high density, low cost interconnects.

The ideal solution would incorporate the low cost, mass-produced manufactability of traditional Si VLSI. Silicon continues to be the material of choice for digital integrated circuits. However, because of its poor optoelectronic properties, efforts to incorporate integrated optical emitters and detectors have met with limited success. The most effective optoelectronic devices have been demonstrated using GaAs and InP. However, GaAs and InP have been unable to match Si in density or cost for VLSI applications.

A new technique for combining GaAs and InP-based optoelectrical devices with Si VLSI has been developed in the Microelectronics Research Center at Georgia Tech. Using epitaxial liftoff, small (100 x 100 μm) GaAs and InP-based light emitting diodes and detector have successfully been separated from their lattice growth substrates. The deposition of these thin film devices onto a silicon host containing circuitry has also been demonstrated. Operating wavelengths for InGaAs and InGaAsP are selected for which Si is transparent, allowing through-wafer transmission.

This technique, which has been demonstrated for simple optoelectronic interconnect, offers the promise of low cost and mass producibility. In moderate volume, inexpensive optical devices could be integrated en masse, on Si circuits, using procedures no more complex than existing VLSI processing steps.

The offset-cube topology can exploit this technology to form an extremely simple three-dimensional optoelectronic interconnect. Processing elements are designed and fabricated using existing Si VLSI techniques. Bonding pads are provided only for power contacts. (Probe pads are provided for testing.) Holes in the overglass allow GaAs and InP-based emitters and detectors to be attached in a post-processing step. Silicon-based driver circuits connect parallel buses from routers on the chip to the faster optical devices (0.1 – 1.0 Gbits/second).

After the Si chips containing the optical devices are fabricated and tested, they are attached to a larger silicon substrate. This provides physical support and also participates in power distribution and cooling. A fully populated substrate forms one plane of the system. Completed substrates are then stacked to create the third dimension. To facilitate manufacturing, all chips and substrates are identical.

Each chip is broken into four quadrants which overlap with eight neighboring chips (four in the plane above, four in the plane below). Although any number of transmitter and receivers can be included in each quadrant, the minimum case requires two transmitter/receiver pairs, as shown in Figure 5.

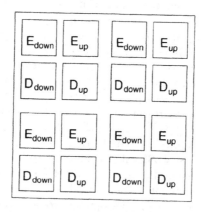

Fig. 5. Chip Device Pattern

In order for transmitter/receiver pairs to be correctly aligned, the chips must be offset. To achieve this using identical plane substrates, a spacing equal to one half the chip width plus inter-chip spacing is added to two non-opposing sides of the substrate. Then alternating planes are rotated 180^0 during assembly, providing the correct device alignment. Figure 6 shows the substrate pattern.

System I/O is provided by I/O layers which inject data directly into the network on the top and bottom surfaces of the stack. These layers can interface to high-bandwidth electrical or optical connections. Alternatively, the input surface can be covered by visible light detectors for direct focal-plane imaging. The

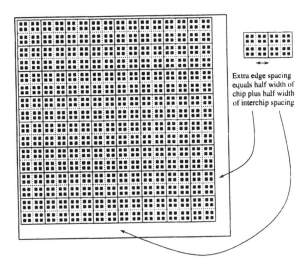

Extra edge spacing
equals half width of
chip plus half width
of interchip spacing

Fig. 6. Substrate Pattern for 8 x 8 Chip Layer

output surface can incorporate a frame buffer for direct video output. The sides of the stack are used for power distribution and cooling connections. Due to the dense packaging, liquid cooling between layers is anticipated. Optical clock distribution is also incorporated into this system. In-line detectors on each layer detect broadcast clock signals from the bottom of the stack via the through-wafer transmission technique employed by the network. A large scale interconnection network implemented using this technology requires consideration of several new issues.

1. Unlike the wire density limits for wire networks, optical channels are limited entirely by characteristics of the transmitter and receiver. The communication medium (i.e., the space through which light travels) does not enforce any fundamental density or bandwidth limits.
2. The channel delay is not determined by channel length. Since the messages travel fast (near c), and the channel length is small (around $1mm$), the time of flight in a channel is around three picoseconds. The channel delay is dominated by transmitter and receiver response time (around $10nS$).
3. Power and heat dissipation are the dominant issues in communication costs. GaAs LEDs have a low quantum efficiency ($< 3\%$). GaAs lasers are more efficient (75%), but still dissipate several milliwatts during operation. The cumulative effect of thousands of lasers operating in a few hundred cm^3 will require special consideration.

5 Research Status

A high-throughput message-passing architecture and offset cube network have been specified. An experimentation environment including several simulators and programming tools has been constructed and is being refined and enhanced.

Our first test chip combining basic digital router structures with high speed analog drivers and amplifiers has been fabricated through MOSIS, digitally tested, and has been integrated with optical devices for an initial demonstration [12]. A through-wafer optoelectronic channel without digital logic has already been demonstrated in [2].

A five year prototype target (which would be undertaken with industrial collaboration) contains 32 100 Mbit/sec transmitter/receiver pairs. Four 50 MIPS processing elements are included on each chip. A processing plane contains 64 chips (256 nodes, 12,800 MIPS) and measures approximately 10 cm by 10 cm. 16 planes contain 1024 chips (4096 nodes, 204,800 MIPS) and fit inside a cube 10 cm on a side. 819.6 Gbits/sec of I/O bandwidth is available from the top and bottom surfaces of the cube.

References

1. L. S. Bergman, W. H. Wu, A. R. Johnston, R. Nixon, S. C. Esener, C. C. Guest, P. Yu, T. J. Drabik, M. Feldman, and S. H. Lee. Holographic Optical Interconnects for VLSI. *Optical Engineering*, 25:1109–1118, October 1986.
2. K. H. Calhoun, C. B. Camperi-Ginestet, and N. M. Jokerst. Vertical Optical Communication Through Stacked Silicon Wafers Using Hybrid Monolithic Thin Film InGaAsP Emitters and Detectors. *IEEE Photonics Technology Letters*, 5(2):254–257, February 1993.
3. R. T. Chen, H. Lu, D. Robinson, M. Wang, G. Savant, and T. Jannson. Guided-wave Planar Optical Interconnects Using Highly Multiplexed Polymer Waveguide Holograms. *Journal of Lightwave Technology*, 10:888–897, July 1992.
4. N. C. Craft and A. Y. Feldblum. Optical Interconnections Based on Arrays of Surface-emitting Lasers and Lenslets. *Applied Optics*, 31:1735–1739, April 1992.
5. J. L. Cruz-Rivera, E. V. R. DiBella, D. S. Wills, T. K. Gaylord, and E. N. Glytsis. Parallelized Implementation of the Maximum Likelihood Expectation Maximization Algorithm on a Fine-grained Optically Interconnected Architecture. to be submitted to *IEEE Transactions on Medical Imaging*, 1994.
6. William J. Dally. Performance Analysis of k-ary n-cube Interconnection Networks. *IEEE Transactions on Computers*, C-39(6):775–785, June 1990.
7. William J. Dally, Andrew Chien, Stuart Fiske, Greg Fyler, Waldemar Horwat, John Keene, Rich Lethin, Michael Noakes, Peter Nuth, and D. Scott Wills. The Message Driven Processor: Am Integrated Multicomputer Processing Element. In *ICCD '92 International Conference on Computer Design, VLSI in Computers & Processors*, pages 416–419, 11-14 October 1992.
8. Jose Duato. A New Theory of Deadlock-Free Adapative Routing in Wormhole Networks. *IEEE Transactions on Parallel and Distributed Systems*, 4(12):1320–1331, December 1993.
9. G. C. Fox et al. Matrix Algorithms on a Hypercube I: Matrix Multiplication. *Parallel Computing*, 4(1), 1987.
10. J. M. Kallis, L. B. Duncan, S. P. Laub, M. J. Little, L. M. Miani, and D. C. Sandkulla. Reliability of the 3-D Computer Under Stress of Mechanical Vibration and Thermal Cyling. In *Proceedings of the IEEE International Conference on Wafer Scale Integration*, pages 65–72, 1989.

11. R. K. Kostuk, J. W. Goodman, and L. Hesselink. Design Considerations for Holographic Optical Interconnects. *Applied Optics*, 26:3947–3953, September 1987.

12. W. Stephen Lacy, Christophe Camperi-Ginestet, Brent Buchanan, D. Scott Wills, Nan Marie Jokerst, and Martin Brooke. A Fine-Grain, High-Throughput Architecture Using Through-Wafer Optical Interconnect. In *Proceedings of First Annual Workshop on Massively Parallel Processing and Optical Interconnect*, pages 27–36, 26-29 April 1994.

13. W. Stephen Lacy, Jose Cruz-Rivera, and D. Scott Wills. A Scalable Optical Interconnection Network for Fine-Grain Parallel Architectures. *to be submitted to IEEE Transactions on Computers*, October 1994.

14. M. J. Little, R. D. Etchells, J. Grinberg, S. P. Laub, J. G. Nash, and M. W. Yung. The 3-D Computer. In *Proceedings of the IEEE International Conference on Wafer Scale Integration*, pages 55–64, 1989.

15. Y. S. Liu and J. Bristow. Hybrid Integration of Electrical and Optical Interconnect for MCMs Applications. In *Proceeding of the IEEE Lasers and Electro-Optics Summer Topical Meeting on Hybrid Optoelectric Integration and Packaging*, page 10, July 1993.

16. Michael Noakes and William J. Dally. System Design of the J-Machine. In *Sixth MIT Conference of Advanced Research in VLSI*, pages 179–194. MIT Press, 1990.

17. Daniel A. Reed and Richard M. Fujimoto. *Multicomputer Networks: Message-Based Parallel Processing*. Scientific Computation Series. MIT Press, 1987.

18. Gregory K. Wallace. Overview of the JPEG (ISO/CCITT) Still Image Compression Standard. In Richard Feinberg, editor, *Current Overviews in Optical Science and Engineering I*, pages 358–371. SPIE Optical Engineering Press, Bellingham, Washington, 1990.

19. D. Scott Wills, Huy Cat, Jose Cruz-Rivera, W. Stephen Lacy, James M. Baker, John Eble, Abelardo Lopez-Lagunas, and Mike Hopper. High Throughput, Low Memory Applications on the Pica Architecture. *submitted to IEEE Transactions on Parallel and Distributed Systems*, May 1994.

20. D. Scott Wills and Matthias Grossglauser. A Scalable Optical Interconnection Network for Fine-Grain Parallel Architectures. In *1993 International Conference on Parallel Processing*, pages I–154 – I–157, 16-20 August 1993.

21. D. Scott Wills and Matthias Grossglauser. A Three-Dimensional Optical Interconnection Network for Fine-Grain Parallel Architectures. In *Proceeding of the IEEE Lasers and Electro-Optics Summer Topical Meeting on Hybrid Optoelectric Integration and Packaging*, pages 21–22, 26-28 July 1993.

22. D. Scott Wills, W. Stephen Lacy, Huy Cat, Michael A. Hopper, Ashutosh Razdan, and Sek M. Chai. Pica: An Ultra-Light Processor for High-Throughput Applications. In *ICCD '93 International Conference on Computer Design, VLSI in Computers & Processors*, pages 410–414, 3-6 October 1993.

Three-Dimensional Network Topologies †

John Nguyen[1], John Pezaris[2], Gill Pratt[2], and Steve Ward[2]

[1] University of Michigan
[2] Massachusetts Institute of Technology

johnn@eecs.umich.edu
pz, gill, ward@lcs.mit.edu

Abstract. This paper presents the derivation and performance results of several new three-dimensional topologies. Various transformations can be applied to the conventional six-neighbor mesh in order to construct these topologies, which vary both in number of neighbors (degree) and logical connectivity. Analysis shows that after normalization for constant pin-count, lower-degree topologies yield lower latencies for long messages on unloaded networks, while higher-degree topologies possess higher bandwidth capacities. Although simulation results generally verify these findings, we also observe a surprising amount of difference in the performance between distinct topologies of the same degree.

1 Introduction

The past few years have seen a rise in popularity of multiprocessors using direct networks that span two or three dimensions. Such networks typically follow the topology of a two or three-dimensional mesh or torus. Although topologies other than the mesh have been studied for two-dimensional space[7], there have been few investigations of alternate topologies in three-dimensional space. This paper proposes five such alternate topologies and presents some analytical and empirical performance results.

We restrict our study to direct topologies whose nodes all possess the same number of neighbors, or *degree*. Furthermore, the node degree for any topology remains constant no matter how many nodes are in the network. Thus non-constant degree topologies such as hypercubes are not considered. Also eliminated are indirect topologies such as butterflies and fat-trees.

Since high-degree topologies require a larger number of channels on each switch, we must somehow normalize performance to the hardware complexity required by the degree of the topology. This can be accomplished by requiring a constant switch complexity through reducing the channel width of higher-degree topologies. On such topologies, the narrower data path can in turn degrade performance by increasing the number of flits required by long messages. Conversely, a network requiring a small number of channels per node allows one to increase

---

† This research is sponsored by DARPA contract #DABT63-93-C-0008.

the data path size without increasing switch complexity and thus possibly decrease the latency of long messages. Many of the topologies that are presented here can be viewed as an attempt to reduce the degree of each node.

In the following sections, we present several new three-dimensional topologies as well as a formal definition of a topology, derive analytical results to predict performance, and discuss results of some routing simulations.

2 Topologies

We present in this section five topologies can be derived from various modifications to the conventional six-neighbor mesh. These modifications include splitting each six-neighbor node into several nodes as well as adding and removing links from the six-neighbor topology. Although physical representations are presented for clarity, the topologies are really defined by the logical connectivity of the nodes. The following section will focus on a more formal treatment of topologies.

Topology A: In the standard three-dimensional mesh, each node is represented as a point (n_1, n_2, n_3) in the cartesian three-dimensional space where each n_i is an integer. The six neighbors of a node are defined as nodes with points corresponding to $+1$ and -1 offsets in one of the three axes. Such a network is illustrated in Figure 1.

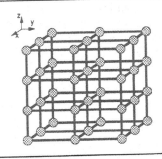

Figure 1: 6-neighbor cartesian mesh (Topology A)

Topology B: A second topology can be formed by inserting a node at each point $(n_1 + \frac{1}{2}, n_2 + \frac{1}{2}, n_3 + \frac{1}{2})$ to the set of integral-coordinate nodes. The neighbors of a node (x, y, z) can then be defined as the eight nodes represented by coordinates $(x \pm \frac{1}{2}, y \pm \frac{1}{2}, z \pm \frac{1}{2})$, as shown in Figure 2. This topology can also be formed by adding diagonal links in the directions $(1, 1, 1)$ and $(-1, -1, -1)$ to Topology A. The equivalence of the two modifications will be discussed in the next section.

The remaining four topologies can be viewed as modifications that are derived by splitting each node of the six-neighbor mesh of Topology A into several *subnodes*. In particular, four-neighbor topologies can be formed by splitting each

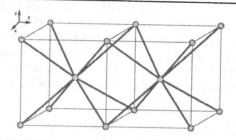

Figure 2: 8-neighbor topology (Topology B)

six-neighbor node into two subnodes, each with three external neighbors and one internal neighbor. Likewise, three-neighbor topologies can be formed by dividing each six-neighbor node into six subnodes, each with one external neighbor and two internal neighbors. For the following derivations, we label the six ports of a node in Topology A as $-x$, $+x$, $-y$, $+y$, $-z$, and $+z$. The pair $-x$ and $+x$ are called *opposing* ports, as are the pairs $-y$, $+y$ and $-z$, $+z$.

Topology C: The first four-neighbor topology can be derived by splitting each six-neighbor node into two subnodes, each of which contains exactly two opposing ports. Without loss of generality, let the first subnode be assigned to ports $\{-x, +x, -z\}$, and let the second subnode be assigned to ports $\{-y, +y, +z\}$. The two subnodes are then connected by a vertical link, forming the topology of Figure 3. Alternately, one can derive this topology by removing x links in odd z planes and removing y links in even z planes of the six-neighbor mesh. Each node has four neighbors, with two in the directions $(0, 0, \pm 1)$. Nodes on even z planes contain neighbors in the directions $(\pm 1, 0, 0)$, while nodes on odd z planes contain neighbors in the directions $(0, \pm 1, 0)$.

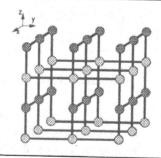

Figure 3: 4-neighbor topology with opposing ports (Topology C)

Topology D: The second four-neighbor topology can also be formed by splitting each six neighbor node into two subnodes, but with a different grouping where each subnode contains no opposing ports. For example, let the first subnode be assigned to ports $\{-x, -y, -z\}$, and the second subnode be assigned to ports $\{+x, +y, +z\}$. If one connects the two subnodes with a vertical link, then the topology can be viewed as the removal of alternating x and y links from the six-neighbor mesh, as shown in Figure 4.

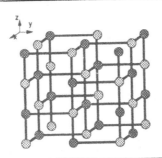

Figure 4: 4-neighbor topology with no opposing ports (Topology D)

If the orientation of links of the above topology are modified, then we obtain the same physical representation as the structure of carbon atoms in a diamond crystal. Two views of the diamond topology are shown in Figure 5, with the picture in Figure 5b representing the view from the top (z direction) of Figure 5a. In this two-dimensional projection, the number next to each node represents its z coordinate modulo 4, while an arrow represents a link that travel upwards towards the reader. The nodes in this lattice can be viewed as a subset of the integral nodes, specifically, nodes (n_1, n_2, n_3) such that $n_1 \bmod 2 = n_2 \bmod 2 = n_3 \bmod 2$. Since all links are diagonal, all neighbor offsets are in the set $(\pm 1, \pm 1, \pm 1)$. Like the previous topology, there are two types of nodes, each with four neighbors. The first type of node has an even number of $+$'s in all its neighbor offsets, while the second type has an odd number of $+$'s in all its neighbor offsets.

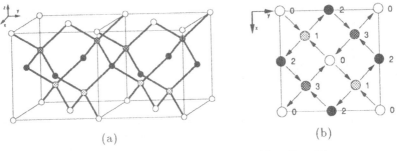

(a)   (b)

Figure 5: 4-neighbor diamond lattice (Topology D)

Topology E: This topology is created by splitting each node in the 6-neighbor mesh into six subnodes. Each subnode is associated with one of the 6-neighbor links. A ring is then formed among the six subnodes, with the constraint that no direct connections are formed between two subnodes with opposing links (for example, subnodes with $+x$ and $-x$ links are not connected). The resulting 3-neighbor topology is shown in Figure 6a. A two-dimensional projection of this topology can be formed by viewing the topology from the left upper front corner, producing the view shown in Figure 6b. Again, numbers on nodes represent the height of the node, while arrows represent links that travel out of the page.

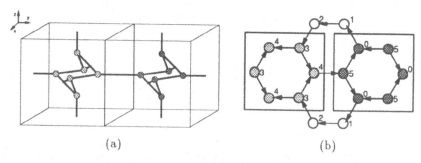

(a)   (b)

Figure 6: 3-neighbor Topology E

Topology F: The final topology is formed once again by splitting each node in the 6-neighbor mesh into six subnodes. Again, the subnodes are associated with the 6-neighbor links and are formed into a ring. However, this ring follows the constraint that subnodes with opposing links are always connected (for example, subnodes with $+x$ and $-x$ links are connected). The resulting topology is shown in Figure 7.

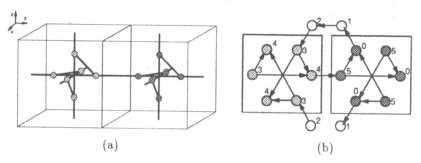

(a)   (b)

Figure 7: 3-neighbor Topology F

3 Topology isomorphism

Since topologies are defined in terms of the logical node connectivity, many physical representations may exist for a particular topology. However, it may be very difficult to determine whether some of these physical representations are indeed equal. In this section, we present a strategy for formally defining topologies in terms of the logical connectivity. From this, a technique can be derived to detect isomorphism between different physical representations of topologies. Readers who are primarily interested in the performance comparisons between topologies may wish to defer this section until later.

A topology $T = [L, M]$ is defined as a set of links L and a set of paths M that can be reached by some traversals of the links from a *reference node*. We define the group $S(T)$ to represent all paths using the links in L. Thus each link in L can be viewed as generators for $S(T)$, and the group operator is merely the concatenation of paths. Since the links can be represented by vectors in space, $S(T)$ must be abelian (commutative).

As an example, consider Topology A (T_A), whose links can be defined as the set $\{X, Y, Z\}$. The mapping f_A from logical links to physical links can be defined as: $f_A(X) = (1, 0, 0)$, $f_A(Y) = (0, 1, 0)$, $f_A(Z) = (0, 0, 1)$. Any element in $S(T_A)$ can be represented in the form $X^a Y^b Z^c$, which is translated to physical coordinates as the path from $(0, 0, 0)$ to (a, b, c). For a more complex example, consider Topology B (T_B). Let the links of T_B be $\{W, X, Y, Z\}$, with the mapping f_A to physical links as: $f_B(W) = (\frac{1}{2}, \frac{1}{2}, \frac{1}{2})$, $f_B(X) = (\frac{1}{2}, -\frac{1}{2}, -\frac{1}{2})$, $f_B(Y) = (-\frac{1}{2}, -\frac{1}{2}, \frac{1}{2})$, $f_B(Z) = (-\frac{1}{2}, \frac{1}{2}, -\frac{1}{2})$. Again, the group $S(T_B)$ can be represented by the elements of the form $W^a X^b Y^c Z^d$. However, there is an important difference: whereas each representation $X^a Y^b Z^c$ of $S(T_A)$ represents a different element for different values of a, b, c, the same is not true for $S(T_B)$. Notably, for any a, $W^a X^a Y^a Z^a$ is equal to $W^0 X^0 Y^0 Z^0$ or the identity element, representing a null path. This can be verified by using the mapping to vectors.

In the above two examples, each path in $S(T)$ from the reference node is also in the set of topology paths M. However, this is not the case for other topologies, such as the diamond topology T_D. Although four links $\{W, X, Y, Z\}$ also exist for T_D, with $S(T_D) = S(T_B)$ and $f_D = f_B$, the topologies are different. This can be explained by observing that not all paths in $S(T_D)$ from the reference node are legal. Indeed, any of the eight links $\{W^{\pm 1}, X^{\pm 1}, Y^{\pm 1}, Z^{\pm 1}\}$ are legal from any node in T_B, while only four of the links are available from any node in T_D. Thus only a subset of the paths in $S(T_D)$ can be considered legal paths from the reference node. In this case, we allow links $\{W, X, Y, Z\}$ to be used at any even number of hops from the reference node, and links $\{W^{-1}, X^{-1}, Y^{-1}, Z^{-1}\}$ to be used at an odd number of hops away. From this, we derive the constraint that any legal path for T_D must be of the form $W^a X^b Y^c Z^d$ where $a+b+c+d \in \{0, 1\}$. Note that the case of $W^a X^a Y^a Z^a = W^0 X^0 Y^0 Z^0$ for T_B is no longer relevant for T_D.

In summary, a topology T is defined as a tuple $[L, M]$ consisting of links and paths from a reference node. The links of L can be used as generators for an abelian group $S(T)$ which defines all paths from the reference node. The set M

is a subset of $S(T)$ and represents the actual legal paths that can be taken from the reference node to form the topology.

This formalism of a topology can then be used to prove isomorphism between different physical representations of topologies. As an example, let us consider the two representations of Topology D, one formed from removing alternate x and y links from the six-neighbor mesh, and the other defined as the physical structure of the diamond lattice. Since a definition for T_D is already derived above, we can show isomorphism merely by showing two consistent mappings to the two physical representations. The mapping to the diamond lattice representation is already discussed above, with $f_D(W) = (\frac{1}{2}, \frac{1}{2}, \frac{1}{2})$, $f_D(X) = (\frac{1}{2}, -\frac{1}{2}, -\frac{1}{2})$, $f_D(Y) = (-\frac{1}{2}, -\frac{1}{2}, \frac{1}{2})$, $f_D(Z) = (-\frac{1}{2}, \frac{1}{2}, -\frac{1}{2})$. The second mapping can be defined as follows: $f_D'(W) = (0, 0, -1)$, $f_D'(X) = (1, 0, 0)$, $f_D'(Y) = (0, 1, 0)$, $f_D'(Z) = (0, 0, 1)$. Note that the restriction of using $\{W, X, Y, Z\}$ on an even number of hops from the reference node and $\{W^{-1}, X^{-1}, Y^{-1}, Z^{-1}\}$ on an odd number of hops is consistent with the illustration in Figure 4.

4   Analytical comparisons

We first compare topologies by applying the conventional analytical measurements of maximum latency and minimum bisection bandwidth. In the following comparisons, we assume that pin-count forms the primary constraint on complexity of the routing chip, and thus normalize the topologies by keeping the pin-count constant. For a number of pins P, a k-neighbor topology requires $k+1$ ports for connections to neighbors and the local processor. Thus the number of bits in the communication path for each channel is $P/(k+1)$.

4.1   Latency

For a given topology, let the volume growth function $V(r)$ be the number of nodes reachable within a distance r from a center node. The set of nodes counted by $V(r)$ can be viewed as a "sphere" of radius r in the given topology. Thus for an n-dimensional topology, $V(r)$ grows as r^n. The maximum latency l_{max} of a topology can then be measured as the maximum distance between any two nodes in the "sphere", and can be calculated using the inverse of the growth function: $l_{max} = 2V^{-1}(N)$ for N nodes. The following section discusses strategies for computing the volume growth of different topologies and presents some results of these computations.

For Topology A, the "sphere" of radius r actually resembles the shape of an octahedron with vertices at $(\pm r, 0, 0)$, $(0, \pm r, 0)$, and $(0, 0, \pm r)$. The number of nodes in the octahedron can then be estimated by multiplying its volume by the density of nodes in space. The volume of the octahedron is equal to twice the volume of the pyramid formed from all points above the plane $z = 0$, which has base area $2r^2$ and height r. The volume of the octahedron is thus $\frac{4}{3}r^3$, and since the density of nodes in space is equal to one per unit volume, the number of nodes in the sphere grows as $\frac{4}{3}r^3$.

For Topology B, the shape of the "sphere" becomes a cube with diagonal $\sqrt{3}r$. The volume of such a cube is r^3, and the density of nodes is 2 per unit volume, yielding $2r^3$ nodes in a sphere of radius r.

For other topologies, the volume growth functions are computed by curve-fitting experimentally-derived results. Figure 8 shows the volume growths and maximum latencies of each topology for large radii.

Topology	# neighbors	Volume growth	Max latency
A	6	$1.33r^3$	$1.82N^{\frac{1}{3}}$
B	8	$2.00r^3$	$1.58N^{\frac{1}{3}}$
C	4	$1.33r^3$	$1.82N^{\frac{1}{3}}$
D	4	$0.83r^3$	$2.13N^{\frac{1}{3}}$
E	3	$0.40r^3$	$2.71N^{\frac{1}{3}}$
F	3	$1.06r^3$	$1.96N^{\frac{1}{3}}$

Figure 9: Topology volume growth

From Figure 9, it is clear that topologies with lower degrees possess higher latencies. However, maintaining constant pin-count also allows these topologies to possess wider data paths which can reduce the latency for large messages. For a message of length L bits, the maximum number of cycles required to send the message across an unloaded network using wormhole routing can be defined as:

$$\frac{L(k+1)}{P} + 2V^{-1}(N)$$

The graphs in Figure 10 illustrate the latencies for different sizes of networks when sending small and large messages. Note that higher-degree topologies require significantly more time to send long messages across small networks. Also note that for topologies with the same degree, Topology C outperforms D, and Topology F outperforms E.

4.2 Bisection bandwidth

The maximum latency results give an indication of the performance of a topology when the network is lightly loaded. However, a fair evaluation also requires a measure of the capacity of a topology to handle a larger density of message transmissions. The bisection bandwidth is an attempt to analytically estimate this capacity by measuring the lowest number of separated links when a network is divided into two equal halves. In this section, we represent the bisection bandwidth for each topology as a function of the form Br^2, computed as the number of links crossed when a sphere of radius r is split into two equal halves.

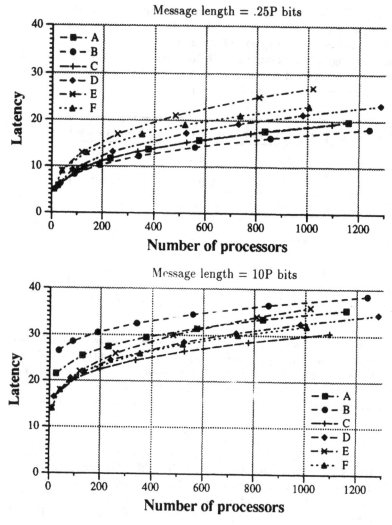

Figure 10: Maximum latency on an unloaded network

The bisection bandwidth of Topology A can be computed by considering the number of links that would be cut by a horizontal plane near $z = 0$. For such a division, the only links that would be cut are in the z direction, and can be computed by considering the number of nodes in the plane $z = 0$ of a radius-r "sphere". Since such a "sphere" takes the shape of an octahedron for Topology A, the cross-section at the plane $z = 0$ takes the shape of a diamond with vertices at $(\pm r, 0, 0)$ and $(0, \pm r, 0)$. The number of nodes in the plane can then be estimated by multiplying the area of the plane by the density of nodes.

The area of the plane is the area of a square with diagonal $2r$, while the density of each node is equal to one per square unit of area. Thus the number of nodes is equal to $2r^2$. The bisection bandwidth of Topology B can be derived with a similar strategy, and is equal to $4r^2$.

For other topologies, the bisection bandwidth is once again derived by curve-fitting computed results. Figure 11 presents bandwidth results as a function of radius and number of nodes, as well as the bandwidth normalized to a constant pin-count P.

Topology	# neighbors	Bandwidth(r)	Bandwidth(N)	Normalized Bandwidth(N)
A	6	$2.00r^2$	$1.65N^{\frac{2}{3}}$	$0.236PN^{\frac{2}{3}}$
B	8	$4.00r^2$	$2.52N^{\frac{2}{3}}$	$0.280PN^{\frac{2}{3}}$
C	4	$1.00r^2$	$0.83N^{\frac{2}{3}}$	$0.166PN^{\frac{2}{3}}$
D	4	$0.75r^2$	$0.85N^{\frac{2}{3}}$	$0.170PN^{\frac{2}{3}}$
E	3	$0.32r^2$	$0.59N^{\frac{2}{3}}$	$0.148PN^{\frac{2}{3}}$
F	3	$0.65r^2$	$0.63N^{\frac{2}{3}}$	$0.156PN^{\frac{2}{3}}$

Figure 12: Bisection bandwidth

The last column of Figure 12 represents the capacity of each topology for a given number of nodes when the channel width is limited by pin-count. This function is further illustrated by the graph in Figure 13, derived from simulation results of bisection bandwidth for particular spheres of each topology. Note that topologies with higher degrees tend to have higher bandwidths, with little difference between topologies of the same degree.

5   Routing simulation

Although the analytical results just presented give an indication of the performance of topologies under some scenarios, their accuracy is constrained by some significant assumptions. The latency measurement only represents delays for the unrealistic case when no contention arises in routing. The bisection bandwidth measurement, on the other hand, assumes the overly-pessimistic situation of total non-locality in communication. Rather than relying on these extremes, we focus instead on a random routing simulation to measure message latencies. Even though this method is not as accurate as a simulation of true program traces, it gives us a more realistic measurement of topology performance.

The results presented in this section are obtained from a uniformly random routing simulation. At every clock tick, each node has a certain probability (the *injection rate*) of injecting a message to a random destination. In order to achieve

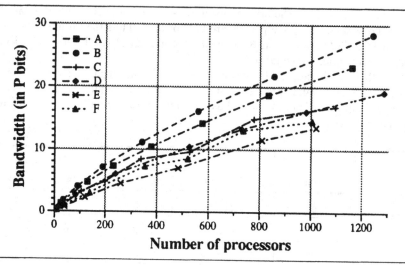

Figure 13: Normalized bisection bandwidths

a minimal and fully adaptive routing algorithm [8], a routing table of size $N \times N$ is precomputed which contains all links that can be taken for any minimal path between each pair of possible source and destination nodes.‡. The table can be computed in time $O(N^3)$ by employing a dynamic programming approach similar to those for computing shortest paths in a graph. Deadlock avoidance is accomplished by imposing no limits on the number of messages that can be placed on a link, thus in effect allowing an infinite number of virtual channels. Although an abort-and-retry approach [5] could potentially be used, we had no easy way of ensuring that no livelocks would arise using such techniques.

Figure 14 shows the simulated average latency of short messages (length P bits) using "spheres" of 256 processors. For each topology, the number of pins are held constant, causing each message to be of length $k + 1$ flits for a degree-k topology with $k + 1$ ports. Observe that latencies for low loads are very similar. For larger loads, Topology B performs best, followed by Topology A, as indicated by the bisection bandwidth measurements. However, Topology D performs significantly better than Topology C, while Topology F is only able to support a much lower load than any other topologies. This discrepancy with the bisection bandwidth results will be discussed later in this section.

In order to observe any difference in latency due to the higher channel widths of lower-degree topologies, results from a simulation on longer messages (length $5P$ bits) is shown in Figure 15. For light loads, a difference in latency exists between the higher-degree topologies A and B and other topologies. As the load increases, the higher bandwidth of some topologies impose lighter contention penalties on the latencies, resulting in various crossover points in the graph.

---

‡ Minimal routing algorithms that do not rely on tables also exist for topologies A-D[9]

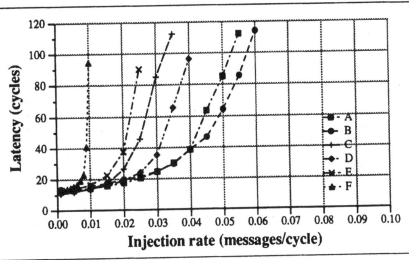

Figure 14: Simulated latencies for messages of length P bits

These crossover points can be used to influence the design decisions for a machine. For example, let us examine the crossover point between topologies A and D at the injection rate of 0.003 messages per cycle. A machine that is optimized for applications with loads lower than an injection rate of 0.003 should employ Topology D, while one that expects much higher loads should be built using Topology A. Note however that the vertical value of the crossover point may also determine its applicability. Although Topology B outperforms Topology A for loads higher than 0.007, one may question whether such a load is relevant since the latencies are already over 140 cycles per message. In order to optimize for such high load demands, it may be more advantageous to employ other factors to improve the speed of the network with respect to the processors.

From the routing simulation results, we see that some topologies do not perform at high loads nearly as well as others with similar bisection bandwidths. This can be partially explained by observing that an adaptive routing scheme works best if a message header has many choices of physical links at each node. With a large number of choices, the header can be assigned to the link with the least contention and improve latency. Even when topologies have similar bisection bandwidths, the average number of choices at each node can differ significantly. Figure 16 shows the number of choices of links that a source node has in routing to a destination node, averaged over all sources and destinations of a 256-node "sphere". Note that a number near 1 implies that there are very few routing decisions. This may explain the relatively poor performance of topologies C and F with respect to topologies of the same degree.

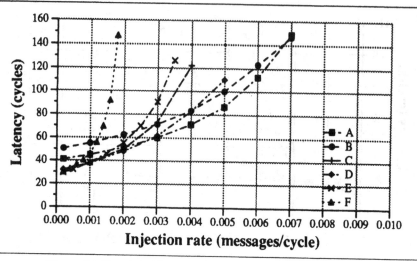

Figure 15: Simulated latencies for messages of length $5P$ bits

Topology	# neighbors	Average choices
A	6	2.19
B	8	2.72
C	4	1.45
D	4	1.53
E	3	1.23
F	3	1.15

Figure 17: Average number of routing choices

6   Conclusion

We have shown that by applying various transformations to the six-neighbor mesh, one can derive new topologies with different characteristics. Despite the existence of many physical representations of individual topologies, a consistent logical definition can be formed based on the connectivity of nodes. This definition can in turn be used to prove isomorphism between different physical representations.

In order to normalize topologies to maintain similar switch complexity, we keep the pin-count constant and vary the channel widths of each topology according to the number of neighbors for each node. Analytical techniques can then be applied to compute maximum latency and bandwidth for comparison. As expected, lower-degree topologies require a larger radius than higher-degree topologies and thus incur higher latencies for very short messages on large networks. However, for long messages, the overhead of sending the message becomes predominant, resulting in superior performance for lower-degree topologies. Simulated bisection bandwidth results predict that higher-degree topologies are able to sustain higher loads even with smaller channels.

We presented the results of a minimal and fully-adaptive routing scheme using unlimited virtual channels to avoid deadlock. On a medium-sized machine, no differences in latency is detectable for small messages on low loads. For larger messages, lower-degree topologies possess lower latencies as predicted. As the message injection rate increases, the average latency of lower-degree topologies increase very quickly, whereas higher-degree topologies can tolerate higher loads, also as predicted by bisection bandwidth. However, some large differences in load tolerance exist between topologies of similar degree and bisection bandwidth. Although there could be many reasons for this, we speculate that one explanation involves the lower number of routing choices of topologies that exhibit poor load tolerance.

The above results are meant as a preliminary comparison of topology performance. As illustrated, the attractiveness of different topologies vary significantly with different message lengths and injection rates. Before any conclusions can be reached about the preferred topology, comparisons using relevant applications and realistic machine models must be performed.

References

[1] Anant Agarwal. Limits on interconnection network performance. *IEEE Transactions on Parallel and Distributed Systems*, 2(4):398–412, 1991.

[2] Thomas H. Cormen, Charles E. Leiserson, and Ronald L. Rivest. *Introduction to Algorithms*. MIT Press, Cambridge, Massachusetts, 1990.

[3] William Dally. Virtual channel flow control. *IEEE Transactions on Parallel and Distributed Systems*, 3(2):194–205, 1992.

[4] William Dally and Charles Seitz. Deadlock-free message routing in multiprocessor interconnection networks. *IEEE Transactions on Computers*, C-36(5), 1987.

[5] Jae H. Kim, Ziqiang Liu, and Andrew A. Chien. Compressionless routing. In *The 21st Annual International Symposium on Computer Architecture*, pages 289–300, 1994.

[6] D. Linder and J. Harden. An adaptive and fault tolerant wormhole routing strategy for k-ary n-cubes. *IEEE Transactions on Computers*, C-40(1):2–12, 1991.

[7] Allen D. Malony. Regular processor arrays. In *The 2nd Symposium on the Frontiers of Massively Parallel Computation*, pages 499–502, 1988.

[8] Lionel M. Ni and Philip K. McKinley. A survey of wormhole routing techniques in direct networks. *Computer*, 26(2):62–76, 1993.

[9] Gill Pratt, Steve Ward, John Nguyen, and Chris Metcalf. The diamond interconnect. In press.

[10] Supercomputing Research Center. Five year review, March 1991.

[11] Steve Ward, et al. A scalable, modular, 3D interconnect. In *1993 International Conference on Supercomputing*, pages 230–239, 1993.

Support for Multiple Classes of Traffic in Multicomputer Routers *

Jennifer Rexford and Kang G. Shin

Real-Time Computing Laboratory
Department of Electrical Engineering and Computer Science
The University of Michigan
Ann Arbor, MI 48109-2122

Abstract. Emerging parallel real-time and multimedia applications broaden the range of performance requirements imposed on the interconnection network. This communication typically consists of a mixture of different traffic classes, where *guaranteed* packets require bounds on latency or throughput while good average performance suffices for the *best-effort* traffic. This paper investigates how multicomputer routers can capitalize on low-latency routing and switching techniques for best-effort traffic while still supporting guaranteed communication. Through simulation experiments, we show that certain architectural features are best-suited to particular performance requirements. Based on these results, the paper proposes and evaluates a router architecture that tailors low-level routing, switching, and flow-control policies to the unique needs of best-effort and guaranteed traffic. Careful selection of these policies, coupled with fine-grain arbitration between the classes, allows the guaranteed and best-effort packets to share network bandwidth without sacrificing the performance of either class.

1 Introduction

Although multicomputer router design has traditionally emphasized providing low-latency communication, modern parallel applications require additional services from the interconnection network [1, 2]. Multimedia and real-time applications, such as scientific visualization and process control, necessitate control over delay variance and throughput, in addition to low average latency [3]. While *guaranteed* traffic necessitates deterministic or probabilistic bounds on throughput or end-to-end delay, *best-effort* service often suffices for the remaining traffic. For example, control or audio/video messages may mandate explicit performance guarantees, while data transfer may tolerate delay variability in exchange for improved average latency.

* The work reported in this paper was supported in part by the National Science Foundation under Grant MIP-9203895 and an Office of Naval Research graduate fellowship. Any opinions, findings, and conclusions or recommendations expressed in this paper are those of the authors and do not necessarily reflect the views of the funding agencies.

Handling this mixture of disparate traffic classes affects the suitability of architectural features in multicomputer routers. While the router alone cannot satisfy application performance requirements, design decisions should not preclude the system from providing necessary guarantees. Servicing guaranteed traffic requires control over network access time and bandwidth allocation, so the router should bound the influence best-effort packets have on these parameters. The software, or even the hardware, can then utilize these bounds to satisfy quality-of-service requirements through packet scheduling and resource allocation for communicating tasks. Additionally, the design should not unduly penalize the performance of best-effort packets.

Modern parallel routers significantly reduce average latency by avoiding unnecessary packet delay at intermediate nodes; however, these low-latency techniques often impinge on control over packet scheduling. In particular, cut-through switching [4, 5] decentralizes bandwidth allocation and packet scheduling by allowing an incoming packet to proceed directly to the next node in its route if a suitable outgoing link is available. Other multicomputer router features, such as FIFO queueing and adaptive routing, further complicate the effort to provide predictable or guaranteed service.

Research in networking considers techniques for the effective mixing of multiple traffic classes in a communication fabric [6, 7]. However, the design trade-offs for parallel machines differ significantly from those in a heterogeneous, distributed environment. In parallel machines, router design trade-offs reflect the large network size and the tight coupling between nodes. Speed and area constraints motivate single-chip solutions, including designs that integrate the processing core and the communication subsystem [8–11]. Regular topologies facilitate efficient offset-based routing, avoiding the costs of implementing and maintaining a table-driven scheme at each node.

While these implementation constraints restrict some router design options, the tighter coupling between nodes enables multicomputer routers to consider more diverse routing and switching techniques for handling different traffic classes. The shorter, wider communication links in most parallel machines result in much lower packet transmission delays, compared to distributed systems. These low-latency channels broaden the spectrum of flow-control schemes that can be implemented efficiently. The fine-grain interaction between and within the nodes necessitates effective mapping of application tasks onto the interconnection network [12]. Effective router techniques for handling multiple traffic classes should provide useful software abstractions to parallel applications.

The remainder of this paper is organized as follows. Section 2 presents a simulation model for studying the impact of routing and switching on interconnection network performance. Using this model, Section 3 investigates how switching schemes affect the network's ability to service multiple traffic classes. Based on these results, Section 4 proposes and evaluates a router architecture that allows best-effort packets to capitalize on low-latency routing and switching techniques without compromising the performance of guaranteed traffic.

This architecture uses virtual channels [13] to logically partition the inter-

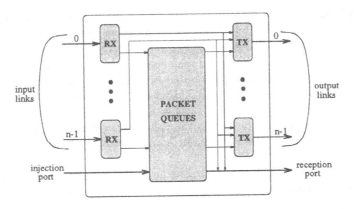

Fig. 1. Router model

connection network into multiple virtual networks that each employs different low-level policies for managing communication. Fine-grain, demand-slotted arbitration between the virtual networks regulates the intrusion of best-effort traffic on guaranteed packets, while allowing packets from either class to consume available link bandwidth. By tailoring the routing, switching, and flow-control policies for each virtual network, this architecture can accommodate the diverse performance requirements of parallel real-time and multimedia applications.

2 Evaluation Framework

The efficacy of a router architecture hinges on the policies for routing, switching, queueing, and resource arbitration. Supporting both guaranteed and best-effort traffic in a single design requires careful consideration of these low-level policies and how they influence the interaction between traffic classes. Evaluating design options for multicomputer routers requires the ability to vary low-level architectural parameters in a single unified framework. This section presents a flexible router model and simulation environment, which is used in Sections 3 and 4 to address effective architectural support for multiple traffic classes.

Packets enter the router from an injection port and n incoming links and depart the router through the reception port and n outgoing links, as shown in Figure 1. Each physical link multiplexes traffic for c virtual channels at the granularity of a flit cycle, while the injection and reception ports handle packets on behalf of the nc outgoing and incoming virtual channels, respectively. A crossbar connects the packet buffers and the incoming channels to the output links. Although each physical link services at most one virtual channel in each flit cycle, multiple virtual channels can be active at the injection and reception ports; this enables the model to represent router designs that have multiple physical or logical injection/reception ports [10, 14, 15].

Upon receiving the header flits of an incoming packet, the receiver (RX) decides whether to buffer, stall, or forward the packet, based on the routing and switching policies and prevailing network conditions. By treating outbound virtual channels as individually reservable resources, the model can invoke a variety of routing and switching schemes through flexible control over reservation policies. The routing algorithm selects candidate outgoing virtual channels, while the switching scheme determines whether or not an incoming packet waits to acquire a selected outgoing virtual channel or buffers instead. Once a packet reserves an outgoing virtual channel, it competes with other virtual channels for access to the physical link (TX) through an arbitration policy. The model includes several arbitration policies, including round-robin and priority-driven schemes.

The router model is evaluated in the pp-mess-sim (point-to-point message simulator) environment [16,17]. Implemented in C++, pp-mess-sim is an object-oriented discrete-event simulation tool for evaluating multicomputer router architectures. Using a high-level specification language, the user can select the network topology, internal router policies, and the traffic patterns generated by each node. These communication patterns stem from a collection of independent traffic classes, each with its own performance metrics and packet characteristics. The simulator allows the derivation of packet length, interarrival times, and target nodes from a variety of stochastic processes.

To evaluate traffic mixing, the simulator associates each traffic class with a particular routing algorithm and switching scheme on a set of virtual channels. The tool includes an extensible set of routing-switching algorithms that interact with the router model through a well-defined set of instructions. This enables specification of routing-switching combinations separate from the router model. These algorithms can formally query the status of the router in order to execute state-dependent routing and switching decisions. The simulator supports wormhole, virtual cut-through, and packet switching, as well as hybrid schemes, each under a variety of routing algorithms.

The experiments in this paper evaluate an 8×8 torus (8-ary 2-cube) network carrying 16-flit packets using dimension-ordered routing; similar performance trends occur for other network and message sizes. Each traffic class independently generates packets at each node with exponentially-distributed inter-arrival times and uniform random selection of destination nodes. The simulator collects performance data only after receiving at least 200 packets from each traffic class on each source node to allow the network to reach steady state. Each traffic class then accumulates performance data for 2000 packets from each node, with each source continuing to generate packets until data collection completes throughout the network. For all results shown in the paper, the standard error of average latency is less than 10 cycles for the 95% confidence interval.

3 Evaluation of Switching Schemes

In defining how packets flow through the network, the various switching schemes use different resources at nodes along a packet's route. This section evaluates the ability of wormhole, virtual cut-through, and packet switching to meet different

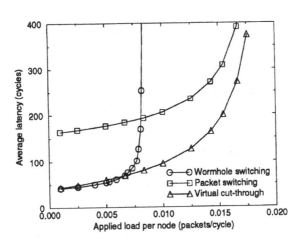

Fig. 2. Average packet latency

performance requirements in multicomputer routers. Each switching scheme is best-suited for certain traffic classes with particular characteristics and performance requirements [14, 18]. To effectively support multiple traffic classes, the router should bound both network access time and the service rate for guaranteed packets. These bounds provide necessary abstractions for the scheduling and mapping of communicating tasks. Best-effort packets, on the other hand, may forego these restrictions in exchange for lower latency and reduced buffer requirements.

3.1 Average Latency

Traditional *packet switching* requires an arriving packet to buffer completely before transmission to a subsequent node can begin. In contrast, cut-through switching schemes, such as *virtual cut-through* [4] and *wormhole* [5], try to forward an incoming packet directly to an idle output link. If the packet encounters a busy outgoing channel, virtual cut-through switching buffers the packet, while a blocked wormhole packet stalls pending access to the link. While first-generation multicomputers employed packet switching, most existing research and commercial routers utilize cut-through switching for lower latency and reduced buffer space requirements [19]. The usage of memory and link resources determines both average packet latency and the influence an in-transit packet can have on other network traffic.

Figure 2 shows the average end-to-end packet latency for the three switching schemes as a function of the packet injection rate. In the simulation experiments, virtual cut-through and packet switching utilize one virtual channel for each physical link and store buffered packets in output queues in the router. Wormhole packets employ deadlock-free routing on a pair of virtual channels [20] with demand-driven, round-robin arbitration amongst the virtual channels; each virtual channel can hold a single flit pending access to the output link. Even with this small amount of memory resources, wormhole switching performs well at low loads, slightly outperforming virtual cut-through switching. At high loads, virtual cut-through and packet switching performance gradually merge, as high network utilization decreases the likelihood that an in-transit packet encounters an idle output link.

By removing blocked packets from the network, virtual cut-through and packet switching consume network bandwidth proportional to the offered load. In contrast, a blocked wormhole packet stalls in the network, effectively dilating its length until its outgoing channel becomes available. As a result, wormhole networks typically utilize only a fraction of the available network bandwidth [13, 21], as seen by the early saturation of the wormhole plot in Figure 2. At higher loads, this effect enables packet switching to outperform wormhole switching, even though packet switching introduces buffering delay at each hop in a packet's route. While adding virtual channels can increase wormhole throughput [13], channel contention still creates dependencies amongst packets spanning multiple nodes.

The sensitivity of wormhole networks to slight changes in load, including short communication bursts [22], complicates the use of wormhole switching for guaranteed traffic. Still, wormhole switching is particularly well-suited to best-effort packets, due to its low latency and minimal buffer space requirements. While flow-control costs limit the utility of wormhole switching in distributed systems, parallel machines can dynamically transfer or stall wormhole flits without complicating buffer allocation for other traffic. Section 4 describes how, with effective flow-control and arbitration schemes, best-effort packets can employ wormhole switching without compromising the performance of the guaranteed traffic.

3.2 Predictability

While the router should provide low average latency for best-effort packets, guaranteed communication requires predictable network delay and throughput. Figure 3 shows the coefficient of variation for packet latency for the three switching schemes, where the coefficient of variation measures the ratio of the standard deviation to the mean [23]. Since latency characteristics vary depending on the distance between source-destination pairs, the graph shows results only for packets traveling a fixed distance in the network. While each source generates traffic with uniform random selection of destination nodes, data collection for Figure 3 includes only packets traveling exactly five hops.

Across all loads, packet switching incurs the least variability since packets deterministically buffer at intermediate nodes. Coupled with static routing, a packet-switched transfer utilizes deterministic memory and channel resources at fixed nodes and links along the route. This greatly simplifies the allocation and scheduling of resources throughout the interconnection network. In contrast, virtual cut-through imparts variable load on memory resources at intermediate

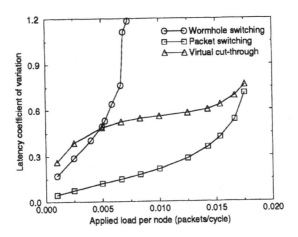

Fig. 3. Latency coefficient of variation (5-hop packets)

nodes by basing the buffering decision on the status of the output links. At high loads, virtual cut-through and packet switching merge, as in Figure 2, due to the decreasing likelihood of packet cut-throughs.

Wormhole switching, though conceptually similar to virtual cut-through, has quite different characteristics. Since a blocked wormhole packet never buffers, it imparts no memory demands on intermediate nodes, but instead consumes unpredictable amounts of channel bandwidth. In Figure 3, wormhole latency variation increases dramatically with rising load, even under a moderate injection rate below saturation throughput. Below the saturation load, wormhole switching results in a low average latency, as seen in Figure 2, but a portion of the traffic incurs larger delay due to pockets of channel contention and the small amount of buffer resources. In addition to a large coefficient of variation, wormhole traffic suffers a large standard deviation of packet latency, as shown in Figure 4.

Depending on the number of active virtual channels at each link, flits within a single wormhole packet may encounter different service rates. Demand-driven arbitration for access to the physical links, while important for low average latency, complicates the effort to export a predictable flit or packet service rate to a static or run-time scheduling algorithm. While adding virtual channels can reduce contention, additional virtual channels also increase the potential variability in the number of flits awaiting access to each physical link, further complicating the flit service rate.

3.3 Packet Scheduling

The router must have control over packet scheduling and bandwidth allocation to ensure that guaranteed packets meet their latency and bandwidth requirements.

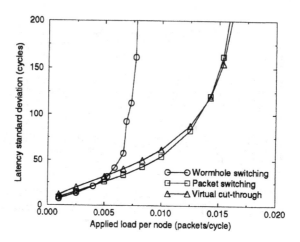

Fig. 4. Latency standard deviation (5-hop packets)

Virtual cut-through and packet switching generate physical queues in each node, facilitating priority-based scheduling amongst competing packets. In contrast, stalled wormhole packets form logical queues spanning multiple nodes. While these decentralized queues complicate packet scheduling, a wormhole router can influence resource allocation through the virtual channel reservation and arbitration policies. Priority assignment of virtual channels to incoming packets improves predictability; adaptive arbitration policies can further reduce variability by basing flit bandwidth allocation on packet deadlines or priority [13, 24–26].

While assigning priorities to virtual channels provides some control over packet scheduling, this ties priority resolution to the number of virtual channels. If packets at different priority levels share virtual channels, the application must account for blocking time when a lower priority packet holds resources needed by higher priority traffic. While adding more virtual channels can improve priority resolution, this also incurs increased latency overhead and implementation complexity for the router [27]. In addition, the router must enforce the multiple priority levels at its injection and reception ports to avoid unpredictable stalling at the network entry and exit points.

Providing separate buffers for each priority level is effective for coarse-grain priority assignment, but this approach incurs significant cost for fine-grain resolution. With *packet* queues at each node, the router can effectively utilize fine-grain priorities, such as deadlines, to assign access to output links [7, 28]. Instead of providing separate logic and buffer space for each priority level, the router can include a single priority queue for each output link [29, 30]. By buffering packets at each node, packet switching enables the router to schedule traffic to provide latency or bandwidth guarantees [28]. For example, suppose a guaranteed packet enters an intermediate node well in advance of its deadline. The scheduler may wish to detain this packet, even if its outgoing link is available, to avoid unexpectedly overloading the subsequent node.

4 Controlled Traffic Mixing

Best-effort and guaranteed traffic have conflicting performance goals that complicate interconnection network design. The effective mixing of guaranteed and best-effort traffic hinges on controlling the interaction between these two classes. In particular, best-effort packets cannot consume arbitrary amounts of link or buffer resources while guaranteed packets await service.

4.1 Router Architecture

As seen in Section 3, wormhole and packet switching exercise complementary resources in the interconnection network, with wormhole switching reserving virtual channels and packet switching consuming buffers in the router. Hence, the combination of wormhole switching for best-effort traffic and packet switching for guaranteed communication enables effective partitioning of router resources. However, since the traffic classes share network bandwidth, the router must regulate access to the physical links to control the interaction between the two classes.

Assigning the best-effort and guaranteed packets to separate virtual networks can regulate this interaction between the traffic classes. The router divides each physical link into multiple virtual channels, where some virtual channels carry best-effort packets and the rest accept only guaranteed traffic. Virtual channels provide an effective mechanism for reducing the interaction between packets while still allowing traffic to share network bandwidth [8–10, 14, 31]. Exporting the virtual channel abstraction to the injection and reception ports further prevents intrusion between packets at the network entry and exit points [10, 14, 15].

By tailoring the routing, switching, and flow-control policies for each virtual network, multicomputer routers can support traffic classes with conflicting performance requirements. Packets on separate virtual networks interact only to compete for access to the physical links and ports. This bounds network access time for guaranteed packets, independent of the amount or length of best-effort packets. The communication software, or hardware, can then build on these underlying abstractions to provide various services, such as connection-oriented communication with latency or bandwidth guarantees. Fine-grain flow control on the wormhole virtual network enables best-effort flits to capitalize on slack link bandwidth left unclaimed by guaranteed packets.

4.2 Fair Arbitration

Figures 5, 6, and 7 evaluate the effect of increasing best-effort load on the performance of both best-effort and guaranteed traffic in this router architecture. In these experiments, the router interleaves three virtual channels on each link,

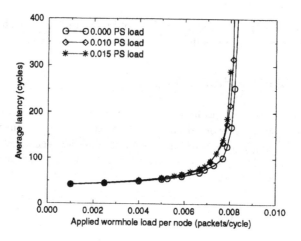

Fig. 5. Average wormhole latency

with two virtual channels allocated to best-effort packets for deadlock-free wormhole routing and one dedicated to guaranteed traffic using packet switching. Each
curve shows the impact of changing best-effort load in the presence of a fixed rate
of injection for guaranteed packets. The router employs round-robin arbitration
amongst the active virtual channels contending for each link.

Figure 5 shows the average latency for the best-effort, wormhole packets,
under three different injection rates for the packet-switched (PS) traffic. Note
that the curve for zero packet-switched load corresponds to the wormhole latency
data in Figure 2. As the amount of wormhole traffic increases, best-effort packets
incur larger latency due to increased channel contention within the best-effort
virtual network. Even with fairly heavy packet-switching load, the best-effort
packets maintain low average latency until reaching the saturation throughput.
The presence of packet-switched traffic does not significantly limit this achievable best-effort throughput, since the wormhole virtual network saturates due
to virtual channel contention, not a shortage of network bandwidth.

As seen in Figures 6 and 7, both the average latency and predictability of
the guaranteed packets are largely unaffected by the best-effort traffic, due to
fine-grain arbitration amongst the virtual channels. For both packet-switched
loads, the mean and standard deviation of end-to-end latency closely match the
corresponding values in Figures 2 and 4, even as the wormhole traffic exceeds
its sustainable load. Channel contention on the best-effort virtual network does
not impede the forward progress of guaranteed packets, since blocked wormhole
packets temporarily stall in their own virtual network instead of depleting physical link or buffer resources. Demand-driven arbitration ensures that either class
of traffic can improve throughput by capitalizing on the available link bandwidth.

While the separate virtual networks limit the interaction between the traf-

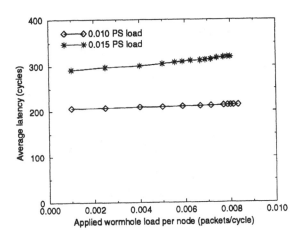

Fig. 6. Average packet switching latency

fic classes, the arbitration for access to the physical link still permits active best-effort virtual channels to increase delay for the guaranteed packets. This is manifested in Figures 6 and 7 by the slight increase in packet-switching latency and standard deviation in the presence of a heavier load of wormhole traffic. More significantly for the guaranteed traffic, fair arbitration amongst the virtual channels varies the service rate afforded both traffic classes, providing slower guaranteed service under increasing best-effort load.

4.3 Tighter Bounds for Guaranteed Traffic

The router can further minimize intrusion on guaranteed traffic by imposing priority arbitration between the virtual networks, where guaranteed packets always win arbitration over the best-effort packets. For a guaranteed packet, this effectively provides flit-level preemption of best-effort traffic across its entire path through the network. Unlike the results in Figures 6 and 7, assigning priority to guaranteed traffic removes any sensitivity to the best-effort load. Priority arbitration enables a guaranteed packet to travel at the same rate through each link in its journey, independent of the number of active best-effort virtual channels. This abstraction enables the scheduler to allocate resources based only on the worst-case requirements of the guaranteed traffic, while still enabling best-effort traffic to dynamically consume unused link bandwidth.

However, priority arbitration can exact a heavy toll on the best-effort packets, particularly at higher loads, as illustrated by Figure 8. This graph shows the average latency of best-effort wormhole packets in the presence of three different packet-switching loads under priority arbitration for the physical links. Unlike Figure 5, Figure 8 shows significant degradation of the performance of best-effort packets, since the strict priority-based scheme restricts their forward progress.

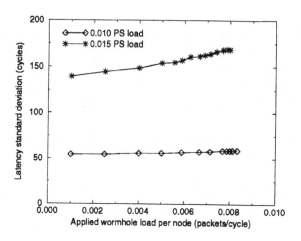

Fig. 7. Packet switching latency standard deviation

Even in the absence of livelock, lengthy blocking of wormhole flits increases contention delays in the best-effort virtual network.

Priority arbitration varies the service rate for the best-effort packets depending on the load of guaranteed traffic. To reduce contention, the best-effort virtual networks could employ adaptive routing to enable these packets to circumvent links and nodes serving a heavy load of guaranteed packets. Alternatively, the router could aid the forward progress of best-effort packets by ensuring predictable access to the physical link, even in the presence of guaranteed packets. The router can allow up to α best-effort flits to accompany the transmission of a guaranteed packet. Since the guaranteed traffic employs packet switching, a guaranteed packet holds the physical link for a bounded time proportional to its packet length ℓ. In effect, this dilates each guaranteed packet to a service time of at most $\ell + \alpha$ cycles, while dissipating contention in the best-effort virtual network. When no guaranteed packets await service, pending best-effort flits have free access to the outgoing link.

This permits forward progress for best-effort packets while still enforcing a tight bound on the intrusion on guaranteed traffic, without restricting packet size. Such a credit-based scheme preserves necessary delay abstractions for the scheduling of guaranteed traffic. For additional flexibility, a writeable register in each router would allow the system to set α when downloading tasks to the processing nodes. For example, the compiler could test the schedulability of the guaranteed communication under several candidate α values, selecting an α that does not disrupt the delay or bandwidth bounds for the guaranteed packets. This enables the compiler to determine the appropriate trade-off between the best-effort performance and the admission of guaranteed traffic for a given application.

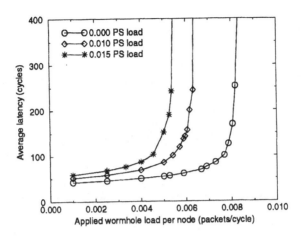

Fig. 8. Average wormhole latency with priority arbitration

5 Conclusions and Future Work

Parallel real-time and multimedia applications impose diverse communication requirements on multicomputer interconnection networks. The conflicting performance goals of best-effort and guaranteed traffic affect the suitability of routing, switching, and flow-control schemes. In this paper, we show that low-level control over routing and switching, coupled with fine-grain arbitration, enables multicomputer routers to effectively mix guaranteed and best-effort communication. This allows best-effort traffic to capitalize on flexible routing and switching schemes that improve average performance, without compromising the predictable, timely delivery of guaranteed packets.

Effective mixing of best-effort and guaranteed traffic requires a combination of low-level hardware support and higher-level protocols. This paper has addressed effective multicomputer router hardware for enabling the development of such higher-level protocols. Arbitration and flow-control schemes enable the router to export bounded network access delay, packet service time, and throughput for guaranteed traffic, even in the presence of best-effort flits. Hardware or software protocols can then build on these abstractions to allocate communication resources and schedule guaranteed packets [6, 7, 28].

Traditionally, real-time systems have employed packet switching, coupled with scheduling algorithms, for predictable performance. However, in tightly-coupled parallel machines, this approach unduly penalizes best-effort packets. As future work, we plan to compare the proposed router architecture to approaches that employ a single switching scheme, such as wormhole, virtual cut-through, or packet switching. Studying realistic communication patterns and scheduling algorithms should lend more insight into the cost-performance trade-offs in the proposed router model.

References

1. D. Cohen, G. G. Finn, R. Felderman, and A. DeSchon, "The use of message-based multicomputer components to construct gigabit networks," *Computer Communication Review*, vol. 23, no. 3, pp. 32–44, July 1993.

2. R. Cypher, A. Ho, S. Konstantinidou, and P. Messina, "Architectural requirements of parallel scientific applications with explicit communication," in *Proc. Int'l Symposium on Computer Architecture*, pp. 2–13, May 1993.

3. D. Ferrari, "Client requirements for real-time communication services," *IEEE Communications Magazine*, pp. 65–72, November 1990.

4. P. Kermani and L. Kleinrock, "Virtual cut-through: A new computer communication switching technique," *Computer Networks*, vol. 3, no. 4, pp. 267–286, September 1979.

5. W. J. Dally and C. L. Seitz, "The torus routing chip," *Journal of Distributed Computing*, vol. 1, no. 3, pp. 187–196, 1986.

6. J. J. Bae and T. Suda, "Survey of traffic control schemes and protocols in ATM networks," *Proceedings of the IEEE*, vol. 79, no. 2, pp. 170–189, February 1991.

7. C. M. Aras, J. F. Kurose, D. S. Reeves, and H. Schulzrinne, "Real-time communication in packet-switched networks," *Proceedings of the IEEE*, vol. 82, no. 1, pp. 122–139, January 1994.

8. W. J. Dally and P. Song, "Design of a self-timed VLSI multicomputer communication controller," in *IEEE Int'l Conf. on Computer Design: VLSI in Computers*, pp. 230–234, 1987.

9. W. J. Dally, J. A. S. Fiske, J. S. Keen, R. A. Lethin, M. D. Noakes, P. R. Nuth, R. E. Davison, and G. A. Fyler, "The Message-Driven Processor: A multicomputer processing node with efficient mechanisms," *IEEE Micro*, pp. 23–39, April 1992.

10. C. Peterson, J. Sutton, and P. Wiley, "iWarp: A 100-MOPS LIW microprocessor for multicomputers," *IEEE Micro*, pp. 26–29,81–87, June 1991.

11. D. Talia, "Message-routing systems for transputer-based multicomputers," *IEEE Micro*, pp. 62–72, June 1993.

12. M. G. Norman and P. Thanisch, "Models of machines and computation for mapping in multicomputers," *ACM Computing Surveys*, vol. 25, no. 3, pp. 263–302, September 1993.

13. W. Dally, "Virtual-channel flow control," *IEEE Trans. Parallel and Distributed Systems*, vol. 3, no. 2, pp. 194–205, March 1992.

14. J. Dolter, S. Daniel, A. Mehra, J. Rexford, W. Feng, and K. G. Shin, "SPIDER: Flexible and efficient communication support for point-to-point distributed systems," Technical Report CSE-TR-180-93, University of Michigan, October 1993. To appear in *Proc. Int. Conf. on Distributed Computing Systems*, June 1994.

15. J. H. Kim and A. A. Chien, "Evaluation of wormhole routed networks under hybrid traffic loads," in *Proc. Hawaii Int'l Conf. on System Sciences*, pp. 276–285, January 1993.

16. J. Dolter, *A Programmable Routing Controller Supporting Multi-mode Routing and Switching in Distributed Real-Time Systems*, PhD thesis, University of Michigan, September 1993.

17. W. Feng, J. Rexford, A. Mehra, S. Daniel, J. Dolter, and K. Shin, "Architectural support for managing communication in point-to-point distributed systems," Technical Report CSE-TR-197-94, University of Michigan, March 1994.

18. J. Rexford, J. Dolter, and K. G. Shin, "Hardware support for controlled interaction of guaranteed and best-effort communication," in *Proc. Workshop on Parallel and Distributed Real-Time Systems*, April 1994.

19. X. Zhang, "System effects of interprocessor communication latency in multicomputers," *IEEE Micro*, pp. 12–15,52–55, April 1991.

20. W. J. Dally and C. L. Seitz, "Deadlock-free message routing in multiprocessor interconnection networks," *IEEE Trans. Computers*, vol. C-36, no. 5, pp. 547–553, May 1987.

21. J. Ngai and C. Seitz, "A framework for adaptive routing in multicomputer networks," in *Symposium on Parallel Algorithms and Architectures*, pp. 1–9, June 1989.

22. W. Dally and H. Aoki, "Deadlock-free adaptive routing in multicomputer networks using virtual channels," *IEEE Trans. Parallel and Distributed Systems*, vol. 4, no. 4, pp. 466–475, April 1993.

23. R. Jain, *The Art of Computer Systems Performance Analysis*, John Wiley & Sons, Inc., 1991.

24. B. Tsai and K. G. Shin, "Sequencing of concurrent communication traffic in a mesh multicomputer with virtual channels," to appear in *Proc. Int'l Conf. on Parallel Processing*, August 1994.

25. J.-P. Li and M. W. Mutka, "Priority based real-time communication for large scale wormhole networks," in *Proc. International Parallel Processing Symposium*, pp. 433–438, April 1994.

26. J.-P. Li and M. W. Mutka, "Real-time virtual channel flow control," in *Phoenix Conference on Computers and Communication*, April 1994.

27. A. A. Chien, "A cost and speed model for k-ary n-cube wormhole routers," in *Proc. Hot Interconnects*, August 1993.

28. D. D. Kandlur, K. G. Shin, and D. Ferrari, "Real-time communication in multi-hop networks," in *Proc. Int. Conf. on Distributed Computer Systems*, pp. 300–307, May 1991.

29. H. J. Chao and N. Uzun, "A VLSI sequencer chip for ATM traffic shaper and queue manager," *IEEE Journal of Solid-State Circuits*, vol. 27, no. 11, pp. 1634–1643, November 1992.

30. K. Toda, K. Nishida, E. Takahashi, N. Michell, and Y. Yamaguchi, "Implementation of a priority forwarding router chip for real-time interconnection networks," in *Proc. Workshop on Parallel and Distributed Real-Time Systems*, April 1994.

31. S. Konstantinidou, "Segment router: A novel router design for parallel computers," to appear in *Proc. Symposium on Parallel Algorithms and Architectures*, June 1994.

32. M. W. Mutka, "Using rate monotonic scheduling technology for real-time communications in a wormhole network," in *Proc. Workshop on Parallel and Distributed Real-Time Systems*, April 1994.

Multidestination Message Passing Mechanism Conforming to Base Wormhole Routing Scheme*

Dhabaleswar K. Panda, Sanjay Singal, and Pradeep Prabhakaran

Dept. of Computer and Information Science
The Ohio State University, Columbus, OH 43210-1277
Tel: (614)-292-5199, Fax: (614)-292-2911
E-mail: {panda,singal,prabhaka}@cis.ohio-state.edu

Abstract. A new concept of *multidestination wormhole* mechanism is proposed which allows a message to be propagated along any *valid path* in a wormhole network *conforming* to the underlying *base* routing scheme (ecube, planar, turn, or fully adaptive). Two schemes are developed and evaluated to perform fast *multicasting* and *broadcasting* in 2D/3D meshes/tori using this new mechanism. Not only do these schemes demonstrate superiority over Umesh [10] and Hamiltonian Path [9] schemes, they indicate an *interesting* result that the cost of multicast can be *reduced* or kept *near-constant* as the degree of multicast *increases*. Variations of the proposed schemes to take advantage of routing-adaptivity are also presented. These results are the first ones in the wormhole-routing literature to propose multicasting schemes with such reduced overhead and provision for taking advantage of adaptivity. It lays a new foundation in building high-performance wormhole architecture for supporting fast collective communication operations.

1 Introduction

The wormhole-routing switching technique is becoming the trend in building future parallel systems due to its inherent advantage of low-latency communication [6, 12]. Intel Paragon, Cray T3D, Ncube, J-Machine, and Stanford DASH are representative systems falling into this category. Such systems are being used for supporting either distributed-memory, shared-memory, or distributed-shared memory programming paradigms. In order to support these paradigms, these systems need fast implementation of collective communication operations (*broadcast, multicast, global combine,* and *barrier synchronization*) [11].

Traditionally, the wormhole-routed systems have supported only *point-to-point* (unicast) message passing mechanism with one destination per message. This leads to costly implementation of collective communication and synchronization operations on these systems with *multiple phases* of unicast message

---

* This research is supported in part by the National Science Foundation Grant #MIP-9309627.

exchange. Some examples are: broadcasting algorithms by Van de Geijn[2], multicasting algorithms using Umesh operations by McKinley [10], and complete exchange algorithm by Bokhari [3]. To reduce the number of phases, a Hamiltonian Path-based scheme has been proposed by Ni[9]. This scheme uses a modified router organization to support propagation of multidestination messages (a message with multiple destinations) and allows a message to be consumed at a destination node while being forwarded to the next node concurrently. However, the message propagation is restricted to a Hamiltonian Path in the network to prevent deadlock.

Though Hamiltonian path-based routing demonstrates significant potential, its development has been in a different track compared to e-cube [6] and adaptive routing schemes [5, 7, 8]. Though today's commercial and experimental systems (Intel Paragon, Cray T3D, Ncube-3, and Stanford DASH) use only e-cube routing, a natural extension for these machines in near future will be to go for adaptive routing. In order to implement Hamiltonian-path-based routing, these machines need to go through a complete set of router modification. Hence, it is less likely that a system in near future will be able to take advantage of the potential of Hamiltonian-path-based routing.

In this paper, we take an approach to bridge this gap by defining a new framework of *Base-Routing-Conformed-Path* (BRCP) model. This model utilizes multidestination message-passing mechanism. Unlike the Hamiltonian-path-based scheme, this model allows a multidestination message to be propagated through any *path* in the network as long as it is a *valid* path *conforming* to the base-routing scheme. For example on a 2D mesh with e-cube (row-column) routing, a valid path can be any row, column, or row-column. If the network supports planar-adaptive routing scheme, a message can also be propagated along a diagonal path. Similar flexibility exists for networks supporting fully-adaptive routing and turn model.

To demonstrate the potential of this new mechanism, we develop and present two schemes for multicast, an important collective communication operation [12]. These schemes perform far better compared to the Umesh and Hamiltonian-path-based schemes even for systems with e-cube routing. As the number of destinations for a multicast *increases*, we show that the cost of multicast can in fact be *reduced*. With increase in adaptivity in the network, the schemes perform even better. It is shown that this model can be very easily implemented in the existing routers by incorporating minor additional logic to the router and hence, can be incorporated into near-future wormhole-routed systems to obtain significant performance gain with minimal increase in cost.

2 Base-Routing-Conformed-Path (BRCP) Model

This section explains multidestination message passing and introduces BRCP model. Intrinsic benefits of this model together with deadlock-freedom properties and architectural supports are discussed.

2.1 Multidestination Wormhole Mechanism

The concept of wormhole message passing mechanism with multiple destinations was used in [9] to perform fast multicast operations with Hamiltonian-Path-based routing. Under this mechanism, the header of a worm consists of multiple destinations. The *sender* node creates these destinations as an ordered list, depending on their intended order of traversal. As soon as the worm is injected into the network, it is routed based on the address in the leading header flit corresponding to the first destination. Once the worm reaches the router of the first destination node, the flit containing this address is removed by the router. Now the worm is routed to the node whose address is contained in the next header flit (second destination in the ordered list). While the flits are being forwarded by the router of the first destination node to its adjacent router, they are also copied flit-by-flit to the system buffer of this node. This process is carried out in each intermediate destination node of the ordered list. When the message reaches the last destination, it is not routed any further and gets completely consumed by the last destination node.

2.2 Paths Conforming to Base Routing

The list of destinations in a multidestination worm is ordered by the sender node. This *ordering* depends on two parameters: 1) the *intended traversal* of the message to a set of destinations and 2) the *feasibility* of the intended path to be traversed by the worm in the network. Obviously, the first parameter depends on the application and the second one is determined by the routing constraint of the underlying network. Consider a multidestination worm with n destinations from a source s with an ordered destination list $\{d_1, d_2, \ldots, d_{n-1}, d_n\}$ (the first and the last destinations are d_1 and d_n, respectively). The validity of this worm depends on the underlying routing scheme. Assume the network supports a deadlock-free routing scheme $\mathcal{R}$ which can be e-cube [6], planar-adaptive [5], turn-model [8], fully-adaptive [7], or any other routing scheme. The Base-Routing-Conformed-Path (BRCP) model is defined as follows:

Definition 1 *A multidestination worm with an ordered destination list $\{d_1, d_2, \ldots, d_{n-1}, d_n\}$ in a network supporting routing scheme $\mathcal{R}$ conforms to this base routing iff the destination set $\{d_1, d_2, \ldots, d_{n-1}\}$ can be covered as intermediate nodes on one of the possible paths from s to d_n under the routing constraint $\mathcal{R}$.*

Figure 1 shows examples of multidestination worms under BRCP model. For example, in an ecube system (assuming messages are routed first along row and then along column), a multidestination worm can cover a set of destinations in row/column/row-column order. It is to be noted that a set of destinations ordered in a column-row manner will be an *invalid* path under BRCP model for e-cube systems. Similarly, in a planar adaptive system, a multidestination worm can cover a set of destinations along any diagonal in addition to the flexibility supported by the ecube system. Such additional paths are shown as bold lines in the figure. If the underlying routing scheme supports west first turn model, it can provide further flexibility in covering a lot of destinations using a single worm. For this turn model example, a non-minimal west first routing scheme is assumed. If the base routing scheme supports non-minimal routing then the traversal of multidestination worms can also conform to non-minimal paths [13].

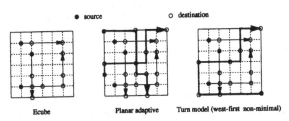

Fig. 1. Examples of multidestination worms under BRCP model conforming to different base routing schemes in a 2-D mesh. In addition to ecube paths, added flexibility for new paths under planar and west first routing schemes are shown in bold lines.

2.3 Intrinsic Benefits

The significant benefit of BRCP model comes from the fact that a message can be delivered to multiple destinations with the same overhead as that of sending it to a single destination, if the destinations can be grouped into a single worm under BRCP model. Even the simplest e-cube routing scheme can take advantage of this model by grouping destinations on row, column, or row-column. As the adaptivity of the base routing scheme increases, more and more destinations can be covered by a single multidestination worm. As the number of destinations per source *increases* in operations like multicast and broadcast, *less* number of multidestination worms are needed to cover them compared to the unicast-based schemes. If the set of destinations demonstrate some spatial organization (row, column, diagonal, or block) then a suitable scheme based on the underlying routing constraint can be developed to cover them using as few multidestination worms as possible. Similarly, depending on the technological parameters (the ratio of communication start-up time to link-propagation time), a programmer/compiler can optimize on the grouping to implement the required collective communication operation with minimal time. Hence, this model opens up an entirely new framework together with its challenges for developing optimal algorithms to implement collective communication operations with minimal time. In this paper, we emphasize on this framework by developing and evaluating algorithms for single-source multicast and broadcast operations.

2.4 Deadlock-Freedom and Architectural Supports

The BRCP model assumes that the base routing scheme $\mathcal{R}$ is free from deadlock under unicast message passing. Since the propagation of multidestination worms under BRCP model conforms to routing restrictions of $\mathcal{R}$, there is no additional channel (link) dependency in the network when both unicast and multidestination worms co-exist. However, added dependency across multidestination worms may arise if each node in the system has limited number of *consumption channels*[1, 12]. We illustrate this deadlock property through examples and propose solutions to achieve deadlock-freedom.

Consider the Hamiltonian Path-based scheme[9] with dual-path implementation. From a given source, the high-path (low-path) is used for sending messages to higher (lower) numbered destination nodes. Consider the example shown in Fig. 2a where two destination nodes B and D are common to two worms W1 and W2 moving in the high- and low-paths, respectively. Assume each router-processor interface has only one consumption channel. Based on the movement of worms, assume a situation where the consumption channels at nodes B and D are taken up and being held by the worms W1 and W2 (it is shown against the consumption channels in parenthesis), respectively. It can be easily seen that such a situation will lead to deadlock in the system. Hence, the dual-path implementation assumes an implicit 2 consumption channels per node. Similar observations have also been made in [4].

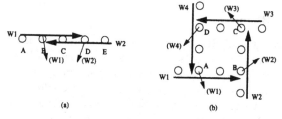

Fig. 2. Examples of deadlock through consumption channel dependency in a) Hamiltonian-path model and b) BRCP model. Bold arrows indicate worm propagation and thin ones represent consumption channels being held by the worms indicated in parenthesis.

Let us consider our BRCP model. Since the set of paths allowed by e-cube routing is always a subset of the paths allowed by other routing schemes, we first analyze the consumption channel dependency in e-cube systems. Figure 2b illustrates an example of deadlock where the corner nodes (A, B, C, and D) are common destinations to a pair of multidestination worms passing through the node. For example, node A is a common destination for worms W1 and W4. If each router-processor interface has only one consumption channel, it can be easily verified that this situation will lead to deadlock. Now the problem is how many consumption channels are needed at each router interface to make the BRCP model deadlock-free?

The solution to the above problem depends on how many different worms can compete for a consumption channel at a node. If the base routing scheme requires v virtual channels per physical channel to provide deadlock-free unicast communication, there might be $2nv$ worms trying to enter a node concurrently in a k-ary n-cube system [12]. This leads to an *upper bound* of $2nv$ consumption channels per node. The following theorem provides us the *minimum* number of consumption channels required for e-cube systems.

Theorem 1 *A k-ary n-cube system with e-cube routing $\mathcal{R}$ requires $(n+1)$ consumption channels per node to support deadlock-free communication under the BRCP model.*

Proof: The BRCP model can be made deadlock-free if we can eliminate all possible dependencies between multidestination worms. The maximum number of multidestination worms entering a node is $2n$. We can allocate a dedicated consumption channel per each pair of positive and negative dimensions. One extra channel can be used as an 'escape' channel. Now, similar to the arguments made by Duato [7], it can be easily shown that a solution of $(n+1)$ consumption channels per node provides deadlock-freedom. ∎

This result indicates that only 3 consumption channels per node are required for a 2D e-cube mesh. This is only one extra compared to the Hamiltonian-path model. Similarly, a 3D e-cube system will require 4 consumption channels. For adaptive routing schemes supporting v virtual channels per physical channel to provide deadlock-free unicast communication, we hypothesize that $(n+1)v$ or $(nv + 1)$ consumption channels are sufficient to provide deadlock-free communication under the BRCP model [14]. Since these consumption channels are needed to provide deadlock-freedom instead of increasing network throughput [1], these can be configured as *virtual* consumption channels instead of *physical* consumption channels. It is to be noted that systems like Intel Paragon already have provision to use up to two physical consumption channels for each router. As the technology is moving towards 64-bit processors with 64/128 bits-wide processor-memory bus and 16/32 bit-wide communication channels, it is not impossible to provide $4-8$ physical consumption channels with more number of virtual consumption channels per node. Hence, the BRCP Model is a feasible solution for near-future wormhole-routed systems.

3 Multicasting and Broadcasting

In this section, we address how to implement single-source multicasting and broadcasting under the BRCP model. We present two schemes to accomplish it.

3.1 Hierarchical Leader-based Scheme (HL)

Given a multicast destination set, this scheme tries to group the destinations in a hierarchical manner so that minimum number of unicast/multidestination worms are needed to cover all destinations. Since the multidestination worms conform to paths supported by the base-routing, the grouping scheme takes into account system dimension, topology, routing, adaptivity, and spatial positions of the destination set to achieve the best grouping. Once the grouping is achieved, multicast takes place by traversing from the source in a reverse hierarchy.

Consider a multicast pattern from a source s with a destination set D. Let L_0 denote the set $D \cup \{s\}$. The hierarchical scheme, in its first step, partitions this set L_0 into disjoint subsets with a *leader* node representing each subset. The leader node is chosen in such a way that it can forward a message to the members of its set using a single multidestination worm under the BRCP model. For example, if a system implements *ecube* routing, then the partitioning is done such that the nodes in each set lie on a *valid* ecube path. These paths can be either row, column, or row-column. If the system supports some form of adaptive routing then the partitioning scheme can use added paths provided by the base-routing, as discussed in Section 2.

Let the leaders obtained by the above first step partitioning be termed as *level-1* leaders and identified by a set L_1. This set L_1 can be further partitioned into disjoint subsets with a set of *level-2* leaders. This process of hierarchical grouping is continued as long as it is profitable. We will define this profitability aspect shortly. Assuming the grouping is carried out for m steps, we will have m sets of level i leaders, $1 \leq i \leq m$. It is to be noted that the sets satisfy the following inclusion property: $L_m \subset L_{m-1} \subset \ldots L_1 \subset L_0$. Similarly, a *level-i* leader is also a *level-(i-1)* leader, $2 \leq i \leq m$.

After the grouping is achieved, the multicast takes place in two phases. In the first phase, the source performs unicast-based multicast [10] to the set L_m in $\lceil \log_2 (|L_m| + 1) \rceil$ steps. The second phase involves m steps of multidestination message-passing. It starts with the leaders in the set L_m and propagates down the hierarchical grouping in a reverse fashion to cover the lower-level leaders and finally, the members of the leaders in the set L_1. It is to be noted that if the source happens to be the sole level m leader, then the first phase is eliminated. This leads to:

Observation 1 *A multicast operation can be achieved in $(\lceil \log_2 (|L_m| + 1) \rceil + m)$ communication steps under the BRCP model if the destination set can be grouped into m levels under the hierarchical grouping scheme.*

While doing the above grouping, an issue that needs to be addressed is what level of grouping is *profitable* in order to reduce the multicast latency. Since the first phase of the multicast involves unicast-based multicast to the set L_m, an effort needs to be made to reduce the size of the set L_m. However while going from L_{m-1} to L_m, one more step of multidestination communication gets introduced into the multicast latency. Hence, it can be seen that when $\log_2 (|L_{m-1}|) > \log_2 (|L_m|) + 1$, it is profitable to go through an additional level of grouping. This ensures that the final grouping leads to minimum multicast latency assuming the communication startup cost is dominant (a common trend in current generation systems). Now we illustrate this scheme through examples for e-cube and planar-adaptive routed 2D meshes.

E-cube Routed 2D Meshes: Consider a 2D mesh with e-cube routing as illustrated in Fig. 3a. Given a destination set, the first level grouping can be done along dimension 0 to obtain the level-1 leaders (L_1) as shown in the figure. The L_1 leaders now can be grouped along dimension 1 to form L_2 with two level-2 leaders. We thus have six level-1 leaders and two level-2 leaders in this example. It is to be noted that each level-2 leader is also a level-1 leader. The multicast takes place in two phases. In the first phase, the source uses the Umesh algorithm [10] to send out unicast messages to the two level-2 leaders. In the next phase, these two level-2 leaders send out multidestination worms along dimension 1 to cover the level-1 leaders. Finally, all the level-1 leaders (including the level-2 leaders) send out multidestination worms along dimension 0 to cover the remaining destinations. Thus, the multicast takes 4 communication steps.

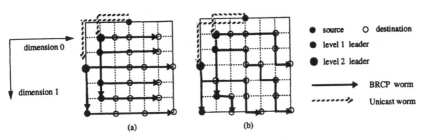

Fig. 3. An example multicast in a 2-D mesh using (a) ecube dimension order grouping and (b) planar adaptive grouping under hierarchical leader-based scheme.

Taking Advantage of Adaptivity: If the system uses some kind of adaptive routing scheme (planar, turn model-based, or fully), then the grouping can be designed to take advantage of it. Figure 3b shows such a grouping for a 2D mesh supporting planar-adaptive routing. It can be noted that compared to e-cube grouping, this grouping reduces the number of level-1 leaders by 1. However, the number of level-2 leaders remains the same. These numbers are sensitive to the spatial positions of the destinations. Since the set of valid paths supported by planar-adaptive routing is more than that of e-cube routing, it is expected that the BRCP model for a planar-adaptive routed system will perform at least as good as that of an e-cube system. We emphasize more on this aspect while presenting simulation results.

Before going to the second scheme, we present the complexity of multicast and broadcast for e-cube systems using hierarchical-leader-based scheme. Earlier we observed that for a $k \times k$ mesh, the maximum number of level-2 leaders can be k. This leads to:

Theorem 2 *The upper bound in number of communication steps to implement arbitrary single-source multicast in a $k \times k$ mesh using multidestination worms is $\lceil \log_2 (k + 1) \rceil + 2$.*

Broadcasting: It is to be noted that as the degree of multicast increases, better grouping can be achieved while reducing L_1 to L_2. The best case is achieved for broadcast, when all L_1 leaders (the elements of the left-most column) are reduced to a single L_2 leader. This indicates that broadcast from any arbitrary source can be done in 3 steps. Figure 4 shows these three steps. This leads to:

Observation 2 *One-to-all broadcasting from any arbitrary source in a n-D mesh can be implemented in $(n + 1)$ communication steps using multidestination worms under hierarchical grouping scheme.*

3.2 Multiphase Greedy Scheme(MG)

In this section, we present an alternative greedy scheme which attempts to minimize the multicast latency by sending as many multidestination messages as

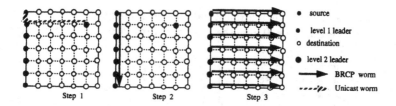

Fig. 4. Broadcast in a 2-D mesh using ecube dimension order grouping under hierarchical-leader-based scheme.

possible in each step. At the end of each step, the destinations which have received message act as secondary sources to accelerate the multicasting.

Consider a $k \times k$ mesh. Let s be the source and D be the set of destinations. Similar to the hierarchical-leader-based scheme, the destinations can be partitioned into maximum k disjoint columns with a leader node representing each column. Contrary to the hierarchical-scheme, here we do not emphasize on the leader node to be an end node in the column. As long as the leader node receives the message, it can forward the message to the remaining destinations in its column. Since the leader node is not an end node, it may take one or two steps of multidestination message passing for a leader node to cover the destinations in its column.

Now the objective is to transfer the message from the source to the respective leader nodes using minimum number of steps. A greedy approach is used to achieve this. Consider the column having the largest number of destinations. If we can cover these destinations in the first phase, then all these destinations can act as secondary sources to transfer messages to the leader nodes of the remaining columns during the second phase. For example, let the column having the largest number of destinations have m destinations in it. Once we cover these destinations in the first phase, we will have $(m+1)$ sources to cover leader nodes of additional $(m+1)$ columns in the second phase. Such process is carried out until no more columns are left to be covered. Each phase logically consists of two steps. The leader node together with the destinations either *above* or *below* it can receive the message in the first step through a single multidestination message. In the second step, the leader node uses another multidestination worm to cover the remaining nodes in the column. To achieve best performance, the second step of each phase can be overlapped with the first step of the next phase. An example multicasting for a 2D mesh using this greedy scheme and overlapped steps is shown in Fig. 5.

Theorem 3 *The number of steps for multiphase greedy scheme to perform single-source multicast for a destination set D in a $k \times k$ mesh is less than or equal to $\lceil log_t(2k) \rceil + 2$ if $t > 1$ and $\lceil log_2(k) \rceil + 2$ if $t \leq 1$, where $kt \leq |D| \leq k(t+1)$ and t is an integer.*

Proof: Due to space limitation, we only provide a sketch of the proof here. The readers are requested to refer to [14] for the details. Since a greedy approach

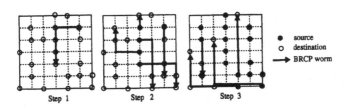

Fig. 5. An example multicasting in a 2D mesh using multiphase greedy scheme.

is used, the number of destinations covered in the first few steps determine the overall complexity. As soon as the leaders of all columns are covered, it takes two more steps to finish the multicast. Since the column having the largest number of destinations is chosen in the first step, based on the pigeon hole principle, it can be observed that at least $\lfloor t/2 \rfloor$ destinations are covered at the end of first step of phase 1. All these destinations act like secondary sources and try to cover the leaders of other columns and those leaders try to cover destinations in their respective columns. Hence, at the end of first step of phase 2, the number of destinations covered are $\lfloor \frac{t^2}{2} \rfloor$. Since there are maximum k leaders, the number of steps required for multicast is $r+2$, where r is equal to the smallest b satisfying $\lfloor t^b/2 \rfloor \geq k$. If $t \leq 1$, the number of columns covered gets at least doubled in each step leading to the result. ∎

Broadcasting: Similar to the hierarchical scheme, one-to-all broadcasting from arbitrary source can also be achieved in 3 steps using multiphase greedy-scheme. Figure 6 shows an example of such broadcasting.

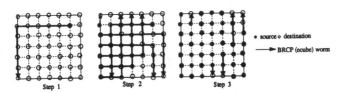

Fig. 6. Broadcasting in a 2D mesh under multiphase greedy scheme.

Impact of Adaptivity: For a single-source multicast, the first two steps of this scheme are guaranteed to be contention-free. The first step only involves a single message from the source to the column having largest number of destinations. During the second step, the secondary sources fall into disjoint rows and hence the communication is contention-free. However, from the third step onwards, as shown in Fig. 5, it may happen that multiple secondary sources trying to reach different leader nodes fall into the same row. Under e-cube routing, this will lead to contention. However, if the system supports adaptive-routing then the contention in these steps will get reduced as shown in the simulation section. The current scheme only considers column-wise grouping. To exploit adaptivity, paths conforming to the base routing can also be used to reduce the multicast cost further.

4 Effect of changes in topology

In this section we show how our schemes can be adopted to higher dimensional systems and can also take advantage of changes in system topology to accomplish multicast faster.

Multidimensional Meshes: For an n-dimensional system, the HL scheme can have up to n ecube dimension order groupings. Assuming m grouping steps are used, the number of communication steps required to perform multicast will be $\lceil \log_2 (|L_m| + 1) \rceil + m$. The MG scheme can be extended for n-dimensional meshes by considering 'columns' along the nth dimension. The maximum number of columns in this case would be k^{n-1} where k is the width of the mesh. Similar to the analysis presented earlier, the number of communication steps will be bounded by $\lceil \log_t k^{n-1} \rceil + 2$ if $t > 1$ and $\lceil \log_2 k^{n-1} \rceil + 2$ if $t \leq 1$, where $kt \leq$ number of destinations $\leq k(t+1)$ and t is an integer.

Systems with Irregular Topologies: The HL scheme with ecube grouping can take advantage of irregularly shaped meshes by performing grouping along the larger dimension first. For example, with a 2D mesh of size $k_1 \times k_2$, $k_1 < k_2$, grouping along the k_2 dimension first will reduce the level-2 leaders to be maximum k_1, as opposed to k_2 otherwise. Generalizing this for an n-dimensional irregular mesh, it can be seen that grouping should take place from the largest dimension to the smallest in order to get the least number of leaders at the final step. The MG scheme performs better for rectangular meshes compared to a square mesh of equal size if the larger dimension is along the columns. In this case, the number of destinations covered in each step is likely to be higher leading to less number of columns to be covered. This reduces the multicast latency significantly.

Wrap-around Tori: The HL scheme can take advantage of wrap-around connections to reduce multicast latency. For a 2D system, the level-1 leaders can be chosen appropriately (need not be the end nodes along the rows) so that they will lead to a better grouping in level-2. Similar criteria can be used for multidimensional and adaptive-routed systems so that the grouping uses minimum number of steps and leads to minimum number of leaders in the last step. The MG scheme can take advantage of wrap-around connections by allowing a leader of a column to cover all destinations in its column in one step using a single worm. Similarly, a worm along a row can cover all destinations in its row in one step. This indicates that if the algorithm reaches a stage when there exists a set of sources which can cover all the rows, the multicast can be completed in one more step. Thus, for a $k \times k$ torus, the number of communication steps can be reduced to $\lceil \log_t k \rceil + 1$ if $t > 1$ and $\lceil \log_2 k \rceil + 1$ if $t \leq 1$, where $kt \leq$ number of destinations $\leq k(t+1)$ and t is an integer.

5 Simulation Experiments and Results

To verify the effectiveness of our multicasting schemes, we simulated single-source multicasting on a CSIM-based [15] simulator test bed. This test-bed implements flit-level simulation and can be configured for different topological and technological parameters. We compared our scheme with Hamiltonian Path-based scheme [9] and Umesh algorithm [10]. For all simulation experiments, we assumed system parameters representing the current trend in technology. The following parameters were used: t_s (communication start-up time) as 1.0 microseconds, t_p (link propagation time) as 5.0 nsec, and t_{node} (router delay) as 20.0 nsec. For all multicast operations, message size was kept constant at 50 flits. For each experiment we randomly chose the source as well as a given number of destinations. Each experiment was repeated 30 times and the average latency was determined.

5.1 Overall Comparison for 2D Meshes with E-cube Routing

Figure 7 compares our schemes with the Umesh and the Hamiltonian path schemes. The most *interesting* and *unique* aspect to be noted is that as the number of destinations per source *increases*, the BRCP model demonstrates its superiority over the Umesh and the Hamiltonian schemes by *reducing* the multicast latency. For less number of destinations (10-20%), the cost of single-source multicast remains almost same for all the schemes. While the hierarchical-leader-based scheme is able to *reduce* the cost as the degree of multicast increases, the multiphase greedy scheme allows it to remain *near-constant* over a wide range of destinations. This demonstrates the potential of the BRCP model to support dense communication operations faster.

As the degree of multicast increases, the BRCP model provides flexibility for better grouping and hence, reduces the multicast cost. For less number of destinations, the sparsity is high and the schemes behave equally to that of the Umesh or the Hamiltonian scheme. The multiphase greedy scheme demonstrates lower latency than the hierarchical scheme because it is able to take advantage of multidestination message passing in each phase where as the hierarchical scheme uses it only in later phases. It is also to be noted that the multiphase scheme has higher grouping complexity than the hierarchical scheme. Hence, it is a question of trading-off between grouping complexity and multicast latency. Being a greedy scheme, it also reflects on the lower-bound of single-source multicast latency using the BRCP model. For applications with multicast patterns known statically at the compile time, one can go for the multiphase greedy scheme. Where as the hierarchical scheme with very little grouping complexity can be used for multicast patterns known both statically and dynamically.

5.2 Effect of Adaptivity

We studied the effect of adaptivity on 2D meshes with e-cube and planar-adaptive routing. For the hierarchical leader-based scheme(hl), as discussed in Section 2, multiple levels of grouping can be done to achieve profitability. We considered the following grouping sequences: (e, e), (e, p), and (e, e, p); where e and p stand for e-cube and planar-adaptive grouping, respectively. The grouping

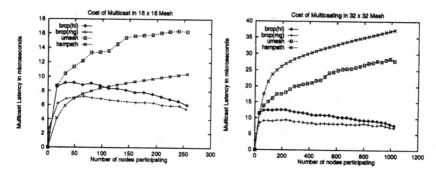

Fig. 7. Comparison of the BRCP model-based single-source multicasting schemes (hierarchical leader-based (hl) and multiphase greedy (mg)) with Umesh and Hamiltonian Path-based schemes on 2-D meshes.

(e, p) indicates that for a given set of destinations, grouping was first done according to e-cube paths (e) followed by planar-adaptive paths (p). We simulated the same multiphase greedy algorithm (mg) on systems with e-cube and planar-adaptive routing to study the impact of adaptivity in reducing contention.

Figure 8 shows the effect of adaptivity on both schemes for two different mesh sizes. It is to be noted that (e, e, p) grouping performed better than (e, e) grouping for hierarchical leader-based scheme. Here the increase in adaptivity was used to cover a set of leaders through paths conforming to planar-adaptive routing, which were not feasible under e-cube routing. Similarly, (e, p) grouping performed better than (e, e) grouping. For small number of destinations, the multiphase greedy scheme encountered more number of steps and the adaptivity helped to reduce contention in these steps.

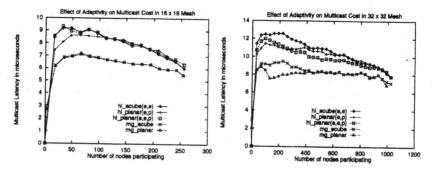

Fig. 8. Reducing the cost of single-source multicasting by increase in adaptivity in 2D meshes.

5.3 Comparison for 3D Meshes

Figure 9 shows how the hierarchical leader-based scheme performed in 3D meshes compared to other schemes. This scheme was able to perform multicast with a reduced cost by factors of 2-4 and 2-6 compared to the Umesh and the Hamiltonian-path schemes, respectively.

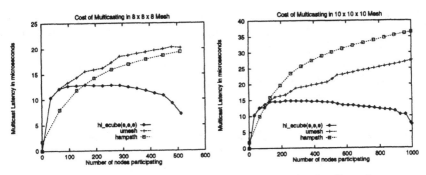

Fig. 9. Comparing cost of single-source multicasting in 3D meshes.

5.4 Effect of Irregular Topology and Wraparound

We also studied the effect of irregular topologies and wrap around as discussed in section 4. Between two systems 32x8 and 16x16, our proposed schemes were able to implement multicast efficiently on 32x8 system by taking advantage of the longer dimension. Similar observations were also made for systems with wrap-around connections. Due to the space limitation, we are not able to report these results here and the readers are requested to refer to [14] for details.

6 Conclusions and Future Research

In this paper we have introduced a new multidestination worm mechanism conforming to the base routing scheme of wormhole systems. The power of this mechanism is illustrated by developing and presenting two schemes with varying complexity in order to implement single-source multicast and broadcast operations. On e-cube meshes, these schemes reduce multicast and broadcast latency up to a factor of 6, compared to the existing Hamiltonian-path and Umesh schemes available in the literature. It has also been shown that these schemes can take advantage of routing adaptivity, irregularity in system topology, and spatial distribution of destination nodes to further reduce the cost of multicast.

The presented framework provides the following two *unique* and *interesting* results: 1) the cost of multicast can be *reduced* or kept *near-constant* as the degree of multicast *increases* and 2) the cost of multicast can be *reduced* by taking advantage of adaptive paths in the underlying network. Such results are the first ones in the literature. These results suggest a guideline that high-performance wormhole communication architectures can be developed by supporting multi-destination message passing conforming to base-routing. The unicast message passing can always be implemented as a subset operation under this mechanism. Such design will lead to efficient implementation of collective communication operations with less number of messages and will increase network throughput for a combined unicast and collective communication traffic.

In this paper, we have studied the impact of multidestination mechanism for single-source multicast and broadcast patterns. We are extending our work to other collective communication patterns like multiple-source multicast, barrier-synchronization, parallel-prefix, and reductions, etc. Since multicast is a basic mechanism for implementing cache-coherency in distributed-shared-memory systems, we are extending this framework to see how scalable distributed-shared-memory systems can be designed with low cache-coherency overheads.

References

1. S. Balakrishnan and D. K. Panda. Impact of Multiple Consumption Channels on Wormhole Routed k-ary n-cube Networks. In *Proceedings of the International Parallel Processing Symposium*, pages 163–167, April 1993.
2. M. Barnett, D. G. Payne, and R. Van de Geijn. Optimal Broadcasting in Mesh-Connected Architectures. Technical Report TR91-38, Dept. of Computer Science, Universityof Texas at Austin, Dec 1991.
3. S. H. Bokhari and H. Berryman. Complete Exchange on a Circuit-Switched Mesh. In *Proceedings of the Scalable High Performance Computing Conference*, pages 300–306, 1992.
4. R. V. Boppana, S. Chalasani, and C. S. Raghavendra. On Multicast Wormhole Routing in Multicomputer Networks. manuscript, Jan 1994.
5. A. A. Chien and J. H. Kim. Planar-Adaptive Routing: Low-Cost Adaptive Networks for Multiprocessors. In *Proceedings of the International Symposium on Computer Architecture*, pages 268–277, 1992.
6. W. J. Dally and C. L. Seitz. Deadlock-Free Message Routing in Multiprocessor Interconnection Networks. *IEEE Trans. on Computers*, pages 547–553, May 1987.
7. J. Duato. A New Theory of Deadlock-Free Adaptive Routing in Wormhole Networks. *IEEE Trans. on Parallel and Distributed Systems*, 4(12):1320–1331, 1993.
8. C. J. Glass and L. Ni. The Turn Model for Adaptive Routing. In *Proceedings of the International Symposium on Computer Architecture*, pages 278–287, 1992.
9. X. Lin, P. K. McKinley, and L. M. Ni. Performance Evaluation of Multicast Wormhole Routing in 2D-Mesh Multicomputers. In *Proceedings of the International Conference on Parallel Processing*, pages I:435–442, 1991.
10. P. K. McKinley, H. Xu, A.-H. Esfahanian, and L. M. Ni. Unicast-based Multicast Communication in Wormhole-routed Direct Networks. In *Proceedings of the International Conference on Parallel Processing*, pages II:10–19, 1992.
11. Message Passing Interface Forum. *MPI: A Message-Passing Interface Standard*, Mar 1994.
12. L. Ni and P. K. McKinley. A Survey of Wormhole Routing Techniques in Direct Networks. *IEEE Computer*, pages 62–76, Feb. 1993.
13. D. K. Panda and P. Prabhakaran. Multicasting using Multidestination-Worms Conforming to Base Wormhole Routing Scheme. Technical Report OSU-CISRC-11/93-TR37, Dept. of CIS, The Ohio State University, 1993.
14. D. K. Panda, S. Singal, and P. Prabhakaran. Multidestination Message Passing Mechanism Conforming to Base Wormhole Routing Scheme. Technical Report OSU-CISRC-6/94-TR33, Dept. of CIS, The Ohio State University, 1994.
15. H.D. Schwetman. Using CSIM to Model Complex Systems. In *Proceedings of the 1988 Winter Simulation Conference*, pages 246–253, 1988.

Multi-Address Encoding for Multicast*

Chi-Ming Chiang and Lionel M. Ni

Department of Computer Science, Michigan State University
A714 Wells Hall, East Lansing, MI 48824-1027
{chiangm,ni}@cps.msu.edu

Abstract. Efficient implementation of multicast communication is critical to the performance of message-based scalable parallel computers and switch-based high speed networks. This paper deals with address issues occurring in the message header for the transmission of multicast messages. Multi-address encoding is becoming critical to system performance as the scale of networks is getting larger and the demand of multicast communication is getting higher. Several multi-address encoding schemes are investigated and explored. Although the proposed multi-address encoding schemes can be applied to networks with different switching techniques, the emphasis of this paper is on the emerging wormhole routing technique.

1 Introduction

Multicast communication, which refers to the delivery of a message from a single source node to a number of destination nodes, is a frequently used communication pattern in distributed-memory parallel computers and computer networks. Efficient implementation of multicast communication is critical to the performance of message-based scalable parallel computers and switch-based high speed networks. For example, a number of collective communication services, such as broadcast and barrier synchronization, defined in the Message Passing Interface (MPI) effort exhibit multicast communication pattern [1]. Note that an application-level broadcast within a process group is a system-level multicast. Multicast communication is also demanded in high speed networks, such as ATM switches, for various network applications [2, 3].

Multicast communication has been extensively studied for distributed-memory multicomputers based on direct network architectures, such as mesh and hypercube topologies. Past work included both hardware and software approaches [4, 5, 6] for wormhole routing and virtual cut through switching techniques. A theoretical study of multicast communication for 2D mesh and hypercube can be found in [7]. Multicast communication for extra stage multistage interconnection networks (MINs) was studied in [8]. In ATM switches, Liew [9] proposed a multicast algorithm for Clos networks, and the multicast support in [10] involves three segments: *copy* network, *distribution* network, and *routing* network.

---

* This work was supported in part by NSF grants CDA-9121641 and MIP-9204066, and DOE grant DE-FG02-93ER25167.

No matter what kind of topology a network is, a message header for multicast communication must carry the destination set information needed for routers/switches to make appropriate routing decisions. In some networks, such a header is needed in a sender-initiated control message in order to establish a multicast circuit; while in some other networks, such a header is used in all data messages. Nevertheless, the header information is an overhead to the system and should be minimized in order to reduce communication latency and to increase effective network bandwidth. Basically, a multicast message header carries multiple destination addresses (multi-address) information. A destination address can be either a physical address or a relative address. A relative address is usually used to represent the relative location to the source address. Each address may be further represented by a number of dimensions. For example, in a 2D mesh network, each address may have two dimensions — one for each dimension. In this paper, we don't further distinguish different types of addresses. Unless otherwise specified, an address refers to all details of the address.

The objective of this paper is to investigate different multi-address encoding schemes in multicast messages. This issue is becoming critical to system performance as the scale of networks is getting larger and the demand of multicast communication is getting higher. Although the proposed multi-address encoding schemes can be applied to networks with different switching techniques, such as circuit switching, store-and-forward switching, and cell relay, the emphasis of this paper will be on the emerging wormhole routing technique adopted in almost all new generation scalable parallel computers [11, 12].

A good multi-address encoding scheme should consider to minimize the message header length overhead, to reduce the header processing time (or routing decision making time), and to support cut-through switching. These issues are discussed in Section 2. Six multi-address encoding schemes which can be applied to different network topologies are described in Section 3. Section 4 discusses some potential problems, such as wormhole bubbles and multiple receptions, that may raise when the encoding scheme is decoded at switches/routers. Some generic decoding algorithms are also described. Section 5 concludes the paper.

2 Header Encoding Design Considerations

Each multicast message header must have a number of flits to carry the necessary routing information, where each flit is a flow control unit. It could be an address or a region (to be discussed later) depending on the encoding scheme. The total number of flits or header length is usually not only dependent on the number of destinations but also on the selected multi-address encoding scheme. The function of switches or routers is taking a message from an input channel, making a routing decision, and forwarding (with possibly replicating) the message to one or more output channels. The terms switches and routers will be used interchangeably in the paper. A good multi-address encoding scheme should not only shorten the message header length, but minimize communication latency and ease routing decision. The following header design issues are considered.

The length of a message header can be either fixed or variable in terms of the number of destinations. The length of a variable length header is dynamically adjusted by routers as the message header is processed. For the fixed one, the length may be a function of the location of routers in the network.

In cut through switching, should each switch buffer the whole message header before making the routing decision? For a large message header, it implies a large buffer to hold the whole message header and a longer communication latency. In wormhole routing, a message is divided into a number of flits, and the minimum capacity of each buffer is one flit. Since a message header may be composed of many flits, it is desirable that the routing decision in each router can be made as soon as possible to minimize the buffer requirement. Ideally, a message header can be processed on the fly on the flit basis.

For a variable length header, the number of destination addresses (or regions to be discussed later) is another design parameter. It may be impractical and inefficient to use a counter to indicate the number of destinations (or regions) because the counter flit is usually placed at the beginning of a message header. Since the value of counters may be changed by switches if the destination address set is split into different subsets, it will prohibit the processing of message headers on the fly by switches. An alternative approach is to have an *end-of-header* (EOH) flit to indicate the end of an address header. Some known hardware and software techniques, such as code violation and address stuffing, may be used to implement the EOH flit.

Both tree-based multicast, in which a router is able to replicate an input message through multiple output channels, and path-based multicast, in which a message traverses along a certain path picking up by the destination nodes along the path, may be considered to implement multicast communication [5]. Usually, path-based multicast is used in direct networks, such as multi-dimensional meshes, and tree-based multicast is used in indirect (switch-based) networks, such as multistage interconnection networks. In both approaches, the message header may have to be modified by those intermediate routers. Deadlock avoidance is critical to the design of multicast routing methods.

3 Multi-Address Encoding Schemes

Six multi-address encoding schemes are described in this section. The message header format of these schemes are shown in Figure 1.

3.1 All Destination Encoding

This is an intuitive method used in [13], in which all destination addresses are carried by the header as shown in Figure 1(a). Assuming that all addresses are sorted in ascending order, the EOH flit can be all 0's. If the only destination address is all 0's, the second all 0's indicates the EOH. If the routing requires that the addresses be arranged in a certain order, such as path-based multicast [5], the EOH flit may be represented by replicating the last address. However,

(a) All Destination Encoding

$addr_1$	$addr_2$	$\cdots\cdots\cdots$	$addr_m$	EOH

(b) Bit String Encoding

b			$\cdots\cdots\cdots\cdots\cdots\cdots\cdots\cdots$		e

(c) Multiple Region Broadcast Encoding

$b_1 : e_1$	$b_2 : e_2$	$\cdots\cdots\cdots$	$b_k : e_k$	EOH

(d) Multiple Region Stride Encoding

$b_1 : e_1 : s_1$	$b_2 : e_2 : s_2$	$\cdots\cdots\cdots$	$b_k : e_k : s_k$	EOH

(e) Multiple Region Mask Encoding

$b_1 : e_1 : m_1$	$b_2 : e_2 : m_2$	$\cdots\cdots\cdots$	$b_k : e_k : m_k$	EOH

(f) Multiple Region Bit String Encoding

$b_1 : e_1 : T_1$	$b_2 : e_2 : T_2$	$\cdots\cdots\cdots$	$b_k : e_k : T_k$	EOH

Fig. 1. The message header format of six address encoding schemes.

for tree-based multicast, it is easier to generate the same EOH flit for all replicated outgoing messages. In this case, the EOH flit could be an unused address or use other methods. Clearly, all destination encoding is good for a small number of irregular addresses as its header length is proportional to the number of addresses.

3.2 Bit String Encoding

The major drawback of the all destination encoding scheme is its significant header overhead when the number of destinations is large. One way to limit the size of a header is to have a bit string to indicate destinations, where each bit corresponds to a destination ranged between node b and node e as shown in Figure 1(b). Since the number of nodes in a system is predefined, there is no need of an EOH field. In some network topologies, such as multistage interconnection networks, the bit string length can be a function of the number of reachable nodes from a given switch, which is still independent of the number of destinations. Apparently, the bit string encoding scheme is inefficient when the system is large and the number of destinations is small. However, it is flexible in handling a large number of irregular destination addresses.

Usually, it is extremely difficult for a router to make the routing decision on the fly based on the incoming bit string information and to produce the bit string information for each output port. Thus, a router usually has to buffer the entire bit string in order to make the routing decision and to generate output bit strings. This is named *buffered bit string*. Although the buffered bit string encoding scheme allows distributed routing, each router requires a large flit buffer and the communication latency is also increased.

To eliminate a large flit buffer, a *hierarchical bit string* may be used. This is a source routing method in which the source node has to determine the complete multicast tree information. In this scheme, the input message header has $1 + k$ flits for a router with k output ports. The first flit has k bits corresponding to k output ports. A "1" in a bit position indicating that the corresponding output port should forward a copy of the message. The remaining k even sized flits carry bit string information for each output port. The bit string information is recursively defined because each bit string becomes an input to the next router. Note that if these bit string flits are not even sized or have less than k flits, it will be very difficult to determine the delimiter between two adjacent flits. Obviously, the hierarchical bit string encoding scheme can perform routing on the fly and requires a small flit buffer in each router. However, the header length is much longer than the buffered bit string method.

3.3 Multiple Region Broadcast

In order to enforce communication locality and minimize communication interference among processors from different process groups, processors belonging to the same process group are usually allocated in a contiguous region, if possible. Thus the multicast addresses can be confined within a region, and each region is specified by two fields: $(b_i : e_i)$, the beginning and ending addresses of the region, respectively. This is referred to as *region broadcast* and is used in some ATM switches and NEC Cenju-3 [14].

Figure 2(a) shows the specification of a single region broadcast, where the beginning address must be no greater than the ending address. An example is given in Figure 2(b). When a message enters a switch, it buffers the complete region flit and then directs the message to corresponding output port(s). The header is revised at every switch where the message is replicated. For example, the incoming header at the shadow switch is (4:6), and the outgoing headers for upper and lower ports are (4:5) and (6:6), respectively.

However, depending on the processor allocation scheme and application program characteristics, not all process groups can have all their nodes in a contiguous region. The single region broadcast thus cannot achieve the multicast in a single multicast communication. Two approaches may be used. One method is to send multiple single region broadcast messages in sequence to different disjoint regions. Another method is to add extra hardware (e.g., the copy network used in [10, 15]) and to introduce the concept of dummy addresses. Here, we generalize this scheme to multiple regions by allowing multiple region specification in the header.

The multiple region broadcast, see Figure 1(c) for its header format, forwards the message to every node covered by each region. The EOH flit can be specified as a region containing an address with all 1's follows by an address with all 0's (i.e., address violation). In fact, any pair of addresses can be an EOH as long as the second address is smaller than the first address.

Figure 3(a) illustrates an example of multiple region broadcast. Consider 64 nodes organized as a 2D array. For some 2D matrix applications, it may require

(a) Single Region Broadcast

(c) Single Region Stride Multicast

begin	end

begin	end	stride

(b) An example of region broadcast

(d) An example of region stride

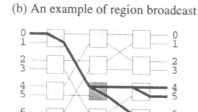

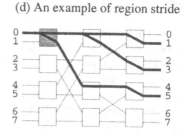

Fig. 2. Single region broadcast and single region stride, where the source node is 0 and the destination sets are {4, 5, 6} and {1, 3, 5}, respectively.

the source node (3,2) to send a message to all nodes in the same column and in the same row. If the source node can also be a destination, the header for node (3,2) is (3:3,0:7; 0:7,2:2). Otherwise, the header will be (3:3,0:1; 3:3,3:7; 0:2,2:2; 4:7,2:2).

Fig. 3. Multicast to the same row and column in (a) 2D mesh and (b) linear array architectures.

3.4 Multiple Region Stride

In some applications, a source node may wish to send a message to all odd-numbered destinations or to all even-numbered destinations. In other words, the destination addresses have a constant distance between two adjacent addresses. Thus, the addresses (or flit) can be specified by three parameters: $(b_i:e_i:s_i)$, the beginning address, the ending address, and the stride value. Note that for a multi-dimensional address, each dimension may have its own stride value. This encoding scheme is referred to as *region stride multicast*.

Figure 2(c) shows the specification of a single stride-region. Consider a stride-region, $(b{:}e{:}s)$, where $(b \leq e)$ and s is the stride value. The message is forwarded to node $\{d | d = b + i \times s, i = 0, 1, \ldots, \lfloor (e-b)/s \rfloor \}$. Figure 2(d) shows an example in which destinations are $\{1, 3, 5\}$ and the source node is 0. The header can be either $(1{:}5{:}2)$ or $(1{:}6{:}2)$. The header is also revised when the message is replicated. For example, the incoming header is revised to $(1{:}3{:}2)$ and $(5{:}5{:}2)$ for the outgoing messages to upper and lower ports of the shadow switch, respectively.

Similarly, this encoding scheme can be generalized to *multiple region stride*. The header format is shown in Figure 1(d). To be consistent with the stride-region flit specification, the EOH flit may contain three fields. Same as multiple region broadcast, an address with all 1's followed by an address with all 0's may be used to indicate the EOH, where the third stride field is irrelevant.

Consider the same multicast example illustrated in Figure 3(b). If the processors are organized in a linear order, such as NEC Cenju-3 and IBM SP-1, all nodes in the same row are not in a contiguous region. The multiple region stride encodes these destinations as $(2{:}58{:}8; 24{:}31{:}1)$ if the source node is also a destination; otherwise, the header is $(2{:}18{:}8; 34{:}58{:}8; 24{:}25{:}1; 27{:}31{:}1)$.

3.5 Multiple Region Mask

Another regular pattern of destination addresses that typically occurred in k-ary n-cube networks is subcube. Let $d_{n-1} \ldots d_1 d_0$ represent a node in a k-ary n-cube, where $0 \leq d_i \leq k - 1$ (note that this definition can be easily extended to a more general cube network in which the radix of each dimension may be different). Any subcube can be described by a binary mask, m, with an address, b. The binary mask m defines the size and dimensions of the subcube, i.e., the number of ones in m and the location of each dimension with $m_i = 1$. The address b defines which subcube among those subcubes, i.e., b_i's where $m_i = 0$. This approach is used in the nCUBE-2 [16]. In a more general case, we define a subset of a subcube with three fields: $(b{:}e{:}m)$, where $b_i = e_i$ when $m_i = 0$ and for those i's with $m_i = 1$, b_i and e_i specify the lower and upper bounds of the subcube, respectively. The multiple region mask shown in Fig. 1(e) extends this approach to allow that a message be destined for multiple subsets of subcubes.

Consider a binary 4-cube with eight destinations $\{0100, 0101, 0110, 0111, 1100, 1101, 1110, 1111\}$. The multiple region mask encodes the header to $(0100{:}1111{:}1011)$, which is a complete 3-cube. When the destinations are $\{0110, 0111, 1100, 1101, 1110\}$, a subset of the 3-cube is specified as $(0110{:}1110{:}1011)$.

3.6 Multiple Region Bit String

Both multiple region broadcast and multiple region stride are suitable for destinations that can be divided into a number of clusters and with a regular address pattern within each cluster. If the destinations are not in any regular shape, the header encoded by previous encoding schemes may be too large (e.g., many disjoint regions). The multiple region bit string encoding scheme shown in Figure 1(f) is proposed to reduce the header overhead under such a situation. In general, a region bit-string flit is specified as (b, e, T), where b and e ($b \leq e$) indicate the beginning and ending addresses, and T is a binary bit string. Each bit in T corresponds to a node within b and e. A node is a destination if the corresponding bit is 1. Both b and e are destinations and T has $(e - b + 1)$ bits[2].

Consider a system with 16 nodes and the destinations are $\{0,1,3,4,6,12,13,15\}$. With multiple region broadcast, it require five regions. With multiple region bit string, one possible specification is (0:6:1101101;12:15:1101). Apparently, in multiple region bit string, the length of each region is not fixed and is determined by the values of b and e. Depending on the flit buffer capacity, the system has to limit the maximum value of $e - b$. The EOH flit can contain two fields, a field with all 1's followed by one with all 0's. Although the multiple region bit string is more flexible and can handle addresses with irregular patterns, it may be difficult to determine the most efficient number of regions and the router design may be more complicated.

4 Multi-Address Decoding

Consider a generic network switch/router with k input ports and k output ports as shown in Figure 4(a) with $k = 4$. The interconnection of routers defines the network topology. Each router may or may not have a local processor depending on the system architecture. When a multicast message arrives at a router via an input port, the router examines the header and may enable a number of output ports depending on the routing strategy. The message is replicated and forwarded to all enabled output ports. A critical issue is how to define a new header information for each enabled output port. If not handled properly, the same message may be received repeatedly by the same processor as shown in Fig. 4(b).

In distributed routing, if a router is able to process the input message header on the fly, it will buffer one header flit, make the routing decision, and deposit a new message header flit information to a selected output port. When an address or a region is forwarded to its associated output port, the other enabled ports will be idle since there is no address or region to be forwarded to these output ports. Such an idle on timing is referred to as *wormhole bubble*. Note that a wormhole bubble does not necessarily imply an empty or a null flit. With self-timed design, a wormhole bubble implies a timing delay to the next flit. However, for ease of explanation, the wormhole bubble is represented as an individual flit in the following figures as **B**.

When a router replicates a message, the message header will be revised and an output message header is generated for each enabled output port (or each replicated message). Figure 4(a) shows an example replicating a message into two

---

[2] Since the first and last bits are always 1 in T, these two bits may be removed from T.

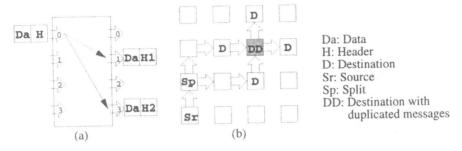

Fig. 4. (a) A generic switch/router with four input/output ports, and the message is forwarded via both output ports 1 and 3. (b) The receiving of a duplicated message when the header is not handled properly and alternate routing paths are allowed.

messages, the headers $H1$ and $H2$ are different. Usually, the destination address set is divided into a number of disjoint address subsets, one for each replicated message. This approach can avoid multiple receptions of the same message, which is especially important if there are many alternate paths to a destination. The drawback of having disjoint subsets is its less flexibility in forming the header format. However, if the routing path is unique, those destination subsets may overlap. Since a router usually makes its routing decision based on the first field of a region flit, it may ignore any destination which is not reachable from its output port. This approach is more flexible in forming the header format.

For a single region which contains a number of addresses, the region may be split into several regions by a router. Each region is directed to an enabled output port. It is possible that two or more disjoint regions are directed to the same output port. Thus, the number of regions in the new header may be larger than the incoming one. Therefore, placing the number of regions in the header may not be feasible.

For each of the six multi-address encoding schemes, this section will describe some generic address decoding algorithms that may be performed by a router. Given a header flit, say F, the routing function $Route(F)$ will determine the output port number to be selected to forward the message. Furthermore, we assume that if the processor, if any, associated with a router is one of the destinations, a copy of the message will be sent to the processor. An output port is enabled if a copy of the message is to be forwarded through the port. At the end of message transmission, all output ports will be disabled. These behavior will not be further described in the following algorithms.

4.1 All Destination Decoding

For each incoming flit, d, Figure 5 shows the corresponding decoding algorithm. When sending information through an enabled port, it implies that the corresponding output channel is available; otherwise, the message transmission will be pending until the port is available. Avoiding deadlock is another critical design issue. The solution is dependent on the network topology, routing strategy, and is beyond the scope of this paper.

Algorithm: all destination decoding
   Input: An address d.
   Output: append d to the header of the selected output port.
   Procedure:
   begin
      if $d = EOH$ then send EOH to all enabled ports; exit;
      $j:=Route(d)$;
      send d to port j;
   end

Fig. 5. All destination decoding algorithm.

For example, the addresses of a message into a router is $\{2, 3, 5, 7, 15, B, B\}$ as shown in Figure 6(a), where B indicates wormhole bubble and E represents EOH. Let the reachable nodes from port i be node $i \times 4$ to node $i \times 4 + 3$, where $0 \leq i \leq 3$. We further assume that there are 16 nodes in the system. The router enables port 0 and forwards address 2 when address 2 is decoded. The address 3 is forwarded to port 0. While the address 5 is decoded, port 1 is enabled and address 5 is forwarded to port 1. There is a wormhole bubble on port 0. The process is repeated until the header is split completely as shown in the figure. Port 2 is not enabled since there is no destination via this port.

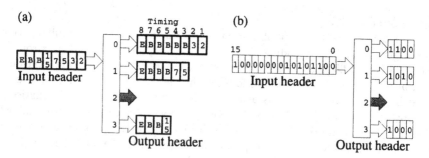

Fig. 6. Examples: (a) all destination and (b) bit string decoding.

4.2 Bit String Decoding

Buffered Bit String. A router stores the entire bit string and then detects each bit which has a 1 to enable the corresponding output port. If there are more than one output port that can reach the destination, the router selects exactly one port. The length of each bit string is dependent on the corresponding port and the number of nodes reachable from that port. The router also knows the reachable node for a given bit position. The buffered bit string decoding algorithm is given in Figure 7. An example based on the previous example is shown in Figure 6(b).

```
Algorithm: buffered bit string decoding
    Input:   Binary bit string, T.
    Output: Bit string, Dⱼ, for each enabled output port j.
    Procedure:
    begin
        for every bit, tᵢ, in bit string T do
            (j, k):=Route(i);
            (* route through port j, bit position k *)
            d_{j,k} := tᵢ;
        endfor
        enable port j with Dⱼ ≠ 0 for all j;
    end
```

Fig. 7. Buffered bit string decoding algorithm.

Hierarchical Bit String Decoding. In hierarchical bit string, the first field (k bits) of an incoming bit string indicates the enabling or disabling of the k output ports of a k-port router. The following bits are divided into k fields, one for each output port. For each field, it is forwarded to the next router if the associated port is enabled. Otherwise, it is eliminated at the router. The decoding algorithm is too simple to be described here, and the corresponding example is shown in Figure 8(a).

4.3   Multiple Region Broadcast Decoding

As shown in Figure 1(c), the header in multiple region broadcast contains several regions. All nodes covered by all regions should receive a copy of the message. Thus, the router may have to divide a region into several sub-regions, and each sub-region is directed through an appropriate output port. The algorithm for decoding each region is given in Figure 9.

   In this decoding algorithm, the router checks the beginning address of a region and searches for the first address, e', which cannot be reached by the same output port. A sub-region is then identified for that output port. The process repeats until all sub-regions have been identified. For example, consider an incoming header of (2:5; 7:8) shown in Figure 8(b). The router splits the first

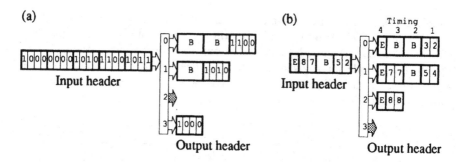

Fig. 8. Examples: (a) hierarchical bit string decoding and (b) multiple region broadcast decoding.

```
Algorithm: multiple region broadcast
Input:     A region (b, e).
Output:  Send each sub-region to an output port.
Procedure:
begin
   if (b, e)=EOH, send EOH to all enabled ports; exit;
   while (b ≤ e) do
      (j, e'):=Route(b,e);
      send region (b, e') to port j;
      b = e' + 1;
   end while;
end;
```

Fig. 9. Multiple region broadcast decoding algorithm.

region to (2:3) and (4:5) for ports 0 and 1, and the second region to (7:7) and (8:,8) for ports 1 and 2, respectively.

4.4 Multiple Region Stride Decoding

The method to handle multiple region stride is similar to that of multiple region broadcast. A router divides the region into several sub-regions, where each sub-region is directed to a single output port. As indicated in Figure 1(d), there is an additional field, stride, in each region to indicate the distance between two adjacent nodes. The decoding algorithm is similar to Fig. 9, except replacing (b, e) and (b, e') by (b, e, s) and (b, e', s), respectively. Note that the stride value is never changed.

Consider the example in Figure 10(a), the incoming header is $\{(1:5:2), (6:10:1)\}$, which indicates that nodes 1, 3, 5, 6, 7, 8, 9, and 10 are destinations. The router splits the first region to (1:3:2) and (5:5:2) for ports 0 and port 1 and the second region to (6:7:1) and (8:10:1) for ports 1 and 2, respectively.

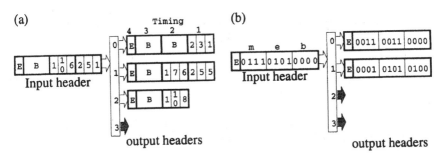

Fig. 10. Examples: (a) multiple region stride decoding and (b) multiple region mask decoding.

4.5   Multiple Region Mask Decoding

The method to handle multiple region mask is similar to that of multiple region broadcast and multiple region stride. A region is divided by the router into several sub-regions, where each sub-region is directed to an associate output port. Not only the beginning and ending address but also the mask will be changed by the router to avoid duplicated receiving.

An example of a binary 4-cube is given in Figure 10(b). The input header specifies six destinations {0000, 0001, 0010, 0011, 0100, 0101}. The router forwards a copy of the message to port 0, which defines a 2-cube with header (0000:0011:0011), and another copy to port 1, which defines a 1-cube with header (0100:0101:0001).

4.6   Multiple Region Bit String Decoding

As shown in Figure 1(f), there are three fields in a region. The decoding algorithm is also similar to that of multiple region broadcast except the representation of regions. The tricky part is in the partitioning of a region into sub-regions. When a single output port can reach several non-contiguous regions, the router can mark those bits that correspond to unreachable nodes to 0 instead of splitting the region. The corresponding algorithm is shown in Figure 11.

Let an incoming header be (2:7:110101) which indicates that nodes 2, 3, 5, and 7 are destinations, as shown in Figure 12. The router enables port 0 since bits 0 and 1 in the input bit string are 1's, and port 1 since bits 3 and 5 are 1's.

5   Conclusions

As the scale of networks getting larger and the demand of multicast communication getting higher, the overhead of message header is becoming critical which implies that multi-address encoding is becoming critical. Several multi-address encoding and decoding schemes were investigated and explored in this study.

```
Algorithm: multiple region bit string
    Input:    A region (b, e, T).
    Output:  Send each sub-region to an output port.
    Procedure:
    begin
        if (b, e, T)=EOH, send EOH to all enabled ports; exit;
        while (b ≤ e) or (T = 0) do
            (j, e', T'):=Route(b, e, T);
            send region (b, e', T') to port j;
            t_i := 0 if t_i is covered by T';
            b := corresponding node of the first non-zero t_i;
        end while;
    end;
```

Fig. 11. Multiple region bit string decoding algorithm.

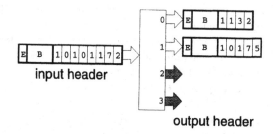

output header

Fig. 12. An example of multiple region bit string decoding.

Although the emphasis is on wormhole routing, the proposed schemes can be applied to networks with different switching techniques. Some other network topology dependent encoding schemes are possible.

As indicated earlier, different encoding schemes have their own advantages and disadvantages. The choice of an appropriate encoding scheme is dependent on many factors, such as network topology, network size, routing strategy, processor allocation strategy, switching technique, and frequent multicast communication patterns. A complicated system may be able to simultaneously support different encoding schemes. In this case, another indication field is needed to indicate which encoding scheme is used in the associated multicast message.

This paper only addressed the basic concept of various multi-address encoding and decoding schemes. When implementing a scheme in a network, depending on the corresponding network characteristics, additional level of header optimization is possible. In [17], we illustrate how to implement each of the above encoding/decoding schemes in a multistage interconnection network and how to further optimize the header overhead. More research is needed to study other network topologies, to evaluate the performance and cost tradeoffs among different encoding schemes, and to design efficient and deadlock-free multicast routing algorithms.

References

1. Message Passing Interface Forum, "MPI: A Message-Passing Interface Standard," tech. rep., University of Tennessee, Mar. 1994.

2. H. T. Kung, "Gigabit local area networks: A systems perspective," *IEEE Communications Magazine*, pp. 79–89, Apr. 1992.

3. J. Hui, "Switching integrated broadband services by Sort-Banyan networks," *Proceedings of the IEEE*, pp. 145–154, Feb. 1991.

4. Y. Lan, A. H. Esfahanian, and L. M. Ni, "Multicast in hypercube multiprocessors," *Journal of Parallel and Distributed Computing*, pp. 30–41, Jan. 1990.

5. X. Lin and L. M. Ni, "Deadlock-free multicast wormhole routing in multicomputer networks," in *Proceedings of the 18th Annual International Symposium on Computer Architecture*, pp. 116–125, May 1991.

6. P. K. McKinley, H. Xu, A. H. Esfahanian, and L. M. Ni, "Unicast-based multicast communication in wormhole-routed networks," in *Proceedings of the 1992 International Conference on Parallel Processing*, vol. II, pp. 10–19, Aug. 1992.

7. X. Lin and L. M. Ni, "Multicast communication in multicomputers networks," *IEEE Transactions on Parallel and Distributed Systems*, pp. 1105–1117, Oct. 1993.

8. C.-M. Chiang, S. Bhattacharya, and L. M. Ni, "Multicast in extra-stage multistage interconnection networks," in *Proceeding of the Sixth IEEE Symposium on Parallel and Distributed Processing*, (Dallas, Texas), Dec. 1994. (accepted to appear).

9. S. C. Liew, "Multicast routing algorithms for 3-stage CLOS ATM switching networks," in *Proceedings of the 1991 Globecom*, pp. 1619–1625, 1991.

10. J. S. Turner, "Design of a broadcast packet switching network," *IEEE Transactions on Communications*, vol. 36, pp. 734–743, June 1988.

11. W. J. Dally and C. L. Seitz, "The torus routing chip," *Journal of Distributed Computing*, vol. 1, no. 3, pp. 187–196, 1986.

12. L. M. Ni and P. K. McKinley, "A survey of wormhole routing techniques in direct networks," *IEEE Computer*, vol. 26, pp. 62 – 76, Feb. 1993.

13. Y. Lan, L. M. Ni, and A. H. Esfahanian, "A VLSI router design for hypercube multiprocessors," *Integration: The VLSI Journal*, vol. 7, pp. 103–125, 1989.

14. N. Koike, "NEC Cenju-3: A microprocessor-based parallel computer," in *Proceeding of the 8th International Parallel Processing Symposium*, pp. 396–401, Apr. 1994.

15. T. T. Lee, "Nonblocking copy networks for multicast packet switching," *IEEE Journal on Selected Areas in Communications*, vol. 6, pp. 1455–1467, Dec. 1988.

16. NCUBE Company, *NCUBE 6400 Processor Manual*, 1990.

17. C.-M. Chiang and L. M. Ni, "Encoding and decoding of address information in multicast message," Tech. Rep. MSU-CPS-ACS-90, Michigan State University, Department of Computer Science, May 1994.

Routing Algorithms for IBM SP1

Bülent Abali[1] and Cevdet Aykanat[2]

[1] IBM Thomas J. Watson Research Center,
P.O.Box 218, Yorktown Heights, NY 10598
[2] Bilkent University, 06533 Ankara, Turkey

Abstract. Scalable multicomputers are based upon interconnection networks that typically provide multiple communication routes between any given pair of processor nodes. Routes must be selected for communication so that the load is distributed evenly among the links and switches to prevent congestion in the network. We describe the route selection algorithm used in the IBM 9076 SP1 multicomputer. We then describe a new algorithm for reducing network congestion and compare the two algorithms.

1 Introduction

Scalable multicomputers are based upon interconnection networks that typically provide multiple communication routes between any given pair of processor nodes. Multiple routes provide low latency, high bandwidth, and reliable interprocessor communication. In such networks, the selection of the routes is important because of its impact on the communication performance. Routes must be selected so that the communication load is distributed evenly among the links and switches to prevent congestion in the network. In this paper we describe the route selection algorithm used in the IBM 9076 SP1 multicomputer. We then describe an experimental algorithm for reducing network congestion and compare the two algorithms. In the next section we give an overview of the SP1 network architecture. In Section 2 we describe the SP1 routing algorithm. In Section 3 we describe the experimental routing algorithm and compare the two algorithms in Section 4.

1.1 The SP1 Network Architecture

The 9076 SP1 is a commercially available multicomputer whose communication architecture is based upon the Vulcan architecture [1]. The SP1 processor nodes attach to a multistage interconnection network consisting of 8 input 8 output non-blocking switches [1]. The switch chip shown in Fig.3 consists of 8 receiver and 8 transmitter modules, an unbuffered 8 × 8 crossbar, and a 1-KByte large central queue. Each input and output port consists of 8 data lines and 2 control lines. Processor nodes communicate by sending and receiving message packets. Packets are of variable length with up to 255 bytes in size. The method of packet transfer is similar to *wormhole routing* [2], with the difference in that when a packet is blocked the packet bytes are not buffered in place but they are temporarily transferred to the central queue until the blocked output port is cleared up. The method of packet transfer also differs from *virtual cut-through* technique [3, 2] in that flow control is byte based, not packet based. When there is no output contention packet bytes pass through the switch chip via crossbar in 5 clock cycles. Packets are formatted such that the first byte of each packet indicates the packet length, followed by a number of routing bytes, followed by data. The *source routing* technique is used for routing packets [4]. In this technique, the source processor node determines the complete route and puts the respective route bytes in the packet. As the packet proceeds to its destination, each switch chip examines the first route byte of the packet and determines the destination output port. The switch chip also strips off the portion of the routing information pertaining to itself. The packet has no route bytes remaining upon arriving at the destination node. In the SP1 implementation, the switch chip operates at 40 MHz, resulting in a peak bandwidth of 40 MB/s per port and ports may be interconnected with links over 100 feet in length enabling the easy construction of large networks.

In the network implementations, the switch chip input port i and output port i are paired together to form a full duplex bidirectional channel. The resulting 4×4 bidirectional switch element can forward a packet to any of the 8 output ports, including the output ports on the same side with the input port (called "turn-around routing"). In this respect, the SP1 network topologies differ from more commonly known unidirectional multistage interconnection networks (MIN) such as the Omega and indirect binary n-cube [5, 6]. Bidirectionality enhances the modularity, fault-tolerance, and diagnosis of the network as described in [1]. Eight switches placed in a 2-stage configuration interconnected with a shuffle form the switch board as shown in Fig. 4. The switch board provides full connectivity; it can route a packet from any 32 input ports to any 32 output ports. Switch boards may be interconnected in various ways to construct larger networks. A 16 node network is constructed using only one switch board with the 16 processor nodes attached to the left hand side of the board and the 16 ports on the right hand side unused. A 32 node network is constructed using two switch boards whose right hand sides are interconnected with straight wires. Examples of 128 node and 256 node networks are shown in Figs. 5 and 6. Custom network topologies of any size can be easily constructed due to the link technology used.

2 The SP1 Routing Algorithm

We developed the SP1 routing algorithm originally for the Vulcan prototype [1]. A modified version of the algorithm is also being used in IBM's recently announced SP2 multicomputer. The SP1 routing algorithm is a simple algorithm that selects a single shortest path between each pair of processor nodes, although multiple shortest paths may exist. In this respect, the SP1 routing algorithm is comparable to the commonly known XY routing algorithm for 2-

dimensional meshes and the *e-cube* routing algorithm for hypercubes [2]. In a 2-dimensional mesh, the XY routing algorithm uses the single route that goes along the X dimension first and then along the Y dimension, although two nodes have $(h_x + h_y)!/h_x!h_y!$ different shortest paths from one to another, where h_x and h_y are the internode distances in the X and Y dimensions, respectively. In the hypercube topology, the e-cube algorithm uses the single route that goes along the increasing order of dimension, although two nodes with a Hamming distance of k have $k!$ shortest paths from one to another.

The shortest path routing is not necessarily the best choice for all communication patterns [7]. However, in the absence of any information on communication patterns, we decided to use the shortest paths since fewer switches and links would be used. We use the modified *Breadth-First Search* algorithm shown in Fig. 1 for building a breadth-first spanning (BFS) tree rooted at each source node (*src*), and then we follow the spanning tree paths to find the shortest paths from the source node to the rest of the processor nodes. The algorithm is originally due to [8] and uses a first-in, first-out (FIFO) queue Q for the breadth-first search. We added a simple static load balancing strategy to ensure that links are included in the selected routes in a balanced manner. The network graph $G = (V, E)$ is represented by a linked list of vertices. Each vertex $v \in V$ represents a processor node or a switch, and each arc $e \in E$ represents a half duplex link. Only the non-faulty links and switches are represented in G. The direction of an arc indicates the direction of message transmission. Each switch vertex has a maximum in-degree of 8 and an out-degree of 8, and each processor vertex has an in-degree of 1 and an out-degree of 1. The *u.parent* field indicates the parent of vertex u in the spanning tree, and *u.distance* indicates the distance of vertex u to the root (the source node) of the tree. The *u.port[i]* field represents the vertex attached to the output port i of vertex u, and hence also represents the arc from vertex u to vertex *u.port[i]*.

Load balancing is facilitated by the *u.portusage[i]* field which indicates how many times an output port has been used during route generation. While building a spanning tree from a given source node, each time a source–destination path is found the *portusage* field is incremented for each output port in that path. Usage count of the ports determine the order of breadth-first search from the next source node, such that from a given vertex v we first visit the vertices adjacent to the least frequently used output ports (i.e. with the smallest counts), which is accomplished by sorting the port usage counts in lines 10–17.

The routes are stored in a route table in each processor's memory. The route table approach enables routing to be done in a topology independent fashion. Note also that by design the SP1 routing algorithm does not assume a topology, whereas the e-cube and the XY routing algorithms assume hypercube and 2-dimensional mesh topologies, respectively. Topology independence is important for fault-tolerance and scalability; missing links and switches are handled properly by the SP1 routing algorithm, and larger networks of different topological properties can be implemented easily without having to change the routing hardware or the algorithm. Although, the SP1 routing algorithm attemps to in-

```
RTG(G) /* Route Table Generator */
  1      for each vertex u ∈ V[G]
  2          for i = 0 to 7
  3              u.portusage[i] ← 0
  4      for each vertex src ∈ V[G]
  5          BFS_RTG(G, src)


BFS_RTG(G, src)
  1      for each vertex u ∈ V[G]
  2          u.visit ← WHITE
  3          u.distance ← 0
  4          u.parent ← NIL
  5      src.visit ← GRAY
  6      ENQUEUE(Q, src)
  7      while Q ≠ ∅
  8          u ← head[Q]
  9          if u.type = SWITCH then
 10              for i = 0 to 7
 11                  index[i] ← i
 12              for j = 7 to 1
 13                  for i = 0 to j − 1
 14                      if u.portusage[i] > u.portusage[i + 1] then
 15                          tmp ← index[i]
 16                          index[i] ← index[i + 1]
 17                          index[i + 1] ← tmp
 18              for j = 0 to 7
 19                  i ← index[j]
 20                  v ← u.port[i]
 21                  if v ≠ NIL  AND v.visit = WHITE  then
 22                      v.visit ← GRAY
 23                      v.distance ← u.distance + 1
 24                      v.parent ← u
 25                      v.parentport ← i
 26                      ENQUEUE(Q, v)
 27          if u.type = PROCESSOR then
 28              TRACEBACK(G, u)
 29          DEQUEUE(Q)
 30          u.visit ← BLACK


TRACEBACK(G, u)
  1      while u.distance ≠ 0
  2          v ← u.parent
  3          i ← u.parentport
  4          v.portusage[i] ← v.portusage[i] + 1
  5          u ← v
```

Fig. 1. The SP1 algorithm for route selection

clude the links in the routes in a balanced manner, it does not base the routing decisions on any measured or estimated network traffic. Therefore, it is a *non-adaptive* algorithm. Adaptive switches are known to perform better than non-adaptive switches in general with somewhat increased switch complexity [9, 7]. However, in the experiments we observed that the SP1 routing algorithm realizes many commonly used communication patterns without link conflicts for some network topologies.

In the SP1 multicomputer, network topologies are generally designed to be deadlock-free [2] with shortest path routes. For example, all the topologies used in the experiments reported in this paper are deadlock-free with shortest path routes. However, we have some experimental topologies that may cause deadlock cycles due to "turn-around routing" where a packet enters and leaves a switch from the same side. In such cases we eliminate the deadlock causing routes by putting routing restrictions on some switches while generating the routes.

3   An Experimental Routing Algorithm

We developed an experimental algorithm for adaptive route selection in SP1 like networks. We were motivated by the fact that although the SP1 switch chip was not designed for adaptive routing, software control of route selection and existence of multiple routes between any pair of nodes would allow us to make better routing decisions if estimates of the network traffic were available. We assumed that the network traffic is represented by a Node Interaction Graph (NIG). NIG is a directed graph whose vertices represent the processor nodes, while arcs represent interprocessor communication. NIG arcs may have weights indicating the amount of information transmitted from the source node to the destination node. The NIG model may appear unrealistic for general applications since it does not model the temporal interactions between the processor nodes. However, a large class of applications such as iterative solution of systems of equations that arise in numerical computing may be represented with NIGs (see [10, 11] for examples). When all vertices of an NIG have an in-degree and out-degree of 1, then it is a *permutation routing* problem. NIGs may be obtained in several ways, such as the users or compilers supplying NIGs based on the expected program behavior, or the operating system supplying NIGs based on the history of system workload. However, these are system level issues that we will not attempt to solve, but briefly discuss here. It is probably difficult for a user to generate NIGs unless communication patterns of the parallel program are well known or unless parallel program profiling tools are available. Compiler generated NIGs would be more convenient. It was suggested that NIGs may be derived during the data partitioning phase of a parallelizing compiler. The issue of multiple NIGs and their respective route tables may be dealt with easily. In SP1 route tables are stored in processor nodes memory. When the routing problem (NIG) changes, switching to a new route table is simply a matter of changing a pointer to the new route table base. Another issue is when to run the experimental routing algorithm described: in SP1, the operating system may perform a logical to physical node number mapping before loading programs to the nodes (described in Section 4.2). Therefore, to get good results the experimental routing algorithm must be executed using the physical node numbers obtained from the mapping.

In the experimental routing algorithm, we formulate the route selection problem as minimization of the cost function

$$\text{cost} = \sum_{\ell \in L} W_\ell^2 + K \sum_{s \in S} W_s^2 \qquad (1)$$

where L is the set of all links, W_ℓ is the total flow through link ℓ, S is the set of all switches, and W_s is the total flow through switch s. The nonlinear cost function penalizes the links and switches with higher flow. For example, n messages each with a unit flow routed over one link will contribute n^2 units to the cost, whereas the n messages routed over n different links will contribute n units to the cost. We used an exponent of 2 merely for convenience. An exponent of 3 made no appreciable difference in results. $K \geq 0$ is the weight of the total switch penalty and it is a hardware dependent constant. $K \neq 0$ is used to minimize switch sharing. In some switch designs, messages sharing the switch resources such as a central queue may impact the performance and this may be taken into account in the cost function by a nonzero constant K that is derived empirically or by analysis. A cost function similar to Eq. 1 was used in [12] for routing in networks with virtual cut-through capability. However, Eq. 1 differs from that of [12] such that the second term due to switch sharing does not exist in [12]. Furthermore, the distance metric that we use in our algorithm is based on the number of network hops, whereas in [12] it is based on the link utilization.

A brief sketch of the adaptive algorithm is given in Fig. 2. The objective is to minimize the cost. For each communication arc $(s, d, f) \in E(NIG)$ an initial route is selected, where f is the required amount of flow from node s to node d. The total cost is calculated after the initial selection of routes. Then, sequentially for each arc $(s, d, f) \in E(NIG)$, the previously selected route is ripped up and a new route with smaller incremental cost is selected from the set of routes $R[s][d]$. The procedure is repeated iteratively until the cost converges to a local minimum. The algorithm is guaranteed to converge because the cost is monotonically non-increasing. If the cost from previous iteration does not change, the algorithm does not terminate immediately but allows a different set of routes with the same cost to be tried a bounded number of times ($NTRY = 2$ in this case) in anticipation of further cost reduction in the next iteration. For the topologies we used, the route set $R[s][d]$ consists of all deadlock-free shortest-path routes from node s to node d. However, in richer topologies a restricted subset of the routes between nodes s, d may also be considered, because the number of routes may get quite large increasing the execution time.

4 Results and Conclusions

We have implemented the experimental route selection algorithm and compared its performance to the SP1 routing algorithm using a set of communication work-

```
ROUTER(NIG, G)
  1    Let R be the set of all routes, where R[i][j]
          is a set of all possible routes from node i to j
  2    for each arc e = (src, dst, flow) ∈ E(NIG)
  3        Select an initial route r ∈ R[e.src][e.dst]
  4        Add e.flow to the links and switches on the path of route r
  5        Update cost
  6    previous_cost ← ∞
  7    n_trials ← NTRY ← 2
          (to try the same cost a number of times)
  8    while previous_cost > cost OR n_trials ≠ 0
  9        previous_cost ← cost
 10        for each arc e = (src, dst, flow) ∈ E(NIG)
 11            cost ← ROUTE_ONE_EDGE(e, G, R)
 12            if cost = previous_cost then
 13                n_trials ← n_trials - 1
 14            else
 15                n_trials ← NTRY
```

```
ROUTE_ONE_EDGE(e, G, R)
  1    Rip up previously selected route for e and update cost
  2    Find a route r ∈ R[e.src][e.dst] with the smallest incremental cost.
       If there are multiple such routes, then select one randomly
  3    Update G and cost
```

Fig. 2. The adaptive algorithm for route selection

loads. Results given in Tables 1 through 3 show how well the two algorithms deal with network congestion. Note that results are based on simulations. They are not based on actual measurements on SP1. The FLOW metric in the tables denotes the maximally loaded link in the network for given workload and network size. Figs. 7-9 summarize the relative performance of the experimental routing algorithm over the SP1 routing algorithm based on the FLOW metric, as described in more detail in Section 4.2.

4.1 Workloads and Methods

In the simulations, we used standard network topologies available from IBM for 16, 32, 64 node systems. For 128, 256, and 512 node networks we used topologies shown in Figs. 5 and 6. The 256 node topology has all the nodes connected to the left hand side of the network with the right hand side ports remaining unconnected. The 512 node topology is constructed from two 256 node networks shown in Fig. 6 whose right hand sides are interconnected with straight wires. Not shown in the figures is the 256-A topology which consists of 8 second stage boards instead of the 16 used in Fig. 6.

We used a number of communication workloads (NIGs): in the RANDOM-F workload each node i sends a unit size message to a randomly selected node j. RANDOM-V is similar except that message sizes randomly vary between 1 and 10 units. DOLOOP refers to a commonly used communication pattern in parallel programs coded in Fortran. Each node executes

```
1    DO I = 1, N − 1
2         each node J = 0...N − 1 sends message to node (I + J)(modN)
3         where N is the number of processors
4    CONTINUE
```

Note that each iteration of the loop corresponds to one NIG graph. EXOR refers to a communication pattern that provides conflict free routing in hypercubes as shown in [13]. It is similar to the DOLOOP, except that the order of exchange is different

```
1    for i = 1 to N − 1
2         each node j = 0...N − 1 sends message to node i EXOR j
3         where N is the number of processors
```

NCUBE refers to a commonly used communication pattern in divide and conquer type algorithms. Given 2^n processor nodes, each node sends to n other nodes

```
1    for i = 0 to n − 1
2         each node (j_{n−1}...j_i...j_0) sends to node (j_{n−1}...\overline{j_i}...j_0)
```

where $(j_{n-1} \ldots j_i \ldots j_0)$ is the binary representation of a processor's node number and $(j_{n-1} \ldots \overline{j_i} \ldots j_0)$ is the i-th bit complemented. We derived the remaining workload from BCSSTK9, BCSPWR10, BLCKHOLE, and JAGMESH9 matrices of Harwell-Boeing sparse matrix collection. We mapped task graphs obtained from the sparse matrices to processor graphs using Kernighan-Lin heuristic to minimize communication [14]. We then assumed that the processors communicate using the DOLOOP algorithm. The resulting NIGs resemble the NIGs for DOLOOP with the exception that the arcs have variable weights. We report here only the results for BCSSTK9. Others were similar.

In the tables, the COST column refers to the minimum cost obtained by the algorithms as given by Eq. 1. We set the constant $K = 0$ in the simulations since switch sharing does not incur any penalty in the SP1 switch. As a performance metric we also included the maximally loaded link in the network given in the FLOW column. Note that smaller cost does not necessarily mean smaller maximum link flow. However, in practice we have not observed a case of maximum link flow increasing with decreasing cost.

4.2 Results

The main result of the paper regarding the SP1 algorithm is shown in Table 1 which indicates that the SP1 routing algorithm generates conflict free routes for 16, 32, and 512 node topologies for DOLOOP, EXOR, and NCUBE workloads. FLOW columns show that the maximum link load is 1.0 indicating conflict free routing. The experimental routing algorithm was most effective with the RAN-DOM workloads; the maximum link load was smaller by a factor of 2 to 3 compared to the SP1 routing algorithm. For the BCSSTK9 workload the difference between the two algorithms was negligible, most probably due to the fact that the NIGs were sparse and used the DOLOOP algorithm. Thus messages rarely shared any links or switches. The results in Tbl. 1 are summarized in Fig. 7 by dividing the SP1 algorithm max. link load by the experimental algorithm max. link load averaged over the six workloads. A ratio of 1.0 or greater in Fig. 7 indicates that the experimental algorithm performs better. Going back to Tbl. 1, we see that for the 16 and 32 node DOLOOP cases the experimental algorithm performed worse than the SP1 routing algorithm suggesting a weakness of the experimental algorithm: since it is a local minimization heuristic, the quality of results depend very much on the initial selection of the routes. To fix this problem we modified the experimental routing algorithm such that instead of selecting the initial routes randomly in Line 3 of Fig. 2, we selected the routes generated by the SP1 routing algorithm as the initial routes. Results of this experiment are reported in Tbl. 2 which indicate that the experimental routing algorithm always performs better than or equal to the SP1 routing algorithm for individual cases. However, the averages did not change significantly except for the 256-C and 512 node cases as shown in Fig. 8.

We performed a third set of simulations reported in Table 3 and Fig. 9 to test the effects logical to physical node mapping. In SP1, each user is presented with a logical sequence of node numbers from 0 to N-1. The logical node number observed by a user program is not necessarily equal to the physical node number of the underlying node. A logical to physical node number mapping is performed by the system. This is necessary because some nodes may already have been allocated to other users, and some nodes may be down, and therefore cannot be allocated. To test the effects of mapping on routing we randomly interchanged the node numbers. Although random mapping will not happen in practice, we tried it as a worse case for the SP1 routing algorithm and to see how well the experimental algorithm adapts to the mapping. Results show that the DOLOOP, EXOR, and NCUBE communication patterns could not use the conflict-free routes generated with the SP1 algorithm anymore and the experimental routing algorithm performed better.

4.3   Conclusions

Simplicity is the main advantage of the SP1 routing algorithm. It selects the routes in a balanced manner and in a topology independent fashion which is useful in large networks possibly with broken links and switches. Among the workloads that we used, the experimental algorithm improved the performance over the SP1 algorithm most significantly when node interactions were random. In general the experimental algorithm will be useful for networks in which the route selection is under software control such as in the SP1 network and when the problem has known routing loads in advance. Compilers appear to be good candidates for producing that information. For future work it would be interesting to try the experimental algorithm not only by simulations but also by actual implementation on SP1 for real problems. Also interesting to see is how well the experimental algorithm performs compared to a network with adaptive switch hardware.

Acknowledgements

We wish to thank Craig Stunkel of IBM Research for his valuable discussions. We also would like to thank D.G. Shea and C.J. Tan of IBM Research for their support, and finally the anonymous reviewers for their suggestions.

References

1. C. B. Stunkel, D. G. Shea, B. Abali, M. M. Denneau, P. H. Hochschild, D. J. Joseph, B. J. Nathanson, M. Tsao, and P. R. Varker, "Architecture and Implementation of Vulcan," in *Proc. Int. Parallel Processing Symp.*, pp. 268–274, April 1994. An extended version is also available as Research Report RC19492 from the IBM T.J. Watson Research Center.
2. W. J. Dally and C. L. Seitz, "Deadlock-Free Message Routing in Multiprocessor Interconnection Networks," *IEEE Transactions on Computers*, vol. C-36, pp. 547–553, May 1987.
3. P. Kermani and L. Kleinrock, "Virtual Cut-Through: A new computer communications switching technique," *Computer Networks*, vol. 3, pp. 267–286, September 1979.
4. A. S. Tanenbaum, *Computer Networks*. Englewood Cliffs, NJ: Prentice-Hall, 1981.
5. D. H. Lawrie, "Access and alignment of data in an array processor," *IEEE Transactions on Computers*, vol. C-24, pp. 1145–1155, December 1975.
6. M. C. Pease, "The indirect binary n-cube microprocessor array," *IEEE Transactions on Computers*, vol. C-26, pp. 458–473, May 1977.
7. S. A. Felperin, L. Gravano, G. D. Pifarre, and J. L. C. Sanz, "Routing Techniques for Massively Parallel Communication," *Proceedings of the IEEE*, vol. 79, pp. 488–503, April 1991.
8. T. H. Cormen, C. E. Leiserson, and R. L. Rivest, *Introduction to Algorithms*. NY: McGraw-Hill, 1990.
9. R. V. Boppana and S. Chalasani, "A Comparison of Adaptive Wormhole Routing Algorithms," in *Proceedings of the 20th Ann. Int. Symp. on Computer Architecture*, pp. 351–360, May 1993.
10. T. Bultan and C. Aykanat, "A New Mapping Heuristic Based on Mean Field Annealing," *J. Parallel and Distributed Comput.*, vol. 16, pp. 292–305, 1992.
11. C. Aykanat, F. Ozguner, F. Ercal, and P. Sadayappan, "Iterative Algorithms for Solution of Large Sparse Systems of Linear Equations on Hypercubes," *IEEE Trans. Comput*, vol. 37, no. 12, pp. 1554–1567, 1988.
12. D. D. Kandlur and K. G. Shin, "Traffic Routing for Multicomputer Networks with Virtual Cut-Through Capability," *IEEE Transactions on Computers*, vol. 41, pp. 1257–1270, October 1992.
13. B. Abali, F. Ozguner, and A. Bataineh, "Balanced Parallel Sort on Hypercube Multiprocessors," *IEEE Trans. Parallel and Distributed Systems*, vol. 4, pp. 572–581, May 1993.
14. B. W. Kernighan and S. Lin, "An efficient heuristic procedure for partitioning graphs," *Bell System Tech. J.*, vol. 49, pp. 291–307, 1970.

171

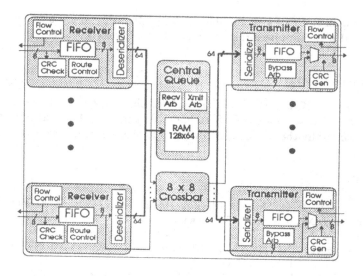

Fig. 3. The Switch Chip Block Diagram.

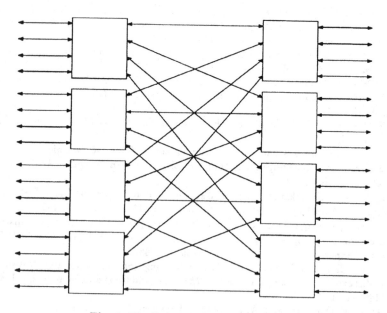

Fig. 4. The Switch Board consisting of 8 Switch Chips

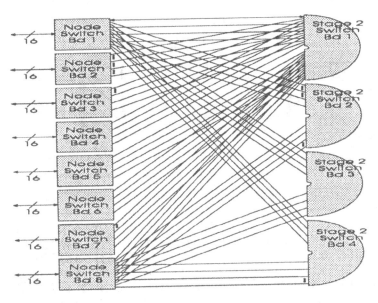

Fig. 5. A 128 node network consisting of 8 first stage and 4 second stage switch boards.

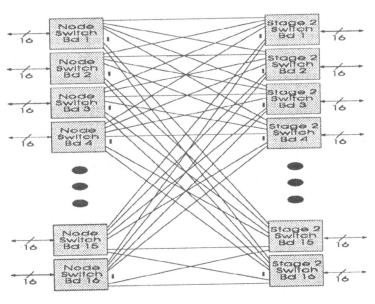

Fig. 6. A 256 node network consisting of 16 first stage and 16 second stage switch boards.

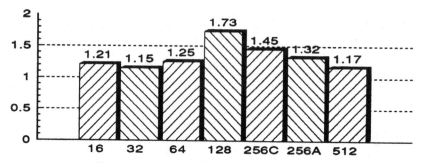

Fig. 7. Ratio of SP1 FLOW over EXP FLOW averaged over the six workloads given in Table 1

# NODES	16 NODES		32 NODES		64 NODES		128 NODES	
WORKLOAD	FLOW	COST	FLOW	COST	FLOW	COST	FLOW	COST
RANDOM-F SP1	2.10	30.4	2.50	86.0	3.20	250.2	3.50	712.0
RANDOM-F EXP	1.20	25.2	1.70	73.2	2.00	198.0	2.00	571.6
RANDOM-V SP1	15.30	1169.8	18.50	3348.7	22.00	9469.4	27.50	26914.1
RANDOM-V EXP	9.30	947.8	10.20	2836.3	13.00	7384.2	10.90	21566.7
DOLOOP SP1	1.00	25.6	1.00	74.3	3.19	247.7	3.87	863.2
DOLOOP EXP	1.13	26.1	1.55	77.5	2.73	244.6	1.93	575.4
EXOR SP1	1.00	32.0	1.00	82.3	3.40	307.2	2.55	949.7
EXOR EXP	1.00	32.0	1.00	82.3	3.40	302.9	1.52	571.9
NCUBE SP1	1.00	32.0	1.00	74.7	2.50	236.0	1.60	588.8
NCUBE EXP	1.00	32.0	1.00	74.7	2.50	234.0	1.20	442.4
BCSSTK9 SP1	61.71	21521.7	36.31	11841.4	28.67	6225.3	13.37	2183.5
BCSSTK9 EXP	61.71	21521.7	36.31	11841.4	26.88	6077.8	12.15	2080.8
# NODES	256 NODES-C		256 NODES-A		512 NODES			
WORKLOAD	FLOW	COST	FLOW	COST	FLOW	COST	FLOW	COST
RANDOM-F SP1	4.50	1874.8	4.20	1741.0	4.80	4348.8		
RANDOM-F EXP	2.00	1503.8	2.00	1374.0	2.00	3504.2		
RANDOM-V SP1	33.80	67670.2	30.00	62225.3	32.30	158898.9		
RANDOM-V EXP	14.00	53969.6	16.20	47799.3	17.20	126871.5		
DOLOOP SP1	1.96	1421.3	3.03	1521.3	1.00	3166.2		
DOLOOP EXP	1.95	1503.8	3.07	1633.7	2.01	3498.2		
EXOR SP1	1.76	1438.5	3.29	1779.8	1.00	3184.9		
EXOR EXP	1.76	1406.0	3.29	1804.2	1.88	3222.2		
NCUBE SP1	1.33	1045.3	2.00	1194.7	1.00	2267.4		
NCUBE EXP	1.33	1032.0	2.00	1205.3	1.43	2282.3		
BCSSTK9 SP1	5.00	584.2	4.96	561.2	2.38	219.5		
BCSSTK9 EXP	4.96	583.7	4.96	561.2	2.38	219.6		

Table 1. Comparison of the SP1 routing algorithm and the experimental routing algorithm which uses random initial routes.

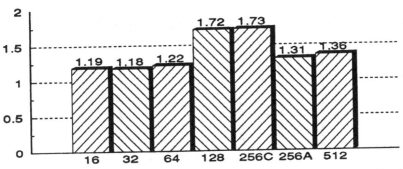

Fig. 8. Ratio of SP1 FLOW over EXP FLOW averaged over the six workloads given in Table 2

# NODES	16 NODES		32 NODES		64 NODES		128 NODES	
WORKLOAD	FLOW	COST	FLOW	COST	FLOW	COST	FLOW	COST
RANDOM-F SP1	2.10	30.4	2.50	86.0	3.20	250.2	3.50	712.0
RANDOM-F EXP	1.30	26.2	1.90	75.4	2.00	199.0	2.00	572.6
RANDOM-V SP1	15.30	1169.8	18.50	3348.7	22.00	9469.4	27.50	26914.1
RANDOM-V EXP	9.90	957.0	10.50	2839.7	14.00	7437.0	11.70	21584.7
DOLOOP SP1	1.00	25.6	1.00	74.3	3.19	247.7	3.87	863.2
DOLOOP EXP	1.00	25.6	1.00	74.3	2.92	241.5	1.83	552.6
EXOR SP1	1.00	32.0	1.00	82.3	3.40	307.2	2.55	949.7
EXOR EXP	1.00	32.0	1.00	82.3	3.40	302.9	1.52	560.5
NCUBE SP1	1.00	32.0	1.00	74.7	2.50	236.0	1.60	588.8
NCUBE EXP	1.00	32.0	1.00	74.7	2.50	234.0	1.20	438.0
BCSSTK9 SP1	61.71	21521.7	36.31	11841.4	28.67	6225.3	13.37	2183.5
BCSSTK9 EXP	61.71	21521.7	36.31	11841.4	26.88	6077.8	12.15	2080.8

# NODES	256 NODES-C		256 NODES-A		512 NODES			
WORKLOAD	FLOW	COST	FLOW	COST	FLOW	COST	FLOW	COST
RANDOM-F SP1	4.50	1874.8	4.20	1741.0	4.80	4348.8		
RANDOM-F EXP	2.00	1503.8	2.00	1376.8	2.10	3512.6		
RANDOM-V SP1	33.80	67670.2	30.00	62225.3	32.30	158898.9		
RANDOM-V EXP	15.00	54114.4	17.00	47788.7	17.10	126901.1		
DOLOOP SP1	1.96	1421.3	3.03	1521.3	1.00	3166.2		
DOLOOP EXP	1.09	1373.8	3.02	1521.3	1.00	3166.2		
EXOR SP1	1.76	1438.5	3.29	1779.8	1.00	3184.9		
EXOR EXP	1.00	1389.7	3.29	1779.8	1.00	3184.9		
NCUBE SP1	1.33	1045.3	2.00	1194.7	1.00	2267.4		
NCUBE EXP	1.00	1024.0	2.00	1194.7	1.00	2267.4		
BCSSTK9 SP1	5.00	584.2	4.96	561.2	2.38	219.5		
BCSSTK9 EXP	4.96	583.7	4.96	561.2	2.38	219.5		

Table 2. Comparison of the SP1 routing algorithm and the experimental routing algorithm which uses the initial routes selected by the SP1 routing algorithm.

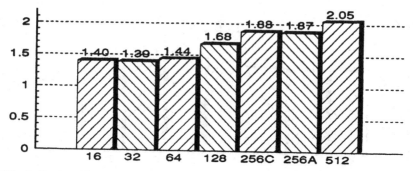

Fig. 9. Ratio of SP1 FLOW over EXP FLOW averaged over the four workloads given in Table 3

# NODES	16 NODES		32 NODES		64 NODES		128 NODES	
WORKLOAD	FLOW	COST	FLOW	COST	FLOW	COST	FLOW	COST
DOLOOP SP1	2.00	30.4	2.74	92.5	3.21	240.3	3.74	712.3
DOLOOP EXP	1.13	25.9	1.87	78.1	2.00	191.5	2.00	565.0
EXOR SP1	2.13	30.9	2.81	92.0	3.13	240.2	3.63	714.1
EXOR EXP	1.67	27.3	1.94	80.1	2.00	193.2	2.00	566.5
NCUBE SP1	2.25	30.5	3.00	92.0	3.00	253.3	3.71	728.6
NCUBE EXP	1.50	26.0	2.00	78.0	2.00	201.3	2.00	572.6
BCSSTK9 SP1	82.08	41564.3	51.46	30824.4	30.25	15574.1	14.49	6979.4
BCSSTK9 EXP	76.83	40468.7	44.21	28000.8	28.02	13817.9	12.38	6158.5

# NODES	256 NODES-C		256 NODES-A		512 NODES			
WORKLOAD	FLOW	COST	FLOW	COST	FLOW	COST	FLOW	COST
DOLOOP SP1	4.26	1850.6	4.21	1705.7	4.76	4319.3		
DOLOOP EXP	2.00	1488.5	2.02	1359.2	2.03	3487.1		
EXOR SP1	4.24	1850.0	4.24	1706.6	4.73	4311.7		
EXOR EXP	2.01	1493.1	2.01	1362.1	2.03	3495.4		
NCUBE SP1	4.25	1862.5	4.25	1719.0	4.78	4322.0		
NCUBE EXP	2.00	1496.2	2.00	1375.5	2.00	3487.8		
BCSSTK9 SP1	5.87	2791.8	5.88	2477.2	2.69	646.2		
BCSSTK9 EXP	5.10	2396.8	5.10	2075.1	2.39	564.0		

Table 3. Comparison of the SP1 routing algorithm and the experimental routing algorithm with random mapping of tasks onto processors

Congestion-Free Routing on the CM–5 Data Router

Steve Heller

Thinking Machines Corporation
245 First Street
Cambridge, MA 02142

Abstract. Even though the CM–5 data router employs randomization, some permutations can be routed more quickly than random permutations with the same bisection requirements. In this paper we describe a class of permutations called congestion-free permutations and show how they can be used to accomplish important communication problems including all-to-all personalized communication, hypercube dimension-exchange, block transfer, and others.

1 Introduction

When a message is delivered by the CM–5 data router (DR)[6], the first half of the path is randomly chosen subject to availability. The idea is to convert all communication patterns into random patterns. But some permutations with the same bisection requirements as random permutations can be routed more quickly than random permutations, even in the presence of this kind of randomization. We call a class of these permutations **congestion-free**. We describe the class of congestion-free permutations and show how they can be used to accomplish many important communication problems quickly on a hypertree including all-to-all personalized communication, hypercube dimension-exchange, block transfer, and others.

Section 2 reviews the topology and the routing algorithm of the CM–5 DR. Section 3 introduces the notion of congestion with some examples, and Sect. 4 shows that some permutations are congestion-free. We conclude in Sect. 5.

2 Hypertree Topology and Routing

The topology of the CM–5 DR, which will be referred to as the hypertree, is a realization of Leiserson's fat tree [6, 7].

We can think of a hypertree as a three dimensional structure akin to a solid tetrahedron oriented with two horizontal edges; the bottom edge is aligned left-right, and the top edge, front-back, as shown in Fig. 1. The processors are connected at the leaves, along the bottom left-right edge, and the roots of the tree are found on the top front-back edge. For additional details about the topology, the reader is referred to [7]. The hypertree shown in Fig. 1 corresponds to an actual CM–5 as nodes at the first two levels have two parents. For simplicity and unlike the CM–5, in this paper we will assume that the hypertree has uniform bandwidth at all levels unless otherwise noted, *i.e.*, the upward branching factor is assumed to be four at all heights.

When a message is inserted into the network, it rises to a common ancestor of the source and destination nodes. Given any source and destination node pair, we can easily identify the set of lowest-common ancestors, and from any one of them, the downward path to the destination node.

The choice of lowest common ancestor is made dynamically, to minimize congestion. Once the lowest common ancestor is reached however, the downward path to the destination node is fixed. It is possible to push messages in the tree higher than a lowest common ancestor; nonetheless, there will be a unique downward path from the highest point down to the destination node.

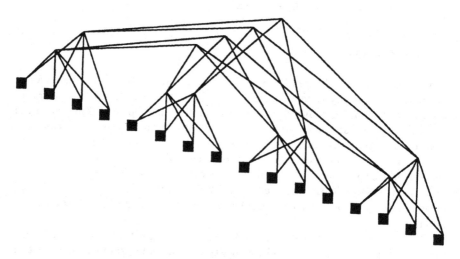

Fig. 1. The CM–5 Hypertree

3 Congestion

In this section, we discuss congestion and congestive permutations. All random and most regular permutations are subject to a certain amount of congestion when routed in a hypertree. Nonetheless, there exists a class of permutations that can be routed with no congestion.

3.1 Definitions

When two messages reach a single router switch simultaneously, and both require the same output link, we say they **collide**. The presence of one or more collisions in the network creates **congestion**. A permutation is **congestion-free** if it admits no collisions, even with the randomization of the upward paths.

Collisions can occur only on the downward paths within hypertrees. Upward-bound messages cannot collide with each other, because they have no routing constraints. Any message at any router node can take any upward link until it reaches a common ancestor of the source and destination nodes. Once a message reaches an ancestor and begins its descent, however, it is on a fixed downward path. If two downward-bound messages reach the same router node at the same time, both may require the same output link. Thus they collide and cause congestion.

3.2 Distinctions

We treat congestion differently than back-pressure from flow control. Back-pressure occurs when a channel has flow turned off due to congestion further ahead or due to a node's failing to empty the network fast enough. Back pressure can stall both upward-bound and downward-bound messages.

Virtual-channels [2] change the flavor of congestion problems as colliding messages can share the same physical communication resources. We assume that virtual-channels are not in use.

3.3 A Closer Look

Let's take a closer look at a root node when routing a random permutation. Each root node is connected to four sub-trees, each sub-tree covering one quarter of the processors. Each sub-tree presents a message to the root node, and each message is destined for a different sub-tree than the one from which it emerged. The chance that all four messages are destined for different quarters of the machine is about eleven percent. The rest of the time, at least one message must wait. If we could guarantee that every switching node was always presented with a local permutation, no messages would ever need to wait. By local permutation, we mean that each incoming message wishes to leave on a different output.

Each time a message ascends one level in the tree, it can proceed to any one of its four parents, as all four parents subtend the same subtree i.e., have the same reachability. Each step up involves a random choice. Once the destination node is a descendent of the node reached, the message can descend. Although all nodes have four children, there is never a choice on the way down — think of this as descending a simple quadtree. The height to which a message rises is a function of the most significant bit differentiating the source and the destination nodes. No matter what choices were made on the way up, the sequence of choices on the way down is a function of the destination node address.

Let's consider a cyclic shift by one. Processor P_i sends a message to processor P_{i+1}. Three fourths of the messages turn around at the first level (height one, or simply H1) of switches, and there is no congestion. Of the remaining messages, three-fourths turn around with no congestion at H2. Let's slow down here, as something subtle just happened. Consider a group of sixteen processors. Each of the four messages that rose to H2 independently chose one of four nodes. One in sixty-four times they'll choose the same node, and six in sixty-four times they'll choose different nodes. However, no matter what the choices are, two messages will never need the same child output port. It is also clear that the messages descending from H2 will not interfere with the messages turning around at H1.

And so it goes all the way up the tree. Cyclic shift by one is a congestion-free permutation. What about cyclic shift by k? Suppose p denotes the number of processors in the machine, and $k = 3p/8$. Then each quarter of the nodes sends half its messages one quarter to the right, and half two quarters to the right; each quarter divides all its messages equally between two other quarters. All messages go through a root, and a root node will only see a local permutation one-eighth of the time, so a root node is congested seven-eighths of the time. If we could specify upward paths, we could avoid congestion entirely, but this orchestration is not possible on the CM–5 DR as it has serious implications with respect to robustness in the presence of failures.

Figure 2 shows the bandwidth achieved for various shift distances on a 256 node machine. The figure reports experimental results, not simulation. The upward spikes correspond to congestion-free rotations and will be explained by the theory developed in this paper.

4 Congestion-Free Permutations

In the previous section we saw that some permutations are congestive. In this section we describe a class of congestion-free permutations.

Lemma 1. *The identity permutation is congestion-free if all messages are sent to the top of the hypertree.*

Proof. Regardless of the upward path chosen, when a message reaches the top, it has only one possible downward path to reach its destination node. Since we are sending messages to ourselves, the downward path from the top to the destination node is the same as the upward path taken from the source node to the top, but in reverse. Since there is no congestion on the way up, there is no congestion on the way down — the upward path is a reservation for the downward path. Hence, the identity permutation can be routed with no congestion.

A **block transfer** is a partial permutation where $P_i \ldots P_{i+k-1}$ send data to $P_j \ldots P_{j+k-1}$ respectively. An **aligned block transfer** is when k is a power of two and both i and j are multiples of k.

Block transfers are used to ship data from one group of processors to another. On the CM–5, block transfers are used among partitions and I/O devices as well as between them.

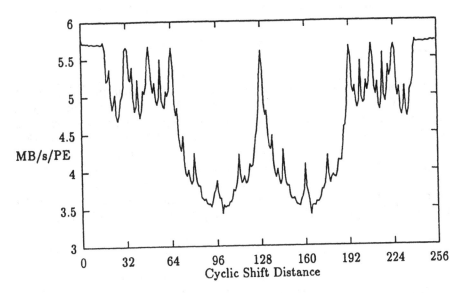

Fig. 2. Communication Rates at all Cyclic Shift Distances on a 256 node CM–5

Lemma 2. *Aligned block transfers are congestion-free.*

Proof. The proof is similar to the proof for the identity permutation, but when the data reaches the least common ancestors, it turns around and takes translated rather than identical downward paths.

Lemma 3. *The left-right exchange permutation, where all the processors from the left half of the machine exchange messages with processors from the right half of the machine, i.e., $P_0 \ldots P_{n/2-1}$ exchange with $P_{n/2} \ldots P_{n-1}$ respectively, is congestion-free.*

Proof. The top of the tree is the least-common ancestor for all paths, so all messages must go across the top. At each step, a top node will receive one message from each quarter of the machine. The messages from $Q_0 Q_1 Q_2 Q_3$ will want to go to $Q_2 Q_3 Q_0 Q_1$ respectively, so there are no collisions. And the rest of the route, *i.e.*, the way down, is like the identity route with messages descending in different quarters. We are effectively doing four aligned and non-interfering block transfers at the same time; they pass each other at the top, and proceed on their way. So, this left-right exchange, which can be described concisely by flipping the high bit of the processor addresses, is congestion-free.

Lemma 4. *All quarter permutations that preserve the order of messages within a quarter are congestion-free.*

These permutations are generated by two permutations: S_n and E_n, which shuffle and exchange the quarters:

$$S_n : Q_0Q_1Q_2Q_3 \rightarrow Q_1Q_2Q_3Q_0$$

$$E_n : Q_0Q_1Q_2Q_3 \rightarrow Q_1Q_0Q_2Q_3$$

An interesting class of permutations, named bit-matrix-multiply/complement or **BMMC** in [1] and affine transformations in [3], is generated by multiplying an address by a boolean matrix, and then by a complement vector using mod 2 arithmetic. BMMC includes shuffle, transpose, bit-reverse, and many other regular permutations. As an example, vector reverse is described by an identity matrix and a complement vector containing only ones.

All twenty-four quarter permutations can be put in one-to-one correspondence with the six non-singular two-by-two boolean matrices crossed with the four binary strings of length two, *i.e.*, these permutations are in BMMC.

$$
D = \begin{pmatrix} A_{n-1,n-1} & A_{n-1,n-2} & & \\ A_{n-2,n-1} & A_{n-2,n-2} & 0 & \\ & & 1 & \\ & 0 & & \ddots \\ & & & & 1 \end{pmatrix} S \bigoplus \begin{bmatrix} C_{n-1} \\ C_{n-2} \\ 0 \\ \vdots \\ 0 \end{bmatrix}
$$

Lemma 5. *All permutations described by BMMC and restricted to two-by-two blocked diagonal characteristic matrices are congestion-free.*

A permutation is said to map a tree to itself when hierarchical groupings are preserved: siblings remain siblings, first cousins remain first cousins, and kth cousins remain kth cousins.

Lemma 6. *All permutations that map the tree into itself are congestion-free.*

Proof. We can play the same game as we did in the quarter permutations by performing any permutation at all leftmost nodes one level down from the top corresponding to the leftmost node one level below the root, and the permutations will be generated by S_{n-1} and E_{n-1}, defined analogous to S_n and E_n, but on the sixteenths of the machine. In fact, we can permute any group of nodes at a given left-right position one level down by first using S_n to put the subtrees to be manipulated on the left, by applying S_{n-1} and E_{n-1} as needed, and then using S_n to put them back in place, and the reasoning goes through, and there is no congestion. In fact, all permutations generated by S_n, E_n, S_{n-1} and E_{n-1} are congestion-free. They are not all in BMMC, however. If we perform identical permutations on all nodes one level down, we do stay in BMMC, and these permutations have a characteristic matrix with two two-by-two non-singular blocks on the diagonal in the upper left corner and the rest identity, and a complement vector with the first four positions possibly non-zero.

We can play the same game all the way down the tree. All permutations generated by $S_n, \ldots, S_1$ and $E_n, \ldots, E_1$ are contention free. And, if at each level a single permutation is used, we are in the subset of BMMC that is described by two-by-two blocked diagonal characteristic matrices with arbitrary complementation.

$$
D = \begin{pmatrix}
A_{n-1,n-1}\ A_{n-1,n-2} & & & \\
A_{n-2,n-1}\ A_{n-2,n-2} & & 0 & \\
& A_{n-3,n-3}\ A_{n-3,n-4} & & \\
& A_{n-4,n-3}\ A_{n-4,n-4} & & \\
& 0 & \ddots & \\
& & & A_{1,1}\ A_{1,0} \\
& & & A_{0,1}\ A_{0,0}
\end{pmatrix} S \oplus \begin{bmatrix}
C_{n-1} \\
C_{n-2} \\
C_{n-3} \\
C_{n-4} \\
\vdots \\
C_1 \\
C_0
\end{bmatrix}
$$

Corollary 7. *Hypercube dimension-exchange $X_{2^i}(P_j) = P_j\ XOR\ 2^i$ corresponding to flipping a single address bit (the ith) is congestion-free.*

Corollary 8. *Hypercube multi-dimension-exchange $X_i(P_j) = P_j\ XOR\ i$ corresponding to flipping several address bits (encoded in i) is congestion-free.*

Proof. All such hypercube [multi-]dimension-exchange permutations correspond to the subset of BMMC with an identity characteristic matrix and a complement vector corresponding to the address bits to be flipped. These permutations are congestion-free.

Corollary 9. *Any rotation of the form $R_{\pm a4^i}(P_j) = P_{j\pm a4^i\bmod p}$, $a = 1, 2$, or 3, is congestion-free.*

Proof. They are all mappings of the tree to itself.

Rotations of the form $R_{\pm a4^i}(P_j) = P_{j\pm a4^i\bmod p}$, $a = 1, 2$, or 3, are important as they subsume unit distance shifts in all dimensions when grids are embedded in hypertrees.

In all the permutations discussed so far, each processor sends all its data to one other processor. In such a situation, there is no need to worry about the order in which message packets are inserted into the network. However, if a processor is sending messages to more than one processor, insertion order is an issue[4]. The order in which a processor inserts messages into the network is called the **schedule**. In the permutations considered so far, all schedules are equivalent.

When every processor sends a message to every processor, we are performing an All-to-All Personalized Communication (AAPC) [5]. It would be foolish to choose a schedule in which all processors sent their messages strictly in order. This identity schedule, where at step i P_j sends a message to P_i, would start by flooding processor zero, and, in turn, all processors. By restricting consideration to schedules that perform a permutation at each step, we avoid this problem, yet there are many of these schedules to choose from.

We can start by having each processor send a message to itself, then to one processor to the right, then to two to the right, etc, performing a cyclic ring shift at each step. At step i P_j sends a message to $P_{(i+j) \bmod p}$, where p is the number of processors. We refer to this schedule, which performs a sequence of cyclic shifts at increasing distances, as the diagonal schedule; as we have seen, it is not congestion-free for most shift distances.

Theorem 10. *All-to-all personalized communication has a congestion-free schedule on a hypertree.*

Proof. In an AAPC, each processor has a message for each processor. Suppose at step i P_j sends a message to $P_{j \text{ XOR } i}$. At each step we are performing a hypercube multi-dimension-exchange, and therefore the schedule is congestion-free. Each processor has an opportunity to send a message to each processor, as its set of destinations is the permutation of $0 \ldots p - 1$ given by XORing with its own processor address. Hence, this schedule accomplishes AAPC with no congestion.

4.1 The Actual CM–5 Hypertree

Each processing node in an actual Thinking Machines Corporation CM–5 has two 20MB/sec ports to the hypertree, known as the left and right DRs. Each of the first two levels decreases the bandwidth available by a factor of two, and all subsequent levels maintain the bandwidth, leaving 10MB/sec/proc across the top. Physical routing information occupies about four bytes, and we set aside anywhere from zero to four bytes for a local offset, leaving sixteen to twenty bytes for data in a maximal size packet. In these calculations we assume that four bytes of physical routing information, four bytes of offset, and sixteen bytes of data are present in each packet, giving a maximum of 6.67MB/s/proc if there is no congestion and no software overheads. The transpose code in Thinking Machines Corporation's scientific subroutine library, the CMSSL, runs within ten percent of this figure in some cases.

Figure 3 shows the bandwidth achieved for two random and three congestion-free schedules as a function of permutation and bytes sent per processor. The rates in Fig 3 were derived from a C* program running on a sixty four node CM–5. In the processor random permutation, each node sends data to exactly one other node using a series of messages. In the element random permutation, each node sends data to any number of nodes; each message has a random destination.

5 Conclusion

The dream of the router designer is to build a network with guaranteed high bandwidth and low latency and therefore predictable performance. The CM–5 hypertree uses randomization in hardware to reduce all routing problems to random ones. We have shown that, even in the presence of randomization, there are some permutations that can be routed faster than random ones, and, as a

	128 bytes sent/node	1280 bytes sent/node	12800 bytes sent/node
processor random	0.44	1.73	2.45
element random	1.44	3.02	3.06
self XOR 1	1.13	3.28	3.68
self XOR 4	1.12	3.29	3.68
self XOR 16	1.12	3.30	3.68

Fig. 3. Congested and Non-Congested Bandwidth MB/s/node on a CM–5

result, we can quickly route a class of important permutations including all-to-all personalized communication, hypercube dimension-exchange, block transfer, and others.

We have left a few lose ends. We have not extended our proofs to the actual CM-5 hypertree, which loses overall bandwidth at higher levels. We have not found the complete class of congestion-free permutations. We have also been a bit sloppy in exactly what kind of randomization happens on upward paths.

While we dream of efficiency and predictability, our experience found that there has been no substitute for cleverness. Of course, the next generation of routers hope to provide efficiency and justice for all without the need to be tricky.

References

1. T.H. Cormen. Fast permuting on disk arrays. In *Brown/MIT VLSI Conference* (1992)
2. W.J. Dally. Virtual-channel flow control. *IEEE Transactions on Parallel and Distributed Systems* (1992)
3. A. Edelman, S. Heller, and S.L. Johnsson. Index transformation algorithms in a linear algebra framework. Technical report, Thinking Machines Corporation (1992)
4. S. Heller. Reducing dynamic congestion in networks. Unpublished (1993)
5. S.L. Johnsson and C.T. Ho. Optimum broadcasting and personalized communication in hypercubes. *IEEE Transactions on Computers* (1989)
6. C.E. Leiserson. Fat-trees: Universal networks for hardware-efficient supercomputing. In *IEEE Transactions on Computers* (1985)
7. C.E. Leiserson, Z.S. Abuhamdeh, D.C. Douglas, C.R. Feynman, M.N. Ganmukhi, J.V. Hill, W.D. Hillis, B.C. Kuszmaul, M.A. St. Pierre, D.S. Wells, M.C. Wong, S.W. Yang, and R. Zak. The Network Architecture of the Connection Machine CM–5. In *Symposium on Parallel Algorithms and Architectures* (1992)

ROMM Routing: A Class of Efficient Minimal Routing Algorithms

Ted Nesson[1] and Lennart Johnsson[1,2]

[1] Harvard University, Cambridge, MA 02138, USA
[2] Thinking Machines Corporation, 245 First Street, Cambridge, MA 02142, USA

Abstract. ROMM is a class of Randomized, Oblivious, Multi–phase, Minimal routing algorithms. Our conjecture is that ROMM routing offers a potential for improved performance compared to fully randomized algorithms under both light and heavy loads. Our conjecture is also that ROMM routing offers close to best case performance for many common permutations. These conjectures are supported by extensive simulations of binary cube networks for a number of routing patterns. We show that $k \times n$ buffers per node suffice to make k–phase ROMM routing free from deadlock and livelock on n–dimensional binary cubes.

1 Introduction

Efficient data motion has been critical in high performance computing as long as computers have been in existence. Parallel computers use a sparse interconnection network between processing nodes with local memories. Minimizing the potential for high congestion of communication links is an important goal in the design of routing algorithms and networks. Moreover, the packaging technology introduces constraints on the data motion bandwidth at module boundaries, such as chips and boards.

These constraints suggest that preserving locality of reference with careful data allocation and minimizing network load by using minimal algorithms are desirable objectives. However, minimality in routing and preservation of locality of reference in data mapping are no guarantees for a minimal routing time, particularly under heavy load. In fact, non–minimal routing algorithms and data allocations which do not preserve locality of reference may utilize more of the available network bandwidth and decrease the congestion of communication links. Here we report on a class of minimal algorithms designed to keep the risk of severe congestion low for arbitrary routing patterns, yet to behave like optimal algorithms for some important regular patterns on binary cubes.

We introduce ROMM, a class of Randomized, Oblivious, Multi–phase, Minimal routing algorithms. Though the technique is general, the results here are limited to ROMM routing on binary cube networks. We study the performance of ROMM algorithms for light and heavy network loads. Under light loads, path lengths, and possibly link congestion, may be important factors. Under heavy loads, bandwidth utilization and link congestion may be the dominant factors.

2 Related Work

There are three common approaches to the message routing problem:

1. *Oblivious* – The path taken by a message depends only on the source and destination of the message. The path is *not* influenced by other messages.
2. *Adaptive* – The path taken by a message is influenced by other messages, usually in an attempt to minimize the total routing time.
3. *Customized* – Message routing is based on global knowledge of the problem.

Routing algorithms are also *randomized* or *deterministic*. In a randomized algorithm the path selection, the scheduling of messages, or both, use randomization. In a deterministic algorithm, the paths and schedules are determined without randomization.

The Intel Paragon, CalTech Mosaic, MIT J–Machine, Cray T3D, and CMU iWarp all use deterministic, oblivious routing. Such routing is relatively easy to implement and usually performs well, though performance may decay rapidly under heavy load. Also, these algorithms have poor worst–case behavior[3]. For any N–node, degree d network, there exist permutations for which any deterministic, oblivious routing strategy requires time $\Omega(\sqrt{N}/d)$ [13].

Valiant and Brebner proposed two phase randomized routing in which a random node is used as an intermediate destination [33, 32]. The algorithm can route *any* permutation on the n–dimensional binary cube in $O(n)$ steps with high probability. Tsantilas showed that the constant factor is approximately two [31]. The disadvantages of the algorithm are that all data locality is lost and buffers of size $O(n)$ are required in each node. Variants which use fixed size buffers have been proposed [19, 31]. In the Connection Machine CM–5 [29], randomization is employed in the first routing phase in the fat–tree network [18].

An improvement of the routing time by approximately a factor of two can be achieved by randomizing the allocation of the address space, as suggested by Ranade et al. [24, 25]. This approach is being implemented by Abolhassan et al. [1]. Fixed size buffers suffice, but data locality is still lost. Randomized allocation is an option for some operations on Connection Machine systems [30].

Adaptive routers which do not employ randomization have been proposed by Ngai and Seitz [21], G. Pifarre et al. [23], and Dally and Aoki [4], among others. A survey of adaptive routing for binary cubes is provided in [6]. Adaptive routing is used on the Connection Machine CM–1, CM–2, and CM–200 [7]. However, questions about the effectiveness of adaptive routing have been raised [22].

The Zenith [15] and Chaos [16] routers are randomized, adaptive routers. They use the links between source and destination in a random order, avoiding loss of locality. The Zenith router is minimal; the Chaos router is non–minimal. A prototype of the Chaos router has been implemented [2].

Customized algorithms exist for a variety of permutations on binary cubes, such as matrix transposition and bit–reversal [12], binary–to–Gray code conver-

---

[3] For example, bit–transpose and bit–reversal exhibit worst–case behavior on the binary cube

sion [9], bit–complement [26] and shift operations on arrays [10]. Some of these optimal algorithms are available on Connection Machine systems [30].

The outline of rest of this paper is as follows. Section 3 provides some basic definitions. Section 4 presents ROMM routing. Section 5 describes our test criteria and presents simulation results. Section 6 provides several analytical results. Our results show that ROMM routing, for some representative permutations, performs better than fully randomized routing and as well as, or not much worse than, best case routing. For the selected problems, non–minimality and adaptivity are not required for good routing performance.

3 Definitions

In this paper, we focus on binary cube networks. An extensive discussion of the binary cube and related networks can be found in [17].

Definition 1 (Binary Cube). The n-*dimensional binary cube*, C_n, has $N = 2^n$ nodes of degree n and $n2^{n-1}$ bidirectional links. Nodes are labeled with the n–bit binary numbers $0, 1, \ldots, 2^{n-1}$. Nodes are linked in the ith dimension if their labels differ in bit i only. For example, a link in dimension i connects nodes $X = x_{n-1}x_{n-2}\ldots x_i \ldots x_1 x_0$ and $X' = x_{n-1}x_{n-2}\ldots \overline{x}_i \ldots x_1 x_0$, where $\overline{x}_i$ denotes the complement of x_i. For ease of notation, let $\text{BIT}(X, i) \stackrel{\text{def}}{=} x_i$.

The binary cube C_n has a number of desirable features. The degree, though not fixed, is only $n = \log_2 N$. The diameter is n, and the average distance between two random nodes is $n/2$. The bisection width is $2^{n-1} = N/2$.

Definition 2 (Hamming Distance). Given two nodes in C_n, the *hamming distance* between the nodes is the number of bits in which the nodes' labels differ. It is also the shortest distance (in links) between the nodes.

Definition 3 (Routing Algorithm). A *Routing Algorithm* provides rules for transporting messages from source to destination through the network. It may be *oblivious*, *adaptive*, or *customized*, as well as *deterministic* or *randomized*. A routing algorithm is *minimal* if all messages use shortest paths. It is *optimal* if it finishes in time equal to the lower bound for any algorithm.

Definition 4 (Routing Set $\mathcal{D}$). We define the routing set to be the set of all dimensions that must be routed for all messages in some set M:

$$\mathcal{D} = \bigcup_{m \in M} \{i : \text{BIT}(\text{source}(m), i) \neq \text{BIT}(\text{dest}(m), i)\}$$

Definition 5 (Virtual Channels). A virtual channel consists of a communications link between adjacent nodes together with an input and output buffer. Virtual channels may share physical communications links, but the buffers are private. Virtual channels can be used to make routing deadlock–free [5].

4 ROMM Routing

ROMM algorithms route each message from source to destination in k phases, $k \leq n$. During each phase, a subset of the dimensions in the message's routing set are traversed. The dimensions traversed in each phase are determined by randomly selecting, for each message, $k-1$ intermediate nodes $R_1, R_2, \ldots, R_{k-1}$, on some minimal path between the source and destination[4]. For the binary cube, the number of links traversed in the ith phase is simply the Hamming distance from R_{i-1} to R_i. Within each phase, the e–CUBE algorithm [27] is used for routing. e–CUBE, or *dimension order* routing, is a minimal algorithm which traverses the dimensions in a message's routing set in descending order[5]. Figure 1 shows an example of ROMM routing for $k = 4$. We denote the ROMM algorithm with k phases as k–PHASE.

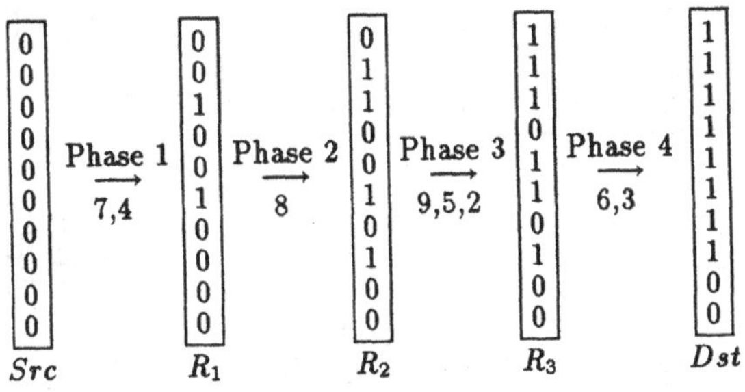

Fig. 1. Using ROMM with $k = 4$ to route from 0000000000 to 1111111100 in C_{10}.

Minimality ensures that the bandwidth demand on the network is minimized given the data distribution. As k increases, more randomization becomes possible. This results in more path choices for a message, reducing the likelihood of congestion for many, but not all permutations, as we will see in our simulations.

e–CUBE is provably deadlock–free and livelock–free on C_n. We can obtain deadlock and livelock freedom for k–PHASE ROMM algorithms by employing k virtual channels per physical link, as proven below. These properties hold for *wormhole* [5], *virtual cut-through* [14], and *store-and-forward* [28] routing.

Theorem 1. *k virtual channels per physical link are necessary and sufficient to ensure deadlock and livelock freedom for k-PHASE ROMM routing on binary cubes.*

Proof. We assume no barrier synchronization between phases. We first show that k virtual channels are sufficient. Label the bth buffer of the dth dimension at the ith node by concatenating the binary values of b, d, and i, where messages in the pth phase use buffer $b = k - p - 1$. When a message moves without changing phases, b is unchanged and d decreases (because e–CUBE is used).

---

[4] We will use R_0 and R_k as shorthand for the source and destination nodes.

[5] We choose to use descending order; ascending order is equally valid.

When a message changes phases, b decreases. In either case, the buffer label decreases. Hence, there are no cyclic buffer dependencies, ensuring deadlock freedom [5]. Because all paths are minimal, every link traversal makes progress, so the algorithm is also livelock–free.

The k virtual channels per physical link are also necessary to ensure deadlock freedom, assuming all physical links have the same number of virtual channels. If fewer than k virtual channels are used, then at least two phases must share the same virtual channel, and deadlocked configurations can be constructed. ☐

An example of the buffer arrangement for 2–PHASE is shown in Figure 2. We will now look at some other factors which can affect performance.

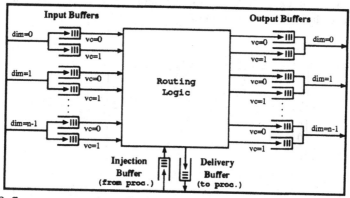

Fig. 2. Buffer arrangement for 2–PHASE, with 2 virtual channels per physical link. The labels *dim* and *vc* indicate the dimension and virtual channel numbers.

4.1 Choosing the Intermediate Destinations

Typically, we expect congestion to decrease as k increases (at the cost of additional virtual channels), but this may depend on the problem and the method of selecting the R_i's. We have studied three ways of selecting the R_i's:

1. **Even Splitting** (*split_even*): The R_i's are selected such that the same number of dimensions (within one) are routed in each phase.
2. **Recursively Splitting the Remaining Path** (*split_rem*): R_i is picked randomly on a minimal path from R_{i-1} to R_k, the final destination.
3. **Recursively Splitting the Longest Path** (*split_long*): R_i is picked by randomly splitting the longest existing path, based on $R_0, R_1, \ldots, R_{i-1}$. This differs from *split_rem*, which was restricted to the remaining path.

Using *split_even* for the example in Figure 1, the dimensions routed in each phase might be, for example, {7,4}, {8,5}, {9,2}, and {6,3}. Using *split_rem*, one would expect something like {9,7,4,2}, {8,5}, {6}, and {3}. An analysis of each of the methods provides the following theorems (proofs can be found in [20]):

Theorem 2. *For a* k-PHASE *ROMM algorithm using* split_even, *the number of paths available to a message traveling distance* d *is* $\frac{d!}{((\frac{d}{k})!)^k}$.

Theorem 3. *For a* k-PHASE *ROMM algorithm using* split_rem, *the expected number of paths available to a message traveling distance* d *is*

$$\frac{d!}{(\frac{d}{2^1})!(\frac{d}{2^2})!(\frac{d}{2^3})!\cdots(\frac{d}{2^{k-2}})!(\frac{d}{2^{k-1}})!(\frac{d}{2^{k-1}})!}.$$

Theorem 4. *For a* k-PHASE *ROMM algorithm using* split_long, *the expected number of paths available to a message traveling distance* d *is* $\frac{d!}{((\frac{d}{k})!)^k}$.

The *split_even* method guarantees the maximum number of paths for a k-PHASE ROMM algorithm. The *expected* behavior of *split_long* is the same as *split_even*, but *split_rem* is substantially worse. Note that phases which traverse no links can occur, but no delays happen since there is no synchronization between phases. Our experiments use *split_even* because its behavior seems best.

4.2 Buffer Depths

For a k-PHASE ROMM algorithm, each physical link has associated with it k incoming and outgoing buffers of depth d_{in} and d_{out}, respectively. For heavy loads, deeper buffers help performance by reducing back pressure. In our packet routing simulations, we set d_{in} to 1 packet and varied the value of d_{out}[6]. Results suggested limited performance gains above 4 packets.

4.3 Other Routing Policies

ROMM algorithms specify the paths messages follow, but do not specify policies for other routing decisions (e.g., scheduling). We will now address some of these issues. In our model, a routing step consists of scheduling and transmission stages. During the scheduling stage, the buffers are examined sequentially, all routing decisions are made, and packets are moved amongst the buffers. Then, during the transmission stage, every outgoing link may transmit up to one packet. We will refer to the n physical links and k virtual channels for k-PHASE on C_n using the notation from Figure 2. Messages in the pth phase use virtual channel $vc = p - 1$. Buffers are FIFO queues unless otherwise stated.

Incoming/Outgoing Link Management The router examines arriving messages and redirects them to outgoing buffers or the delivery buffer. There are $k \times n$ incoming and outgoing buffers. Figure 3 shows the processing order for incoming buffers (scheduling stage) and outgoing buffers (transmission stage). In the scheduling stage, virtual channels within a dimension are visited in ascending order. This favors messages in earlier phases, but every message is guaranteed service eventually. In the transmission stage, no buffer is favored over any other.

---

[6] Outgoing links at one node are incoming links at another, so it is not necessary to provide buffer depth at both ends.

Incoming Buffer Processing	Outgoing Buffer Processing

Incoming Buffer Processing

for $i = 0$ to $k \times n - 1$ **do**
$\quad i' \leftarrow (i + \textit{offset}) \bmod (k \times n)$;
$\quad dim \leftarrow i' \textbf{ div } k; \quad vc \leftarrow i' \bmod k$;
$\quad$ process buffer IN[dim, vc];

Outgoing Buffer Processing

for $dim = 0$ to $n - 1$ **do**
$\quad$ **for** $vc = 0$ to $k - 1$ **do**
$\quad\quad vc' \leftarrow (vc + \textit{offset}) \bmod k$;
$\quad\quad$ process buffer OUT[dim, vc'];

Fig. 3. Pseudo–code describing the order in which incoming (left) and outgoing (right) buffers are processed. The variable *offset* is incremented after each routing step.

Injection/Delivery Policy Messages in the injection buffer compete with incoming messages for the outgoing buffers. We have studied methods which prioritize existing messages over new ones and vice versa. Simulations have not revealed any obvious differences, so for this paper, our simulations favor the existing messages. When the injection buffer contains multiple messages, we route the first message for which there is space in the desired outgoing buffer[7]. It is possible to inject more than one packet per routing step, but simulations suggest this hurts performance under heavy load. The delivery buffer absorbs all packets which arrive in a routing step. Thus, no delays are incurred during delivery.

Computing the Intermediate Destinations The R_i's can be determined dynamically (i.e., R_{i+1} is determined at node R_i) or precomputed (i.e., the message header holds all the R_i's). *split_even* and *split_rem* may use either approach, but *split_long* must precompute the R_i's. Figure 4 shows message structures and the number of bits required for both approaches. In contrast, e–CUBE requires n bits and Valiant's algorithm requires $2n$ bits. When the R_i's are precomputed, the header can represent a large fraction of the message size. This problem can be reduced by encoding the R_i's and/or removing the R_i from the header once it's reached. Both techniques add routing logic. When the R_i's are determined dynamically, the header is smaller, but more computation is required at phase boundaries. For wormhole or virtual cut–through routing, this expense can be amortized over the number of flits. Our simulations used precomputed R_i's.

Fig. 4. Message structures for k–PHASE ROMM routing using dynamically determined R_i's (left) and precomputed R_i's (right).

5 Performance

The focus of our simulations has been on understanding the merits of ROMM algorithms, as compared to e–CUBE and fully randomized routing, as suggested by Valiant and Brebner [33, 32]. To accomplish this, we considered a representative set of routing problems.

---

[7] As a result, messages in the injection buffer may not be serviced in FIFO order.

5.1 Test Problems

As test cases, we used permutation routing problems which occur frequently in scientific and engineering programming on multiprocessors and have very different routing characteristics. The permutations are described below.

Shift operations on arrays (e.g., CSHIFT in Fortran 90) are used often. Regular grids are subgrids of binary cubes [10, 8, 3], so distance one shifts require one link traversal when Gray code mappings are used. Shifts of distance 2^j $(j > 0)$ require two link traversals. This mapping is ideal for light loads, but for heavy loads, other approaches may be better. In contrast, the ideal embedding for Fast Fourier Transform is a binary code mapping, for light loads. Hence, conversion between the two mappings is an important operation [9]. Bit–complement is an operation that may occur in distributed matrix multiplication [11], as well as when performing vector reversals. Data is routed from node i to node $2^n - i$, the complement of i. Matrix transpose is a problem for which e–CUBE exhibits worst case performance. We also include random permutations, which are representative of the average case behavior over all permutations [17]. Some of these permutations' characteristics are summarized in Table 1. Note that CSHIFT–1 has the lowest average distance, while bit–complement has the highest.

Table 1. Routing characteristics for some common permutations on C_n.

Permutation	Min. Dist.	Max. Dist.	Avg. Dist.
Binary–to–Gray	0	$n - 1$	$\frac{1}{2}(n - 1)$
Bit–Complement	n	n	n
CSHIFT–1	1	1	1
CSHIFT–2^j	2	2	2
Random	0	n	$\frac{1}{2}n$
Transpose	0	n	$\frac{1}{2}n$

5.2 Simulations

Using a high–level simulator for store–and–forward (packet) routing, we collected data for the 256 node binary cube C_8. We used even splitting to determine paths (see Section 4.1). Incoming, outgoing, and injection buffer depths were 1, 4, and 5 packets, respectively. Other policies were implemented as described earlier (see Section 4.3). Times are reported as the number of routing steps. We compared the performance of e–CUBE, VALIANT, 2–PHASE, and 4–PHASE for the test problems.

5.3 Probabilistic Loading

To understand the behavior of the algorithms under increasing loads, we used probabilistic injection. In this model, each node tries to inject a packet with some probability during each step[8]. Hence, the maximum applied load is one

---

[8] For "random", we pick one permutation, π, and route all packets from i to $\pi(i)$.

packet injected per routing step. Although this model may not accurately reflect real network traffic, it is helpful in understanding the performance behavior for different loads. We collected data on the average throughput and average latency for each of the test problems. The results are shown in Figures 5 and 6.

Because of its simplicity, the e-CUBE algorithm is often used in routers. For several of the test cases, e-CUBE has ideal performance (i.e., throughput grows linearly with load, and latency is the maximum Hamming distance). However, for transpose, e-CUBE exhibits lower throughput and higher latency, even at moderate loads. The same problem, albeit less severe, occurs for random permutations. This behavior occurs because e-CUBE provides only one path for a given source and destination (i.e., there is no load balancing). Hence, if e-CUBE causes congestion at an edge, doubling the load will double the congestion. This is most visible in the case of transpose, for which some edges are traversed by $\frac{\sqrt{2^n}}{2}$ packets when injecting only one packet per node.

The Valiant–Brebner algorithm, VALIANT, addresses the load balance issue by routing each packet via a random node, effectively converting one problem into two random ones. Hence, VALIANT has similar behavior for all of the permutations. For loads up to 75%, throughput grows linearly with load. Above 75%, congestion effects appear, and the throughput curve flattens out, dropping off at 100%, except for transpose. For transpose, higher loads have less impact because a substantial number of nodes do not generate packets[9]. Hence, the overall load is lower. However, the main problem with VALIANT is latency. On average, VALIANT paths are n links long, twice the length of "average case" paths. This is particularly noticeable for CSHIFT problems, where the minimal path lengths are very short. However, VALIANT is not without value. It outperforms most of the algorithms on full transpose problems.

2-PHASE and 4-PHASE provide both minimality and randomness, with 4-PHASE offering more randomization. For problems other than transpose, ROMM algorithms exhibit behavior comparable to e-CUBE, for loads up to 50%. For bit-complement problems, throughput flattens out and latency increases above 50% load, because any randomness perturbs the perfectly pipelined behavior of e-CUBE. However, the degradation is less significant when the operation is limited to half of the bits. Also, for bit–complement on half of the bits, the advantages of minimal algorithms over VALIANT are more pronounced. For binary–to–Gray and CSHIFT problems, 2-PHASE and 4-PHASE exhibit performance either equal to or close to e-CUBE for all but the highest loads. However, ROMM algorithms have a real advantage for problems like transpose and random. For transpose on all bits, both 2-PHASE and 4-PHASE outperform e-CUBE significantly. Although VALIANT, which does well on this problem, has slightly better throughput than 4-PHASE, it usually has higher latency. For transpose on half of the bits, the ROMM algorithms are better, because VALIANT's non-minimal paths degrade performance when routing is localized. For random problems, we observe behavior similar to transpose, but to a lesser degree. In general, 4-PHASE outperforms 2-PHASE because it offers more randomization.

---

[9] For matrix transpose, $\sqrt{N}$ nodes are on the diagonal and generate no packets.

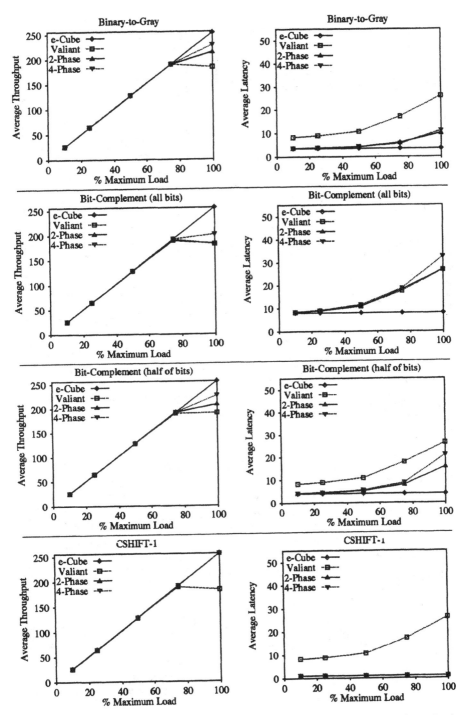

Fig. 5. Graphs of average throughput (packets delivered per routing step) vs. load and average latency (routing steps) vs. load for Binary-to-Gray, Bit–Complement (all bits), Bit–Complement (half of bits), and CSHIFT–1 permutations.

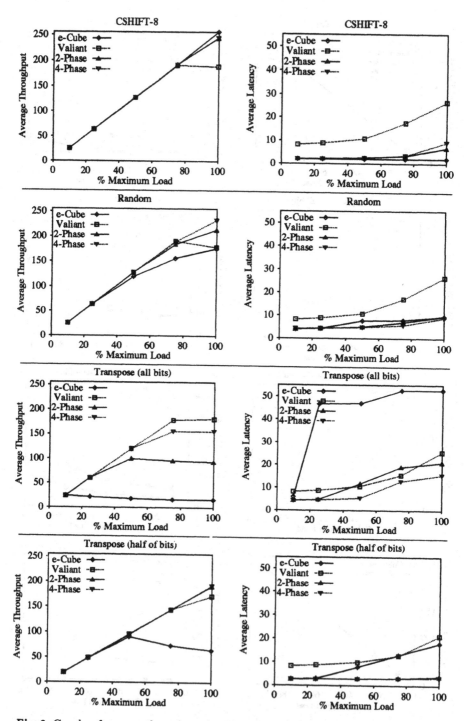

Fig. 6. Graphs of average throughput (packets delivered per routing step) vs. load and average latency (routing steps) vs. load for CSHIFT–8, Random, Transpose (all bits), and Transpose (half of bits) permutations.

5.4 Heavy Loading

In many parallel programs, computation and communication phases are separated. During communication phases, large blocks of data are sent to specific locations. To model this, we injected 500 messages at each node and waited for delivery of all messages. Note that until a node has sent its messages, it tries to inject each step. Table 2 shows the time required for the test cases.

Table 2. Times to route 500 messages for different problems and algorithms.

Permutation	Total Time (Routing Steps)			
	e-CUBE	VALIANT	2-PHASE	4-PHASE
Binary-to-Gray	506	810	1009	825
Bit-Complement (all bits)	507	823	785	814
Bit-Complement (half of bits)	503	827	725	680
CSHIFT-1	500	852	500	500
CSHIFT-8	501	846	572	564
Random	1637	846	1080	827
Transpose (all bits)	> 4000	792	1591	961
Transpose (half of bits)	1072	670	525	506

As discussed earlier, e-CUBE runs without congestion for binary-to-Gray, bit-complement, and CSHIFT problems. In these cases, randomization can perturb the well pipelined behavior of e-CUBE, introducing congestion. VALIANT is usually worse, since non-minimality does not help the problem. The ROMM algorithms have the advantage of minimality, which is useful, except for full bit-complement. However, randomization still introduces congestion, though typically not as badly as VALIANT. For CSHIFT-1, ROMM algorithms are congestion-free, and for CSHIFT-8, some congestion occurs.

For transpose and random problems, e-CUBE performs less well. As mentioned in Section 5.3, any edge congestion inherent in the problem for load one is multiplied by 500. In particular, transpose performance is extremely poor. VALIANT, 2-PHASE, and 4-PHASE all do much better. For transpose on half of the bits, the ROMM algorithms are better than VALIANT due to minimality. In most cases, the ROMM algorithms have an advantage over VALIANT and are competitive with e-CUBE. This is especially noticeable for 4-PHASE.

6 Analysis

In our work, a fundamental goal is to understand how much randomness is required to reduce link congestion to acceptable levels. We now present some results which provide more insight into the observed behavior of ROMM algorithms.

Table 3 shows the expected maximum edge load for transpose problems, using e-CUBE and k-PHASE[10]. The data suggest that $k \geq 3$ may be sufficient to reduce

---
[10] The values in the table were computed by a C program.

congestion to acceptable levels. Table 4 provides some bandwidth–based lower bounds on routing time for n–PHASE. These bounds are obtained by dividing the bandwidth required (see Table 1) by the bandwidth available to n–PHASE (The analyses can be found in [20]). For e–CUBE, this bound is always L. In some cases, the n–PHASE bound is better, indicating more usable bandwidth.

Table 3. Expected maximum edge loads for transpose, using e–CUBE and k–PHASE.

		Expected Maximum Link Load						
n	e–CUBE	k–PHASE ROMM						
		$k=2$	$k=3$	$k=4$	$k=5$	$k=6$	$k=7$	$k=8$
2	1.00	0.50						
4	2.00	0.83	0.83	0.67				
6	4.00	1.37	1.17	0.97	0.90	0.90		
8	8.00	2.21	1.50	1.40	1.26	1.26	1.23	1.23
10	16.00	3.55	2.01	2.01	1.80	—	—	—

Table 4. Lower bounds for routing L packets per node on C_n, using n–PHASE.

Routing Problem	Mileage Required	Usable Bandwidth	Lower Bound
Binary–to–Gray	$\frac{(n-1)N}{2}\cdot L$	$1.36\cdot\frac{(n-1)N}{2}$	$\frac{L}{1.36}$
Bit–Complement	$nN\cdot L$	nN	L
CSHIFT–1	$N\cdot L$	N	L
CSHIFT–2^j	$2N\cdot L$	$2N$	L
Random	$\frac{nN}{2}\cdot L$	$\sim nN$	$\sim\frac{L}{2}$
Transpose	$\frac{nN}{2}\cdot L$	nN	$\frac{L}{2}$

7 Future Work

The simulation results reported here are for packet routing only. Virtual cut–through and wormhole routing will be examined. We also plan comparisons with adaptive methods. Intermediate node selection and a number of routing policies affect performance. We plan to investigate these further through experimentation and by developing quantitative models to describe the implementation cost and performance behavior of ROMM. Finally, we plan to study ROMM on other networks, such as meshes and tori.

8 Conclusions

We have presented a class of randomized, oblivious, multi–phase, minimal routing algorithms, ROMM, which combines the advantages of fully randomized routing and deterministic, minimal routing. ROMM algorithms exhibit close to optimal performance under both light and heavy loads. Freedom from deadlock and livelock is achievable using $k \times n$ buffers per node for k–PHASE ROMM routing on the n–dimensional binary cube. The simplicity and efficiency of ROMM routing makes it a viable alternative to deterministic and adaptive methods.

9 Acknowledgements

We would like to acknowledge the support of the National Center for Supercomputing Applications, the Navy Research Laboratory, Washington D.C., the Massachusetts Institute of Technology, and the Northeast Parallel Applications Center for providing access to Connection Machine systems. We would also like to acknowledge the support of the Office of Naval Research through grant N00014-93-1-0192 and the Air Force Office of Scientific Research through grant F49620-93-1-0480.

References

1. F. Abolhassan, R. Drefenstedt, J. Keller, W. Paul, and D. Scheerer. On the Physical Design of PRAMs. *Computer Journal*, 36(8):756–762, December 1993.
2. K. Bolding et al. The Chaos Router Chip: Design and Implementation of an Adaptive Router. In *Proceedings of VLSI '93*, September 1993.
3. M.Y. Chan. Embedding of grids into optimal hypercubes. *SIAM J. Computing*, 20(5):834–864, 1991.
4. W. Dally and H. Aoki. Deadlock-Free Adaptive Routing in Multicomputer Networks Using Virtual Channels. *IEEE Trans. on Parallel and Distributed Systems*, 4(4):466–475, April 1993.
5. W. Dally and C. Seitz. Deadlock-Free Message Routing in Multiprocessor Interconnection Networks. *IEEE Trans. on Computers*, C-36(5):547–553, May 1987.
6. P. Gaughan and S. Yalamanchili. Adaptive Routing Protocols for Hypercube Interconnection Networks. *COMPUTER*, 26(5):12–23, May 1993.
7. W. Daniel Hillis. *The Connection Machine*. MIT Press, Cambridge, MA, 1985.
8. Ching-Tien Ho and S. Lennart Johnsson. Embedding meshes in Boolean cubes by graph decomposition. *J. of Parallel and Distributed Computing*, 8(4):325–339, April 1990.
9. Ching-Tien Ho, M.T. Raghunath, and S. Lennart Johnsson. An efficient algorithm for Gray-to-binary permutation on hypercubes. *Journal of Parallel and Distributed Computing*, 20(1):114–120, 1994.
10. S. Lennart Johnsson. Communication efficient basic linear algebra computations on hypercube architectures. *J. Parallel Distributed Computing*, 4(2):133–172, April 1987.
11. S. Lennart Johnsson. Minimizing the communication time for matrix multiplication on multiprocessors. *Parallel Computing*, 19(11):1235–1257, 1993.
12. S. Lennart Johnsson and Ching-Tien Ho. Matrix transposition on Boolean n-cube configured ensemble architectures. *SIAM J. Matrix Anal. Appl.*, 9(3):419–454, July 1988.
13. C. Kaklamanis, D. Krizanc, and T. Tsantilas. Tight Bounds for Oblivious Routing in the Hypercube. In *Proc. of the 2nd Annual ACM Symp. on Parallel Algorithms and Architectures*, pages 31–36. ACM Press, July 1990.

14. P. Kermani and L. Kleinrock. Virtual Cut–Through: A New Computer Communication Switching Technique. *Computer Networks*, 3:267–286, 1979.

15. S. Konstantinidou. Adaptive, Minimal Routing in Hypercubes. Technical Report TR-89-11-01, Computer Science Dept., Univ. of Washington, Seattle, WA, 1989.

16. S. Konstantinidou and L. Snyder. The Chaos Router: A Practical Application of Randomization in Network Routing. In *Proc. of the 2nd Annual ACM Symp. on Parallel Algorithms and Architectures*, pages 21–30. ACM Press, July 1990.

17. T. Leighton. *Parallel Algorithms and Architectures: Arrays, Trees, and Hypercubes*. Morgan Kaufmann, San Mateo, California, 1992.

18. C. Leiserson et al. The Network Architecture of the Connection Machine CM-5. In *Proc. of the 4th Annual ACM Symp. on Parallel Algorithms and Architectures*, pages 272–285. ACM Press, July 1992.

19. Y.-D. Lyuu. *An Information Dispersal Approach to Issues in Parallel Processing*. PhD thesis, Harvard University, 1990.

20. T. Nesson and L. Johnsson. ROMM: Randomized, Oblivious, Multi–Phase, Minimal Routing. Unpublished Manuscript, Harvard University, December 1993.

21. J. Ngai and C. Seitz. A Framework for Adaptive Routing in Multicomputer Networks. In *Proc. of the 1st Annual ACM Symp. on Parallel Algorithms and Architectures*, pages 1–9. ACM Press, June 1989.

22. M. Pertel. A Critique of Adaptive Routing. Technical Report CS-TR-92-06, Dept. of Computer Science, California Institute of Technology, Pasadena, CA, 1992.

23. G. Pifarré, L. Gravano, S. Felperin, and J. Sanz. Fully-Adaptive Minimal Deadlock-Free Packet Routing in Hypercubes, Meshes, and Other Networks. In *Proc. of the 3rd Annual ACM Symp. on Parallel Algorithms and Architectures*, pages 278–290. ACM Press, July 1991.

24. Abhiram Ranade. How to emulate shared memory. In *Proceedings of the 28th Annual Symposium on the Foundations of Computer Science*, pages 185–194. IEEE Computer Society, October 1987.

25. Abhiram G. Ranade, Sandeep N. Bhatt, and S. Lennart Johnsson. The Fluent abstract machine. In *Advanced Research in VLSI, Proceedings of the fifth MIT VLSI Conference*, pages 71–93. MIT Press, 1988.

26. Quentin F. Stout and Bruce Wagar. Passing messages in link-bound hypercubes. In Michael T. Heath, editor, *Hypercube Multiprocessors 1987*. Society for Industrial and Applied Mathematics, Philadelphia, PA, 1987.

27. H. Sullivan and T. Brashkow. A Large Scale Homogeneous Machine. In *Proc. of the 4th International Symp. on Computer Arch.*, pages 105–124. IEEE, 1977.

28. A. Tannenbaum. *Computer Networks*. Prentice Hall, Englewood Cliffs, New Jersey, second edition, 1989.

29. Thinking Machines Corp. *CM-5 Technical Summary*, 1991.

30. Thinking Machines Corp. *CMSSL for CM Fortran, Version 3.0*, 1992.

31. A. Tsantilas. A Refined Analysis of the Valiant-Brebner Algorithm. Technical Report TR-22-89, Center for Research in Computing Technology, Harvard University, Cambridge, MA, 1989.

32. L. Valiant. A Scheme for Fast Parallel Communication. *SIAM Journal on Computing*, 11(2):350–361, May 1982.

33. L. Valiant and G. Brebner. Universal Schemes for Parallel Communication. In *Proc. of the 13th Annual ACM Symp. on the Theory of Computing*, pages 263–277. ACM Press, May 1981.

Packaging and Multiplexing of Hierarchical Scalable Expanders

Frederic T. Chong, Eric A. Brewer,
F. Thomson Leighton and Thomas F. Knight, Jr.

MIT Laboratory for Computer Science
MIT Artificial Intelligence Laboratory

545 Technology Square
Cambridge MA 02139
{ftchong,brewer,ftl}@lcs.mit.edu, tk@ai.mit.edu

Abstract. Multistage networks are important in a wide variety of applications. Expander-based networks, such as multibutterflies, are a tremendous improvement over traditional butterflies in both fault and congestion tolerance. However, multibutterflies cost at least twice as much in chips and wiring as butterflies. It is also impossible to build large multibutterflies due to their wiring complexity.

We show that we can build an expander-based network that has comparable cost to a butterfly with the same number of endpoints, yet has substantially better fault and congestion performance. Specifically, we introduce a hierarchical construction that dramatically reduces wiring complexity and makes large expanders buildable. We are able to exploit the hierarchical structure to find large numbers of logical wires to multiplex over a smaller number of physical wires. Since many of the wires in an expander-based network are used to provide alternate paths, not useful bandwidth, substantial multiplexing can be done without significantly degrading performance. We present simulation results to support our conclusions. In comparing a butterfly with the comparable 2-to-1 multiplexed metabutterfly, we found that the metabutterfly performed better by nearly a factor of two on random traffic and greater than a factor of five on worst-case traffic.

1 Introduction

Butterflies and related regular, multistage interconnection networks have been broadly used in many applications, but exhibit extremely poor performance un-

Acknowledgments: This work was supported in part by National Science Foundation grant CCR-8716884; by ARPA contracts N00014-91-J-1698 and N00014-92-J-1799; by Air Force Contract AFOSR F49620-92-J0125; by NSF Experimental Systems grant MIP-9012773; by a NSF Presidential Young Investigator Award; by an Office of Naval Research Graduate Fellowship; by an equipment grant from Digital Equipment Corporation; and by grants from AT&T, LSI Logic and IBM.

der faults, congestion, and worst-case permutations. Recent work has shown that randomly wired expander-based networks, such as multibutterflies, are a substantial improvement. They possess tremendous fault tolerance and very low congestion even under high loads. Unfortunately, the wiring complexity of such networks becomes physically problematic as they become large. Further, multi-butterflies use at least twice as many wires and chips as butterflies for the same number of endpoints.

This work addresses the cost and complexity of expander-based networks. We present a sequence of multistage networks, shown in Figure 1, that trans-forms the traditional butterfly network into a new network, called a *multiplexed metabutterfly*, that requires similar hardware but provides substantially better performance and fault tolerance. The following sections cover this sequence in detail, but it is useful to first walk through it at a high level:

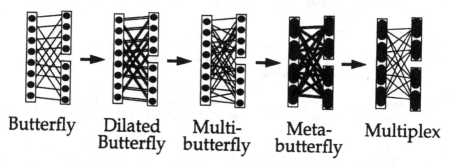

Butterfly   Dilated Butterfly   Multi-butterfly   Meta-butterfly   Multiplex

Fig. 1. Our sequence of transformations from the butterfly to the multiplexed metabutterfly

---

Butterfly: Simple and easy to build, but provides no fault tolerance and suffers from internal congestion.

Dilated Butterfly: Doubles each wire of the butterfly to achieve some fault and congestion tolerance, but the extra hardware could be used much more effectively.

Multibutterfly: Same number of wires as the dilated butterfly, but provides tremendous fault and congestion tolerance through the use of random wiring. It has strong theoretical underpinnings for its performance and fault toler-ance. Although the advantages are probably worth the extra hardware for large sytems, the random wiring makes large multibutterflies impractical because of the wiring complexity. This represents the state of multistage networks prior to our work.

Metabutterfly: Uses the same amount of hardware as the multibutterfly, but constrains the randomness of the wiring to ensure that large versions are practical. Despite the limited randomness, we proved that all the theoretical properties hold [BCL94]. In this paper we present evidence that the fault and congestion tolerance is identical in practice as well. The metabutterfly thus provides all of the benefits of the multibutterfly without the wiring complexity, thus allowing very large networks.

Multiplexed Metabutterfly: Although the metabutterfly provides superior performance and far superior fault tolerance over the traditional butterfly, it also uses twice as many wires. However, these wires really only provide alternate paths rather than additional bandwidth. Thus, we can use multiplexing to reduce the number of wires substantially without proportionally reducing performance. It is important to note that the multiplexing option was enabled by the limited randomness, which allows wires to be grouped together into cables. These cables can then be multiplexed onto thinner cables or onto optical fiber. The goal of the multiplexed metabutterfly is the performance and fault tolerance of the metabutterfly with hardware requirements close to those of the traditional butterfly. We show through simulation that this goal is achievable.

2 Butterflies

In this context, it is useful to view the traditional butterfly as the simplest form of a splitter network, as shown in Figure 2. A *splitter network* is composed of multiple stages of routers. It is helpful to view routing a message through a splitter network as a sorting function through equivalence classes of fewer and fewer routers. Specifically, for the ith stage there are r^i equivalence classes, each with r^{s-i} routers, where r is the *radix* of the routers (the number of directions among which the router selects) and s is the number of stages in the network. Each equivalence class is connected to r equivalence classes in the next stage. An individual splitter consists of an equivalence class and its r associated equivalence classes in the next stage.

The dilated butterfly, shown in Figure 3, is also a splitter network. The only difference from the traditional butterfly is that each wire has been split into two, so that one can fail or be busy without affecting the other. Looking at it as a splitter network, each splitter now has two wires to the equivalence classes in each of the r directions.

3 Multibutterflies

A multibutterfly also has two wires in each direction, but they are not constrained by the butterfly wiring pattern. The only constraint is the equivalence classes: each of the r pairs of wires must go to a distinct equivalence class, but they can go to any node in their class. For the multibutterfly, these nodes are selected randomly from their equivalence class. The key reason for random selection is that it ensures that the resulting network is an *expander graph* (with

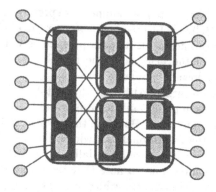

Fig. 2. A butterfly viewed as a splitter network. The butterfly is radix 2 and three splitters are shown outlined in round rectangles.

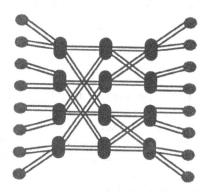

Fig. 3. A dilated butterfly with radix 2 and multiplicity 2.

high probability), which leads to very strong theoretical properties that are also valuable in practice.

A bipartite graph with M inputs and N outputs is an (α, β, M, N)-*expander* if every set of $S \leq \alpha M$ inputs reaches at least βS outputs. For a radix-r splitter network to have expansion, each splitter must achieve expansion in each of the r directions. Figure 4 shows an M-input, radix-2 splitter with expansion. To achieve expansion, a splitter network must have routers with redundant connections in each of its r directions. We refer to this redundancy, d, as the *multiplicity*; so far we have implicitly assumed $d = 2$ as it is the most practical, but higher multiplicity leads to better fault tolerance at a higher hardware cost. Given multiplicity d, the degree of any node is dr.

A multibutterfly is a splitter network in which each splitter is an $(\alpha, \beta, M, \frac{M}{r})$-expander in each of the r directions, where M is the number of inputs of the splitter.

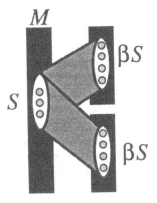

Fig. 4. A splitter with expansion.

Bassalygo and Pinsker [BP74] first studied splitter networks with expansion. Recently, numerous results have been discovered that indicate that multibutterflies are ideally suited for message-routing applications. Among other things, multibutterflies can solve any one-to-one packet routing [Upf89], circuit-switching [ALM90], or non-blocking routing problem [ALM90] in optimal time, even if many of the routers in the network are faulty [LM89]. No other networks are known to be as powerful.

The reason behind the power of multibutterflies is that expansion roughly implies that βk outputs must be blocked or faulty for k inputs to be blocked, and thus it takes β^j faults to block one input j levels back. In contrast, *one* fault in a radix-2 butterfly blocks 2^j inputs j levels back. As a consequence, problems with faults and congestion that destroy the performance of traditional networks can be overcome easily in multibutterflies. (For a survey of the research on multibutterflies see [Pip93] [LM92].)

3.1 Wiring Complexity

Multibutterflies are generally constructed by randomly wiring redundant connections between equivalence classes of each splitter. Although deterministic constructions are known [WZ93], none are known to produce expansion comparable to random wiring.

Unfortunately, random wiring (as well as the known constructions of good expanders) scales poorly in practice. For example, a 4K-endpoint machine with multiplicity $d = 2$ has 8K wires in the first stage, almost all of which would be long cables with distinct logical endpoints. For comparison, a fat-tree [Lei85] might have a similar number of cables for the root node, but there are few logical endpoints, so huge groups of wires can be routed together. The groups connect to many boards, but the boards are located together and the connection of cables to boards is arbitrary and thus low labor. In the multibutterfly, the cables cannot be grouped and the connection of cables to boards is constrained. The other early stages also suffer from this problem.

At first glance, it appears that this wiring complexity is inherent to both expanders and random wiring. Indeed, given a splitter with M boards of input routers, M boards of output routers, and k routers per board, we can expect each board to be connected to about $\Theta(\min(M, dkr))$ other boards when using random wiring. For typical values of M, d, k, and r, this means that we would need to connect nearly *every* input board to nearly *every* output board in a randomly wired splitter. Clearly, this becomes infeasible as M gets large and thus the randomly wired multibutterfly does not scale well in the practical setting where the network consists of boards of chips. A similar problem arises at the level of cabinets of boards for very large machines.

In what follows, we show how to (randomly) construct a special kind of expander for which there is no explosion in cabling cost. In particular, we show how to build a multibutterfly for which each board is connected to only dr other boards, no matter how large M and k become, thereby achieving full scalability. In effect, there are a few fat cables connected to each board instead of many thin cables. At the same time, the resulting network will still have all the same nice routing properties as a randomly wired multibutterfly. Hence, we will gain wiring scalability without sacrificing performance.

4 Random k-extensions

The wiring complexity of large expanders can be dramatically decreased by constructing them hierarchically. A *hierarchical expander* is an expander constructed from the application of a sequence of *random k-extensions* to an expander.

Given a directed graph $G \equiv (\mathcal{V}, \mathcal{E})$, an integer $k \geq 1$, and a set of permutations of $[1,k]$, $\Pi = \{\pi_e | e \in \mathcal{E}\}$, we define the k-*extension of G induced by Π* to be the graph $G' \equiv (\mathcal{V}', \mathcal{E}')$ where:

$$\mathcal{V}' \equiv \{\langle v, i \rangle \mid v \in \mathcal{V}, \ i \in [1, k]\} \text{ and}$$
$$\mathcal{E}' \equiv \{(\langle u, i \rangle, \langle v, j \rangle) \mid$$
$$(u, v) \in \mathcal{E} \text{ and } \pi_{(u,v)}(i) = j\}$$

We define a *random k-extension of a graph G* to be a k-extension induced by some Π such that each $\pi_e \in \Pi$ is an independently and uniformly chosen random permutation of $[1,k]$. Equivalently, a random k-extension of a graph G can be obtained by selecting randomly and uniformly over all of the $(k!)^{|\mathcal{E}|}$ possible k-extensions of G. Figure 5 shows an example of a random 3-extension.

5 Metabutterflies

We apply random k-extensions to a multibutterfly to build a scalable, hierarchical network, the *metabutterfly*. Each splitter of the metabutterfly is a random

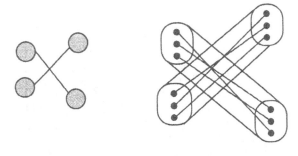

Fig. 5. A random 3-extension (right) of a graph (left).

k-extension of the corresponding splitter of the multibutterfly, with the possible exception of the last few stages. The value of k may differ for each splitter.

For example, a 1024-node metabutterfly can be implemented with a 64-extended 16-node multibutterfly plus 16 64-node multibutterflies for the output metanodes. The total counts of nodes, wires, and stages are each the same as for a 1024-node multibutterfly; the only difference is the wiring pattern. Figure 6 shows a radix-2 64-input metabutterfly that is an 8-extended 8-input multibutterfly. This example has a two-level hierarchy, but deeper hierarchies are possible and actually make sense for very large networks.

5.1 Metabutterfly Theoretical Properties

Brewer, Chong, and Leighton [BCL94] have proven that any (α, β, M, N)-expander with $\alpha M \geq 1$ can be scaled with a random k-extension into an $(\alpha', \beta', kM, kN)$-expander with probability at least $1 - 2e^{-\alpha M}$, where $\alpha' = \frac{\alpha^2}{\beta^2 e^4 + 4\alpha}$ and $\beta' = \beta - 2$. This means that we have a method of scaling expanders with very little change in β, and some degradation in α.

5.2 Metabutterfly Performance

Although the theoretical bounds on α degrade with each level of hierarchy, we now demonstrate empirically that the performance and fault tolerance of metabutterflies is identical to that of multibutterflies. We use the methodology of previous studies [CED92] [CK92] and investigate performance with uniformly distributed router failures within each network.

We compared performance for a 1024-endpoint multibutterfly and for 1024-endpoint metabutterflies with metanode sizes of 8, 16, and 64. The routers had a radix of 4 and a multiplicity of 2. We used a synthetic load based upon shared-memory applications. Figure 7 shows that the performance of all four networks is statistically indistinguishable.

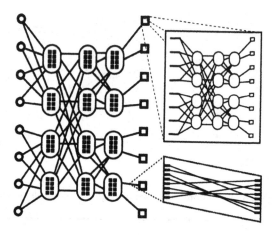

Fig. 6. A radix-2, multiplicity-2, 64-endpoint metabutterfly with metanodes of size 8. Each circle on the left contains 8 inputs, and each oval metanode contains 8 routers. Each router (solid square) is a 4 × 4 switch. Each output metanode (hollow square), shown expanded at the top right, is an 8-input multibutterfly; each channel, shown expanded at the bottom right, contains 8 wires. Typically, the metanodes correspond to boards.

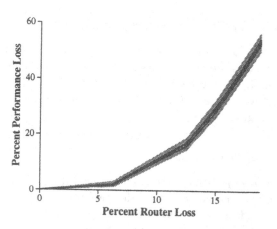

Fig. 7. The four curves represent performance for a 1024-endpoint multibutterfly and 1024-endpoint metabutterflies with metanodes of size 8, 16, and 64. The shaded area represents the aggregate 95 percent confidence interval of the curves.

6 Multiplexing

Now that we have established the attractive theoretical and empirical properties of our construction, we would like to use it to reduce the wiring and chip cost of expander-based networks. We will use multiplexing techniques to reduce the number of wires in the metabutterly to be comparable to the number in a butterfly with the same number of endpoints. However, we will still have d times more cables. This complexity is unavoidable and is the cost of providing the multiplicity that gives our networks their performance and fault tolerance.

From wire utilization studies, we discovered that many of the wires in an expander-based network are only used to provide alternate paths, not raw bandwidth. To reduce wiring cost, we would like to provide alternate paths with logical wires that are multiplexed over a smaller number of physical wires. Recall that we have replaced the many thin cables of the multibutterfly with a small, constant number of fat cables in the metabutterfly.

With large cables, the option of multiplexing becomes both more cost effective and more likely to deliver good performance. For example, optical fiber would provide enough bandwidth to replace very large cables. Note that a packet routing scheme across such fiber would provide little degradation in performance until the load reached bandwidth limits. The number and capacity of fibers can be designed to accommodate expected load rather than peak load. The larger the original cable being multiplexed, the more likely the average load will be significantly lower than the peak load. We can exploit such differences to build more cost-effective networks.

Figure 8 shows the performance of a radix-4 (r), dilation-2 (d), 5-stage, 1024-endpoint metabutterfly with metanodes of size 64 (k) under various multiplexing conditions and using the same benchmark as in Section 5.2. Even though the benchmark loads the network heavily, a large portion of the curve is flat. In other words, many of the physical wires can be eliminated from the metabutterfly without significant performance degradation. For comparison, Figure 8 also shows the performance of a butterfly on this benchmark, which performs almost two times worse than the comparable metabutterfly.

The butterfly is plotted directly over the multiplexed metabutterfly with approximately the same amount of wiring (2-to-1 multiplexing). Note that our multiplexing techniques do not apply in the end stages, since metanodes are of size one. These last two stages have twice as much hardware as the butterfly, but this hardware is necessary for fault and congestion tolerance. Fortunately, these end stages have high physical locality and can be fabricated without expensive wiring, such as on PC boards. We are able to multiplex where it matters the most, in the beginning stages where the wires are long and expensive. Further, the effect of the end stages on network cost diminishes as we build larger networks.

Figure 9 shows the performance of the same multibutterfly (metanodes of size 64) under multiplexing and the same benchmark except that destinations are chosen by bit-inverse rather than randomly. Regular networks such as the butterfly perform very poorly on such permutations, but randomized networks perform much better. Once again, we see little performance degradation up to

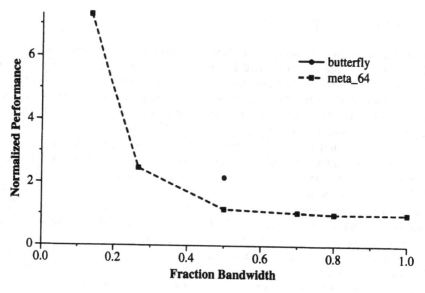

Fig. 8. Multiplexed performance with random destinations. The performance of a full butterfly plotted above the comparable 2-to-1 multiplexed metabutterfly.

a high degree of multiplexing. For comparision, we can see that the butterfly performs poorly on this permutation, over five times worse than the comparable metabutterfly.

Note that the bit-inverse benchmark degrades more severely with multiplexing than the random benchmark. This is because all the messages in any given input metanode are destined for only one of r equivalence classes of destinations (for a 1024-endpoint, radix-4 network, the r equivalence classes are: 0-255, 256-511, 512-767, and 768-1023). If a metanode in the first stage of routers is not connected to metanodes that together have messages to all r equivalence classes, then all of the routers in that first-stage metanode will have underutilized channels in the directions leading to the equivalence classes with no messages. With our random metachannel wiring between input metanodes and first-stage metanodes, about 10 percent of our channels are underutilized. We can fix this problem for bit-inverse by guaranteeing that each first-stage metanode reaches an equal number of input metanodes from each of the r equivalence classes. The bad cases would still exist, but would be randomized to permutations less likely to be used. We are also investigating more advanced resource arbitration policies that will reduce the performance degradation in these bad cases.

In summary, the 2-to-1 multiplexed metabutterfly outperforms the comparable butterfly, but has a factor of d higher cabling complexity. Recall, however, this higher complexity also results in extremely high fault tolerance. The butterfly has no fault tolerance.

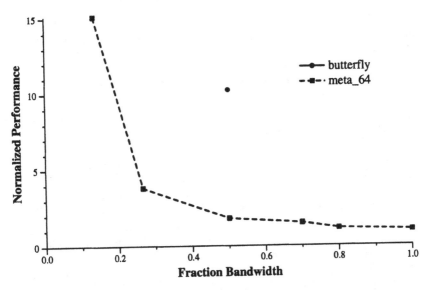

Fig. 9. Multiplexed performance with bit-inverse destinations. The performance of a full butterfly plotted above the comparable 2-to-1 multiplexed metabutterfly.

6.1 Randomized Multiplexing

Observe that, since the logical wires within each metachannel cable were assigned via a random permutation, we really do not care to which logical wire a packet belongs. We can perform *randomized multiplexing*, where the message packets across a cable are demultiplexed to random destinations. This results in increased efficiency in terms of bandwidth used on the physical wire or optical fiber. In traditional multiplexing, packets must either be assigned to fixed time slots or have extra headers identifying their destination upon demultiplexing. The use of fixed time slots is inefficient because there may be empty slots. Every destination must have a slot, but not every destination receives a packet at all times. The use of headers is also inefficient because the headers take up bandwidth. With randomized multiplexing, only the actual packets are sent and demultiplexing proceeds by assigning any packet to any free destination.

An important result of randomized multiplexing is that only one type of metabutterfly cable is needed. The randomization is provided by the multiplexing hardware, not the physical cables. Having only one standard type of cable greatly simplifies manufacturing and assembly.

This notion of time-varied multiplexing is similar to the time domain switching used in STS switches in the telephone community. However, the random nature of our logical wire clusters provides novel opportunities for efficient implementation. In fact, randomized multiplexing results in networks with a stronger, more dynamic form of randomness than networks with physical connections.

This dynamic randomness may provide a fairer share of resources in the face of faults or congestion, especially in the early stages of the network where expansion has less effect. Over time, dynamic randomness allows every router on the input side of the cable to reach every router on the output side, effectively providing each input-side router with enormous multiplicity over time. We have yet to quantify the benefits of randomized multiplexing.

7 Multiplexed Implementations

We have now established the tools and motivation to construct expander-based networks comparable in cost to butterflies. In this section, we describe three implementations. All three optimize for average bandwidth as suggested in Section 6. The three differ, however, in cost, fault-tolerance, and latency. The first implementation reduces wiring costs through multiplexing. The second replaces each metanode with a single high-multiplicity switch. The third replaces each metanode with a number of high-multiplicity switches.

First, the obvious implementation, shown in Figure 10 uses a multiplexing chip or chips at the endpoints of every metachannel. Pin limitations would limit the number of routers and channel wires multiplexed by any one chip. This implementation could use either conventional or randomized multiplexing. Latency would depend upon whether an optical or electrical technology was used. The critical nature of the multiplexing chips reduces fault tolerance, as does the reduced number of physical channels. However, this implementation is at least as fault tolerant as the small multibutterflies used to wire the metastructure.

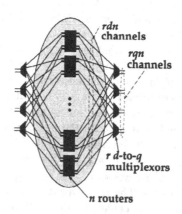

Fig. 10. Multiplexors at metachannel endpoints.

The multiplexed metanode in Figure 10 can be viewed as a single, large radix-r, multiplicity-qn switch. Our original structure switches rdn channels internally, but only rqn channels are visible externally. Such a structure reduces internal collisions, but directly switching the external inputs and outputs with high-multiplicity switches will have even fewer internal collisions. Our next two implementations focus on such direct switching. Note that multiplexing technology will still be required between the network endpoints and the metanodes, as well as between the end stages of the network and the metanodes.

Our second implementation replaces each metanode with a single time-domain ATM switch such as the AN2 [AOST93]. The high-bandwidth, high-switching capabilities of such an ATM switch make them ideal for metanode implementation. Although ATM switches could support randomized multiplexing, such ATMs are actually powerful enough to implement a radix-r, multiplicity-dq switch, where q is the number of physical channels per directions, $q \leq n$, and the metanode to be implemented had radix r, multiplicity d, and size n. Once the functionality of a metanode can be fit in a single switch, a high-multiplicity switch makes more sense than a randomly multiplexed switch. Fault-tolerance is once again comparable to that of the small multibutterflies formed by the metanodes. Latency, however, is high in optical technologies.

The ATM switch represents the extreme case in which a metanode is implemented by a single high-multiplicity switch. In our third implementation, we implement metanodes with several high-multiplicity switches, each simulated by a cascade of routing chips. The goal is to use the same number of chips, each with the same number of pins, as the corresponding portion of the conventional butterfly. A metanode in our first implementation would have n chips each with rdw input and rdw output pins, where the width, w, is the number of bits in a channel. An equivalent portion of a butterfly would have n chips with only rw inputs and rw outputs. Therefore, we have nrw input pins and nrw output pins in total to implement our metanode.

In order have a multiplicity of d, we must reduce the number of routers from n to $\frac{n}{d}$. This gives us dw pins per physical channel. However, each chip can only have rw inputs and rw outputs. Therefore, we must implement each of our radix-r, multiplicity-d, width-w routers with d cascaded chips, each with radix r, multiplicity d, and width $\frac{w}{d}$. Figure 11 compares a cascaded metanode to the equivalent butterfly hardware. The resulting metanode is a radix-r, multiplicity-n router. Since the original metanode had dn channels in each direction, our cascade implementation effectively performs d-to-1 multiplexing.

The cascading of router chips is described in [DeH93]. Basically, a set of d cascaded width-$\frac{w}{d}$ chips work in tandem to simulate a single width-w router. Since pad delays dominate high-performance switches, latency of these cascaded routers should be comparable to those of the original butterfly. Fault tolerance is much better than the butterfly, but can be substantially worse than our other two implementations. For a given chip failure probability P_f, a cascaded metanode remains operable with probability $(1 - P_f)^d$. We still have the fault tolerance of the underlying metanode small multibutterfly, but we have increased our metanode failure probability by a power of d. This is a problem with cascaded routers, but should be manageable at small values of d. Alternatively, we could try to use error-correcting codes, but we would need to use an extra $\mathcal{O}(\log n)$

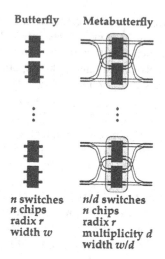

Fig. 11. Implementing a metanode (right) with a cascaded routers and hardware equivalent to the butterfly (left).

chips in each *n*-chip cascade to tolerate a single chip failure.

In summary, we have described methods to build multiplexed metabutterflies that are comparable in cost to butterflies. Our direct switching implementations are simpler and may result in fewer collisions in the heavily loaded case. However, our first implementation, involving multiplexed metanodes, can provide higher bandwidth in the lightly loaded case by providing all of a metanode's bandwidth to a small number of active logical channels.

8 Conclusion

We have presented a sequence of transformations from the traditional butterfly to the dilated butterfly, multibutterfly, metabutterfly, and finally to the multiplexed metabutterfly. Our hierarchical wiring techniques transformed the multibutterfly from a non-scalable network to a the metabutterfly, a highly-scalable network. Our multiplexing techniques resulted in the multiplexed metabutterfly, which can be comparable in cost to a butterfly with the same number of endpoints, but provides nearly twice the performance for random traffic and over five times the performance for worst-case traffic.

Although the multiplexed metabutterfly is less fault tolerant than the metabutterfly, it is far more fault tolerant than the comparable butterfly. Most importantly, the multiplexed multibutterfly provides alternate paths with logical rather than physical wires, achieving high performance without excess hardware cost. Our simulations demonstrate this, revealing little performance degradation even for 2-to-1 multiplexed cables.

We also introduced the notion of randomized multiplexing, which allows us to build metabutterflies with standard cables. Randomized multiplexing also provides extremely high effective multiplicity, which should result in higher performance and is a direction of future study.

References

[ALM90] S. Arora, T. Leighton, and B. Maggs. On-line algorithms for path selection in a non-blocking network. In *Proceedings of the 22nd Annual ACM Symposium on Theory of Computing*, pages 149–158, May 1990.

[AOST93] Thomas E. Anderson, Susan S. Owicki, James B. Saxe, and Charles P. Thacker. High-speed switch scheduling for local-area networks. *ACM Transactions on Computer Systems*, 11(4):319–352, November 1993.

[BCL94] Eric A. Brewer, Frederic T. Chong, and F. Thomson Leighton. Scalable expanders: exploiting hierarchical random wiring. In *Proceedings of the 26nd Annual ACM Symposium on Theory of Computing*, pages 144–152, May 1994.

[BP74] L. A. Bassalygo and M. S. Pinsker. Complexity of optimum nonblocking switching networks without reconnections. *Problems of Information Transmission*, 9:64–66, 1974.

[CED92] Frederic Chong, Eran Egozy, and André DeHon. Fault tolerance and performance of multipath multistage interconnection networks. In Thomas F. Knight Jr. and John Savage, editors, *Advanced Research in VLSI and Parallel Systems 1992*, pages 227–242. MIT Press, March 1992.

[CK92] Frederic T. Chong and Thomas F. Knight, Jr. Design and performance of multipath MIN architectures. In *Symposium on Parallel Architectures and Algorithms*, pages 286–295, San Diego, California, June 1992. ACM.

[DeH93] André DeHon. Robust, high-speed network design for large-scale multiprocessing. Master's thesis, MIT, 545 Technology Sq., Cambridge, MA 02139, February 1993.

[Lei85] Charles E. Leiserson. Fat-trees: Universal networks for hardware efficient supercomputing. *IEEE Transactions on Computers*, C-34(10):892–901, October 1985.

[LM89] Tom Leighton and Bruce Maggs. Expanders might be practical: Fast algorithms for routing around faults on multibutterflies. In *IEEE 30th Annual Symposium on Foundations of Computer Science*, 1989.

[LM92] Tom Leighton and Bruce Maggs. Fast algorithms for routing around faults in multibutterflies and randomly-wired splitter networks. *IEEE Transactions on Computers*, 41(5):1–10, May 1992.

[Pip93] Nicholas Pippenger. Self-routing superconcentrators. In *25th Annual ACM Symposium on the Theory of Computing*, pages 355–361. ACM, May 1993.

[Upf89] E. Upfal. An $O(\log N)$ deterministic packet routing scheme. In *21st Annual ACM Symposium on Theory of Computing*, pages 241–250. ACM, May 1989.

[WZ93] Avi Wigderson and David Zuckerman. Expanders that beat the eigenvalue bound: explicit construction and applications. In *25th Annual ACM Symposium on the Theory of Computing*, pages 245–251. ACM, May 1993.

Guaranteeing Idempotence for Tightly-Coupled, Fault-Tolerant Networks

Ian Eslick, André DeHon, and Thomas Knight Jr.

MIT Artifical Intelligence Laboratory, Cambridge, MA 02139

Abstract. This paper presents techniques for guaranteeing idempotent semantics for classes of network operations in fault-tolerant networks. This is accomplished through operation transformation and message filtering. The conventional response to a failed or corrupted message transmission is to retransmit the failed message. This retry mechanism can lead to duplicate message delivery. If duplicated messages are non-idempotent, duplicate message delivery places the system into an inconsistent state. We explore methods of guaranteeing message idempotence at both the application and network protocol levels.

1 Introduction

In large multiprocessing systems, tolerance to component and wiring failure is an important design consideration. Fault tolerance concerns play a major role in many aspects of a multiprocessor system and features prominently in interconnection network design. If the network is not engineered to tolerate component and link faults, the failure rate of the network increases in direct proportion to the number of components and links in the network. Consequently, as we scale our systems in size, the system's mean time to failure (MTTF) drops dramatically. For systems in non-ideal field conditions, environmental factors may further reduce the MTTF, for example dirt, vibrations and temperature cycling can lead to faulty connections and broken components.

Multiprocessor networks can tolerate static faults, however few provide protection against transient faults. We know that transient faults account for the dominant portion of faults leading to system failure [And85]. The lack of emphasis on transient faults may rise from a variety of causes. Hardware has proven to be sufficiently reliable that hardware based failures are rare. In fact, for most systems which run full-blown operating systems (usually a UNIX style derivative), system software causes the dominant fraction of system failures. While this trend may prove true today, future computing systems will undoubtably find benefit in fault-tolerant computing substrates.

The MIT Transit project has constructed the *Multipath Enhanced Transit Router Organization* (METRO) [DCB+94], a routing switch architecture engi-

Acknowledgments: This research is supported in part by the Advanced Research Projects Agency under contract N00014-91-J-1698.

neered to provide fault tolerance while maintaining high performance in short-haul networking applications. To support fault-tolerant network operation, METRO supports multipath, multistage topologies, stochastic path selection and source responsible, end-to-end messaging protocols. We have developed the Metro End-point Routing Protocol (MRP_ENDPOINT) [DeH93] which provides at-least-once, uncorrupted message delivery in METRO networks.

The MRP_ENDPOINT protocol layer requires that all network messages be *idempotent*, so that multiple receipts of a message by the communications end-point does not yield a semantically different result than the receipt of a single message. Or alternatively stated, the message operation and arguments on the new value yields the new value. That is:

– op(value,[args]) = op(op(value,[args]),[args])

With this guarantee, MRP_ENDPOINT will ensure correct operation in the presence of transient faults.

This paper presents techniques for analyzing and transforming common classes of non-idempotent operations into idempotent operations to guarantee exactly-once delivery semantics. The collection of transformation techniques presented is relevant to any communications system that may duplicate messages. In addition, we discuss general mechanisms in the short-haul networking domain for constructing endpoint protocols that guarantee idempotence to higher layers of the network. In Section 2 we discuss idempotence issues in the context of the METRO architecture, and briefly extend our discussion to include other classes of networks. Section 3 introduces operator transforms and evaluates the complexity and cost of implementation. Section 4 introduces a general mechanisms for ensuring idempotence. We explore optimization and implementation details of these mechanisms in Section 5.

2 Problem Domain and Design Issues

This section describes the essential fault-tolerant features of the METRO architecture and the MRP_ENDPOINT protocol. We will abstract the problem of guaranteeing idempotence by detailing assumptions possible in various short-haul network settings. We argue that the placement of functionality which ensures idempotent network operation must be balanced by between requirements of simplicity and efficiency. In all cases, the performance of low-level network capabilities should never be hidden from programs.

2.1 Fault Tolerance in METRO Networks

The METRO architecture is circuit switched, providing a channel through the network between source and destination. This channel may be quickly reversed at the end of message transmission to allow data to flow back to the source. MRP_ENDPOINT uses this reversed connection to support end-to-end checksum acknowledgments, allowing the source endpoint to quickly verify that the data has been received and checksummed correctly by the destination. The source endpoint employs a simple source responsible retry scheme causing it to retransmit the message under any of the following conditions:

1. The path is blocked due to resource contention in the network
2. The destination node indicates that data was corrupt on arrival
3. The return data stream does not adhere to protocol specifications

The return acknowledgment can be corrupted by transient faults, causing it to deviate from protocol specifications, leading to message retransmission. If the acknowledgment indicates corrupted receipt of a transmission, then the retry mechanism will again retransmit a second message to the destination endpoint. Consequently, MRP_ENDPOINT expects higher level protocols to ensure that only one message will ultimately be acted on by the system.

2.2 Idempotence

To illustrate the problems caused by duplicate non-idempotent message reception, consider an operation that decrements a synchronization counter. For example, dataflow synchronization in Berkeley's TAM [CSS+91] model. Redundant application of synchronization messages causes the synchronization counter to expire early. This may lead to a thread being posted before the data is available for the thread to compute.

Providing idempotence through filtering duplicate messages is an old problem in distributed computing. The transmission Control Protocol (TCP) provides a standard solution to this problem. TCP supports "reliable" data streams by using sequence numbers [Pos81]. When a source needs to communicate with a destination, the source arbitrates with the destination for a valid set of sequence numbers. The source annotates each unique packet of data transmitted to the destination with a different sequence number. The destination node keeps track of all the sequence numbers it has seen so that exactly one copy of each packet arriving at the destination is passed along to higher-level protocols. In this manner, any duplicates arising due to source-responsible retransmission are filtered out, making each message effectively idempotent to protocols running on top of TCP.

While correct, this particular solution is not well-suited for achieving low-latency communications in a large-scale multiprocessor context. Arbitrating for sequence numbers, filtering and reordering packets are together an unnecessary cost that need not be paid in many tightly-coupled networking scenarios. The overhead of these activities in terms of space and processing time can easily prove many times greater than the time and space required for basic message transmission. In these cases, transmission times are often much less than endpoint message handling time, whereas in the distributed computing case TCP style protocols are usually a small fraction of the overall transmission latency. The critical optimization domain in the multiprocessing context is reducing message handling time. This inclines us to work carefully to adopt solutions that are as lightweight as possible.

2.3 Assumptions

Designers constructing network protocols in the multiprocessing setting have the advantage of a constrained domain. As such, they can specialize protocol features and services for their domain to reduce the overhead of making idempotent guarantees. In comparison TCP must service a more general domain. For various topologies, network architectures and protocols we can:

- Ensure that network messages from a node arrive sequentially
- Assume locality implies a limited set of communications per node
- Bound the number of nodes in the machine

Sequential delivery is a policy decision of the network protocol. Each node can wait for confirmation from the destination before transmitting the next message to that node. The cost of making this decision may be small compared to local or wide area networks. For networks with small message sizes, such as the CM-5, this scheme will drastically reduce latency. For the MRP_ENDPOINT protocol, sequential delivery is both a convenient and cheap policy decision due to the underlying features of the METRO network.

A great deal of research is being performed to enforce locality of reference in multiprocessor settings with the aim of promoting high performance. This property by definition limits the practical size of a particular node's working set of communicating nodes.

The third item is an assumption that is often reasonable in practical settings, such as embedded systems or fixed size architectures. While we might want architectures which can scale to attain continual parallelism benefits, particular machines and specialized architectures may have a fixed size. This fixed size again bounds our working set and provides us with a concrete range of expected node ID's.

2.4 Design Considerations

The "end-to-end argument", argued by Saltzer et al. [SRC84], suggests that all functionality in layered communications systems should be pushed out as close as possible to the application which uses that function. If a function will often be duplicated by an application, then low-level implementation becomes redundant and therefore costly. Any decision to include functionality at a lower network layer must be carefully considered, trading off efficiency and complexity.

We illustrate in the following section that fully guaranteeing idempotence at the application level through transformations can entail considerable overhead. Placing this function in the network endpoint protocols allows us to solve the problem once for all applications, providing a convenient abstraction and overhead savings. This incorporation is done without significantly slowing raw network interface performance. Applications which do not require this guarantee may disable it and avoid performance penalties resulting from the additional functionality.

A last concern is that adding additional mechanism to a critical layer of the system makes it more complex from an engineering standpoint. Our design needs to integrate cleanly with existing software mechanisms and have minimal interaction with other system components. We show that having this mechanism in the network endpoint protocols of our tightly-coupled multiprocessor networks satisfies the tradeoffs in the end-to-end arguments and can be done with minimal effort once the design issues are well understood.

3   Transforming Operations

If our network does not guarantee idempotence, or this guarantee constitutes unacceptable overhead, then we must assure that our network messages are idempotent at the application level. We can characterize many common operations in multiprocessor systems as falling into one of the following categories:

- Fetch and Op
- Raw Reads and Writes
- Remote Function Invocation

The following subsections look at each of these categories and see how each either satisfies the idempotence requirement, or may be transformed into an idempotent operation.

3.1   Fetch and Op

A basic and essential messages in any MIMD-style multiprocessor system support synchronization. This often takes the form of a fetch-and-op routine [GS90] [GGK+84]. The fetch-and-op routine proceeds as follows:

1. old_value = value
2. value = op(old_value[,args])
3. return old_value to caller

Operations (1) and (2) have to be executed together, atomically, to achieve the behavior desired from fetch-and-op routines. Fetch-and-ops can only be executed multiple times without causing semantically different behavior if the operation is idempotent.

One important class of operations where this relation does not hold is the decrement and increment operations often used in synchronization. As described earlier in the context of the TAM model, multiple decrements of a synchronization counter will cause the counter to decrement to zero before the program expects, resulting in incorrect behavior.

To avoid this difficulty, we can replace synchronization decrements with bit set operations. Because bit set operations are idempotent, a fetch-and-op based on a bit set is also idempotent. We make a $\theta(logN)$ to $\theta(N)$ space tradeoff to gain correct operation. For small N, this tradeoff won't be noticed as most synchronization variables are usually allocated in multiples of bytes.

A common problem in systems where messages can be delayed arbitrarily is deciding when to deallocate space. We have to assure that no more messages for that variable are going to arrive and overwrite new variable data. The trivial solution is to ignore the problem, and not deal with the overhead of maintaining all synchronization variables. This has obvious disadvantages, especially if there is no bound on the number of such variables.

A more robust solution is to replace a simple bit-set write with a test-and-set such that each variable is coupled with a monotonically increasing sequence number which corresponds to the variables identity. Messages that have carried over from previous allocations of that variable can test the identity of the variable to make sure it can perform the bit-set.

The test-and-set operation is a subset of the fetch-and-op and is used to implement system objects such as mutexes or semaphores. The results of these style operations can lead to a different class of intolerable behaviors than described above. These behaviors primarily take the form of errors rising from negative return results.

For example, if a network operation is trying to get a lock on a remote mutex, the first message may succeed, but the acknowledgment might have been corrupted. On the source node, the network interface is retrying the message, while on the destination, a confirmation of the lock is queued up for transmission back to the source.

The retransmitted test-and-set operation tests the lock and finds that it is locked. The destination node queues a fail message (assuming a non-blocking mutex lock request). If no more failures occur, then the source sees a success message followed by a fail message. Again, depending on the implementation of the program requesting the lock, this could be non-idempotent and lead to program failure.

To illustrate the subtle nature of analyzing these possible interactions, we could alternatively have a test-and-set operation which results in a return only on success. A mutex polling operation might work like this. If success messages are idempotent to the requesting program then the entire exchange is idempotent, and the problem is solved.

3.2   Read/Write

Raw reads and writes are idempotent as multiple writes yield the same value. Multiple remote reads are followed by local writes of the returned read data. Few applications deal directly in such raw reads and writes, and not many systems support such direct access to the network facilities. The Cray T3D is one exception to this rule, and provides this raw read/write interface to the programmer.

More often, raw reads and writes are intimately connected with operations such as data transfer, remote function invocation and synchronization primitives.

Multiple writes also pose a problem if subsequent message copies cross synchronization boundaries and override writes from other nodes in the system which occurred between the first message receipt and subsequent copies.

As the multiple writes issue indicates, these problems are usually addressed by introducing synchronization mechanisms to ensure that reads and writes are properly sequentialized. However, this sequentialization relies on clients of the system obeying the synchronization contract. If the synchronization mechanisms are blocking, then we do not violate the idempotence requirement so long as we check the blocking queue against incoming lock requests to ignore duplicate requests. If the mechanisms are non-blocking, then we encounter the same concerns as mentioned above in the test-and-set case.

3.3 Remote Function Invocation

Remote function invocation is very similar to writes in that they perform side effects into the destination's memory, or into a network messages to be sent back to the source. Fetch-and-op is a special case of the remote function invocation but since it is a common operation with a well defined behavior, it warrants individual attention. The problems are similar, as multiple invocations of the remote function may result in successively different results on both the source and destination nodes.

We can break down the space of possible erroneous results arising from duplicated remote function calls into those arising from multiple non-idempotent side-effects into the remote memory, and those arising from multiple return results. Unfortunately, the possible interactions of these errors and various system components can become quite complex.

It should prove useful to the system or application designer working the short-haul networking setting to see the salient features of these interactions. The potential for multiple function invocation leads to a series of operations being performed on remote data. If the remote function does not side effect into the remote node's memory, we are safe. If it does write into the remote memory, then each operation of the function that side-effects into that memory must be idempotent. This can be assumed if we know that all the data values accessed by the function and the operations on that data will be invariant between duplicate calls, then the function reduces to the case of a simple, deterministic write, and is consequently idempotent.

For return results, the problems created are highly dependent on how these results are integrated into the calling node computation. For example, in the TAM model a return message from a split-phased remote read activates an inlet thread, a small function meant to incorporate the returned data. These inlets usually copy the data from the message into an inlet or frame slot and post a thread on the system queue which is intended to deal with this data. Multiple return results would lead to the same data in the inlet slots, but would cause multiple thread invocations to be queued up on the originating node.

Clearly, handling remote function call duplication problems on a case-by-case basis can be self defeating as the complexity may lead to more system level errors than the idempotent properties will prevent. Though solutions are possible, they are often subtle and difficult to reason about. This indicates that a more general and pervasive guarantee mechanism is needed to handle cases where the solution is not straightforward.

4 Guaranteeing Idempotence

In light of the above transformations and specific solutions, we see that many transformations require complex reasoning about possible interactions of non-idempotent, duplicate messages. Often we must resort to recording some form of message ID which allows us to filter out duplicate messages. However, as the number of objects in our system increases this becomes increasingly expensive and the software complexity hard to manage.

To avoid these difficulties, we propose maintaining sequence numbers as a function of nodes in the system rather than as a function of objects on a node. This reduces the per-node space cost of our idempotence guarantee. With the proper set of assumptions, we can also allow this mechanism to scale nicely with system size and program complexity. Additionally, by accepting limitations on the number of nodes in the system, we can make our mechanism exceptionally lightweight.

4.1 Analysis of Assumptions

A problem that arises in systems which track sequence numbers is knowing when to throw a <node ID:sequence number> pair away, as there is no bound on how long a duplicate message can be blocked within the network. In the METRO architecture, the circuit switched property of the network guarantees that all messages between nodes occur sequentially. That is, any particular message will only arrive at the destination after the prior message has been successfully acknowledged. This is also true of deterministic routing protocols in mesh style networks. Because only one pair need be maintained per node, this constrains the node storage space to be equal to the number of nodes within a particular node's communication group.

Well balanced communication and computation in a large multiprocessor will usually result in any particular node communicating with a small number of neighboring nodes. This is motivated by the low cost of neighbor vs. remote communications in most practical, scalable topologies. To our sequence ID tracking scheme, this means we will only have to track a small collection of <node ID:sequence number> pairs at any particular time.

Alternatively we can place limitations on the number of processors in our system. This is often a limitation of architectures which aren't intended to scale indefinitely or in specialized applications such as an embedded vision system.

This limitation allows us to make the same assumption as with referential locality, but we are able to set a hard limit on the number of nodes we have to track.

4.2 Mechanism

Assuming only the sequential delivery of messages we can implement a software tracking scheme which maintains <node ID:sequence number> pairs which serve as a unique, monotonically increasing sequence identifiers for each node. This protocol will work best when the set of communicating nodes are limited and static. The protocol executes as follows:

1. A message arrives at the destination with <node:number>.
2. Software looks up the node number in a table
3. If present, and the stored sequence ID == message sequence ID, ignore. Otherwise message.seq_ID →
   stored.seq_ID and perform the message operations.

There are a few potential problems with this scheme that warrant a closer look. If the patterns of communication shift, then old stored node ID's will take up memory space, but no longer be essential to ensure correct operation. The problem of knowing when to drop a particular ID can be solved through a LRU policy, arbitrating with nodes that have been idle the longest, once memory constraints require freeing up memory.

A similar problem arises if particular node, such as an I/O node, receives a large number of messages from all over the machine, in this case we have no choice but to cache the ID/number pairs of every communicating machine. As this is likely to be a special case, we can handle this in a more costly manner, keeping the common case execution simple and cheap.

In the case where a node runs out of storage space for ID pairs, it can drop or block all incoming non-matching messages until it can arbitrate with stored nodes to free storage space. Since the congestion caused by backing the computation into the network will slow down the arbitration, we may want to add provisions for an exponential backoff scheme similar to that used in the Ethernet protocol to free routing resources.

While dropping messages works well for source-responsible protocols, it may be much more expensive in mesh style networks. While the solutions rest heavily on the specific features of the network and routing protocol, one possible method of addressing the problem in adaptive routing networks is to bypass messages which have been backed into the network through a virtual channel that gives high priority to space resolution messages.

5 Optimizations and Extensions

With an understanding of the basic mechanisms and problems encountered in guaranteeing idempotent semantics, we can delve deeper into the designs to extract performance enhancements.

If messages arrive at a node sequentially then there are only going to be two distinct types of network messages: duplicate and non-duplicate. Thus we need only cache a single bit for each node we are communicating with. If the bit is identical to the last message, it is a duplicate, otherwise it is the next sequential message from that node. For systems with restricted ranges of node ID's, the node ID storage vectors may be reduced to bit vectors. Lookup of the single bit is done through offset rather than searching a table.

We can provide further speed enhancements through hardware mechanisms. This is a lower level solution than adding mechanism to the software transport layer, and while it provides higher performance, the policies required to flush an ID pair and the need to deal with overflow cases can make the design quite complex.

The principle performance enhancement in hardware comes from adding an associative memory which allows for single cycle lookups of stored <node:ID> pairs. The size of this hardware table is dependent on the expected working set of communicating nodes. Overflow cases should be trapped to software, which can be optimized to reduce the number of stored nodes by releasing those least recently used.

If we make these mechanisms orthogonal to normal message transmissions, we can make our own assurances about the idempotence of our messages and only pay the cost of the general mechanism when used. This is desirable when optimizing for high performance, but requires very complex reasoning about the problem. It is unlikely that in most cases the custom solution is more efficient than the general solution, especially when hardware mechanisms are used.

We can reduce overhead in systems for which sequential delivery is costly by establishing a partial ordering on those message which are non-idempotent, allowing idempotent messages to proceed as available.

6 Conclusions

Having looked at a variety of methods for dealing with message duplication in the multiprocessor, short-haul networking context, we have provided a substantial toolkit of methods and mechanisms for analyzing and addressing the problem of guaranteeing operator idempotence.

The complexity involved in dealing with the transformation of network messages is daunting, such methods are crucial for enforcing correctness in most fault-tolerant networks. For certain classes of networks, we provide mechanisms which avoid the design problems associated with transforming complex operations. Such mechanisms incur a very low cost. These costs can be reduced further if we are allowed assumptions about network traffic, machine size and network guarantees.

References

[And85]   T. Anderson, editor. *Resilient Computing Systems*, volume I, chapter 10, pages 178–196. Wiley-Interscience, 1985. Chapter by: C. I. Dimmer.

[CSS⁺91] David E. Culler, Anurag Sah, Klaus Erik Schauser, Thorsten von Eicken, and John Wawrzynek. Fine-grain parallelism with minimal hardware support: A compiler-controlled threaded abstract machine. In *Proceedings of the Fourth International Conference on the Architectural Support for Programming Languages and Operating Systems*, April 1991.

[DCB⁺94] André DeHon, Frederic Chong, Matthew Becker, Eran Egozy, Henry Minsky, Samuel Peretz, and Thomas F. Knight, Jr. METRO: A router architecture for high-performance, short-haul routing networks. In *Proceedings of the International Symposium on Computer Architecture*, pages 266–277, May 1994.

[DeH93] André DeHon. Robust, high-speed network design for large-scale multiprocessing. Master's thesis, MIT, 545 Technology Sq., Cambridge, MA 02139, February 1993.

[GGK⁺84] A. Gottlieb, R. Grishman, C. Kruskal, K. McAuliffe, L. Rudolph, and M. Snir. Designing an mimd parallel computer. *IEEE Transactions on Computers*, C-32(2):175–189, February 1984.

[GS90] G. Graunke and S.Thakkar. Synchronization algorithms for shared-memory multiprocessors. *IEEE Computer*, 23(6):60–70, June 1990.

[Pos81] (Ed.) Jon Postel. Transmission control protocol – darpa internet program protocol specification. RFC 793, USC/ISI, Information Sciences Institute, University of Southern California, 4676 Admiralty Way, Marina del Rey, California, 90291, September 1981.

[SRC84] J. H. Saltzer, D. P. Reed, and D. D. Clark. End-to-end arguments in system design. *ACM Transactions on Computer Systems*, 2(4):277–288, November 1984.

Design of a Router for Fault-Tolerant Networks

Kevin Bolding and William Yost *

Department of Computer Science and Engineering
University of Washington, Seattle, WA 98195

Abstract. As interconnection networks grow larger and larger, the need for reliable message delivery in the presence of faults grows as well. Unfortunately, most network routing schemes currently in use do not provide graceful tolerance of even the most common faults. Because routing messages around failed components requires non-minimal routing, it makes sense to examine routers which, by design, allow packets to take non-minimal routes. Such routers provide a basic level of fault-tolerance by allowing messages to be routed around faults, without requiring a priori knowledge of their locations. However, the mechanisms can be slow and clumsy at times. We augment Chaotic routing, a non-minimal adaptive routing scheme, with a limited amount of hardware to support fault detection, identification, and reconfiguration so that the network can automatically reconfigure itself when faults occur. We present a high-level design of these mechanisms, driven by the goal of achieving reasonable reliability without exorbitant cost.

1 Introduction

As multicomputers grow larger, the need for fault-tolerant interconnection networks grows as well. Because of the sheer number of components and links in a large multicomputer with thousands of processing nodes, the likelihood of a single failure in the network becomes too large to ignore. For instance, a 64×64-node torus network contains 16,384 links, and the same size hypercube contains 49,152 links. Since these links are often implemented as cables with plug-in connections to PC-boards, they are especially vulnerable to faults. Thus, any interconnection network designed for future large systems must incorporate mechanisms for coping with the relatively large number of faults that will occur.

Most multicomputer networks have built-in redundancy in the form of multiple possible paths from the source to the destination of a message, so it is possible for the network routers to pick paths which avoid faulty network links. Unfortunately, this task is not easily achieved for two reasons. First, routers must make their decisions very quickly, so complicated algorithms cannot be implemented. Second, global information on the presence of faults in the network is not unavailable, so decisions must be based on local information. Because of these constraints, the goal of building a fault-tolerant network router has been difficult to achieve.

Non-minimal adaptive routing has shown promise for providing simple, on-line mechanisms for fault avoidance [15, 2]. However, the fault-tolerance provided by such

---

* This work is supported in part by Office of Naval Research grant N00014–91–J–1007 and National Science Foundation grant MIP9213469.

systems is not entirely robust, and can benefit from supplemental hardware that targets fault-tolerance capabilities. We present hardware and software mechanisms which boost the ability of the Chaos router to avoid faults. These mechanisms are designed to be in-obtrusive and not interfere with the ordinary routing capabilities and performance of the routing network. Although the design presented here is specific to Chaotic routing, many elements of the design are applicable to other routing networks, both minimal and non-minimal, as well.

2 Fault Tolerant Routing

We define "fault tolerant routing" as a method of providing reliable message delivery between any nodes in the network connected by a functional physical path. Interconnection networks vary in the number of redundant paths they provide between nodes. However, in any network, multiple failures may render communication between two nodes impossible regardless of the routing algorithm.

The goal of fault tolerant routing has three parts:

1. Provide reliable message delivery between all pairs of nodes that have some non-faulty path between them.
2. Detect when a fault has occurred, and alert the operating system.
3. Provide mechanisms to reconfigure the network around faulty areas to ensure quick and reliable message delivery to all non-faulty areas of the network.

We use a high-level fault model in this work. Three basic classes of faults are considered: link failures, node failures and router failures, corresponding to each of the components listed in the basic node and router model shown in Figure 1. An error occurs when a packet injected into the network is either not delivered to its destination, or is delivered with corrupted data. Such faults may be either transient in nature, with only temporary effects, or persistent, causing repeatable errors. Fault detection relies on discovering that packets are lost or corrupted. Thus, if a fault occurs which causes neither lost nor corrupted packets, it may not be detected by the mechanisms introduced in this work. Soft errors such as transmission noise affecting the reception of a packet across a link or the loss of state within a router are covered by our model and are detected by the same mechanisms that detect lost or corrupted packets

Link failures refer to a fault in the physical network link between two routers. This class of failures includes common physical failures such as the unplugging of a routing cable or the unseating of a router chip from its socket. It also includes broken bond wires within the chip package. Link failures result in either the corruption of data or the loss of communication between two routers and are easily detected. A link that is found to be faulty will be removed from service by the reconfiguration methods, but the associated routers will continue to operate.

Node failures refer to any failure which causes the processing node attached to a router to refuse to accept packets. The node appears *dead* to the network when such a fault occurs. Such faults are easily detected, although it is not possible to isolate the fault further than identifying the processing node as *faulty*. Such failures can lie either in the node itself, the communication coprocessor, or the links on the path from the node to the

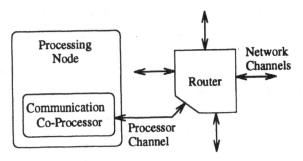

Fig. 1. A node, router, and network links. Failures may occur in any of the components or links.

router. A node that is found to be faulty will be removed from service. The associated router can continue to operate so that network service is unaffected.

A router may fail in different ways, each resulting in varying loss of service. A failure in which packets are routed successfully with proper data, but use an incorrect channel or experience unnecessary delay, is difficult to detect because such behavior is within the realm of normal operation. Fortunately, such failures are not catastrophic because they do not result in corruption or loss of data. Some failures may result in certain channels of the router becoming inoperable, and will appear to be the same as link failures and be treated as such. Finally, a router may fail to operate at all. This is the most severe form of fault in the network because this renders inoperable all network links to the router and isolates the attached processing node from the rest of the network. Fortunately, router failures are expected to be more rare than link or node failures because the routers are not as vulnerable to physical effects as the physical links, and their complexity, determined by number of chips, die size, number of pins or any other measure, is much less than that of the processing node.

3 Related Work

Most current multicomputers use *oblivious* routing [7, 8, 10, 17], in which the path from a message's source to its destination is statically determined. Although such routers can be made very fast due to their simplicity, they are not robust in the presence of faults because there is no natural mechanism for avoiding faulty components. Minimal adaptive routers [4, 6, 16, 12], in which message routing has some degree of adaptivity to congestion or faults, have appeared more recently in research. Two difficulties with these schemes are that the prevention of deadlock becomes complicated and the adaptivity of message routing is limited. Recent extensions of minimal adaptive routers have added fault-tolerant capabilities, once again with the cost of added complexity [4]. Most non-minimal adaptive routers (except deflection routers) have a very natural method of fault-tolerance: faulty links appear the same as congestion, and these routers always steer messages away from congestion by *derouting* messages away from busy links [15, 14, 5]. A shortcoming of these schemes is that the natural derouting mechanisms are, in general, slow to respond when faults are present. Although deflection routers [18, 9] are

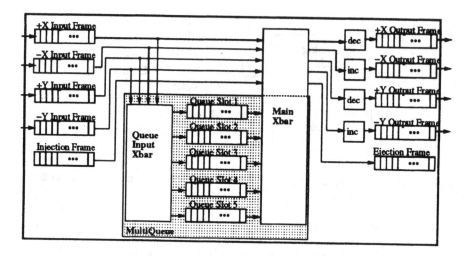

Fig. 2. Two-dimensional Chaos router data path diagram.

quick to deroute messages, their algorithms require all links to be functional and cannot tolerate faults without special hardware considerations.

4 Chaotic Routing

Chaotic routing [14] is a form of non-minimal adaptive routing which uses randomization to prevent livelock without requiring complex protection hardware. It has been shown to be deadlock and livelock free on hypercube and many other types of networks, [1] including all k-ary d-cubes. The enhancements that we propose here are applicable to all chaotic networks. Chaotic routing provides excellent routing performance [3, 11] with a practical design [1].

Figure 2 shows a data path diagram for a two-dimensional (mesh and torus) Chaos router. A Chaos router has three main components: input/output *frames*, a *crossbar*, and the *multiqueue*. Each frame and multiqueue slot is capable of holding one fixed-size (20 16-bit words) packet. The basic operation of the Chaos router is similar to a typical oblivious cut-through packet router [13]: packets enter a router input frame, are connected through the crossbar to an output frame and have their header updated as they exit to reflect their progress. Virtual cut-through allows packets to proceed through the router as soon as their header is received and decoded; it is not necessary for the entire packet to be buffered before moving to the next router. In a Chaos router, packets may be routed to any output channel that brings them closer to their destination. Thus in this mode of operation, the Chaos router acts as a minimal adaptive router.

Chaos routers also include a central buffer, the multiqueue, which stores packets waiting for profitable channels to become free. Packets in the multiqueue have priority over packets in input frames when competing for free channels. Moreover, whenever the multiqueue becomes full, a packet is selected randomly from those in the multiqueue to be sent out the next free output channel, *regardless* of the packet's destination. By this mechanism derouting is accomplished.

4.1 Fault Tolerance

Although the design of the Chaos router was conceived with the primary goals of high performance and low complexity, a basic level of fault tolerance was a natural result of the design. When either a link or a router in a chaotic network persistently fails to respond to its inputs (i.e., becomes "stuck"), the output frames in neighboring routers connected to the faulty components will fail to empty, as the only way for packets to exit is through the failed component. Since packets move into an output frames only when there is space available in that frame, the routers will not route additional packets toward the faulty components.

Packets which have other profitable channels besides the faulty channel will be automatically routed out an alternative minimal path. Those which have no other profitable choices will, after a short delay, be moved into the multiqueue. When the multiqueue fills to capacity, packets will be selected on a random basis to be derouted out the next available output channel. Eventually, packets desiring failed channels will be derouted away from the profitable path and out a non-profitable, but working, channel. From its new location, the routing decision process for the packet will be reinitiated. Thus, even though the minimal paths may be blocked by faults, chaotic routing allows communication to continue by means of the derouting mechanism.

4.2 Shortcomings of the Basic Chaos Router

Although Chaotic routing provides some fault tolerance via the derouting mechanism, there is much room for improvement. First of all, packets can get permanently stuck in the output frames waiting for faulty channels. Packets already in output frames can never be derouted. Moreover, packets may be corrupted or lost due to transient faults, which do not cause the persistent "stuck-at" problems that derouting can handle.

Even when the derouting mechanism is applicable, it works only in a "clumsy" manner, for several reasons. Messages that must be derouted around faulty links may incur large delays as they wait in the multiqueue for their chance to be derouted. Moreover, under light loads, only a small number of packets may get lodged behind a faulty link. The multiqueue may never fill up enough to invoke derouting, leaving the packets stuck in the multiqueue.

Because Chaotic routing provides the promise of fault-tolerant routing, but falls short of the goal, we propose a fault-tolerant Chaos architecture to better cope with the problems caused by faulty hardware.

5 Fault Tolerant Architecture

In order to provide efficient fault detection and recovery, several enhancements must be added to the Chaos router. However, because faults are assumed to be relatively rare, only enhancements which do not significantly affect the normal, fault-free case are considered. The basic strategy for enhanced fault tolerance that we propose depends on several key points.

In order to avoid complexity and to maintain flexibility in the system with regard to procedures relating to fault tolerance, policy decisions were deferred to the software rather than hard wired into the router. For example, the router will perform some fault detection and pass that information to its associated processor, but the decision to enter a diagnostic procedure is left to the processor. In a similar manner, various watchdog timers in the router are programmable to allow the router to be tuned appropriately to maximize efficiency.

The physical context of the Chaos router limits information that it may use for diagnostic purposes to that of a local nature, specifically, internal information, or data on its connecting links. However, the actual cause of a detected problem, for example a missing packet, may be some distance away in the network. Likewise, the effects of a local fault may be felt far away. For these reasons, the Chaos router utilizes a global, synchronous procedure for fault diagnosis.

The overall network fault tolerance is accomplished mainly in system software, which orchestrates fault detection, identification, and recovery at the system level when hardware detects possible faults [2]. The initial fault detection, identification and reconfiguration is performed under the control of the local processor. Diagnostic test procedures result in the generation by each processor of a map defining its local network links as usable or unusable. On a global level, a map of the entire network is compiled from the local information provided by each processor for appropriate use by the system software.

The hardware enhancements help in the four basic phases of the fault-tolerant procedures. A special communication network is needed to allow quick *communication* for fault management. Hardware is also needed for the *detection* of faults and the *diagnosis* of their locations. Finally, once identified, mechanisms for the *reconfiguration* of faulty channels out of the system must be provided.

5.1 Communication

Communication and synchronization related to fault management are provided by a single dedicated bidirectional line per network channel that passes the *red-alert* signal. The primary purpose of this signal is to notify the entire network that a fault may have occurred so that action can be taken to affect recovery. The signal may be asserted by any node in the system, and is propagated to each of the neighbors of the asserting nodes. The router does not originate this signal but passes a signal that it receives from its associated processing node or from any other input channel. Each node that receives the red-alert signal marks the channel from which the red-alert arrived and asserts the signal on all other channels. By this means the red-alert is broadcast to all elements of the network in time proportional to the diameter of the network. Marking the arrival direction allows the node that originated the assertion of the red-alert to control its release. This facilitates control of the red-alert network by this node and allows it to use the red-alert line to signal the phases of the fault diagnosis procedure while maintaining synchronization within the network. A watchdog timer at each node ensures that a stuck red-alert line will not continually force alert status on the network.

The processor channel contains a similar line with some additional functionality. The router may strobe the *Error-detected* line in order to signal to the processing node that the router's fault detection circuitry has detected a possible problem. The processor initiates the red-alert by signalling the router via the Error-detected line. Fault detection signalled to the processor generates a trap condition which, depending upon the context and nature of the fault, may result in the initiation the red-alert by the processor.

5.2 Fault Detection

There are several mechanisms by which the Chaos router detects possible faults. Since the amount of time that a router output frame must wait until granted control of the channel is bounded, watchdog timers on each output channel can indicate that a channel is unresponsive and probably faulty. A timeout will cause the router to strobe the Error-detected line to the processor.

The Chaos channel protocol only requires that the tail of a packet be marked by the assertion of the End-of-message (EOM) signal. Otherwise, transfer of a word is assumed each clock cycle. A channel that failed with a packet in mid-transmission could generate a packet of potentially unbounded length. Because packet-switched routing assumes bounded length packets, we can protect against this situation by counting words for each packet transmission. If a transmission becomes larger than the maximum packet size, the router will terminate the transmission and strobe the Error-detected line.

The body of a message is protected by a checksum, which is generated and verified by the injection and delivery nodes respectively. However, the packet header contains dynamic routing information which is updated on each network hop and cannot be included in the checksum calculation. The router generates new parity for each hop and checks each incoming packet. A packet which fails the header parity check is immediately delivered to the processing node associated with the router which detects the problem, since the routing information is likely to have been corrupted. When a packet is received by the Chaos router, a map of profitable routing directions is generated which is used in making routing decisions. Parity error detection forces the map to indicate that only the delivery channel is profitable.

System Drain. Upon receipt of a red-alert, the router halts the injection of new packets into the network. This requires only that the injection channel from processor to router be disabled. A system drain results, during which packets within the network are delivered and the network empties. The drain is terminated by the expiration of a watchdog timer or when the network is empty.

Figures 3 and 4 show system drain times for 256 and 1024 node torus networks as a function of the number of packets in the network. The worst case drain time is the significant number in setting a drain timeout period. An upper bound on the time that it will take to perform a system drain in a fault-free network can be calculated by assuming a single destination for all packets. If all buffers in each router were filled with packets headed for the same destination, then the bottleneck in the network would be the single delivery channel from the destination router to the destination processing node through which all traffic would have to pass. The rate at which packets could pass on this link

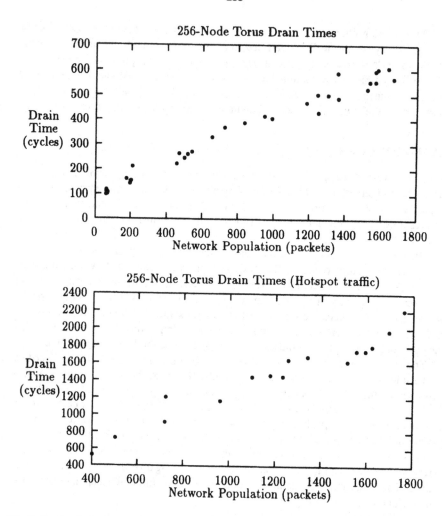

Fig. 3. System drain times for a 16 × 16 node torus network. Packets are injected with uniform random destinations in the top figure, and with traffic containing ten ten-times hotspots in the lower figure.

would determine the drain time. Given a 32 × 32 node network with 15 buffers per router and 20 word packets, it would take $1024 \times 20 \times 15 = 307200$ cycles to drain the network. The drain time in a faulty network may be unbounded. During the system drain phase, the red-alert signal is used to indicate that the drain is incomplete. Each router asserts the signal to indicate that it still contains undelivered packets. The release of the signal by all routers is an indication that the network has drained and the next phase of activity may be entered. If the drain has not completed after the maximum drain period, there must be packets remaining in the network that are undeliverable due to dead destination nodes or a pattern of failures that prevent the packets from reaching their destinations.

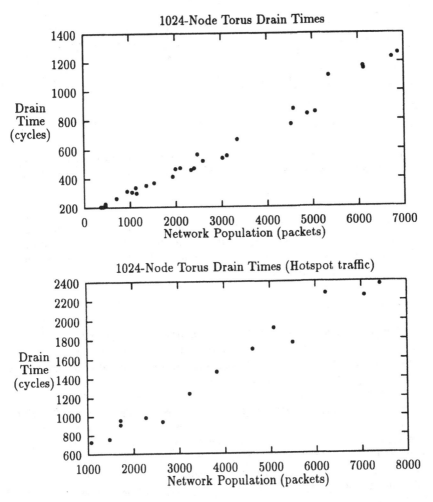

Fig. 4. System drain times for a 32 × 32 node torus network. Packets are injected with uniform random destinations in the top figure and with traffic containing ten ten-times hotspots in the lower figure.

This is indicated by the expiration of a timeout period within each router. In this event, remaining packets will be delivered to the local processing node . All nodes will then enter the diagnosis procedure to check for faults. The fate of those packets misdelivered at the termination of the system drain will be determined at a higher level.

The drain itself provides for some fault detection. One of the characteristics of a non-minimal adaptive router is that packets will not necessarily be delivered in order. The communication coprocessor must reorder the packets in order to reconstruct the message. As a side effect of so doing, missing packets are detected without any significant additional cost in hardware. If the buffer in which the message is reordered overflows

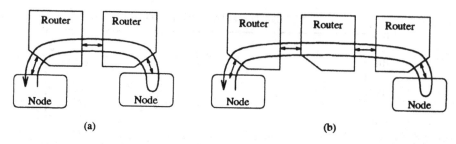

Fig. 5. Fault diagnostic testing. (a) One-hop testing path, which requires nodes to be functional for the link to pass the test. (b) Two-hop testing path allows links to pass the test even if nodes fail.

or if the missing packet doesn't show up within a timeout period, a system drain can be initiated. If the packet is simply slow in arriving, then the drain will facilitate its delivery. If it is in fact missing, then its nonarrival at the end of the drain will be cause to proceed to the fault diagnosis stage.

5.3 Fault Diagnosis

Once a red-alert has been signaled and the system drained, fault diagnosis begins. The goal of diagnosis is to identify as many faults as possible by using a quick distributed algorithm. The procedure is straightforward: All nodes inject test packets destined for each of their neighbors. When a node receives a packet, it sends an acknowledgment back to the sender. This tests the path shown in Figure 5(a) in both directions. If the message is not returned, or is returned corrupted, it could be due to failure of either the link, one or both of the routers, or the receiving processing node. A node that performs a test in which it does not receive a good reply will simply flag the target link as bad. The routers and nodes will be tested by more than one test, since each node is connected to more than one link, and all links are tested. The combination of test results may provide conflicting information about a node or router's status. If this is the case, the operating system will resolve conflicts.

There are two problems with this test design. First, packets intended to be routed on specific links in order to test those links may be derouted around faulty links by the Chaos router and still reach their proper destination without exercising the target link. To avoid this, the router will be configured to disable derouting during the diagnosis phase. This is easily implemented in the router's hardware. The second problem is that, since the processing node must be alive to participate in the testing, a dead node will cause the tests of each of the links from its router to indicate failure. This would render a router attached to a dead or missing node useless. A way to work around this is to add a second phase of testing. In this phase, all two-hop paths would be tested, as in Figure 5(b). More hardware must be functional for this test to succeed, but the intermediate router's attached node does not play any part in the test. Thus, if a link passed the two-hop test, but failed the one-hop test, it can be inferred that the link is working, but that the node is dead. This procedure could be extended with tests of more than two hops, however, the test quickly becomes unwieldy. The number of syndromes that must be decoded based upon test results grows extremely quickly. It appears undesirable to allow extended paths through routers without active associated processors. Because the control of the network fault tolerance is embedded in the local processors, the number of such nodes with inactive processors must be limited in order to maintain reliability, We would recommend that adjacent routers with inactive processors be avoided. This is a policy decision that does not require hardware support by the router.

On-line Testing. The diagnostics described above are only run when the system has been drained and is in a special "diagnostic" state, triggered by one of the fault detection mechanisms. In order to provide more timely fault detection, diagnostics can be run on-line as well. In on-line testing, nodes inject test messages to each of their neighbors, just as above, but during normal network operation. If no response is received after some specified time period, the node can declare a red-alert and enter the off-line diagnostic phase. This solution, unfortunately, requires substantially more hardware support than off-line testing. Test messages must be identified as such so that the network interface recognize them and not attempt to pass them to the processor as normal messages. This is easily done, but requires dedicating space in the header of packets. A larger problem is the requirement that test messages not be derouted. Since on-line test packets must be sent along with ordinary operational packets, the router cannot be put in "no-deroute" mode to solve this problem. To accomplish this, test packets must be marked as such in their header, and hardware must identify these packets and force them along minimal paths. Moreover, since derouting is a critical part of the deadlock-freedom of Chaotic routing, the packets cannot be allowed to create deadlock. This can be solved with additional hardware that destroys test packets after some time limit has been reached. However, because the hardware costs and the complexity of on-line testing are quite large, it is not likely to be a practical addition to the router.

Test Coverage. The diagnostic tests described above provide simple and basic tests of the routing network. The tests will find most static failures in network links, and will detect when nodes fail enough to upset the testing protocol. Router failures are not covered fully. Because the testing path does not cover all of the possible message paths through the router, faults may escape the test. Moreover, only a rudimentary test of the router's ability to correctly route packets is made. Transient faults cannot be found through any form of standard diagnostic testing, and this scheme is no exception to that, though transient errors will be detected by our fault detection scheme. It is our conjecture that most static network failures will lie in faulty links because these require off-chip and board-to-board connections which are especially vulnerable to breakage. Thus, our diagnostics are aimed primarily at link failures and provide a low-cost and quick method of diagnosing such faults.

5.4 Reconfiguration

Once diagnosis is complete, each node has knowledge of the status of the links connected to its router. This data is used to reconfigure the router by marking faulty links as "dead." The router masks out dead channels when making routing decisions. This can be done in a straightforward manner using little extra hardware. A mask corresponding to the functional channels is created at configuration time. When new packets arrive at the router, their profitable channels are determined and logically AND'ed with the functional channel mask, so that they will avoid dead channels. If the packet's profitable channel list is zero, meaning that there are no functional profitable channels, then it must be immediately derouted. This is done by setting the profitable channel list for this packet to the functional channel mask, with the exception that the channel that the packet entered on is excluded. This prevents packets from being derouted immediately back to the source of the previous route. The hardware for this is quite simple: a logical AND, a test for zero, and a register load, so it will barely impact the critical path of packets through the router.

This reconfiguration short-circuits the normal mechanism for derouting packets around faults. Packets do not have to wait to be randomly derouted by the multiqueue to detour around faults, and packets will not get stuck behind faults, even if there is no other traffic in the network.

In order to preserve information on faults for the long term, each node must communicate fault data to a central controller. Since a single controller may be faulty, there can be a set of two or three redundant controllers, each serving the same purpose. Each controller constructs a map of all of the faulty components in the network. This information can be used for several purposes:

- Saving the global information on faults so that it can be taken into account when reconfiguring after a system re-boot.
- Communicating information on faults to the system.
- Alerting the system administrator about new faults.
- Configuring dead or unreachable nodes out of the system completely. Dead nodes should not ever be the destination of any messages.
- Removing messages destined for dead nodes.

By reconfiguring the system around faulty nodes, the network can still run efficiently despite the presence of many faulty components.

6 Summary of Hardware Costs

The total amount of additional hardware that is required to implement this proposal is a small fraction of the basic router cost in hardware. The communication network adds one line per channel and several latches and a small amount of logic for each channel. Considering that each channel must buffer 20 words of 16 bits, the incremental cost is small. The parity checking and generation takes only a few gates per channel. The output channel timers are not large, less than 10 bits and the worst case watchdog timer for any purpose is less than 20 bits. To detect when system drain has completed, each router must be able to report if it is buffering any packets. Again, the internal hardware for this is small. A small state machine is required to control the router during the system drain and the diagnostic procedures. There is also a small cost in augmenting the logic that implements the routing decisions, since the mask of dead channels must be including in that decision. Also, a number of other issues must be handled such as the delivery to the current node of packets with bad header parity as well as the delivery of undelivered packets to the current node at the termination of a system drain. These functions fit smoothly into the basic routing decision circuitry and the incremental cost is small.

7 Remaining Problems

Although our proposed design provides solutions to many problems·of reliability in computer networks, some problems remain. Most of these are due to the difficulty of the problem, the solving of which requires the addition of significant complexity to the network, or the local nature of information available to our solutions. Some known shortcomings are:

- **Orphaned messages.** If a node stops reading messages destined to it from the network, the messages will back up into the network without ever being delivered. We have no way to detect such a problem except by the presence of messages in the network after a system drain times out.
- **Global problems.** While our solutions work fine for isolated faults and *convex-*shaped fault areas, certain patterns of faults can cause situations where messages get stuck in the network. To recognize such fault patterns and solve them requires global techniques.
- **Error correction.** Currently, our system only detects data errors and informs the operating system when one has occurred. Error correction, which requires more hardware and overhead, would reduce the need for applications to re-send messages and re-start applications from checkpoints.
- **Router failures.** Our system centers around data errors and link faults. Coverage of router failures is very limited. The test patterns we use for fault diagnosis do not test the multiqueues at all, and leave many paths through the router untested. Solutions that diagnose router failures will be more complicated, but may not require any additional hardware.

8 Conclusions

The large number of components in massively-parallel multicomputers makes reliability an important issue. However, most interconnection networks currently in use, having been designed exclusively for performance, do not provide even the most basic levels of fault-tolerance. Networks with non-minimal adaptive routing, such as Chaotic routing, are exceptions and provide a good basis for fault-tolerant design. By augmenting the natural fault-tolerant mechanisms with a small amount of hardware, we have designed a router that provides a higher level of fault tolerance.

The architecture of the fault-tolerant Chaos router has been designed with a goal of providing reliable service with nearly the same performance as unprotected Chaos networks. To achieve this, we have added a simple rudimentary communication scheme to assist in fault detection and diagnosis, a small number of hardware timers to check if hardware functions are operable, and some architectural modifications to the routing logic itself to provide efficient routing around network faults. The remaining functions are provided by the network interface and software, in manners which are either efficient or infrequent.

The sum of these parts is a system which provides reliable delivery of messages, as well as automatic detection of errors and diagnosis of fault locations at a reasonable cost.

Acknowledgments

We wish thank Lawrence Snyder for guidance and direction as well as many of the ideas presented in this work. Neil McKenzie's network interface design has also driven many of the issues resulting in this design.

References

1. Kevin Bolding. *Chaotic Routing: Design and Implementation of an Adaptive Multicomputer Network Router*. PhD thesis, University of Washington, Seattle, WA, July 1993.
2. Kevin Bolding and Lawrence Snyder. Overview of fault handling for the chaos router. In *Proceedings of the 1991 IEEE International Workshop on Defect and Fault Tolerance in VLSI Systems*, pages 124–127, November 1991.
3. Kevin Bolding and Lawrence Snyder. Mesh and torus chaotic routing. In *Advanced Research in VLSI and Parallel Systems: Proceedings of the 1992 Brown/MIT Conference*, pages 333–347, March 1992.
4. Andrew A. Chien and Jae H. Kim. Planar-adaptive routing: Low-cost adaptive networks for multiprocessors. In *Proc. Int. Symp. on Computer Architecture*, pages 268–277, May 1992.
5. Bill Coates, Al Davis, and Ken Stevens. The post office experience: Designing a large asynchronous chip. In *Proceedings of the HICSS*, 1993.
6. Robert Cypher and Luis Gravano. Adaptive, deadlock-free packet routing in torus networks with minimal storage. In *Proc. Int. Conf. on Parallel Processing*, pages 204–211, 1992.
7. W. Dally. Wire-efficient VLSI multiprocessor communication networks. In Paul Losleben, editor, *Proceedings of the Stanford Conference on Advanced Research in VLSI*, pages 391–415. MIT Press, March 1987.
8. W. Dally and C. Seitz. Deadlock-free message routing in multiprocessor interconnection networks. *IEEE Trans. on Computers*, C-36(5):547–553, May 1987.
9. Chien Fang and Ted Szymanski. An analysis of deflection routing in multi-dimensional regular mesh networks. In *Proceedings of IEEE INFOCOM '91*, pages 859–868, April 1991.
10. C. Flaig. VLSI mesh routing systems. Master's thesis, California Institute of Technology, May 1987.
11. Melanie L. Fulgham and Lawrence Snyder. Performance of chaos and oblivious routers under non-uniform traffic. Technical Report CSE-93-06-01, University of Washington, Seattle, WA, June 1993.
12. Christopher J. Glass and Lionel M. Ni. The turn model for adaptive routing. In *Proc. Int. Symp. on Computer Architecture*, 1992.
13. P. Kermani and L. Kleinrock. Virtual cut-through: A new computer communication switching technique. *Computer Networks*, 3:267–286, 1979.
14. Smaragda Konstantinidou and Lawrence Snyder. The chaos router: A practical application of randomization in network routing. In *Proc. Symp. on Parallel Algorithms and Architectures*, pages 21–30, 1990.

15. J. Y. Ngai. *A Framework for Adaptive Routing in Multicomputer Networks*. PhD thesis, California Institute of Technology, Pasadena, CA, May 1989.

16. Gustavo D. Pifarré, Luis Gravano, Sergio A. Felperin, and Jorge L. C. Sanz. Fully-adaptive minimal deadlock-free packet routing in hypercubes, meshes and other networks. In *Proc. Symp. on Parallel Algorithms and Architectures*, pages 278–290, 1991.

17. Charles L. Seitz and Wen-King Su. A family of routing and communication chips based on the Mosaic. In *Symp. on Integrated Systems: Proc. of the 1993 Washington Conf.*, pages 320–337, 1993.

18. B. J. Smith. Architecture and applications of the HEP multiprocessor computer system. In *Proceedings of SPIE*, pages 241–248, 1981.

The Reliable Router: A Reliable and High-Performance Communication Substrate for Parallel Computers *

William J. Dally, Larry R. Dennison, David Harris, Kinhong Kan and
Thucydides Xanthopoulos

Artificial Intelligence Laboratory
Massachusetts Institute of Technology
Cambridge, Massachusetts 02139
E-mail: {billd, dennison, harrisd, kinhong, duke}@ai.mit.edu

Abstract. The Reliable Router (RR) is a network switching element targeted to two-dimensional mesh interconnection network topologies. It is designed to run at 100 MHz and reach a useful link bandwidth of 3.2 Gbit/sec. The Reliable Router uses adaptive routing coupled with link-level retransmission and a unique-token protocol to increase both performance and reliability. The RR can handle a single node or link failure *anywhere* in the network without interruption of service. Other unique features include a queueless low-latency plesiochronous channel interface, and simultaneous bidirectional signalling.

1 Introduction

Interconnection networks play a major role in performance and reliability of massively parallel processors (MPPs). Previous work on network switching elements implementing oblivious routing such as the J-Machine Router [2], and the Caltech Mesh-Routing Chips [11] did not address the issue of reliability in part because of the inherent unreliability of oblivious routing. Past work on adaptive elements such as the Chaos Router [9] exploited adaptivity for performance reasons only without providing fault handling mechanisms.

The Reliable Router (RR) exploits adaptive routing for both performance and reliability purposes. It also has mechanisms for continuous link monitoring and link-level retransmission when a link parity error is detected. It also employs a forwarding protocol at the flit level that facilitates packet reconstruction and duplicate detection at the receiving end when a fault occurs. We call this protocol the Unique Token Protocol (UTP) [5].

The coupling of these features (adaptive routing, link monitoring, link-level retransmission and the UTP) enable the RR to handle a single node or link failure *anywhere* in the network without interruption of service.

¹ This research is supported by the Advanced Research Projects Agency under contracts N00014-88K-0738, F19628-92-C-0045, and N00014-91-J-1698.

The Reliable Router avoids the problem of global clock distribution and skew management by using a queueless low-latency plesiochronous channel interface. This mechanism allows each RR chip to be clocked by its own local clock without the need for FIFO buffering on either side of the channel. The penalty is only a very small fraction of link bandwidth.

The RR solves the high pinout problem by using current-mode simultaneous bidirectional signalling [6]. This method has yielded a saving of 92 signal pins over a conventional signalling mechanism.

2 Architectural Overview

The Reliable Router is designed for two-dimensional mesh topologies. Its organization is shown in Figure 1. There is one Input Controller and one Output Controller for every direction. Moreover, there is a processor input/output and a diagnostic input/output. Communication between an input and an output port occurs through a crossbar switch.

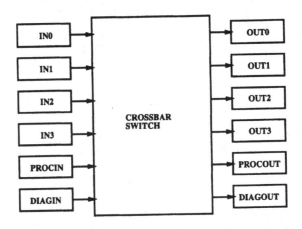

Fig. 1. Organization of the Reliable Router

2.1 Major Object Types

Three types of objects are handled by the architecture. The *packet* is the main unit of information exchange between the sending and receiving end. The Reliable Router can handle packets of arbitrary size. Virtual channels are allocated on a packet basis.

Every packet is broken into 64-bit *flits*. Buffering, forwarding and flow control within the system is performed at the flit level (wormhole routing). Crossbar bandwidth and physical channels are also allocated at the flit level. The first flit of each packet is called *head* flit and contains the address of the packet destination. The format of RR head flits is shown in Table 1.

Bit Field	63:12	11	10	9:5	4:0
Contents	User Info	Priority	Diagnostic	Address in y	Address in x

Table 1. Head Flit Format

Bit Field	22	21	20:18	17	16	15:0
Frame 0	PE	USR0	VCI	BP1	BP0	Data [15:0]
Frame 1	Copied Kind	Copied VCI		BP3	BP2	Data [31:16]
Frame 2	U/D	USR1	Kind	BP5	BP4	Data [47:32]
Frame 3	Freed			BP7	BP6	Data [63:48]

Table 2. Frame Format

Subsequent flits are of type *data* and carry user data. The final flit of the packet is of type *tail* and marks the end of the packet. These is also a flit of type *token* that is injected at the end of each packet to implement the Unique Token Protocol. Each flit contains 64 bits of user data, 8 byte parity bits for end-to-end error detection, and 3 bits that indicate the flit type.

Flits are further broken into *frames* so that they can be transmitted across physical channel links which are only 23-bit wide. Each flit is decomposed in four separate frames as shown on Table 2. Frames carry more information than the data portion, byte parity bits (BP7-BP0) and kind bits (Kind) of each flit. The virtual channel identifier (VCI), flow control information (Copied Kind, Copied VCI, Freed), link status information (U/D, PE) and two user bits (USR1, USR0) are also appended to the frames.

2.2 Functional Description

Most of the functionality of the chip has been pushed into the Input Controller. A simplified block diagram of the Input Controller along with the Arbiter and the Crossbar switch is shown in Figure 2. The Input Controller buffers flits in the Flit Queues (16-flit deep FIFO buffers), computes the next step route in the

Router Module, and directs the flits that are popped from the queues to the appropriate Output Controller through the Crossbar switch.

Flits enter the module after being assembled and synchronized in the Front End and then are stored in a Flit Queue that corresponds to their virtual channel.

If the flit is a head flit and its data payload contains routing information, it is fed through the Router which calculates a possible next step route depending on the destination address and on current availability of output virtual channels. The route is computed in terms of an Output Controller identifier (0-5) and a Virtual Channel identifier (0-4). This routing decision is not final and we call it "optimistic". If another Input Controller wants to route an incoming head flit to the same Output Controller, then the Crossbar Arbiter has to decide which one of the two head flits is allocated the resource.

If, on the other hand, the incoming flit is of type data it does not go through the Router but is stored in one of the Flit Queues waiting to be popped and forwarded to the next node.

Every two cycles a decision must be made as to which Flit Queue – virtual channel – gets a chance to push a flit through the crossbar. A round robin scheduler picks among the eligible virtual channels. A virtual channel is considered eligible in two cases:

Routed case: If the next flit of the channel is data or tail and a route has already been established by assigning an output virtual channel, then the virtual channel is eligible if there are available flit buffers in the neighbor node.

Unrouted case: If the next flit is a head and the Router indicates that a possible next step route can be computed based on channel state information at that time, then the virtual channel is eligible to bid for crossbar bandwidth.

The selection of the virtual channel to be popped is made by the Control box. When a flit is picked to be pushed through the crossbar, the new virtual channel identifier which is computed as part of the next step route is appended by the Flit Munger.

The Output Controllers simply append certain acknowledgment information, compute parity, break the flit into four frames and transmit the frames accross the physical link.

2.3 Architectural Support for Virtual Channels

The Reliable Router has five virtual channels associated with every physical link. Managing five virtual channels at the architectural level may require extra levels of arbitration for allocation of shared resources. Such serialization can cause performance degradation. Early in our architectural design, we decided to replicate one of the most sensitive resources: The Optimistic Router logic. Each Input Controller in the RR has five copies of the routing logic, one for every virtual channel. This decision has eliminated the arbitration for the router along with inefficiencies associated with picking a virtual channel that could not be routed. With just one copy of the routing logic there was no way to determine

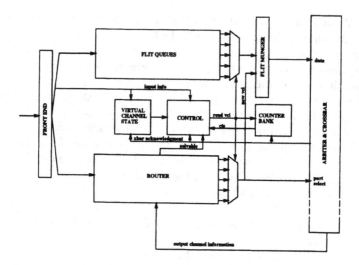

Fig. 2. Input Controller, Arbiter and Crossbar

whether a particular channel could be routed before feeding its head flit through the router.

The only place in the RR where serialization of virtual channels occurs is when the non-idle virtual channels of an Input Controller compete for physical link bandwidth through the crossbar switch. In this case, a round robin scheduler which picks only non-idle virtual channels ensures a fair and efficient arbitration.

3 Adaptive Routing

Past research on adaptive routing has suffered from exponential dependence of resources on network dimension [10], carrying and updating message state along the route [3], and ad hoc fault-handling mechanisms incapable of handling faults along the edges of the network [10], [1]. The RR routing algorithm minimizes resource requirements and message state by using Duato's method [7]. The fault-handling properties of the routing algorithm are decoupled from the adaptive properties by using a different set of virtual channels and a different adaptive algorithm – the Turn Model [8] – for fault-handling. One can think of a network of RRs as the superposition of three separate virtual networks:

A minimally adaptive network. A packet using this network is able to route to any productive channel – a channel which will bring it closer to its destination. This virtual network tries to exploit adaptivity for performance reasons and is susceptible to deadlocks. An example message trace in such a network is shown in Figure 3 (a). The RR allocates two virtual channels to the adaptive network.

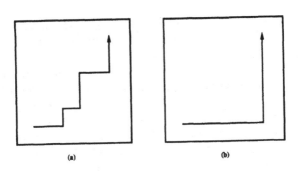

Fig. 3. Minimally adaptive vs. dimension-ordered routing.

A *dimension-ordered network.* Packets in this network are routed in strict dimension order: In every dimension d a packet is routed along that dimension until it reaches a node whose address in dimension d matches the address of the packet destination node in the same dimension. If the addresses match, then the packet continues to route in the next lower dimension where the current channel address and the destination address differ. An example of dimension-ordered routing is shown in Figure 3 (b). The order of dimensions in this example is x, y. Dimension-ordered routing is provably deadlock-free [4]. This virtual network exists in order to break deadlocks introduced in the previous network as suggested in [7]. The RR has two dimension-ordered virtual channels – one used by packets of priority 0 and one used by packets of priority one. We have implemented two packet priorities and associated decoupled resources to avoid software deadlocks.

A *fault-handling network.* This network permits non-minimal adaptive steps and it is used to exploit the fault-handling properties of adaptive routing. We restrict the number of turns a packet can make to make the network deadlock-free [8]. The RR allocates one channel for fault-handling purposes.

All three virtual networks share the same physical network by using different sets of virtual channels. The routing algorithm consists of three separate computations occuring in parallel. The whole route computation takes a single clock cycle. Each computation results in a next step virtual channel from one of the three virtual networks described above:

Adaptive Computation: The switching node attempts to find a non-busy minimally adaptive channel. If such a channel is found, then the message will use it as the next step of its path.

Dimension-Ordered Computation: If no minimal adaptive channel is available, the packet is routed to the unique dimension-ordered channel corresponding to the current position and the destination of the packet. If this channel is busy, the packet blocks for one cycle and tries again to find a channel using the Adaptive Computation.

Fault-Handling Computation: If the dimension-ordered channel is faulty, the packet is routed to a fault-handling channel. This can be any channel, productive or unproductive, except for a channel that will cause the message to make a 180-degree turn. After the packet has been forwarded to the next switching node the algorithm either reverts to picking channels starting from the Adaptive Computation or sticks to Fault-Handling Computation channels only and the packet reaches its destination through fault-handling channels. This decision depends on the packet dimension at the time the Dimension-Ordered Computation fails to select a channel and is essential for the algorithm to be deadlock-free:

If the packet makes a side step to go around a faulty link, this side step will have to be reversed at some point in the future. If the side step is along the y dimension, then the side step can be reversed without violating the order of dimensions x, y, and the packet is allowed to route to dimension-ordered channels after routing on the non-minimal fault-handling channel. If, on the other hand, the side step is along the x-dimension, then the order of dimensions will be violated when the packet tries to reverse this non-minimal step. For this reason the packet continues to route on fault-handling channels until it reaches the destination.

4   The Unique Token Protocol

End-to-end protocols may solve the reliability problem when coupled with adaptive routing, but require extra overhead and the necessary resources do not scale linearly with the size of the machine [5]. For this reason we decided to use link-level retransmission in combination with a unique-token protocol (UTP) [5] to guarantee fault-tolerant exactly-once delivery of all packets in the network. This link-level protocol offers significant advantages over end-to-end protocols because it does not require acknowledgment packets and does not keep copies for possible retransmissions at the packet source. In this way, effective network bandwidth is increased and storage requirements at the nodes decrease. Moreover, the protocol reduces the amount of storage required at the destination nodes for duplicate message detection. These properties allow the protocol resources to scale linearly with the number of network nodes as opposed to end-to-end protocols.

An example of packet forwarding under the UTP is shown in Figure 4 where source node A sends a packet to destination node C. The packet is buffered and forwarded through switching node B. The process must ensure that at least two copies exist in the path between the source node and the destination node at all times. This can be achieved by first copying the packet forward one node, and then allowing the release of the storage in the rearmost node as shown in Figure 4. When the packet is first injected into the network, a token is injected right behind the packet. The invariant that no copies of the packet exist behind the token is always preserved. Packet copying and token passing is carried out exactly as shown in Figure 4. *Note that although multiple copies of the packet are kept in the network, every node receives a packet only once.* Thus, in the absence

248

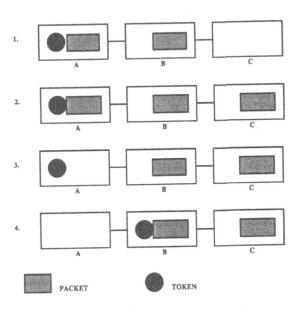

Fig. 4. Buffering and forwarding under the UTP.

of faults, the arrival of the token at the destination implies that the packet has been delivered exactly once.

4.1 Fault Handling

When a node in the network fails, communication between the advance and rear copies of the packet may be severed. Each copy now must make its way to the destination without knowing the fate of the other copy. When packets arrive at the destination they must be marked in such a way so that the destination knows that it needs to look for duplicates. For this reason we establish two types of tokens: Unique, and replica. If the network needs to use multiple paths while forwarding the packet, the token is changed to type replica for all copies of the packet. When the token is changed, forwarding proceeds in the usual way of always keeping two copies of the packet per path.

Such an example is shown in Figure 5. Due to a faulty link, communication between the two copies of the packet has been broken. As a result, each copy changes its token to replica, or generates a replica token and proceeds to the destination using different paths. When the destination receives a packet with a replica token, it knows that it should be looking for duplicates. This scheme is based on the assumption that packets have unique identifiers so that duplicates can be detected and eliminated.

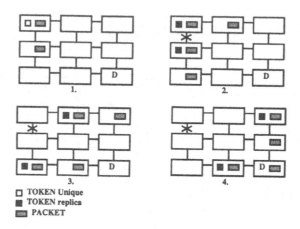

□ TOKEN Unique
■ TOKEN replica
▒ PACKET

Fig. 5. Fault Handling under the UTP

4.2 Flit-Level Implementation of the UTP

The actual implementation of the Unique Token Protocol occurs at the flit level rather than at the packet level. A long packet may span a number of nodes. The flit-level UTP guarantees that each flit of the packet has a copy for retransmission purposes in the neighboring node. A snapshot of a packet in flight under the flit-level UTP is shown in Figure 6. The figure shows a packet that consists of one head flit, seven data flits, and one tail flit. There are a number of things to notice from that figure:

1. There exists a second copy of every data or tail flit in the preceding node.
2. There is only one copy of the token flit. There exist no flits of the specific packet behind its token.
3. The head flit is stored at the head of the flit queue in every node spanned by the packet. It is deallocated only when the token flit leaves the node.

Every node needs a copy of the head flit to ensure retransmission of the partial packet when a link fails after only part of a packet has been transmitted to the next node. The head flit is used to encapsulate the partial packet in the regular packet format and send it to the destination through an alternate route. The head flit of the trailing piece of a partial packet is tagged as a special kind of head flit – in the Reliable Router terminology it is called a *head:restart* flit as opposed to a *head:original* flit. This is necessary for the destination to reconstruct the original packet. It is also assumed that the tail flit of each packet contains the length of the message in flits. Given two partial pieces of a packet, the packet length and the the relative order of the two pieces, the destination can reconstruct unambiguously the original packet.

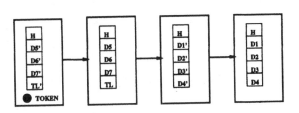

Fig. 6. The UTP at the flit-level

4.3 Architectural Support for the UTP

The implementation of the Unique Token Protocol presents a number of design challenges:

The token must be handled differently from the other flit types. The token can only be forwarded when the Flit Queues have unloaded and invalidated all resident data flits. Moreover, there must be a mechanism to generate a token, back up the pointers in the Flit Queues and reroute the virtual channel when a fault occurs. This functionality is partitioned among the Control, Virtual Channel State and Flit Munger modules of the Input Controller.

The greatest design challenge is that in order to keep two copies of flits at all times within the network, flow control information must make two steps to the back using separate flow control paths. This is shown in Figure 7. Let us assume

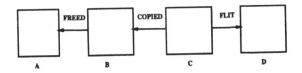

Fig. 7. Flow Control in the Reliable Router.

that node C copies a flit across to node D. It sends a *copied* message to node B using the Copied Kind and Copied VCI fields shown in Table 2. Node B will use this information to invalidate its own copy of the flit. Moreover, reception of a *copied* field in an incoming frame will make node B send a *freed* message to node A using the Freed field of an outgoing frame. Node A will receive the *freed* information and use it to decrement the appropriate counter in its Counter Bank, indicating that the neighboring node (in this case node B) has one flit less in that particular Flit Queue. This backward flow control path is implemented using large buses that broadcast the *copied* and *freed* information to all Input Controllers. Only the Input Controllers that have a virtual channel which is routed to the port where the *copied* or *freed* message was received act upon this information.

5 Plesiochronous Data Recovery

One of the more difficult tasks in putting together a large scale MPP has been the global clock distribution. The RR addresses this problem by using plesiochronous timing. Each router is clocked using a different local oscillator with the same nominal frequency. There is no single global clock – and associated single point of failure – and the clock distribution problem is entirely avoided.

In a system of Reliable Routers, the clocks are all free running. To move data bits, the transmitter sends the clock along with the data. The receiver uses this clock to sample the data wires. Two latches are used to move data from the transmit clock domain to the receive clock domain. However, without some additional protocol, these latches will very quickly undersample or oversample flits.

We use a low-level protocol that imposes a maximum data rate on any wire which is below the minimum carrier rate of any link in the system. The minimum carrier rate is determined by the lowest actual frequency of any of the local oscillators. The transmit limit is implemented in the router by turning off the crossbar one out of a thousand times. The Output Controllers send a non-data frame called a *padding flit* whenever there is no data to send.

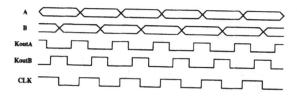

Fig. 8. Plesiochronous Interface

The principle of the interface operation is shown in Figure 8. The receiver delays the input waveform A by 180 degrees and produces waveform B. At any point in time it is always safe to sample from one of the two waveforms. Signals $KoutA$ (Keep out A) and $KoutB$ (Keep out B) are produced by the transmitter clock and indicate the time windows where it is undesirable to sample from the A or B waveforms respectively. The receiver is sampling from one of the two waveforms. When the receiver clock samples a high on the corresponding Keep-out line, the gray area has been entered. As soon as the receiver detects a padding flit on the lines, it will switch and lock on the other waveform. If undersampling occurs, the receiver has missed a padding flit that does not carry any information. If oversampling occurs, the receiver has sampled an extra padding flit which is simply ignored. The finite state machine that controls the multiplexer of the A and B buses ensures that switching occurs only when both buses carry the same data. The latency penalty of this scheme is about 1.5 baud.

6 Bidirectional Signalling

The 6 input and output ports shown in Figure 1 require a large amount of interchip bandwidth. To allow the use of a conventional chip carrier with fewer than 300 pins, we employ simultaneous bidirectional signalling [6]. This method allows bidirectional point to point digital signal communication on the same chip carrier pin and at the same time.

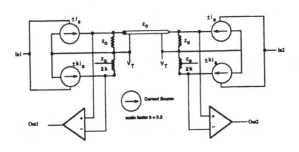

Fig. 9. Simultaneous Bidirectional Signalling

Figure 9 shows the block diagram of a pair of simultaneous bidirectional transceivers. The printed circuit board connection is modelled as a transmission line, with both ends of the line terminated with an internal resistor. A logic 1 or a logic 0 is transmitted as a positive current or a negative current respectively; the signal across the chip boundary is thus a superposition of the two current streams. To receive the digital signal from another transmitter, a local transmitter generates an internal copy of its own transmitted signal as a reference. The reference voltage is then subtracted from the superimposed signal to generate the received signal.

The small voltage swing (i.e. 250mV) of the signalling method calls for different noise reduction techniques:

1. *On-Chip Termination Control* allows the drivers' termination resistors to be fine-tuned for process variations.
2. *Current-Steering* keeps the current drawn by the drivers roughly constant to reduce the noise on the power planes.
3. *Rise-Time Control* staggers the turn-on of successive stages of current drivers to reduce the $L\frac{di}{dt}$ noise induced by the package pins.

To minimize power consumption, the current source for generating the local reference voltage is scaled down, while the reference resistor is scaled up accordingly. All of the 23 bidirectional signals that connect an adjacent pair of Reliable Routers employ the described simultaneous bidirectional signalling method, which amounts to a savings of 92 signal pins over conventional signalling methods. There is also substantial reduction in power and noise over full swing signalling.

7   Physical Implementation

We will be fabricating the Reliable Router on a 144 mm^2 die in a 3-metal layer 1μ CMOS process. The current floorplan is shown on Figure 10.

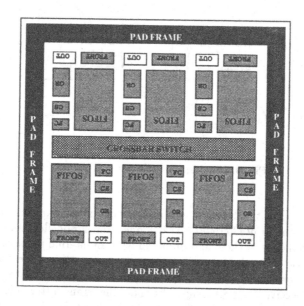

Fig. 10. Reliable Router Floorplan

The gray boxes comprise the Input Controller. Only the biggest modules have been included in the figure. The white boxes named OUT are the Output Controllers. Just by the relative sizing one can tell that most of the functionality in this chip lies in the Input Controllers.

We have employed full custom layout for the FIFOS module (virtual channel flit queues) because of size and special functionality required. This module is the most area intensive block in the whole design. For most of the other blocks such as the Routers (OR), Flow Control (FC), Channel State (CS) and the Front End

(FRONT) semi-custom layout was employed (manual placement and routing of in-house developed standard cells.)

The Reliable Router is designed to run internally at 100 MHz, with the links clocked at 200 MHz. It can achieve a maximum useful bandwidth of 3.2 Gbit/sec per link per direction.

We have currently completed about 90% of the layout. We plan to tape out the design in the very near future.

8 Conclusion

We have introduced the Reliable Router, a network switching element which provides reliable and high performance communication between nodes of parallel computers. The Reliable Router uses a simple and efficient routing algorithm with minimal resource requirements. It also employs a link-oriented retransmission protocol with significant advantages over conventional end-to-end protocols. The coupling of these two features enable the RR to handle a single node or link failure without interruption of service. Other performance features include a queueless low-latency plesiochronous channel interface and simultaneous bidirectional signalling.

References

1. Andrew A. Chien and Jae H. Kim. Planar Adaptive Routing: Low-cost Adaptive Networks for Multiprocessors. In *Proceedings of the 19th International Symposium on Computer Architecture*, pages 268–277, May 1992.
2. William J. Dally et al. The Message-Driven Processor: A Multicomputer Processing Node with Efficient Mechanisms. *IEEE Micro*, April 1992.
3. William J. Dally and Hiromichi Aoki. Deadlock-Free Adaptive Routing in Multicomputer Networks using Virtual Channels. *IEEE Transactions on Parallel and Distributed Systems*, Vol. 4, No.4, April 1993.
4. William J. Dally and Charles L. Seitz. Deadlock Free Routing in Multiprocessor Interconnection Networks. *IEEE Transactions on Computers*, C-36(5):547–53, May 1987.
5. Larry R. Dennison. Reliable Interconnection Networks for Parallel Computers. MIT AI Laboratory Technical Report 1294, October 1991.
6. Larry R. Dennison, Whay S. Lee and William J. Dally. High Performance Bidirectional Signalling in VLSI Systems. In *Research on Integrated Systems: Proceedings of the 1993 Symposium*.
7. Jose Duato. On the Design of Deadlock-Free Adaptive Routing Algorithms for Multicomputers: Design Methodologies. In *Parallel Architectures and Languages Europe Proceedings*, pages 390-405, June 1991.
8. Cristopher J. Glass and Lionel M. Ni. The Turn Model for Adaptive Routing. In *Proceedings of the 19th International Symposium on Computer Architecture*, pages 278–287, May 1992.
9. S. Konstantinidou and L. Snyder. Chaos Router: Architecture and Performance. In *Proceedings of the 18th International Symposium on Computer Architecture*, pages 212–221, May 1991.

10. Daniel H. Linder and Jim C. Harden. An Adaptive and Fault Tolerant Wormhole Routing Strategy for k-ary n-cubes. *IEEE Transactions on Computers*, C-40(1):2–12, January 1991.

11. Charles L. Seitz and Wen-King Su. A Family of Routing and Communication Chips Based on the Mosaic. In *Research on Integrated Systems: Proceedings of the 1993 Symposium*.

Network Interface Support
for User-Level Buffer Management

Cezary Dubnicki, Kai Li, Malena Mesarina

Department of Computer Science, Princeton University, Princeton NJ 08544

Abstract. The network interfaces of existing multicomputers and workstations require a significant amount of software overhead to provide protection and buffer management in order to implement message-passing protocols. This paper advocates a physical memory mapping method in a network interface design that supports user-level buffer management. The method requires only a minimal addition to the traditional DMA-based network interface design and eliminates the need for memory buffer management in the operating system kernel. As a result, the software overhead on message passing is reduced by up to 78% and both receive system call and receive interrupt can be avoided.

1 Introduction

The network interfaces of existing multicomputers and workstations require a significant amount of software overhead to implement message-passing protocols. In fact, message-passing primitives such as the NX/2 [15] *csend/crecv* on many multicomputers often execute more than a thousand instructions to send and receive a message; the hardware overhead of data transfer is negligible. For example, on the Intel DELTA multicomputer, sending and receiving a message requires 67 μsec, of which less than 1 μsec is due to time on the wire [11].

Recent studies and analysis indicate that moving communication buffer management out of the kernel to the user level can greatly reduce the software overhead of message passing. Felten found out that using compiled, application-tailored runtime library for message passing, the latency can be improved by 30% [4]. With a non-traditional design of network interface, the software overhead of message passing primitives for common cases can be reduced to less than 10 instructions [1] without sacrificing protection. An interesting question is whether it is possible to support user-level buffer management with very minimal modifications to the traditional DMA-based network interface designs.

This paper describes a very simple physical memory mapping method to achieve the goal of eliminating the memory buffer management in the operating system kernel. Using this method, we have designed a network interface, called SHRIMP-I, connecting Pentium PCs to Intel Paragon routing backplane. The network interface design is based on the traditional DMA approach with a simple mechanism that allows the message-passing primitives to map physical memory of a send buffer to physical memory of a corresponding receive buffer in software. Our simulations indicate that the physical memory mapping approach can reduce the software overhead of message passing significantly.

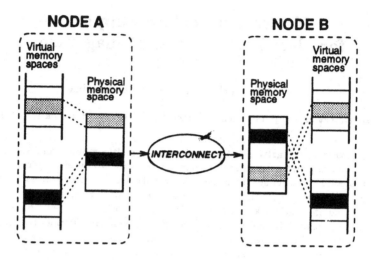

Fig. 1. Virtual memory mapping

2 Main Ideas

To eliminate the buffer management in the operating system kernel we extend a traditional network interface design with the support for virtual memory-mapped communication. The resulting network interface can perform both the traditional style of message passing and virtual memory-mapped communication.

The functionality of the virtual memory-mapped mechanism is to map a piece of sender's virtual memory to an equally sized piece of receiver's virtual memory across a network. The sender process can then communicate with the receiver process through the mapped memory as their send and receive buffers without using kernel memory buffers.

Our idea is to implement virtual memory-mapped communication using *physical memory mapping*, in which physical memory of a send buffer is mapped to physical memory of a receive buffer. Both send and receive buffers are pinned in physical memory. The mapping information is kept in the mapping table data structure maintained by sender's operating system. To support physical memory mapping, each packet carries a physical destination address of a receive buffer. This simple extension to the traditional network interface allows for software implementation of virtual memory mapping. To create a virtual memory mapping from one node to another, this method requires a map system call to set up the appropriate physical mapping information in the mapping table data structure including routing information, the absolute mesh coordinates of the receiver, and destination memory address.

Figure 1 shows how two processes coexist on both sender and receiver nodes. One process is using the gray mapping to send data from Node A to Node B. The other process is using the black mapping to do the same. Since the mapping table data structure resides in the kernel memory, the virtual memory mappings are protected. Since the physical memory used by the two processes is distinct, a context switch between them does not require any action on the mapping table data structure.

After a mapping is established, a send operation simply does a table lookup, builds a packet header with the physical destination memory address, and initiates a DMA transaction. When the message arrives at the receiver's network interface, the physical destination address of the packet will be used to deliver data directly to the destination without CPU assistance.

Such an implementation can transfer data directly between user-level send buffer and user-level receive buffer without going through a memory buffer in the kernel. Since the mapping primitive is implemented as a system call and the mapping is established between two virtual memory address spaces, we can achieve the same level of protection as the traditional message passing approach using memory buffering in the kernel.

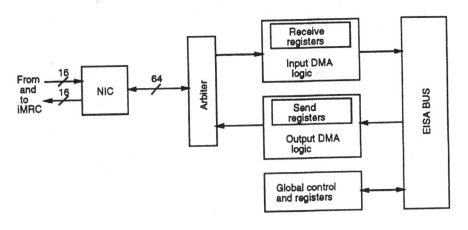

Fig. 2. Data flow block diagram of SHRIMP-I network interface.

3   Network Interface Design

We have designed a simple DMA-based network interface, called SHRIMP-I, which interconnects Pentium PCs with the Paragon routing backplanes. The network interface uses a NIC (Network Interface Chip) to interface with the processor channels of an iMRC on the routing backplane [16].

Figure 2 shows a block diagram of the data flow of the network interface. We use memory-mapped registers to hold packet headers and to control send and receive operations. Global registers implement standard EISA interface (id and control registers). There is also registers' base global register which holds the base physical address of memory-mapped registers. The arbiter arbitrates the bidirectional datapath of the NIC giving a receive higher priority than a send.

Figure 3 shows the packet format. The first 64-bit word of a packet contains destination node for the iMRC routers to route the packet. It is interpreted by the iMRCs and it is stripped at the destination. The second 64-bit word contains packet header. The data of the packet starts from the third 64-bit word. *Version* field of the header identifies the version of network interface which generated this packet, *Destination Address* specifies physical address on the destination machine to receive the data of the packet. *Reserved* field can be used by the operating system. *Action* field indicates what additional actions the destination network interface should perform. There are two bits defining these actions (both are off by default):

- *Destination Address Selection Bit.*
  If this bit is off, store the arriving data starting from the physical address taken from the *Destination Address* field of the packet header. If this bit is on, the receiver's provided destination address register is used to obtain destination address for the incoming packet. *Destination Address* field is ignored in such case.
- *Interrupt Bit.*
  Interrupt the receiving node CPU upon the packet arrival if this bit is on.

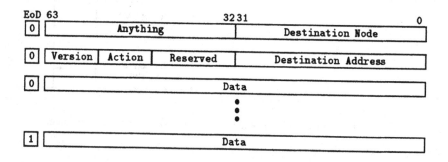

Fig. 3. SHRIMP-I packet format. EoD is the end-of-data bit which is set to 1 for the last word of a packet.

A send operation puts a packet header in the send registers and triggers the send state machine. When the packet arrives, its header will be stored in receive registers. By default, the data of the packet will be delivered to the physical memory indicated by *Destination Address* in the header. The action field of the packet can instruct the receiving logic to deliver data to the physical address provided by the receiver (in a memory-mapped register) and also optionally interrupt the receiving host processor upon the message delivery. If there is an interrupt, the incoming path is frozen until explicitly released by the host processor's write to a special receive control register.

To provide software with flexibility and support debugging, the receiving logic can be programmed to overwrite the actions indicated in the action field of the packet. Specifically, the receive control register can be set to ignore header *Destination Address Selection Bit* and use the physical address from the special receive register as the destination address for the next incoming message. Similarly, the receive control can be programmed to ignore header's *Interrupt Bit* and interrupt after every message (or never interrupt). Finally, the receive logic can be instructed to freeze the incoming path after each packet arrival, which is useful for debugging.

The network interface supports both the traditional message passing and virtual memory-mapped communication. In traditional message passing, the destination address is provided by the receiver and an interrupt is raised upon message arrival (as indicated by action bits in message header). This option will allow the operating system kernel to manage memory buffers and dispatch messages.

Before using virtual memory-mapped communication, mapping phase is needed to map a user-level send buffer to a user-level receive buffer. The mapping step pins both buffers in physical memory. Once a mapping is established, it can be used to send messages without interrupting the receiving host processor. A receive can be performed at user-level without making a system call.

Virtual memory-mapped communication is an optimization which allows for reduction in software overhead on message passing at the expense of additional mapping phase and increased consumption of physical memory caused by pinning of send and receive buffers. If physical memory becomes scarce, virtual memory-mapped communication can be replaced with traditional message passing through kernel-allocated memory buffers.

4   Software Support

The virtual memory-mapped communication for this network interface requires systems calls to create mappings and also primitives to send messages using mapped memory.

There are two systems calls for mapping creation: *map_send* and *map_recv*. Their arguments and costs are similar to the NX/2's *csend* and *crecv* calls:

- **map_send(node_id, process_id, mapid, sendbuf, size)**
  where *node_id* is the the network address of the receiver node, *process_id* indicates the receiving process, *mapid* is a binding identifier (whose function is similar to the message type in the NX/2 send and receive primitives), *sendbuf* is the starting address of the send buffer, and *size* is the number of words in the send buffer. This call is used on the sender side to establish a mapping.
- **map_recv(mapid, recvbuf, size, ihandler)**

where *mapid* is the binding id to match the mapping request by the *map_send* call, *recvbuf* is the starting address of the receive buffer, and *size* is the number of words in the receive buffer. Non-NULL *ihandler* specifies user-level interrupt handler which will be called for every message received. The implementation of this call is to provide the mapping identified by *mapid* with a receiving physical memory address so that the sender side can create a physical memory mapping for the virtual memory mapping.

The mapping calls will pin the memory pages of both send and receive buffers to create stable physical memory mapping between these buffers, as well as to enable data transfers on both sender and receiver sides without CPU involvement.

Every mapping is unidirectional and asymmetric, from the source (sending buffer) to the destination (receiving buffer). A mapping can be established only if the size of the receive buffer is the same as the size of the send buffer. The *mapid* can be viewed as a handle to select a mapping for send operation. It is needed because we allow multiple and overlapped mappings for the same memory.

For security, only objects owned by processes belonging to the same *process task group* can be mapped to each other. The membership of a process in a given task group is fully controlled by the operating system, so all processes within task group trust each other. For example, processes cooperating on the execution of a given multicomputer program usually belong to the same task group.

The send system call is very simple:

```
send( mapid, sendbuf, size )
```

This system call builds a packet for each memory page. It simply looks up the mapping table, selects the destination physical address based on *mapid*, builds a packet header and initiates a send. This call returns immediately after the data is sent out to the network. Since a destination object is allocated in user space, data can be delivered directly to the user without a receive interrupt. User process can figure out the message delivery for example by polling a flag located at the end of the message buffer. In this way we can implement user-level buffer management and avoid the overhead of kernel buffer management, message dispatching, interrupts and receive system calls.

5 Cost and Performance

Compared to the traditional network interface designs, the only addition of the SHRIMP-I network interface is to include the destination physical address of a packet in its header and to have receiving logic to deliver data accordingly. This simple addition makes our network interface very flexible. It supports both the traditional DMA-based message passing and virtual memory-mapped communication with or without interrupting the receiving processor.

Table 1 shows the overhead components of message passing on three kinds of network interfaces: traditional, SHRIMP-I, and SHRIMP-II [1]. The SHRIMP-II network interface implements virtual memory mapping translation in hardware so that the send operation can be performed at user level. SHRIMP-I network interface requires a system call to send a message, but it requires very little addition to the traditional network interface design.

Message passing overheads	Traditional	SHRIMP-I	SHRIMP-II
Send system call	x	x	
Send argument processing	x	x	
Verify/allocate receive buffer	x		
Preparing packet descriptors	x		
Initiation of send	x	x	x
DMA data via I/O bus	x	x	x
Data transfer over the network	x	x	x
Data transfer via I/O bus	x	x	x
Interrupt service	x	optional	optional
Receive buffer management	x		
Message dispatch	x		
Copy data to user space (small)	x		
Receive system call	x		

Table 1. Message passing overheads breakdown of three kinds of network interface designs.

We have implemented the send system call for the SHRIMP multicomputer using the Pentium-based PCs and the SHRIMP-I network interface. We compared the cost of the send system call with that of the *csend/crecv* in NX/2 on the iPSC/2 whose node processors have the same instruction set. For passing a small message (less than 100 bytes), the software overhead of a send for the SHRIMP-I network interface is 104 instructions plus a system call overhead. Interrupting the receiving host processor is optional. However, the software overhead of a *csend* and a *crecv* of NX/2 is 483 instructions plus two system calls (*csend* and *crecv*) and an interrupt.

For passing a large message, the message passing primitives for the SHRIMP-I network interface require only 26 additional instructions for each page transferred. The *csend* and *crecv* of NX/2 require additional network transactions to allocate receive buffer space on the receiving side and must prepare data descriptors needed by the network interface to initiate a send.

The cost of mapping in the SHRIMP-I case is similar to that of passing a small message using *csend* and *crecv* of NX/2. For applications that have static communication patterns [1], the amortized overhead of creating a mapping can be negligible.

We would like to point out that the semantics of *csend/crecv* primitives of NX/2 is richer than the virtual memory-mapped communication supported by the SHRIMP-I interface. Our comparison shows that rich semantics comes with the substantial overhead. Since the SHRIMP-I network interface supports both traditional message passing and virtual memory-mapped communication, it allows user programs to optimize their common cases.

6 Related Work

The traditional network interface design is based on DMA data transfer. Recent examples include the NCUBE [14], iPSC/2 [13] and iPSC/860. In this scheme an application sends messages by making operating system calls to initiate DMA data transfers. The network interface initiates an incoming DMA data transfer when a message arrives and interrupts the local processor when the transfer has finished so it can dispatch the arrived message. The main disadvantage of traditional network interface is that message passing costs are usually thousands of CPU cycles.

One solution to the problem of software overhead is to add a separate processor on every node just for message passing [12, 8]. Recent examples of this approach are the Intel Paragon [9] and Meiko CS-2 [7]. The basic idea is for the "compute" processor to communicate with the "message" processor through either mailboxes in shared memory or closely-coupled datapaths. The compute and message processors can then work in parallel, to overlap communication and computation. In addition, the message processor can poll the network device, eliminating interrupt overhead. This approach, however, does not eliminate the overhead of the software protocol on the message processor, which is still hundreds of CPU instructions. In addition, the node is complex and expensive to build.

Several projects have taken the approach of lowering communication latency by bringing the network all the way into the processor and mapping the network interface FIFOs to special processor registers [2, 6, 3]. Writing and reading these registers queues and dequeues data from the FIFOs respectively. While this is efficient for fine-grain, low-latency communication, it requires the use of a non-standard CPU, and it does not support the protection of multiple contexts in a multiprogramming environment.

An alternative network interface design approach employs memory-mapped network interface FIFOs [10, 5]. In this scheme, the controller has no DMA capability, instead the host processor communicates with the network interface by reading or writing special memory locations that correspond to the FIFOs. This approach results in good latency for short messages. However, for longer messages, the DMA-based controller is preferable, because it makes use of the bus burst mode which is much faster than processor-generated single word transactions. Additionally, processor-independent DMA allows for overlapping communication and computation on the node.

7 Conclusions

This paper describes the new method of reducing the software overhead of message passing. The key idea of this method is to push the buffer management from the kernel to user level. The implementation of this idea is based on virtual memory-mapped communication between user-allocated send and receive buffers. We have designed a new network interface, called SHRIMP-I, which supports virtual memory-mapped communication quite efficiently, and requires only minimal addition to the traditional network interface.

The SHRIMP-I network interface provides users with a set of flexible functionalities. It allows users to specify certain actions such as data delivery locations and performing interrupts at the receiver's side. It supports both the traditional DMA-based message passing and virtual memory-mapped communication.

Although the virtual memory-mapped communication requires map system calls, it can avoid a receive system call and a receive interrupt. For multicomputer programs that exhibit static communication patterns, (transfers from a given send buffer go to a fixed destination buffer), the net gain can be substantial.

We are currently constructing a 16-node multicomputer using the SHRIMP-I network interface. We have built a simulator for software development. We expect the SHRIMP-I network interface to be operational in the summer of 1994. We are also designing a virtual memory-mapped network interface (SHRIMP-II) that allows send operations to perform entirely in user mode [1]. The design of SHRIMP-II network interface is however more complicated than SHRIMP-I.

Acknowledgements

We would like to thank Douglas W. Clark for his help in the evaluation of SHRIMP-I design. We are also grateful to Ed Felten for his helpful comments on the organization of this paper.

References

1. Matthias A. Blumrich, Kai Li, Richard Alpert, Cezary Dubnicki, Edward W. Felten, and Jonathan S. Sandberg. Virtual memory mapped network interface for the shrimp multicomputer. In *Proceedings of the 21st ISCA*, pages 142–153, April 1994.
2. Shekhar Borkar, Robert Cohn, George Cox, Thomas Gross, H.T.Kung, Monica Lam, Margie Levine, Brian Moore, Wire Moore, Craig Peterson, Jim Susman, Jim Sutton, John Urbanski, and Jon Webb. Supporting systolic and memory communication in iWarp. In *Proceedings of the 17th ISCA*, pages 70–81, May 1990.
3. William J. Dally, Roy Davison, J. A. Stuart Fiske, Greg Fyler, John S. Keen, Richard A. Lethin, Michael Noakes, and Peter R. Nuth. The message-driven processor: A multicomputer processing node with efficient mechanisms. *IEEE Micro*, 12(2):23–39, April 1992.

4. Edward W. Felten. *Protocol Compilation: High-Performance Communication for Parallel Programs*. PhD thesis, Dept. of Computer Science and Engineering, University of Washington, August 1993. Available as technical report 93-09-09.

5. FORE Systems. *TCA-100 TURBOchannel ATM Computer Interface, User's Manual*, 1992.

6. Dana S. Henry and Christopher F. Joerg. A tightly-coupled processor-network interface. In *Proceedings of 5th International Conference on Architectural Support for Programming Languages and Operating Systems*, pages 111–122, October 1992.

7. Mark Homewood and Moray McLaren. Meiko CS-2 interconnect elan – elite design. In *Proceedings of Hot Interconnects '93 Symposium*, August 1993.

8. Jiun-Ming Hsu and Prithviraj Banerjee. A message passing coprocessor for distributed memory multicomputers. In *Proceedings of Supercomputing '90*, pages 720–729, November 1990.

9. Intel Corporation. *Paragon XP/S Product Overview*, 1991.

10. Charles E. Leiserson, Zahi S. Abuhamdeh, David C. Douglas, Carl R. Feynman, Mahesh N. Ganmukhi, Jeffrey V. Hill, Daniel Hillis, Bradley C. Kuszmaul, Margaret A. St. Pierre, David S. Wells, Monica C. Wong, Shaw-Wen Yang, and Robert Zak. The network architecture of the Connection Machine CM-5. In *Proceedings of 4th ACM Symposium on Parallel Algorithms and Architectures*, pages 272–285, June 1992.

11. Richard J. Littlefield. Characterizing and tuning communications performance for real applications. In *Proceedings of the First Intel DELTA Applications Workshop*, pages 179–190, February 1992. Proceedings also available as Caltech Technical Report CCSF-14-92.

12. R.S. Nikhil, G.M. Papadopoulos, and Arvind. *T: A multithreaded massively parallel architecture. In *Proceedings of the 19th ISCA*, pages 156–167, May 1992.

13. Steven Nugent. The iPSC/2 direct-connect communication technology. In *Proceedings of 3rd Conference on Hypercube Concurrent Computers and Applications*, pages 51–60, January 1988.

14. John Palmer. The NCUBE family of high-performance parallel computer systems. In *Proceedings of 3rd Conference on Hypercube Concurrent Computers and Applications*, pages 845–851, January 1988.

15. Paul Pierce. The NX/2 operating system. In *Proceedings of 3rd Conference on Hypercube Concurrent Computers and Applications*, pages 384–390, January 1988.

16. Roger Traylor and Dave Dunning. Routing chip set for intel paragon parallel supercomputer. In *Proceedings of Hot Chips '92 Symposium*, August 1992.

Cranium: An Interface for Message Passing on Adaptive Packet Routing Networks*

Neil R. McKenzie, Kevin Bolding, Carl Ebeling and Lawrence Snyder

University of Washington
Department of CSE, FR-35
Seattle WA 98195, USA

Abstract. Cranium is a processor-network interface for an interconnection network based on adaptive packet routing. Adaptive networks relax the restriction that packet order is preserved; packets may be delivered to their destinations in an arbitrary sequence. Cranium uses two mechanisms: an automatic-receive interface for packet serialization and high performance, and a processor-initiated interface for flexibility. To minimize software overhead, Cranium is directly accessible by user-level programs. Protection for user-level message passing is implemented by mapping user-level handles into physical node identifiers and buffer addresses.

1 Introduction

Scalable multicomputer architectures have been converging on a standard organization with four elements: a workstation microprocessor, main memory based on dynamic RAM, a point-to-point interconnection network and a processor-network interface. Both the microprocessors and DRAM chips have become inexpensive and widely available. Multicomputer architects have therefore focused their efforts on the design of a fast network router and an efficient interface.

This report describes Cranium[1], a processor-network interface that supports *message passing* protocols on mesh networks that use *adaptive packet routing* algorithms. The advantage of explicit message passing over the implicit *non-uniform memory access* (NUMA) model is the intrinsic ability to overlap communication and computation. Augmenting the NUMA model with multithreading, scoreboarding, or prefetching makes it possible to overlap communication and computation, but at the cost of much greater hardware complexity than that of a message passing interface.

In the remainder of the introduction, we first describe the benefits and pitfalls of adaptive routing. Then we discuss the tradeoffs of different approaches to network interface design. Finally we summarize our requirements for Cranium.

* This research was supported in part by Office of Naval Research grant N00014-91-J-1007 and National Science Foundation grant MIP-92-13469.
[1] Chaos Router Autonomous Network Interface for User-level Messages

1.1 The case for adaptive routing

It is highly desirable to apply the principles of adaptive packet routing to a practical and realizable multicomputer system.

- Simulation studies show that at high network loads, adaptive routing offers higher bandwidth and lower latency than the standard dimension-order oblivious algorithm, for a given fixed network packet size [1, 2, 4].
- Adaptive routing improves *fault tolerance*, the ability to operate in the presence of failed components [3].
- It is feasible to construct fast, economically competitive adaptive routers, such as the Chaos router [4].

In the network architectures we consider in this article, network packets have bounded length. Therefore, a message that is longer than the maximum network packet size cannot be directly injected into the network; it must be converted into a sequence of packets by the sending node, which then injects them into the network. After the network delivers these packets, the original message is reassembled at the receiving node. A potential drawback to adaptive network routing is the property that packets can overtake other packets in the network. Packets can therefore arrive in an arbitrary order, even if there is only one node actively sending packets and one receiving them. This property is called *out-of-order delivery*. The problem is that there exist message passing protocols that depend on the *in-order delivery* property of the oblivious routers. One common technique is to send a number of data packets followed by a control packet to mark the end of the data. After the receiver detects the arrival of the control packet, it can safely assume that all the data packets have arrived. Under out-of-order delivery, this protocol will not work reliably.

There are two approaches for dealing with out-of-order packet delivery. One approach is to use protocols that assume in-order delivery, and augment *only* the interface hardware to convert the out-of-order stream of packets into a time-sorted stream. Such an interface is required to identify and contain early-arriving packets in a separate buffer space; in effect, it mandates double-buffering, and increases the average packet latency. This kind of interface is inherently expensive, complicated, and slow; therefore it is not practical to implement.

The other approach is to modify the low-level software protocol: instead of waiting for the arrival of the control packet, the receiver simply counts the number of arriving data packets. To accelerate this modified protocol, the network interface hardware provides a set of status bits to indicate to the software that the nth data packet has arrived. Packet counting allows reliable operation that is independent of packet arrival order, and the hardware support in the network interface can be implemented inexpensively; it is the approach we assume in the remainder of this article.

1.2 Processor-initiated interfaces vs. automatic-receive interfaces

Broadly, the network interface has two strategies for handling incoming packets: *processor-initiated* and *automatic-receive*. In the processor-initiated strategy, the processor polls or is interrupted for each packet that arrives from the network. The processor accepts data from network via programmed I/O, optionally, it initiates a direct-memory-access (DMA) operation. In either case, the processor must *rendezvous* with the arriving packet. In the automatic-receive strategy, DMA is required; an intelligent network controller on the receiving node places the packet data in memory automatically. Importantly, interaction with the processor is removed from the critical path of placing the packet in memory. The choice of a processor-initiated interface, an automatic-receive interface, or a combination of the two approaches depends on the network architecture and the tradeoffs among generality, performance and complexity.

- *Generality: processor-initiated is more general.* Because a processor-initiated interface interacts with the processor when a packet arrives, the processor can execute an arbitrary calculation to decide where to put the packet data. An auto-receive interface places the packet directly into memory based on the packet header information alone, without involving the processor.
- *Performance: automatic-receive has better performance.* If we assume the packet-counting scheme outlined in the previous section, then the software overhead for an auto-receive interface is paid *once per message* instead of *once per packet*. The savings in overhead can be substantial if the packet size is small and the message is large. Conversely, the performance advantage may be nil for minimum size (single packet) messages, which are often used for synchronization and global combining operations.

  An auto-receive interface consumes arriving packets right away, whereas a processor-initiated interface incurs a lag time for the processor to service the network. The lag time can vary, including the time it takes the processor to process an interrupt, as well as the time it takes to execute some arbitrary code to compute a destination address for the packet data (e.g. a memory allocator). During the lag time, if there is a subsequent burst of packet traffic destined for arrival at this node, packets are likely to back up into the network. Long lag times at one destination node can actually degrade the performance of the entire network under moderate to heavy traffic loads.
- *Complexity: processor-initiated is simpler.* However, an overly simple solution will limit its performance. Subcircuits such as a DMA controller, a content addressable memory (CAM) and a hardware FIFO are common sources of complexity in the network interface. DMA is required in an auto-receive interface; it is optional in a processor-initiated interface. CAMs are commonly used in an auto-receive interface for validation of the packet header and/or address translation. CAMs are not common in a processor-initiated interface because validation and translation are usually handled in software. A hardware FIFO on the receiving side of the interface helps decouple the network link from the memory bus, and is desirable for containing bursts of packet data that would otherwise back up into the network. For good performance, the receive FIFO needs to be large if the bandwidth of the network link is larger than that of the local memory bus, or if the lag time to service the network is large. Because an auto-receive interface consumes packets right away, it may permit the use of a much smaller FIFO.

1.3 Requirements for Cranium

The requirements for Cranium are threefold[2]. The first requirement is to provide both an *automatic-receive* interface and a *processor-initiated* interface. Automatic-receive is important for supporting a packet-counting protocol compatible with out-of-order packet delivery, serializing packet data in memory, and maintaining high-bandwidth communications. The processor-initiated interface adds flexibility for supporting synchronization, global combining and other situations where message latency is critical but bandwidth is less important.

The second requirement is to *minimize the software latency* for sending and receiving messages. Designers of the older generation of network interfaces considered message passing to be an operating system service. The latency of message passing on a system with *direct user-level access* to the network is reduced by one to two orders of magnitude compared with a similar system-level interface. Felten [5] outlines the basic strategy for safe user-level communication that Cranium supports – system partitioning, hardware validation for message destinations, gang scheduling, saving and restoring the network state, and separate user and kernel level communication.

The third requirement is the ability to *detect faults* in the network at two levels. At the low level, packets include a cyclical redundancy code (CRC) to validate the packet header and payload, to permit the interface to detect corrupted packets directly. At the high level, there must be specific support for the Chaos network. Chaotic routing has the property that delivery time of a particular packet cannot be bounded as long as the network continues to accept the injection of new packets. An absent packet may indicate either a network failure or a heavily loaded network. These two cases are distinguished with the help of a software timer. If the timer expires before all expected packets have arrived, then the software can issue a *drain* command to the network via the interface, which blocks further packet injection. A network drain ensures an upper bound on delivery time for all packets in transit. Either the tardy packets eventually arrive and computation can proceed, or network failure is detected. In the latter case, the interface issues a command to the network for self-diagnosis and possible reconfiguration. See Bolding and Yost [3] for further information on fault detection and recovery in the Chaos network.

Here is the organization of the rest of this report. Section 2 introduces the architecture of Cranium. Section 3 discusses run-time issues and high-level message passing protocols. Section 4 discusses related work on network interface design. Section 5 discusses hardware implementation issues. Section 6 shows our plan for continuing work in this area, and Section 7 is a summary.

---

[2] Although the principles underlying the design of Cranium are presented here in the context of the Chaos router, keep in mind that they are general and apply to all routing algorithms that deliver packets out of order. Features of Cranium that are specific to Chaos are duly noted.

2 Architecture

Cranium is *autonomous*; it schedules and executes its work independently and concurrently with processor execution. Cranium is *multithreaded*; multiple message commands from a single node can be in progress simultaneously. Cranium has *user-level access*; user programs access network interface registers directly via load and store commands. The overhead of sending and receiving messages is minimal, on the order of a few user-level instructions.

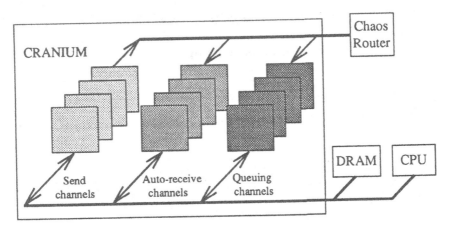

Fig. 1. Cranium architecture

The basic architecture for Cranium is shown in Figure 1. The programming model is a small fixed set of message *channels*. There are three kinds of channels. Messages are sent using the *send channels*. The *auto-receive channels* represent the automatic-receive interface, and the *queuing channels* represent the processor-initiated interface. Each channel represents a complete context for a message, including the physical address of the local message buffer, the remote node name, the number of packets to send or receive, and transfer completion status.

Messages are broken up into packets by the interface at the source node and then reassembled by the interface at the destination node. A packet consists of an 8 byte header and a 32 byte field for payload (user data). The packet header consists of the destination node identifier (2 bytes), source node identifier (2 bytes), a packet sequence number (6 bits), the send channel number (4 bits), the auto-receive channel number (4 bits), the user/system flag (1 bit), the queue flag (1 bit), and two bytes for the CRC.

2.1 Overview of send channels and auto-receive channels

The send channels and the auto-receive channels are symmetric; the programmer model for both sets of channels is nearly identical. At any time, a send channel or auto-receive channel is either in the idle state or in an active state where it is transmitting or receiving packets. The NI_send() command activates a send channel; likewise, the NI_recv() command activates a auto-receive channel. There are 16 send channels and 16 auto-receive channels. Each channel activation represents a block transfer of up to 2K bytes (64 packets, 32 bytes per packet). Send channels tag each outgoing packet with a sequence number, which is used by the auto-receive channels to place incoming packet data into memory in the proper serial order. The processor can test the status of these two types of channels to determine completion status of the transfer. Optionally, Cranium can interrupt the processor when the transfer completes.

2.2 Buffer mapping and node mapping

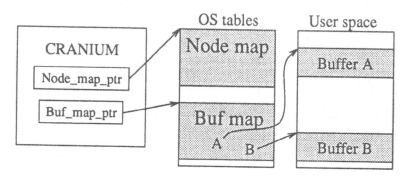

Fig. 2. Protection for safe user-level access via mapping tables

Because Cranium's channels are directly available to the user, there are hard-ware mechanisms for ensuring safe user-level access. Otherwise, a user program might accidentally (or maliciously) interfere with network operation, by spoofing or intercepting messages meant for the operating system, or sending or receiving messages at memory locations outside the user's protection domain. Cranium accomplishes this goal using *mapping tables* that are shared with (and privileged to) the operating system. Figure 2 shows the two mapping tables: the node map and the buffer map. The network interface contains a pair of hardware reg-isters that contain the base physical addresses for each mapping table, called Node_Map_Ptr and Buf_Map_Ptr. An entry in the node map is the physical iden-tifier for a remote node, or zero to indicate an unmapped node entry. An index into the node map (i.e. an offset from the base address of the table) is called a *node handle*. An entry in the buffer map is the physical address of a 2 kilobyte user-space buffer. An index into the buffer map is called a *buffer handle*, which is returned to the user process at the completion of a NI_buffer_map() operating system call. When a buffer is mapped into the network interface, its physical page is also pinned in memory. It makes sense for the programmer to locate all buffer mapping system calls at the beginning of the user program, so that all subsequent network commands are performed at user level.

The buffer mapping feature is very flexible. There is no distinction between a send buffer and a receive buffer; the same buffer can be used to collect a message from one node and then pass it to another node without copying. A single buffer can be used for *multicast*, to send several messages at once to a set of nodes.

Figure 2 shows two user buffers, A and B, that the user program has registered with the operating system and thereby entered into the buffer map. When the user program wishes to send a message to node X using buffer A, it passes X's node handle and A's buffer handle to a Cranium send channel. The interface performs a table lookup on each handle to verify that their corresponding table entries contain valid data. An advantage of using a handle for protection and mapping is that it reduces the amount of data that the user program needs to pass to Cranium. There are 4096 entries for each table, enough to map 8 MB of message buffer space. Handles are only 12 bits instead of 32 or more bits usually required for the address of a user buffer.

2.3 Queuing channels

The queuing channels implement the processor-initiated interface. Packets in the queue are not serialized by the interface; they appear in the order they are ejected from the network. Queue memory is implemented using main memory; queue buffers are locked into the physical memory map. There are several advantages to storing packets in main memory rather than using a deep hardware FIFO[3].

- Main memory is constructed using inexpensive dynamic RAM chips; hardware FIFOs tend to use expensive static RAM.
- The processor is notified *after* the interface places the packet data into main memory, rather than before. The user program can access packet data immediately after notification instead of waiting for the transfer to complete.
- The operating system can change the sizes of the queues dynamically at user program load time, rather than requiring a hardware reconfiguration. The operating system needs to ensure that queue overflow rarely occurs, by making the frequently accessed queues of sufficient size to handle even large bursts of traffic.

There are four queuing channels: the user queue, the user error queue, the system queue and the hardware error queue. Packets that have the queue bit in the packet header enabled are routed to the user queue. The user error queue is used for packets that signal a protocol (soft) error (see Section 2.4). Both the user queue and the user error queue buffers are mapped into user space.

Figure 3 shows the organization of queuing channel memory. For each queuing channel, the channel context is a set of pointers into main memory, called the start pointer (SP), the end pointer (EP), and a pointer to the current (most

---

[3] This use of system memory helps reduce the size of the receiver's hardware FIFO, but it is still necessary for decoupling the network from the memory bus.

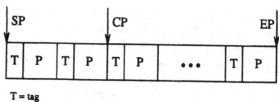

T = tag
P = entire packet (includes header)

Fig. 3. Organization of circular buffer in DRAM for queuing channel

recently arrived) packet buffer (CP). Queue memory is organized as a circular buffer that uses a simple producer-consumer protocol, with Cranium as producer and the processor (i.e. the user program) as consumer.

At initialization, CP and SP both point to the start of the queue buffer. When a packet arrives, Cranium performs a read-modify-write cycle on the tag field (T). If the tag field was 0, then Cranium atomically writes a nonzero value[4] to the tag field, writes the entire packet (including header) into the packet field (P), and advances CP to point to the next tag field. If the tag field was nonzero, then Cranium signals queue overflow and interrupts the processor (see Section 2.4). The user program detects the presence of a packet by polling the tag field. If the packet is present, the user program reads the packet information, processes it, then sets the tag field to zero to release the space back to Cranium.

2.4 Error handling in Cranium

When Cranium encounters a run-time error, it sends an interrupt to the processor. There are two kinds of errors: command errors and packet errors. Command errors are caused by an illegal access to Cranium by the user program, such as trying to initiate a new command on an already active channel, passing the handle of an unmapped node or buffer, or accessing a privileged channel. Packet errors arise when a packet arrives from the network, but Cranium cannot process it normally, so the operating system must intervene. There are several different kinds of packet errors and corresponding error handling mechanisms.

- *Network hardware error.* Symptom: CRC mismatch on incoming packet. Action: the packet is sent to the hardware error queue.
- *Protocol error.* Symptom: either the auto-receive channel for the packet is inactive, or the packet header does not match the expected information in the channel context[5]. Action: the packet is sent to the user error queue.

---

[4] In our implementation, we write a 64-bit timestamp into the tag field to represent the nonzero value (the least significant bit is always 1). Timestamp information can be used by the user program for performance analysis.

[5] For instance, the source node ID in the packet header does not match the source node ID of the auto-receive channel.

— *Queue overflow.* Symptom: the tag field of the current slot of the indicated queue was nonzero (see Section 2.3). Action: A control bit in the NI selects one of two possible actions: *either* hold packet data and wait for an operating system command to remove the packet, *or* simply drop the packet.

3 Run-time support for message passing

The user queue and the auto-receive channels give the user program a wide degree of flexibility in the implementation of efficient message passing primitives. The user queue is the proper mechanism for funneling packets that arrive without prior arrangement; it provides the best support for synchronization, small data transfers and active message handlers [6]. After two nodes synchronize, the auto-receive channels can be used for high bandwidth communication. The restriction with the auto-receive channels is that the processor on the receiving node must initiate an auto-receive channel transfer *before* the processor on the sending node initiates its corresponding send channel transfer. The user queue and user error queue, like the send and auto-receive channels, are available to the programmer at user level. Because these queues are just shared memory, they are accessed directly by loads and stores without touching network interface registers.

Traditionally, run-time support for message passing primitives has been inefficient for two reasons: the architecture of the network interface makes it necessary for user programs to call the operating system to access the network, and messages arriving at destination nodes are stored first into system buffers and later copied into user-space buffers. Cranium enables the user program to eliminate both sources of overhead. First, since Cranium has direct user-level access, there is no system call overhead. Second, the auto-receive channels can be used to place the data directly in user-space buffers in the proper order without copying the data.

3.1 Anatomy of a block transfer

A block transfer of data consists of the following sequence of operations. We assume that the message buffer addresses have already been entered into the buffer map.

— On the destination node, the processor issues an NI_recv() command to a auto-receive channel. The channel is initialized with a node handle and a buffer handle. The network interface performs two table lookups: one on the node handle to get the source node ID, and another on the buffer handle to get the physical destination address for the incoming data.
— On the source node, the processor issues an NI_send() command to a send channel to initialize it with a node handle, a buffer handle, and the packet count. The network interface performs table lookups on the node and buffer handles to get the destination node ID and the physical source address for the outgoing data.

- The source interface creates and injects packets into the network, using the send channel context to create the proper packet header for each packet. The channel's sequence number field is incremented after each packet is sent.
- For each arriving packet, the destination interface validates the packet for correct CRC. Next, the interface confirms that the auto-receive channel selected in the packet header is in the active state. The interface then computes the memory address from the base physical address of the channel, offset by the packet sequence number times the payload size (32 bytes). Finally it places the payload data in memory at this address.

Status information is maintained by the interfaces on both the source and destination nodes. As soon as the send channel has finished injecting all its packets into the network, it goes idle. When all these packets arrive at the destination node, the destination's auto-receive channel goes idle.

3.2 Standard message passing example

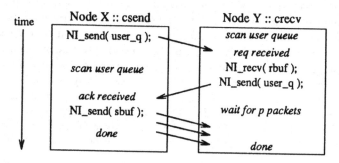

Fig. 4. NX-style message passing example

Most parallel message-passing codes use a standard interface for message passing, such as NX, Express, PVM, and many others [7]. Standard interfaces improve program portability and readability, compared with using the specific message passing primitives provided by the architecture. We now show a simple example of run-time support for Cranium using the semantics of csend() and crecv(), the most basic method of communication under NX [8]. Figure 4 illustrates how the NX commands are implemented in terms of Cranium commands, for the case of medium length messages (between 32 and 32K bytes). In the figure, italics represent pseudocode, and roman type represents NI commands. In this example, X is the source node and Y is the destination node. We wish to transfer up to $32p$ bytes from buffer sbuf on X to buffer rbuf on Y, where $1 \leq p \leq 1024$. Node X executes csend(); at the same time, node Y executes crecv(). The first step is for X to send a packet to Y's user queue to request the block transfer. After Y receives the packet and the message type is matched, Y sets up one or more auto-receive channels, then sends an acknowledge packet back to X's user queue. After X receives the ack packet, X initiates the corresponding number of send channels for the block transfer to Y. After p packets arrive at Y, the message transfer is complete.

For messages smaller than 32 bytes, the block transfer phase is not necessary; the receiver simply copies the small message from queue memory to buffer memory. For messages larger than 32K bytes, there are not enough channels to initiate the entire transfer at once. There must be additional acknowledge packets from Y back to X to denote that it is safe to reuse channels. The loss of performance due to these extra packets is small, because the fraction of bandwidth consumed is only 1/64, and the latency can be hidden by the use of multiple channels.

4 Related work

4.1 Tightly-coupled interfaces vs. bus-based interfaces

A tightly-coupled processor-network interface is one that is integrated onto the same silicon chip as the processor; the instruction set architecture of the processor includes specific instructions for sending and receiving messages. Examples include iWarp [9], MDP (J-machine) [10], and *T [11]. The advantage of tightly-coupled systems is an order of magnitude lower message latency than a comparable bus-based interface. However, there are several disadvantages to this strategy. By placing the interface onto the processor chip, some other functionality must be eliminated or moved off-chip. In the *T design, about 15 per cent of the processor's chip area is dedicated to the network interface [12]. The resulting single-processor performance is less than the fastest possible. Another disadvantage to the tight coupling is the extra amount of engineering effort needed to design and build the interface. Unlike the case for a bus-based interface, this effort cannot be easily amortized across a family of different processors. For these reasons, tightly-coupled interfaces are less able to compete economically and are not as widely used in commercial multicomputer systems as bus-based interfaces. Continuing research in this area may eventually solve these problems. In the meantime, bus-based interfacing remains the most economically viable strategy for implementing multicomputers, using standard workstation processors and memories. Examples of systems using bus-based network interfaces with direct user-level access are CM-5 [13], Shrimp [14], Hamlyn [15] and Cranium.

4.2 Comparison of Cranium with Shrimp and Hamlyn

Cranium is highly similar to the Shrimp processor-network interface [14]. In both systems, messages are sent and received at the cost of only a few user-level instructions. Both systems use a separate phase to map user-space buffers with the operating system and the network interface. Both systems use DMA, rather than the programmed-I/O approach used by the CM-5 interface. Both systems use an automatic receive interface for high throughput. However, Cranium and Shrimp have somewhat different goals. Here are the significant differences between the two designs.

- The automatic receive channels in Cranium are designed to work with a network that delivers packets out-of-order. Shrimp requires in-order packet arrival.

- Cranium's auto-receive channels count the number of packets that arrive. The Shrimp interface does not count packets; furthermore, this information is not even visible at the user level, making it difficult to detect if packets are dropped in the interconnect. Programs running under Cranium can always determine the number of packets that arrive and therefore detect dropped (or late arriving) packets in the Chaos interconnect.

- Once a logical link between two nodes is established under Shrimp, it persists until it is explicitly terminated by the user program. Logical links under Cranium are implicitly broken at the point where all packets regarding that logical link have been sent and received. Under Shrimp, creating and removing a logical link each require an operating system call, whereas Cranium requires only user-mode instructions. However, Cranium requires additional synchronization packets to support long transfers (i.e. the connections need to be created again and again). Thus, their relative performance depends on the behavior of the user program; Shrimp is likely to be more efficient for large transfers where the configuration of links is relatively static, and Cranium is likely to be more efficient for smaller transfers or if the configuration is highly dynamic.

- Cranium is better suited for multicasting than Shrimp is, for two reasons. Cranium has multiple channels to send a set of messages concurrently, whereas Shrimp has only one outgoing DMA context. Shrimp's mapping phase binds a local buffer to a [remote node, remote buffer] pair; Cranium's buffer mapping and node mapping steps are independent and orthogonal. Cranium can send the contents of a single buffer to a set of nodes without copying data or invoking the operating system, which is not possible under the current design of Shrimp.

Cranium is also similar to Hamlyn [15]. Both interfaces are designed to work with a network that deliver packets out-of-order. Both interfaces make use of multiple DMA contexts, called mapping table slots in Hamlyn, similar to Cranium's channels. A proposed implementation of Hamlyn has thousands of slots, compared with the small number of channels we propose for Cranium. All of Hamlyn's communication uses an automatic receive interface; there is no rendezvous interface. However, Hamlyn must still provide the possibility for any node to communicate with any other node. Therefore, $N - 1$ slots per node must be preallocated for any-to-any communication, where N is the number of nodes in the multicomputer. Hamlyn therefore requires the system to "burn" a potentially large number of slots for communication that *might* occur during a computation. For these reasons, we believe that Hamlyn is comparable in features and performance to Cranium, but it is relatively complicated and expensive to implement.

5 Implementation issues

There are a number of implementation issues that space does not permit us to cover in depth. Here, we describe a few of these pertinent issues briefly.

The first issue is to select a processor architecture for the multicomputer node. Ideally the processor should have a 64-bit data bus, to let the user process issue a NI_send() or NI_recv() command in a single memory store operation[6]. It should also have multiprocessor support for cache coherency, with the option of write-update[7]. The cache line size should be 32 bytes to match the size of the packet payload. When a packet arrives, the processor snoops the bus to see if the cache line is mapped into first level cache. The physical address comes from the packet's auto-receive channel in the interface. If snooping on the arriving packet results in a cache hit, then the interface performs a write-update of the packet payload into the first level cache in the processor.

The second issue is a rough estimate of the complexity of an initial implementation of Cranium. The finite state control decomposes into four communicating state machines: a processor-bus interface, a DMA engine, a network-link interface, and a channel scheduler. Here are the approximate memory requirements for each component in Cranium: 100 bits per send channel, 150 bits per auto-receive channel, 100 bits per queuing channel, 200 bits for the channel scheduler, and 320 bits per FIFO stage. Assuming 16 send channels, 16 auto-receive channels, 4 queuing channels, one channel scheduler, and two FIFO stages, the total is about 5K bits. Also required are a 16-bit adder for address calculation, a 64-bit timestamp counter, and CRC logic. An advantage of the channel paradigm is that it eliminates the need for a content-addressable memory, because channels are indexed directly by number.

Cranium and Shrimp have many aspects in common (see Section 4.2), and we anticipate that their relative performance will be similar in many cases. For instance, packet latency under Shrimp (the time to transfer a single packet between two nodes) is on the order of a few microseconds. Actual performance numbers for Cranium will depend on the performance of the network, and the available technology and the amount of optimization in the network interface hardware. An advantage of the mapping table strategy for user-level protection is that a range of implementations for Cranium are possible, such as using regular system DRAM for low cost, or dedicated SRAM to reduce latency.

6 Status and future work

We have completed a preliminary paper design of Cranium. We have also created a visualization tool called visNI to assist in further understanding of the dynamic properties of Cranium, such as bus contention.

---

[6] Each command requires passing approximately 50 data bits from the processor to the interface.

[7] Older processor architectures that do not support multiprocessor cache coherence must flush the entire data cache before sending and after receiving every network packet, causing a loss of performance.

The next phase is evaluation of the Cranium design. Evaluation has two parts: simulation and prototype construction. For simulation, we can take advantage of two existing behavioral simulation tools: a network simulator and a processor simulator. The Chaos network simulator is a very flexible tool for modeling a wide variety of routing algorithms, including chaotic routing, oblivious routing and minimal adaptive routing. The Meerkat processor simulator [16] is a functional simulator for multiprocessors, and is enhanced with timing models for caches, TLBs, register scoreboarding and other processor resources. The simulator is functionally equivalent to a physical multiprocessor prototype system that uses a grid of busses for its interconnect. The simulator estimates execution time to within 5 to 8 per cent of the reference hardware. We are replacing the simulator's bus model with the mesh network simulator. Using the combined simulation strategy, we can begin evaluating simple parallel workloads such as Discrete Fourier Transform and Jacobi iteration. The simulator provides a sanity check for the ideas contained within this article, and will help us decide whether the initial values chosen for the architecture (number of channels, depth of channels, size of mapping tables) represent the best tradeoff between hardware complexity and performance. After the simulator has been constructed, the next step is to construct a hardware prototype. An initial pass at the network interface implementation may involve an inexpensive embedded microcontroller for the channel scheduler and field programmable logic technology such as PALs and FPGAs for the DMA engine, bus interface and network link interface. A higher-speed version may involve a semi-custom solution using sea-of-gates technology.

The current design of Cranium uses the standard gang-scheduling model for safe user-level access [5, 13]. Recently, there has been interest in studying general processor scheduling on multicomputers that have user-level support for message passing [11, 14]. The idea is to let multiple user processes execute at the same time inside the same machine partition. The interaction between adaptive packet routing and general processor scheduling is interesting, and we intend to address this issue in our continuing work with Cranium.

7 Summary

We present a design for a network interface called Cranium. Its architecture meets three design goals: to use both an automatic-receive and a processor-initiated style interface, to support fault detection, and to allow direct user-level access to the network. The automatic-receive interface allows Cranium to accept an out-of-order incoming packet stream, for compatibility with adaptive packet routing networks. Automatic-receive also allows Cranium to handle large numbers of small packets efficiently. A set of queuing channels implements the processor-initiated interface, for added flexibility to support a wide variety of higher level message passing protocols. Protection is implemented by mapping user-level handles into physical node identifiers and buffer addresses. We intend to further evaluate the Cranium design, first by using simulation tools and later by constructing a hardware prototype.

Acknowledgements: we thank our colleagues at the University of Washington for their constructive criticism and input, especially Rob Bedichek, Alex Klaiber, Dave Keppel and the Chaos research team. We also thank Jim Peek at Pyramid Technology, John Wilkes, Greg Buzzard, David Jacobsen and Scott Marovich at HP Labs, Ed Felten at Princeton, and the anonymous reviewers.

References

1. John Y. Ngai and Charles L. Seitz. A Framework for Adaptive Routing in Multicomputer Networks. *Proc. of the Symposium on Parallel Architectures and Algorithms*, May 1989.
2. Kevin Bolding and Lawrence Snyder. Mesh and Torus Chaotic Routing. *Advanced Research in VLSI and Parallel Systems; Proc. of the 1992 Brown/MIT Conference*, March 1992, pp. 333-347.
3. Kevin Bolding and William Yost. Design of a Router for Fault-Tolerant Networks. *Proc. of the 1994 Parallel Computer Routing and Communication Workshop*, Springer-Verlag, Seattle WA, May 1994.
4. Kevin Bolding. *Chaotic Routing: Design and Implementation of an Adaptive Multicomputer Network Router*. PhD dissertation, University of Washington, Dept. of CSE, Seattle WA, July 1993.
5. Edward W. Felten. *Protocol Compilation: High-Performance Communication for Parallel Programs*. PhD dissertation, University of Washington, Dept. of CSE, Sept. 1993. Available as UW CSE technical report TR 93-09-09.
6. Thorsten von Eicken et al. Active Messages: A Mechanism for Integrated Communication and Computation. *19th Annual International Symposium on Computer Architecture*, May 1992, pp. 256-266.
7. Oliver A. McBryan. An Overview of Message Passing Environments. *Parallel Computing* 20(4), April 1994, pp. 417-444.
8. Paul Pierce. The NX Message Passing Interface. *Parallel Computing* 20(4), April 1994, pp. 463-480.
9. Shekhar Borkar et al. Supporting Systolic and Memory Communication in iWarp. *Proc. of the 17th Annual International Symposium on Computer Architecture*, Seattle WA, May 1990, pp. 70-81.
10. William J. Dally et al. The Message-Driven Processor: A Multicomputer Processing Node with Efficient Mechanisms. *IEEE Micro*, April 1992, pp. 23-39.
11. Greg M. Papadopoulos et al. *T: Integrated Building Blocks for Parallel Computing. *Proc. of Supercomputing '93*, Portland OR, November 1993, pp. 624-635.
12. Greg M. Papadopoulos. Personal communication. Supercomputing '93, Portland OR, November 1993.
13. Charles Leiserson et al. The Network Architecture of the CM-5. *Symposium on Parallel Algorithms and Architectures*, 1992, pp. 272-285.
14. Mattias A. Blumrich et al. Virtual Memory-Mapped Network Interface for the SHRIMP Multicomputer. *Proc. of the 21st International Symposium on Computer Architecture*, Chicago IL, April 1994, pp. 142-153.
15. John Wilkes. Hamlyn – an Interface for Sender-Based Communications. Technical Report HPL-OSR-92-13, Hewlett-Packard Company, HP Labs, Operating System Research Dept., November 1992.
16. Robert Bedichek. *The Meerkat Multicomputer*. PhD dissertation, University of Washington, Dept. of CSE, Seattle WA, June 1994.

Optimized Routing in the Cray T3D

Steve Scott and Greg Thorson

Cray Research, Inc.
sls@cray.com, gmt@cray.com

Abstract. The Cray T3D uses a bidirectional, 3D torus interconnection network. Virtual channels are used both to prevent deadlock, and to improve network performance. This paper describes the Cray T3D network and introduces the concept of *virtual channel balance*. We show that balancing the traffic carried by each virtual channel can significantly improve network performance. We also discuss a technique, employing simulated annealing, for assigning virtual channels to routes in order to improve virtual channel balance.

1   Introduction

The interconnection network plays a critical role in the performance of an MPP, especially as the system size increases. A high-performance interconnect also contributes a significant portion of the system cost. Thus, an important design goal is to maximize the utilization of the network.

One way to increase network utilization is by multiplexing multiple virtual channels onto each physical channel [5]. The use of virtual channels can prevent a blocked packet from stalling all of the packets behind it; a packet that does not need the resource on which the blocked packet is waiting may pass the blocked packet *if* it is on a different virtual channel. The extent to which virtual channels improve network utilization thus depends upon the distribution of packets among the various virtual channels.

We have found that the *virtual channel balance*, that is the relative traffic carried by each virtual channel, has a significant effect on overall network performance. Sustained throughput is increased when the traffic load is more evenly spread across the channels. Not only does better balance increase the probability that a packet can pass a blocked packet ahead of it, but it also makes more efficient use of network buffer space, which typically is statically partitioned among the various virtual channels. This paper demonstrates this effect in the context of the T3D, the first MPP system from Cray Research [3].

The problem of non-uniform virtual channel buffer utilization has been previously reported by Bolding [2]. He points out that the virtual channel solution for deadlock avoidance given by Dally and Seitz [4] results in very uneven usage of router buffers. Adve and Vernon have modelled the effect of non-uniform virtual channel usage and shown it to cause significant variations in network performance as viewed by processors in different positions in the network [1].

The remainder of the paper is organized as follows. Section 2 summarizes the T3D network. Section 3 discusses virtual channel balance, and presents a novel method, employing simulated annealing, for assigning virtual channels to routes. Section 4 presents experimental results obtained on a 256-processor T3D. Section 5 summarizes the contributions of the paper.

2   The T3D Network

The backbone of a T3D is a bi-directional, 3D torus interconnection network. The network links are 24 bits wide (16 data, 8 control), and are clocked at 150 MHz, for a raw data capacity of 300 MB/s. The fall through time (per hop latency in the absence of contention) is 2 clocks (13.3 ns). The network ports have the same capacity as the inter-node links, and are shared by two processing elements (PEs) at each node. The PEs are based on the DECchip 21064 $^{(TM)}$ and are also clocked at 150 MHz.

Due to packet overhead, the use of both a request and response packet to transfer a chunk of data and some inefficiency in the port control, the maximum sustained data payload bandwidth per node is approximately 150 MB/s, or 75 MB/s per PE.

In a bi-directional torus, a packet sent to a random destination travels an average of 1/4th the way around each of the torus dimensions. Note that this calculation assumes that some packets travel zero distance in some (or possibly all) dimensions. The average routing distance per *direction* (+X, -X, *etc.*) is 1/8th the dimension's radix, since only half the packets routing in a given dimension will route in each direction.

Therefore, under uniform traffic distribution, the network is balanced (equal port and link utilization) when the radix of each dimension is 8. When the radices are less than 8, the port will generally be the bottleneck, although non-uniform traffic can cause an individual link (or links) to become a hot spot and limit overall throughput. For radices larger than 8, the network links will generally be the bottleneck. The T3D has a maximum radix of 8 in the X and Z dimensions and 16 in the Y dimension.

The T3D network uses deterministic, dimension-order routing (the *e-cube* routing algorithm). The router is physically partitioned into three ECL gate-arrays, one for each dimension, as shown in Figure 1. Packets route in the X dimension first, then Y, then Z.

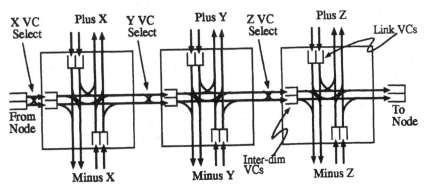

Fig. 1   Virtual channel connections in the T3D router

Virtual channel buffers and their connections are shown for either the request or response channels. Each pair of links represents two virtual channels multiplexed over a single physical connection. The X and Y virtual channels, once chosen, are used when entering and routing in their respective dimensions. The Z virtual channel is used when entering, routing in, and leaving the Z dimension.

Wormhole routing is used, with a flit size of 8 16-bit phits. Some flits, however, are less than 8 phits. These small flits consume a whole flit buffer, but since flit transmission may begin during any clock period, a small flit does *not* consume 8 cycles of physical channel resource. Packet sizes range from 3 to 26 phits, and carry header information plus 0, 1 or 4 64-bit data words.

Virtual channel buffers are one flit deep. Virtual channel acknowledgments are carried upstream via the control signals. Each ack signals that the corresponding VC buffer is being drained and is available for another flit.

The ack turnaround time is less than the time to transmit a full flit (8 cycles). Thus, for packets that are a multiple of 8 phits no bubbles are inherently introduced, and a single virtual channel can utilize 100% of a physical channel's bandwidth. For packets that are not an even multiple of flits, there are 1-, 2- or 3-cycle bubbles introduced on the packet's VC after transmission. In this case, full utilization of the physical channel requires traffic on another VC.

The primary packets used by the workloads in this study are a 26-phit, 4-word write packet and its corresponding 3-phit response. Both of these packets cause a 3-cycle bubble on their virtual channel after transmission across a link. This packet overhead and virtual channel bubbling accounts for the factor of two reduction from peak, raw network bandwidth to maximum sustainable data bandwidth mentioned at the beginning of this section.

Each physical channel carries four virtual channels. Two are used for request traffic, and two are used for response traffic (for simplicity only two virtual channels are shown in Figure 1). Deadlock is avoided by a combination of three features: separate virtual networks for requests and responses remove cyclic dependencies between these traffic classes, dimension-order routing removes cyclic dependencies involving multiple dimensions, and two virtual channels per traffic class are used to remove cyclic channel dependencies involving the wraparound connection within a given dimension.

Routing in the T3D employs end-to-end routing tables. Each node contains a table, stored in dedicated hardware, that provides a routing tag for every destination node in the machine (up to the architected maximum of 2048 processors). The tag specifies a direction, delta, and virtual channel for each of the three dimensions.

The routing tables are loaded by software but are used directly by the hardware. They are indexed by logical PE number, and thus allow a different physical PE to be substituted for a logical PE in the event of a PE failure. They also allow alternate routes to be taken (*i.e.*: the long way around a torus) to avoid faulty links or routers.[1] For the purposes of this paper, we are interested in the ability to specify the virtual channels taken by each route.

3 Virtual Channel Assignments

The routing tables allow us to individually specify the virtual channels used for every source-destination pair in the machine. Thus, two packets traveling along exactly the same segment on a ring (identified by the source and destination nodes on that ring)

---

[1] In a healthy network, the shortest route is always taken. Ties are broken such that the positive direction is taken in a dimension if the source node's ordinate is even in that dimension.

could use different virtual channels, based upon their original source or final destination. In this paper, however, we will ignore a packet's path history and future when assigning it a VC on a given ring. That is, all packets traveling along a given arc of a ring (having the same source and destination on that ring) will use the same virtual channel while on that ring. This allows us to consider each ring in the network individually, making the job of balancing virtual channel traffic much more tractable and allowing solutions for arbitrary networks to be constructed from solutions of the constituent rings.

The primary use of virtual channels in the T3D is to prevent deadlock. Since request and response packets are routed on separate virtual networks, and dimension-order routing breaks cycles between dimensions, we need concern ourselves only with avoiding deadlock within a single ring of the torus. We do this using two virtual channels (VC 0 and VC 1).

We avoid deadlocks by use of logical *datelines*. A dateline is simply an imaginary line cutting a ring that can only be crossed by traffic on the appropriate virtual channel. Since virtual channels are selected via the routing tables, datelines are a purely logical construct; there is nothing built into the hardware to prevent a packet from crossing a dateline on the wrong VC.[1]

A packet stays on the same VC while routing on a given ring, so no traffic ever switches between virtual channels. Therefore, if datelines are enforced for both VC 0 and 1 in both the positive and negative directions for each ring, there can be no cyclic dependencies among VC buffers, and thus no deadlock.

3.1 Virtual channel balance

By convention, we place the VC 1 dateline half way around the ring from the VC 0 dateline in each direction. Since no packet in a healthy network routes more than half way around a ring, at most a single dateline is crossed[2]. Routes that do not cross either dateline are *unconstrained*. These allow us to optimize for virtual channel balance.

Another degree of freedom is the relative placement of the datelines in the positive and negative directions of a ring. Were it not for the inter-dimension VCs (those entering/leaving a ring, as shown in Figure 1), we could completely decouple the positive and negative solutions (in fact, the solution for the positive direction could be flipped and used as the solution for the negative direction). Since we want to balance traffic on the inter-dimension VCs, however, and since these VC buffers are used by both positive-and negative-going traffic on the ring, the two sets of traffic must be considered in tandem and their relative dateline placement matters.

One of the simplest ways to assign VCs (and still avoid deadlock) is to use VC 0 unless a packet will cross the VC0 dateline, else use VC 1. That is, all unconstrained routes use VC 0. The positive VC dateline is node 0, by convention, and the negative VC0 dateline is chosen as node 1. We refer to this as the *naive* assignment. It results in a very unbalanced virtual channel load under the assumption of uniformly distributed traffic on the ring.

---

1 Thus, improper routing tables can lead to deadlock. We make sure to get them right.

2 In a ring with a broken node or link, packets may be routed the long way around in order to avoid the fault. However, there can be no cyclic dependencies in this case because the "ring" no longer forms a circle.

Figure 2 shows the naive VC assignment for an 8-node ring. Routes for each source-destination pair are shown as arcs, with the line type indicating the virtual channel. The figure on the left shows positive and zero-length routes[1]. The VC0 dateline is through node 0 and the VC1 dateline is through node 4. The figure on the right shows negative routes. The VC0 dateline is through node 1 and the VC1 dateline is through node 5. All routes take VC0 except those that cross a VC 0 dateline.

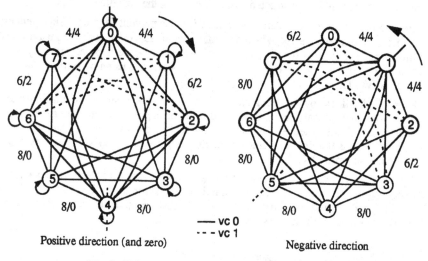

Fig. 2   Naive virtual channel assignment (radix =8)

The pairs of numbers next to each link show the virtual channel balance for that link (VC0 traffic / VC1 traffic), assuming uniform traffic. In both the positive and negative directions, two of the links are perfectly balanced, two carry 75% of their traffic on VC0, and four carry 100% of their traffic on VC0. Table 1 shows the balance for all link and inter-dimension VCs. The VC balance leaving the ring at each node is only important for the Z dimension, as it is the only dimension that has VC buffers leaving the dimension (see Figure 1).

VC *imbalance* is computed by dividing the absolute difference in VC1 and VC0 traffic by the sum of VC1 and VC0 traffic. A perfectly balanced link or inter-dimension VC buffer has an imbalance of 0. The maximum imbalance is 1. Both average and maximum imbalances are shown in Table 1.

As can be seen in the table, the average link imbalance for the naive assignment is 0.625 and the average inter-dimension imbalance is 0.75. The maximum imbalance is 1.0 for both link and inter-dimension VCs. These imbalances can be reduced by use of an *optimized* virtual channel assignment, as discussed in the next section.

---

[1] Zero-length routes cross through a dimension, but do not travel any distance in that dimension (see Figure 1). They are always unconstrained, as they do not introduce any dependencies between intra-VC buffers.

Resource	Node								Avg Imbal	Max Imbal
	0	1	2	3	4	5	6	7		
Positive link	4/4	4/4	6/2	8/0	8/0	8/0	8/0	6/2	0.625	1.0
Negative Link	4/4	4/4	6/2	8/0	8/0	8/0	8/0	6/2	0.625	1.0
Entering Ring	8/0	8/0	6/2	6/2	8/0	8/0	6/2	6/2	0.75	1.0
Leaving Ring	6/2	6/2	6/2	8/0	8/0	8/0	8/0	6/2	0.75	1.0

Table 1   Virtual channel balance for naive assignment (radix = 8)

3.2   Optimizing virtual channel assignment

The problem of optimizing virtual channel assignment requires two inputs. One is an assumption of the traffic distribution on the ring, and the other is a cost function for the "imbalance" in the VC load. Then optimization is simply a matter of assigning VCs to unconstrained routes (source-destination pairs) so as to minimize the cost function.

To increase our flexibility for optimization, we maximize the number of unconstrained routes using two techniques. First, we place the datelines through nodes rather than links. Thus, a route that starts or ends at a dateline node does not *cross* the dateline (this implies, for example, that all length-one routes are unconstrained). We also place positive datelines on even numbered nodes (which send their "half-way-around" traffic in the positive direction) and negative datelines on odd numbered nodes (which send their half-way-around traffic in the negative direction). This reduces the number of routes that cross datelines.

Figure 3 shows an optimized VC assignment for an 8-node ring. For this assignment, we have assumed a uniform traffic distribution. The imbalance cost function is given as follows. We compute the VC imbalance (absolute difference in VC1 and VC0 traffic divided by the sum of VC1 and VC0 traffic) for each link and each inter-dimension VC buffer. We include the VCs leaving the ring as well as those entering the ring (*i.e.*: this is optimized for the Z dimension). The total imbalance cost is the sum of the squares of the link and inter-dimension VC imbalances. Squaring the individual imbalances penalizes links that are highly unbalanced, in an attempt to avoid bottlenecks.

As can be seen by the link balances in the figure, the optimized virtual channel assignment does a much better job of distributing traffic over the two VCs. Table 2 shows the link and inter-dimension VC balances for each node. The average link imbalance is 0.125 and the maximum is only 0.250. The inter-dimension VCs are perfectly balanced. Note that the optimal placement of the negative VC0 dateline is node 1, the same as our assumption in the naive case. This does not hold in general.

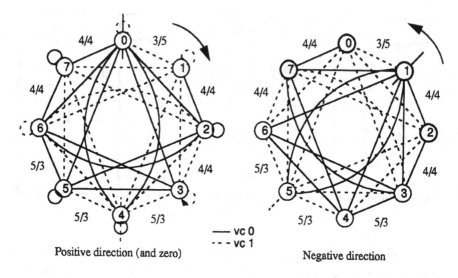

Fig. 3   Optimized virtual channel assignment (radix =8, Z dimension)

Resource	Node								Avg Imbal	Max Imbal
	0	1	2	3	4	5	6	7		
Positive link	4/4	3/5	4/4	4/4	5/3	5/3	5/3	4/4	0.125	0.250
Negative Link	3/5	4/4	4/4	5/3	5/3	5/3	4/4	4/4	0.125	0.250
Entering Ring	4/4	4/4	4/4	4/4	4/4	4/4	4/4	4/4	0	0
Leaving Ring	4/4	4/4	4/4	4/4	4/4	4/4	4/4	4/4	0	0

Table 2   Virtual channel balance for optimized assignment (radix = 8, Z dimension)

3.3   Hierarchically good assignments

Up to this point, we have assumed that the traffic distribution in the machine is uniform (i.e. each node on a ring can be thought to send one packet to every destination node on the ring, including itself). Unfortunately, this assumption is likely to be incorrect in practice. It is likely that many jobs will be run in partitions of the machine (*e.g.* using 64 nodes of a 256-node machine). A useful goal, then, would be to assign virtual channels such that jobs running in sub-partitions of the machine, as well as those using the whole machine, see good virtual channel balance. We refer to this as a *hierarchically good* assignment. We have found that optimizing global VC balance in isolation often leads to poor hierarchical VC balance.

In order to achieve good hierarchical balance, we have modified our cost function and our assumption of traffic distribution. We assume that sometimes one job will be run on the entire ring, and sometimes jobs will be run on smaller partitions of the ring (of course we are only considering a single dimension here; user partitions will include some span in all three dimensions). Partitions are assumed to be naturally aligned powers of two, and partitions of size 2 are ignored. A ring of size 16, for example, might have jobs running on the whole ring, in one of two half-rings, or in one of four quarter-rings.

Our cost function is similar to that used for the globally optimized ring in Section 3.2. In this case, however, we calculate the link and inter-dimension imbalances once for each partition size and then add them all together according to a set of weights. Figure 3 shows a 16-node ring, with one 8-node and one4-node partition. Routes are shown for the positive direction only, assuming the naive virtual channel assignment. Note that with the naive assignment, the 16-node partition is very unbalanced in places and the 8- and 4-node partitions are completely unbalanced (all traffic is on VC0).

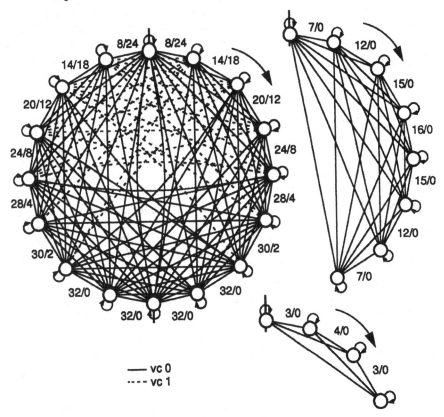

Fig. 4 Hierarchical virtual channel balance (naive assignment, radix =16)

To calculate the VC imbalance for a given link and partition size, we divide the absolute difference in the number of VC1 and VC0 routes over that link by the maximum number of routes crossing any link in the partition (the maximum number of routes crossing a link is 32 for the 16-node partition, 16 for the 8-node partition, and 4 for the 4-node partition). A relative imbalance on a link with less traffic is thus counted less heavily than the same relative imbalance on a more heavily used link. This difference is more pronounced for larger partition sizes.

Similarly, to calculate the VC imbalance for a given inter-dimension VC buffer and partition size, we divide the absolute difference in the number of VC1 and VC0 routes entering or leaving the ring at that node by the maximum number of routes entering or leaving the ring at any node in the partition (16, 8 and 4 for the 16-, 8- and 4-node partitions, respectively).

Once the individual VC imbalances are computed for all nodes and all partition sizes, they are squared and added together to form the total imbalance cost. We use hand-picked coefficients, however, to weight the terms according to their type of traffic and partition size. For example, we ignore the imbalances leaving the ring at each node (by giving them a weight of zero) when computing VC assignments for the X or Y dimension. As another example, we weight inter-dimension VC imbalances less than link VC imbalance for a full partition of 16-nodes, since the intra-dimension traffic is twice as heavy as the inter-dimension traffic in that case. Finally, we can weight the various partition sizes according to how we anticipate the machine being used. If the machine is going to be used primarily for small jobs, we might weight the size-4 partitions in an 8-node ring more heavily than the full partition, resulting in a cost function that was more sensitive to VC balance within a partition and thus favored smaller user partitions.

We have found that it is generally possible to greatly improve the subpartition VC balance while having minimal impact on the VC balance for the whole ring. Results are summarized in Table 3. The *Naive* assignments are as discussed in Section 3.1. The *Globally Optimized* assignments were computed using the cost function of Section 3.2, with no consideration of partition traffic. The *Hierarchically Optimized* assignments were computed as discussed above.

The shaded cells in the table show the average imbalance for link and inter-dimension VCs. The unshaded cells show the maximum link or inter-dimension VC imbalances. Rings of 4, 8 and 16 nodes are shown. For the 8-node ring, results are given for both the X/Y dimensions (which ignore traffic leaving the ring) and the Z dimension. Results for 16 nodes are shown only for the Y dimension.

The first thing to notice from Table 3 is that the globally optimized assignment achieves significantly better balance (lower imbalance) than does the naive assignment for every ring size. The naive assignment has average link and inter-dimension VC imbalances ranging from 0.625 to 1.0 and maximum link and inter-dimension VC imbalances of 1.0 for all ring sizes. The optimized assignment achieves perfect VC balance for the 4-node ring. For full 8- and 16-node rings, it achieves average link and inter-dimension VC balances ranging from 0 to 0.203, with a maximum imbalance of 0.563 for a link in the 16-node ring.

The globally optimized assignments, however, result in poor hierarchical balance. For the 4-node partition of an 8-node X/Y ring, the average link imbalance is 0.417 and average inter-dimension VC imbalance is 0.5. The hierarchically optimized assignment, on the other hand, achieves an average link imbalance of 0.167 and an average inter-dimension VC imbalance of 0. Results are similar for the 8-node Z ring. While the hierarchical assignment significantly improves the subpartition VC balance, it does not degrade the full ring VC balance for either 8-node ring.

Ring Size	Sub-partition Size	Naive				Globally Optimized				Hierarchically Optimized			
		Link Imbal		Inter-dim Imbal		Link Imbal		Inter-dim Imbal		Link Imbal		Inter-dim Imbal	
		Avg	Max	Avg	Max	Avg	Max	Avg	Max	Avg	Max	Avg	Max
4	4	1.0	1.0	1.0	1.0	0	0	0	0	0	0	0	0
8 (X, Y)	8	.625	1.0	.75	1.0	.063	.250	0	0	.063	.250	0	0
	4	.833	1.0	1.0	1.0	417	1.0	.500	.500	.167	.250	0	0
8 (Z)	8	.625	1.0	.75	1.0	.125	.250	0	0	.125	.250	0	0
	4	.833	1.0	1.0	1.0	.333	.750	.313	1.0	.167	.250	0	0
16 (Y)	16	.625	1.0	.625	1.0	.203	.563	0	0	.266	.563	.219	.375
	8	.661	1.0	1.0	1.0	359	.750	.500	.750	.074	.313	0	0
	4	.833	1.0	1.0	1.0	416	1.0	.500	.500	.167	.250	0	0

Table 3 Summary of VC imbalance for all assignment methods

For the 16-node ring, the hierarchically optimized assignment has greater imbalance for the full partition than does the globally optimized assignment. The average link imbalance rises from 0.203 to 0.206 (although the maximum is the same), and the average inter-dimensional VC balance rises from 0 to 0.219. However, the average full ring VC imbalance is still fairly low and there are no highly unbalanced links or inter-dimension VC buffers. Moreover, the subpartition VC balance is significantly improved. The inter-dimensional VCs are perfectly balanced, and the link VCs have low average and maximum imbalances.

While not shown in this paper, the virtual channel balance of Dally and Seitz's original deadlock avoidance scheme [4] is essentially the same as *Naive*.

3.4   Searching the VC assignment space

We have not discussed up to this point how the virtual channel assignment space is searched, only that an assignment is chosen so as to minimize some imbalance cost function. For large rings, however, the search space is prohibitively large for an exhaustive search.

The VC assignment search space is 2^r, where r is the number of unconstrained routes. This, of course, grows exponentially with ring size. For a ring of n nodes, the total number of routes is n^2. When n is a multiple of 4, then $r=n(n+4)/2$; the other $n(n-4)/2$ routes cross a dateline. The search space for 8 nodes is thus 2^{48}, and the search space for 16 nodes is 2^{160}. This space can be pruned somewhat at the possible expense of compromising the solution.

One way to reduce the space is to assign length-one routes independently after the other routes have been fixed. That is for each combination of VCs used by routes length two and up, we assign all the length-one routes so as to minimize the cost function. This is a reasonable compromise, since the VC choice for a length-one route has little effect on the VC choice of other length-one routes. However, even if we ignore length-one routes, the number of unconstrained routes is given by $r=n^2/2$, and the search space for 16 nodes is still an impossible 2^{128}.

Another possible compromise is to assume that the VC assignments are symmetrical with respect to 180 degree rotation. In other words, all positive routes leaving node 0 are mapped to positive routes of the same length but opposite VC leaving node $n/2$, etc. We will not discuss this assumption further, save to say that it does compromise optimality somewhat and it still leaves us with a search space that is intractable for rings much larger than 8 nodes.

We solve this problem by using *simulated annealing* [6] to search for a good assignment. Annealing is a physical process wherein a material is heated and then slowly cooled in order to cure imperfections and reach a well-ordered (low energy) final state. In simulated annealing we use the cost function discussed earlier as an analogy to the energy state of the physical material being annealed. We start with an initial VC assignment and then randomly perturb it. A modification is always accepted if it improves the cost function (*i.e.* lowers the energy state), else it is accepted with some probability that depends upon a *temperature*, which is slowly lowered.

Our simulated annealing algorithm is shown in Figure 3. The initial hot stage avoids local minima in the cost function, and the assignment eventually "cools" into a state that is hoped to be close to the global minimum. The if-statement at the bottom of the repeat-loop controls the speed of the cooling; we cool rapidly until we reach the "interesting" temperature region, then cool more slowly. We used values of HOT=1, TRIES_PER_TEMP=$100n^2$, and COOL=0.9.

```
temp = HOT
repeat
    for tries = 1 to TRIES_PER_TEMP
        pick a random unconstrained route to flip (change VC)
        E = change in cost function from flipping route
        if (E<0)
            accept the modification
        else
            accept the modification with probability e^(-E/temp)
    flips = number of accepted flips at this temperature
    if flips > 0.6*TRIES_PER_TEMP
        temp = temp / 2
    else
        temp = temp * COOL
until flips = 0
```

Fig. 5   Simulated annealing algorithm

This technique has worked very well for us. On a SPARCstation 10, the time to solve a 16-node ring is approximately 3 to 5 minutes, assuming a very gradual rate of cooling. We run the algorithm once for each relative positioning of the positive and negative datelines in order to determine the best placement[1]. A 32-node solution requires about 1/2 hour per negative dateline placement.

The simulated annealing program needs to be run only once per ring size. These results can then be saved and used to construct the routing tables for arbitrary machine configurations. While different "flavors" of routing tables could be used for different machines or workloads – perhaps even switching routing tables between jobs – it is expected that a machine would use a single, default routing table at all times. By using a hierarchically good assignment, the table should work well on a variety of workloads.

4   Experimental Results

In order to determine the practical benefits of improved virtual channel balance, we have modified the routing tables on actual T3D hardware and compared performance on several synthetic benchmarks. The machine available for use was a 256-PE (128-node) T3D configured in an 8×4×4 torus.

The first two benchmarks, *Stride* and *Random*, perform local to remote memory copies. Both perform 512K transfers per PE of 1KB each. We use unoptimized copy routines, so overhead becomes excessive for significantly smaller transfer sizes. In *Stride*, all PEs simply sweep through the logical PEs in order (starting with themselves and wrapping around). In *Random*, each transfer is to a random PE.

Both programs were run in a 4×4×4 partition (128 processors), as well as on the entire machine. For the smaller run, communication in the X dimension is contained within aligned, 4-node partitions on each 8-node ring. Communication in the Y and Z dimensions is, of course, spread over the 4 nodes in each of those dimensions.

Results of the experiments are shown in Table 4. While the mean and variance of request latency would be instructive, only the realized bandwidths were available. Both the globally optimized and the hierarchically optimized VC assignments improve the realized bandwidth in all cases. The relative improvements are greater for the larger partition.

The hierarchically optimized assignment shows a greater improvement relative to the globally optimized assignment for the smaller partition, which is exactly what we would expect. It is also interesting to note that the hierarchically optimized assignment performed slightly better for the larger partition, for which its virtual channel balance equaled that of the globally optimized assignment. From this we can hypothesize that a hierarchically good VC assignment reduces contention even when communication is uniform over the entire ring by improving the mix of virtual channels used on shorter routes. More experimentation would be useful to support this hypothesis.

The improvement from optimizing virtual channel balance is greater for larger network sizes, as can be seen in Table 4. We have also seen that the improvement increases with greater network contention. This is demonstrated by the third benchmark, *Stress*.

---

1 Actually, we only try odd-numbered nodes for the negative dateline placements. This maximizes the number of unconstrained routes, and has been found in practice to produce better VC balance.

Workload	Partition Size	Naive BW	Globally Optimized		Hierarchically Optimized	
			BW	Imp. over Naive	BW	Imp. over Naive
Stride	128	27.3	28.3	3.6%	28.9	5.9%
	256	21.4	24.2	13.1%	24.3	13.6%
Random	128	26.2	27.0	3.1%	28.0	6.9%
	256	21.2	24.1	13.7%	24.3	14.6%

Table 4   Measured bandwidths (MB/s) for communication using various VC assignments

The *Stress* benchmark was extracted from a highly optimized transpose code that performed memory transfers of 2KB from each PE to every other PE. The original program carefully orchestrated which PEs were communicating with which other PEs at each time step, and kept all PEs in lock step by use of fast barriers after each transfer. We removed the barriers and the local memory operations to create the *Stress* benchmark. The result is a workload that creates a lot of network contention.

The results from the *Stress* benchmark are shown in Table 5. The *Stress* benchmark was run only for the full 256-processor machine using the *Naive* and *Globally Optimized* assignments. As can be seen in the table, improvement from optimizing the virtual channel assignment for this code was almost 25%.

Workload	Naive BW	Globally Optimized	
		BW	Imp. over Naive
Stress	19.0	23.7	24.7%

Table 5   Measured bandwidths (MB/s) with high network contention

5   Summary

Virtual channels for all routes in the T3D are selectable via software-writable tables. We have shown that optimizing the virtual channel assignments to achieve good *virtual channel balance* can significantly improve the bandwidth delivered by the interconnection network. We have demonstrated improvements of 13 to 24% under heavy network load on an 8×4×4 torus.

Based upon limited experiments on the 8×4×4 machine, virtual channel balance becomes more important as the network radix grows and as network contention increases. Thus while of significant use in a 3-dimensional torus, good virtual channel balance should be even more beneficial in a 2-dimensional mesh or torus.

A hierarchically good virtual channel assignment attempts to evenly distribute traffic over the available virtual channels for both global communication and for communication among partitions of the machine. We have shown that significant improvements in subpartition virtual channel balance can be made with little or no impact on the global virtual channel balance. Results have shown the hierarchical approach to be quite effective.

We have presented a novel technique, employing simulated annealing, for searching the virtual channel assignment space. This search technique allows us to optimize the virtual channel assignment for large rings, where an exhaustive search would be impossible. The simulated annealing approach is useful for radices of 8 or larger.

Acknowledgments

This paper is an extension of work done earlier by Rick Kessler at Cray. Jim Schwarzmeier provided the *Stress* benchmark.

References

1. Adve, V. S. and M. K. Vernon, "Performance Analysis of Mesh Interconnection Networks with Deterministic Routing," *Transactions on Parallel and Distributed Systems*, pp 225-246, March, 1994.

2. Bolding, K., "Non-Uniformities Introduced by Virtual Channel Deadlock Prevention," *Technical Report UW-CSE-92-07-07*, University of Washington, Seattle, WA, July 12, 1992.

3. Cray Research, Inc., "The Cray T3D System Architecture Overview," HR-04033, 1993.

4. Dally, W. J. and C. Seitz, "Deadlock-Free Message Routing in Multiprocessor Interconnection Networks," *IEEE Transactions on Computers*, pp 547-553, May 1987.

5. Dally, W. J., "Virtual Channel Flow Control," *Proc. 17th International Symposium on Computer Architecture*, pp 60-68, May 1990.

6. Kirkpatrick, S., C. D. Gellatt, Jr. and M. P. Vecchi, "Optimization by Simulated Annealing," Science, pp 671-670, Vol 220, No 4598, May 1983.

R2: A Damped Adaptive Router Design

A. Davis[1], R. Hodgson[2], I. Robinson[2], L. Cherkasova[2], V. Kotov[2], T. Rokicki[2]

[1] Department of Computer Science, University of Utah, Salt Lake City, UT 94112
[2] Hewlett Packard Laboratories, Palo Alto, CA 94303

Abstract. R2 is an attempt to create an interconnection component that provides reliable packet delivery services at low latency under bursty traffic situations and in the presence of certain faults in either the network or processing elements. The R2 design is based on a *damped* adaptive routing scheme that avoids livelock, exhibits improved latency under bursty congestion, while performing similar to deterministic strategies in the lightly loaded case. This paper describes the R2 architecture and presents the results of a simulation study which motivates the damped adaptive routing strategy employed by the R2 switch. [3]

1 Introduction

The work presented here is a natural extension of previous work on a high performance router called the Post Office. The Post Office is a 300,000 transistor CMOS chip that is used to form the interconnect fabric for a prototype scalable parallel multiprocessing system called Mayfly [Davis92]. The Mayfly processing element (PE) architecture was designed to hide communication latency and hence the Post Office was designed primarily with the goal of providing a high capacity fabric. The current interest is to create multicomputer systems that are based on more conventional PE and operating system architectures. From the commercial viewpoint, there is a strong economic motivation to leverage current processing boards and system software into scalable parallel systems. The complexity and multiprocessor specific nature of the Mayfly PE is not a cost effective choice in uniprocessing workstations. Hence the motivation to produce a second revision of the Post Office, called R2, which will be used to interconnect more conventional PE's supporting standard system API's. One effect of this decision is that low latency becomes a more dominant goal than it was in the latency-hiding Mayfly architecture.

An additional requirement of this effort is the need to support a certain level of fault tolerance. Commercial multicomputer applications currently are more focused on the high-availability aspect of multicomputers rather than their performance potential. The fault tolerant requirement imposes a continued need for a certain level of adaptivity [Wille92] in the communications fabric. Adaptivity is costly [AC93, Chien93] both in terms of router complexity and in terms of latency when suboptimal paths are chosen. Several low latency deterministic routers have been developed [Seitz84, Dally89, DS87]. The challenge is to create

---

[3] This work is supported by Hewlett Packard Laboratories

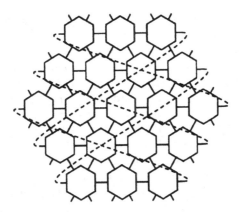

Fig. 1. *R2* Topology

an adaptive routing strategy which performs as well as deterministic variants under light traffic loads but still retains the adaptivity required to provide improved performance under heavy or hot-spot loads and is resilient to certain types of system failures.

The remainder of the paper highlights the R2's behavior and high level aspects of the architecture, and presents the results of a simulation study that motivate the choice for the R2's adaptive routing strategy.

2 The *R2* Interconnect

2.1 Topology

The *R2* interconnect topology is exactly the same as that used by the Post Office and is briefly described here for continuity. The R2 topology is a continuous hexagonal mesh which permits each node in the fabric to communicate with its six immediate neighbors. Figure 1 illustrates an example containing nineteen nodes (only one axis is wrapped for clarity.) A seventh port which is also not shown is called the *PE port* and connects the fabric to the local processing element.

It is convenient to define the size of the interconnect by the number of nodes on each edge of the resulting processing surface. The example shown in Figure 1 represents an $E3$ surface. The total number of nodes in an En interconnect is $3n(n-1)+1$. Each node in the surface is uniquely identified by an integer 3-tuple $< X, Y, Z >$. The labelling scheme and the method for computing the route from an absolute address contained in the packet header is described in [Davis92]. It is important to note that for most of the possible sender receiver pairs there are multiple *best* paths due to the choice of a 2D hexagonal mesh topology, as well as two *no-farther* path options. No-farther paths neither decrease or increase the distance to the receiver. These options will become important in the subsequent description of the R2's adaptive routing mechanism.

Each surface may be sparsely populated in that each potential node site may or may not contain a processing element. If the processing element is missing then shorting each of the axes in the topology will result in reliable packet delivery assuming that no packet destination specifies an empty node site. A processing element consists of 3 components: an R2 switch, a fabric interface component or *FIC*, and a conventional processing board or *PB* containing a CPU, memory, I/O devices, etc. The FIC connects to the main-memory bus of the PB and provides a DMA capability that is consistent with a particular sender based message protocol [Swanson94]. Details of this protocol are suppressed here due to the focus on the R2 switch but the important aspect of this protocol is that each sender owns a portion of memory in each receiver. This implies that establishing a connection requires prenegotiation between the sender and receiver to identify the bounds of that space in the receiver's memory. This prenegotiation also passes a *key* to each sender that can be used to provide a certain measure of security validation for the FIC's DMA transactions.

The R2 switch performs all of the physical delivery aspects of packet routing. The FIC is responsible for validating access permission and for fragmentation, reassembly, and arrived message notification duties. The FIC also contains a small amount of memory that is used to hold protocol tables. These tables allow the FIC to directly place incoming packets into the appropriate address in the receiver memory.

2.2 The R2 Message Model and Packet Format

An R2 packet may vary in size up to a maximum of 40 32-bit words. Each packet must contain a 3 word physical header, a 4 word protocol header, and a single word CRC trailer. The physical header contains information that is processed by the R2 switching fabric. The protocol header contains the information used by the FIC to check for access privileges and deposit the payload in the appropriate location in the receivers memory. The use of a variable packet size reduces the payload transmission time and resource utilization to match the actual tranmission requirements rather than using resources to transmit *padded* packets that would be required if the packet size were fixed.

The R2 interconnect supports two types of messages which are called *normal* and *priority*. Normal messages may be of any length up to 64K packets while priority messages are restricted to a single packet. The FIC design is capable of performing simple remote fetch and op instructions autonomously and constructing a reply to the original sender on certain types of priority messages. More typically priority packets are used for operating system communication and normal messages are used for application interactions.

Adaptive routing in a fault-free R2 fabric is controlled by a sender specified number of *adaptive credits*. Each adaptive credit permits one no-further route option to be taken. The adaptive nature of the R2 fabric implies that packets may arrive out of order, but the sender based protocol implemented by the FIC is able to determine the target address for a packet's payload from a unique message ID and the packet number. The FIC provides notification for message

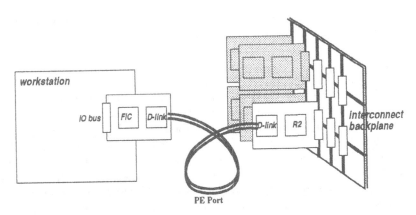

Fig. 2. R2 System Setting

arrival and therefore out of order packets are invisible to the application. The R2 flit size is 16-bits. An *exception eject* field is used for fault handling and when marked forces the packet to be ejected from the fabric at the current PE. A *max hops* field is initially set to the minimum path length to the destination plus the adaptive credit field value by the FIC. The adaptive credit field is decremented on each adaptive route decision which does not take a shortest path, and the max hops field is decremented on every hop. When the adaptive credit field is 0 no further adaptive routing is permitted and when the max hops field goes negative the *rogue* packet will be *exception* ejected from the fabric.

2.3   System Setting

Like the Post Office the R2 switch is intended to be built as a fully asynchronous component. This implies that the R2 to FIC interface is asynchronous as well, but the FIC to PB interface is synchronous with the PB's clock. The result is that each node in the system runs off it's own clock, the FIC is responsible for the resynchronization duties, and the R2 fabric is freed from either clock skew or resynchronization duties. Current prototype efforts are aimed at creating an $E6$ fabric which will be used to connect up to 91 HP 700 series workstations. This system is illustrated in Figure 2.

The backplane board is completely passive and contains no components but implements the wiring interconnections for the $E6$ surface. Each slot in the backplane board may contain an R2 card or a *shunt* card. The R2 card contains an R2 chip and a set of differential drivers for the PE port link. Unpopulated slots will contain a shunt card which simply shorts the axes of the fabric. The FIC card contains a DMA controller, SRAM, and FPGA components that implement the FIC control and interface requirements for the IO bus of the workstation and the R2 Fabric. This packaging is crude and certainly can be improved upon but provides the advantage of permitting the use of existing workstations in an initial testbed prototype. The primary interest of this work is the development of the appropriate streamlined protocol, operating system and API interfaces, the FIC functionality, and the R2 switch.

2.4 The R2 Switch

All normal packets are adaptively routed using virtual cut-through [Fujimoto83] from their inbound port to the desired output port. Priority packets always proceed on best path routes only. The availability of multiple best path routes still provides some freedom from strict deterministic routing delays caused by hot-spot contention. The adaptive credit field is used to limit the total number of adaptive hops. If the number of adaptive credits is positive and all best path ports are unavailable and a no farther path is available then the no farther path is immediately taken and the adaptive credits field is decremented in the packet header. If the adaptive credit field is 0, and all best path ports are busy then the packet will simply wait its turn for a best path forwarding route.

If a priority packet arrives and has no free best path and some best path is currently being used to forward a normal packet then the priority packet will immediately be *embedded* in the normal packet and be forwarded out of the selected best path. This embedding is essentially a virtual channel mechanism and must be supported by appropriate buffers and physical link protocols in the R2 switch. If a priority packet arrives and all best path routes are occupied by priority traffic then the packet waits its turn to be forwarded.

A backpressure mechanism is necessary to avoid persistent saturation of any network [Jain92]. This backpressure signal is used to throttle the rate at which packets can be injected into the interconnect fabric. Increasing the amount of buffering in the fabric increases the capacity of the network. Unfortunately, increasing the buffering capability also inherently delays the backpressure mechanism from being observed at the sending sites. R2's use of virtual cut-through mitigates this effect somewhat but the adaptive routing strategy exacerbates the problem. The R2's backpressure control mechanism is based on a simple progress concept. The first word of the packet header contains both destination and sender addresses. Progress on a packet is defined as having claimed an R2 port on which to forward the packet either to another R2 or to the FIC. If a new packet arrives at an R2 switch and after digesting the first word of this packet and finding that the sender/destination addresses match a previously arrived packet with the same sender/destination address which is not progressing then the new packet is NACK'd (negative acknowledge). This NACK is a backpressure indication to the sender of the new packet.

The R2 switch's datapath is shown in Figure 3. The 6 internal fabric ports and the PE port controllers are connected to a pair of 7 by 15 crossbar switches. The entry crossbar provides a path for an incoming packet on an R2 port to the appropriate packet buffer, while the exit crossbar provides a path for a forwarding packet to the appropriate outbound port. Each packet buffer has a capacity of 40 32-bit words and can therefore hold an entire packet. Each packet buffer is implemented as a FIFO. The R2 switch contains 12 normal packet buffers and 3 priority packet buffers.

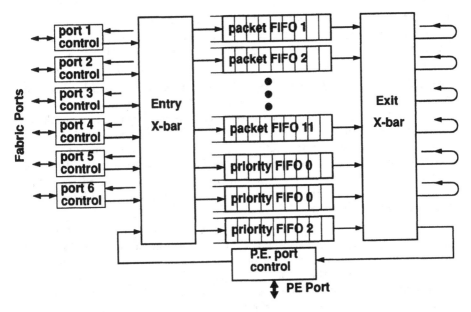

Fig. 3. R2 Datapath

Each packet FIFO has its own routing controller. The forwarding route is calculated from the destination address in the packet header and the *local-ID* held in a control register which specifies the mesh location of the PE with which the R2 is associated. The routing calculation requires 2 subtractions and 2 compares and uses 3 parallel 6-bit subtract-compare ALU's. The control path is a bit too complex to illustrate in detail but is being implemented as a set of communicating asynchronous finite state machines.

The fabric ports are implemented as a single 16-bit flit channel between topologically adjacent R2 switches. This implies that prior to using the fabric channel a sending R2 must acquire *mastership* of the channel. The other option is to provide a pair of unidirectional channels. Assuming a given *wire* budget and port speed, the two channel approach suffers in that the control wire overhead is doubled, channels may be under utilized, each unidirectional channel has half the bandwidth of the twice as wide bidirectional channel, and also requires an increased number of packet buffers to maintain a balanced system. Arbitration and driver turn around times for the shared bidirectional channel does increase latency somewhat but the availability of twice the bandwidth during transmission actually results in decreased packet transfer times. The downside of the single channel approach is that the total capacity of the fabric link is slightly less would be available with the dual channel approach. This effect is only in evidence when the fabric operates near saturation. An operating point that imposes even more severe performance penalties in either case.

All fabric port controllers are identical with the exception that three of the fabric ports have channel mastership arbiters and three do not. Ports with arbiters are called *positive* ports and the others are called *negative ports*. The topology shown in Figure 1 guarantees that a positive port of one R2 is always connected to the negative port of another R2, even when the fabric is sparsely populated. A fabric port consists of 25 wires: 16 for data and 9 for control.

Another key goal of the R2 design is to incorporate a certain level of fault detection and tolerance into the interconnect fabric. One of the goals of the R2 fabric is to make sure that a packet never gets dropped. The reliability of the R2 fabric and the functionality provided by the FIC interface have enabled considerable savings in the software protocol path. The current sender based protocol only requires 67 instructions to be executed for each packet using an FDDI interconnect and requires only a minor modification to the standard Unix API. 90% of this software overhead will be unnecessary when the FDDI interconnect is replaced by the R2 fabric.

The main idea is that if a packet cannot be delivered to its intended destination then it will be ejected from the fabric somewhere as an exception which will then invoke a higher level error protocol that will generate a message to the sender indicating that the intended destination for a particular message could not be accessed. This error handling component of the protocol will be slow but since it is also rare, the lack of performance is not such a problem.

The choice of an asynchronous circuit implementation strategy may provide freedom from maintaining clock synchronization in large multicomputer configurations but it causes several problems from the fault-detection perspective. Most failure detection mechanisms either rely on some timeout mechanism or some calculation which is checked to see if the correct value was returned. Time-out mechanisms are problematic in asynchronous circuit implementations since time in these systems is measured as *sequences* of actions rather than on some absolute or global interval.

The R2 contains *watch-dog* timers that monitor the fabric and PE port links, and if the proper control line protocol is not provided before the watch-dog alarm intervals expire then the offending link is marked as faulty in the R2's fault control register. Failed fabric ports are not a problem since the packet can be adaptively routed to it's destination by another path. In the case where the faulty link is the packet's destination, a *destination suspect* flag is set in the packet and the packet is forwarded to another neighbor of the destination node. If the link to the destination fails and the destination suspect flag is already set in the packet then the packet is marked with the *exception eject* set and forcibly ejected from the fabric to the FIC and PB at its current location. The likely cause of this situation is that the R2 switch at the intended destination has failed. For the intended prototype, providing fault detection and a corresponding error handling mechanism is definitely overkill. The prototype fabric is a single board and the liklihood that an entire R2 switch will fail (as opposed to a particular R2 subcomponent) is remote. However the longer term view is that the R2 and FIC elements will be contained on the PB. If this were the case then the above mechanism is useful.

If the PE port is bad then there is no way the packet can be delivered to its

intended destination by the fabric. In this case the packet exception eject flag
is set and handed to a neighbor R2 switch for ejection to the error handler. All
exception eject packets are treated as error exceptions by the protocol.

3 Simulation Results - Choosing the R2 Adaptive Routing Strategy

The major focus of this simulation study was to determine the impact of varying
degrees of adaptivity in routing strategies on the interconnect performance for
different types of workloads. The existence of multiple best path choices for
routing a message through the R2 topology presents the following options:

A *best path* direction sends a packet to a node which is closer to the packet's
destination. There may be one or two *best path* directions.

A *no farther* direction sends a packet to nodes that are no farther from the destination than the current node. There are always two *no farther* directions.

In order to characterize merits of adaptive routing, the following three routing
strategies are considered:

The *deterministic* strategy uses a single best path at each routing step. In
cases where multiple best paths exist, they are ordered such that only a
single option is possible. This results in a single deterministic path choice.

The *best path* strategy allows the choice of any best path at each hop. Since there
are usually two best path choices, this strategy provides a minimal amount
of adaptivity but does not incur the normal adaptivity penalty caused by a
longer route. For an En interconnect, there may be only a single such path
through n nodes (if both the source and the destination lie on the same axis),
or there may be up to $\binom{n-1}{\lfloor n/2 \rfloor}$ paths through $\lfloor \frac{n+1}{2} \rfloor \lfloor \frac{n+2}{2} \rfloor$ nodes, depending
on the source and destination node location.

The *derouting* strategy allows a packet to use no farther directions as well. The
adaptive credit model is used to prevent livelock and is set to the original
path length minus one. In this simulation the adaptive credit field is decremented on every hop independent of whether a best path or a no farther
path is selected. The initial value therefore guarantees an adaptive option
up to a location adjacent to the final destination.

The main parameters for this *R2* model have been normalized to the rate
at which the ports can toggle. This rate will be dependent both on the design
and the current fabrication technology. Based on experience with the Post Office
and the current design, the R2 switch is expected to be capable of moving a flit
across a port every 5 to 10 nanoseconds. This corresponds to a clock rate in a
synchronous equivalent of 100 to 200 MHz. Hence a time unit can conservatively
be assumed to be 10ns in this case. Specifically:

– Each port permits a byte of information to be transmitted in 1 time unit.
Each full sized standard packet is 160 bytes long and hence takes 160 time

units to transmit. Even though the R2 switch can take advantage of shorter packet payloads, the study here assumes all packets are full sized.

- The PE port has an additional overhead of 80 time units to establish a connection into the interconnect, and 20 time units to establish a connection out of the interconnect. These overheads on PE ports occur before any real packet data is transferred; the actual packet data transfer can then proceed at a rate determined by the port bandwidth.
- To receive a packet header and to compute the next available direction takes 12 time units.

3.1 Uniform Random Traffic and Different Routing Strategies

This first experiment considers uniform random traffic consisting of single-packet messages with a random source and destination node. Under such traffic, the three routing strategies are virtually indistinguishable with respect to message latencies, as shown by Figure 4. In this graph, the horizontal axis represents throughput as a percentage of the PE port bandwidth, and the vertical axis represents the average message latency in time units. It is important to note that 100% of the PE port bandwidth can never be achieved in practice since in this case each node in the multicomputer would only be sending or receiving messages and would never actually process them. In the current design the FIC and the PB's CPU share the main memory bus of the node, and therefore it is unlikely that the average PE port throughput will exceed even 50% in an operational system. However, this simulation study is intended to find the limitations on the system imposed by the interconnect fabric hence the simulation parameters are not bounded by expected operational limits. The interconnect size used was $E6$ with 91 nodes.

The only significant observed difference between the three strategies was with respect to the fabric port utilization, which is a percentage measure of the number of active fabric ports to the total. Given the system setting there are three system attributes that affect saturation. The system can be stalled when either the PE port or the fabric port utilization reaches 100% or when all of the packet buffers are in use. In this instance, under a traffic rate of 95%, the deterministic and best path strategies yielded an internal port utilization of 44%, while the derouting strategy yielded an internal port utilization of 55%. The internal port utilization for the minimal routing strategies (best path and deterministic) coincide on the average because each packet takes a minimal route to its destination. With the derouting strategy, occasional derouting of packets leads to an increase in port utilization due to the elongated path.

3.2 Bursty Traffic

While performance evaluation of packet-switched interconnects has focused on the latency of packets, applications are more concerned with the overall latency of variable-sized messages. Thus, in order to obtain meaningful performance results, *bursty traffic* workloads must be considered. These workloads are based not on

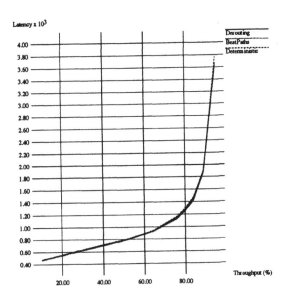

Fig. 4. Average Message Latency for Uniform Random Traffic

packet injection frequency but rather on message injection frequency where a message, depending on its length, causes a burst of packets to be injected as rapidly as possible.

Rather than a lengthy consideration of multiple message length distributions, the treatment here is restricted to bimodal distributions consisting of short messages and long messages. A short message is defined to be from one to five packets in length, where each length has equal probability. Long messages are defined here to be twenty-five packets which is approximately the size of a memory page. Workloads are defined by the percentage of long messages in the workload. For instance, a workload with 10% long messages has an average message length of 5.2 packets. Given a traffic density u between zero and one, new messages are generated using a negative exponential distribution with an average inter-arrival time of $5.2/u$.

A primary goal of the R2 design is to minimize the latency of short messages, possibly trading off long-message latency for short-message latency. Message latency is measured from the moment the message is sent by the application or operating system, as defined by the time the message appears on the FIC's job list, to the moment all the packets of the message have been placed in the receiver's memory and the receiving node has been notified that the message has arrived. Thus, this time includes the time the message waits in the sending node's job queue as well as the time the packets spend in the interconnect fabric and FIC component.

Since a large portion of the message latency is associated with the transport of the packet data and therefore heavily dependent upon the message length,

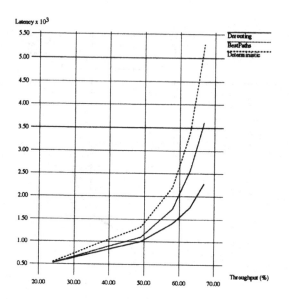

Fig. 5. Normalized Average Message Latency for 10% Long Message Workload

it is helpful to create a *normalized* average message latency metric which is independent of the message length. This normalized message latency is defined as the total message latency divided by the message length. In addition, measurements are kept for the fabric-only component which is referred to simply as the packet latency. Figures 5 and 6 show the normalized average message latency and packet latency corresponding to a workload with 10% long messages using the three different routing strategies. The messages are injected into the interconnect in FIFO order.

Figure 5 indicates that the derouting strategy provides the best overall message latency, followed by the best path and finally the deterministic strategies. Interestingly, the packet latencies illustrated by Figure 6 are in precisely the opposite order, with deterministic providing the best overall packet latency. This phenomena is partly explained by examining the port utilization under the different strategies, as shown in Figure 7. The solid black line represents ideal PE port utilization. The percentage of PE port utilization deviation from that line shows the frequency of packet rejection due to the flow control mechanism. For 67% traffic utilization, the PE port utilization for the derouting strategy is 69%, for the best path strategy it is 73%, and for the deterministic strategy it reaches 77%. This shows that packets for the less adaptive strategies spend more of their time waiting in the message queue. The more adaptive strategies maintain fewer packets in the queue and more packets inside the interconnect for a given traffic load. With so many packets inside the interconnect, contention is higher, and the packets spend longer trying to reach the destination node and competing there for the destination PE port. Thus, the derouting strategy leads to

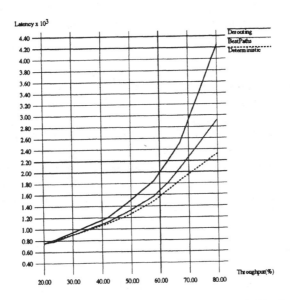

Fig. 6. Packet Latency for 10% Long Message Workload

a higher overall utilization of interconnect fabric resources and provides better overall message latency. The backpressure mechanism under the best path and deterministic strategies has a significant impact, especially under heavier traffic, forcing packets and messages to wait outside the interconnect.

This phenomena is even more pronounced with a higher percentage of long messages. Figure 8 and Figure 9 show the normalized average message latency and packet latency corresponding to a workload with 80% long messages. Figure 10 shows the PE and internal port utilization generated by this workload.

However, the derouting strategy has a few drawbacks. First, at high traffic loads and large interconnects, the internal port utilization rises above the PE port utilization, at which point the internal ports become the bottleneck of the interconnect. Figure 7 and Figure 10 illustrate this. In addition, the ability of a single message to distribute packets across a significant percentage of the interconnect fabric in the presence of contention raises the likelihood of interconnect saturation and deadlock.

4 Conclusion

R2 has been designed to provide a reliable low-latency multicomputer interconnect fabric. One of the key issues in this design was to consider the effects of adaptive routing since adaptivity is required for fault tolerance but has proven problematic with respect to achieving low latency. For uniform random traffic, non-minimal routing does not provide a significant performance advantage over minimal adaptive or deterministic routing strategies. With bursty traffic, however, the use of non-minimal routing can yield a significant decrease in message latency. The derouting strategy reveals some potentially dangerous drawbacks. Adaptivity decreases the efficacy of backpressure because of the larger number of nodes that can be populated with packets from a particular message. In addition, the internal port utilization rises as derouting frequency increases, lowering the effective maximum throughput of the interconnect for large networks. In addition, this higher port utilization threatens a higher likelihood of network saturation and deadlock. A certain level of adaptivity is also necessary to provide a certain level of fault tolerance. The conclusion is that it is necessary to dampen the level of adaptivity in order to achieve a reasonable balance. This conclusion has led to the development of the adaptive credit style routing control in the R2 switch.

References

[AC93] Aoyama, K., Chien, A. A.: The Cost of Adaptivity and Virtual Lanes. Preprint, July 1993.

[CR94] Cherkasova, L. and Rokicki, T.: Alpha Message Scheduling for Packet-Switched Interconnects. To be published.

[Chien93] Chien, Andrew A.: A Cost and Speed Model for k-ary n-cube Wormwhole Routers. In *Proceedings of Hot Interconnects '93, A Symposium on High Performance Interconnects*, August 1993.

[Dally89] Dally, W. J. et al.: The J-Machine: A Fine-Grain Concurrent Computer. In *Proceedings of the IFIP Conference*, North-Holland, pp. 1147–1153, 1989.

[DS87] Dally, W. J., Seitz, C. L.: Deadlock-free message routing in multiprocessor interconnection networks. J. *IEEE Transactions on Computers*, Vol.C–36, No.5, 1987.

[Davis92] Davis A., Mayfly: A General-Purpose, Scalable, Parallel Processing Architecture. J. *LISP and Symbolic Computation*, vol.5, No.1/2, May 1992.

[Fujimoto83] Fujimoto R. M. VLSI Communication Components for Multicomputer Networks.Ph.D. Thesis, University of California at Berkeley, August 1983.

[Jain92] Jain, R.: Myths About Congestion Management in High-speed Networks. Internetworking: Research and Experience, Vol. 3, pp. 101–113, 1992.

[Seitz84] Seitz, C. L.: "The Cosmic Cube". J.*Communications of the ACM*, Vol.28, No. 1, pp. 22-33, January 1984.

[Swanson94] Mark Swanson and Leigh Stoller: "PPE-level Protocols for Carpet Clusters", Technical Report UUCS-94-013, University of Utah, April 1994.

[Wille92] Wille, R.: A High-Speed Channel Controller for the Chaos Router. Technical Report TR-91-12-03, University of Washington, 1992.

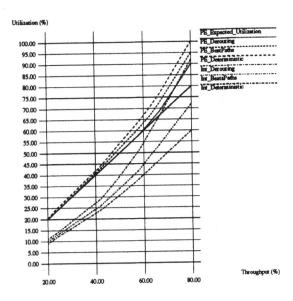

Fig. 7. Port Utilization for 10% Long Message Workload

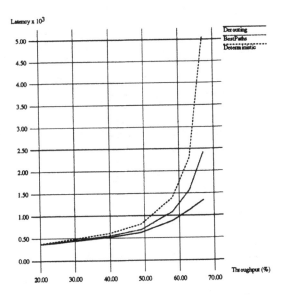

Fig. 8. Normalized Average Message Latency for 80% Long Message Workload

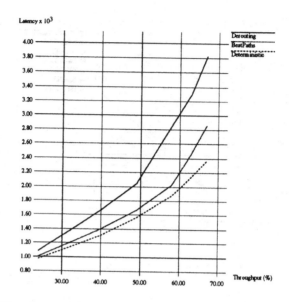

Fig. 9. Packet Latency for 80% Long Message Workload

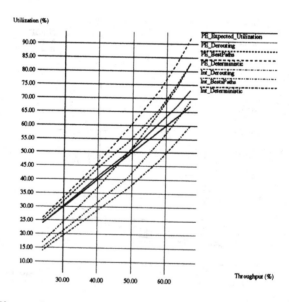

Fig. 10. Port Utilization for 80% Long Message Workload

Arctic Routing Chip*

G. Andrew Boughton

Massachusetts Institute of Technology, Laboratory for Computer Science, Cambridge
Mass 02139, USA

Abstract. Arctic is a 4x4 packet routing chip being developed for the
*T multiprocessor. Arctic can be used to implement a variety of staged
networks and will be used to implement a fat tree network for *T. Arctic
meets the requirements of *T and of a wide class of systems. This paper
discusses the key features of Arctic. These include its buffering scheme
which enables very high utilization of network links and its test and
control system which provides error detection, limited error handling,
and in-circuit testability.

1 Introduction

Arctic is a four input four output packet router implemented on a Motorola
H4CP gate array chip. Arctic has *all* the features necessary for use in a commercial multiboard multiprocessor such as *T [7, 8, 1]. It has high bandwidth (200
MBytes/sec/port), two priority levels, packet sizes up to 96 bytes, and extensive
error detection; it has limited error handling, keeps statistics, can directly drive
long PC traces, and provides significant testing support. While Arctic has special features to support fat tree networks [6], it can also be configured to support
any of a wide variety of other staged network topologies.

Arctic uses a sophisticated buffer management scheme that greatly increases
the effectiveness of its buffers and the utilization of network links. This scheme
is similar to that developed by Joerg for the PaRC routing chip [4, 5] of the
Monsoon multiprocessor.

Arctic has a test and control system that is significantly more sophisticated
than those in most previous chips. This system is accessible through a JTAG
port. It is used to configure the chip, detect errors, count packet flow statistics,
and handle certain errors. It can also be used to access most of the state elements
of Arctic and to run in-circuit chip verification tests.

2 Basic Structure

As is shown in Figure 1, Arctic is composed of four input sections, four output
sections, the crossbar, and the test and control section. There are five clock do-
mains. The crossbar and the output sections are in a single central clock domain.

* The research described in this paper was supported in part by the Advanced Research
Projects Agency under Office of Naval Research contract N00014-92-J-1310.

Each incoming data link has its own clock which drives the corresponding input section. The central clock clocks data out of the buffers.

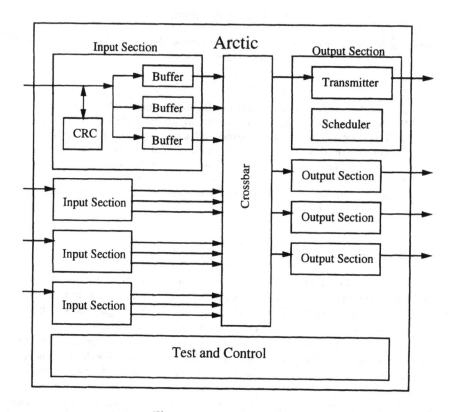

Fig. 1. Arctic Block Diagram

3   Buffering

All buffering in Arctic is located in the input sections. Each input section contains three buffers - each capable of storing a maximum size packet. Each buffer is capable of storing either a priority packet or a normal packet. The last empty buffer is reserved for a priority packet; this ensures that normal packets can not block priority packets. The head of a packet can be transferred out of a buffer before the end of the packet has been received (virtual cut-through with partial cut-throughs allowed). The crossbar has 12 inputs and 4 outputs. Each of the packet buffers in the chip is directly connected to the crossbar. The scheduling scheme used in Arctic ensures that if any buffer in the chip contains a packet destined for a given output then a packet will be transferred to that output as soon as the output becomes available. Any four of the 12 input buffers can be simultaneously transferring to output sections. Packets received on a given input and destined for a particular output are transferred in the same order as they were received, thus in order delivery of packets is maintained along a given network path. Packets received on different inputs and destined for a particular output are scheduled using a round-robin scheme which guarantees that no packet is starved for service. All priority packets waiting for a particular output are transferred before any waiting normal packet is transferred to that output.

This buffering system leads to high utilization of the network links. While an exact analysis of this system is complex, a simple analysis provides an insight of the advantages of this system over a simpler scheme. If Arctic used only a single long FIFO buffer in each of the four input sections then at most four buffered packets would be candidates for output at a given time. The chance that at least one out of four randomly addressed packets is destined for a given output is $1 - (.75)^4$ which is approximately .68. However in Arctic's buffering scheme all of the 12 buffered packets are candidates for output. The chance that at least one out of 12 randomly addressed packets is destined for a given output is $1 - (.75)^{12}$ which is approximately .968. Of course this analysis is not precise (for either buffering system) since it assumes that each of the buffers contains a packet and since it assumes that the buffered packets are randomly addressed, but it does to the first order identify the advantage of Arctic's buffering system over a simpler FIFO system. A longer discussion of a similar analysis of this buffering system can be found in [4].

Related buffering schemes that avoid the problems of a simple FIFO system have been studied by other researchers [2, 10]. The capabilities of these schemes differ from those of the PaRC/Arctic scheme. For example, virtual channel schemes can be used to avoid routing deadlocks in mesh networks and the PaRC/Arctic scheme does not address that issue. However the PaRC/Arctic scheme has a number of features that are not normally provided by virtual channel implementations. A single input section can simultaneously transfer buffered packets to multiple outputs. All the buffers associated with a given input are managed in a single pool rather than using several smaller disjoint pools; this provides more effective buffering. A blocked packet is stored in a single Arctic chip and does not occupy any link (or any virtual channel); this reduces the amount of tree buffering caused by a blocked packet.

For similar reasons the PaRC/Arctic buffering scheme provides better performance than the DAMQ and SAFC schemes discussed in [10, 9]. DAMQ does not allow a single input section to simultaneously transfer buffered packets to multiple outputs. SAFC does not manage in a single pool all the buffers associated with a given input. The performance advantage of these features is discussed in more detail in [4, 10]. The PaRC/Arctic scheme does require a more complex crossbar than the DAMQ and SAFC schemes. However the scheduling circuitry required by the PaRC/Arctic scheme is no more complex than that required by the DAMQ scheme.

4 Link Technology

Arctic supports a network link with a 16 bit wide data path. A clock and a frame signal are sent with the data. A flow control line runs in the reverse direction from the data. Each data bit is transmitted using a single ended GTL driver at 100 Mbits/sec. The design goal is to support printed circuit board transmission lines that are over one meter long. Encoding is used on the frame and flow control lines.

The flow control signal is actually a signal from the receiver indicating that it has freed a buffer and that the buffer is available for use. The transmitter keeps a running count of free receiver buffers. The count is decremented each time a packet is sent and incremented each time a buffer free signal is received. Of course if the transmitter thinks that no buffers are free then it will not send a packet. The count is initialized at startup. The initial value is configurable allowing Arctic to interface receivers with various numbers of buffers. This approach to flow control was suggested by Bob Greiner of Motorola and is related to the *sliding window* scheme used in TCP/IP [3]. This approach works with any amount of link delay. In that respect it is superior to the more common wait line scheme which must take into account link delay. A wait line must be asserted at least two link delays before buffering is exhausted.

Although Arctic's internal data paths are 32 bits at 50 MHz, 16 bit wide link data paths are used to reduce the number of off chip signals. This necessitates the use of a small amount of 100 MHz circuitry in the edges of the input and output sections.

5 Routing

Arctic networks use source based routing; the course of a packet through an Arctic network is completely determined by routing information placed in the packet header by the source. This approach has several benefits. System issues can be considered in the routing of a packet. For example, different packet types (such as I/O packets) can be routed through separate subnetworks. Source based routing is flexible since major changes in network routing policy can be accomplished simply by modifying the route generation algorithm used in the packet sources. Source based routing also supports system reconfiguration including network reconfiguration to isolate broken network hardware.

For a fat tree network, two routing fields in the packet header are used. The source processor places a random bit string in the first and the destination address in the second. As the packet travels from the leaves to the root, each Arctic checks the appropriate prefix of the destination address to determine if the packet must travel farther from the leaves. If this is the case then, since there are several acceptable paths away from the leaves, a portion of the first header field is used to choose an output (away from the leaves). Otherwise a portion of the destination address (the second header field) is used to determine the appropriate output toward the leaves.

The use of a random bit string generated at the source should provide a more globally random distribution of traffic than would be produced if each Arctic dynamically routed packets based on local flow control information. Also since this string is generated at the source, a variety of modifications can easily be made to this fat tree routing algorithm. For example, we can route a packet through a particular subnetwork by fixing certain bits in the first routing field (and placing a random bit string in the remaining portion of the field). Given that the first field determines how the packet is routed from the leaves and given the structure of the fat tree, the fixed bits mean that as the packet travels from the leaves it can only go toward a particular subset of root nodes (the subset is completely defined by the fixed bits). This means that the packet must travel in a subnetwork defined by this subset of root nodes.

Arctic can be configured to implement any of a wide variety of source based routing schemes including the fat tree routing scheme sketched above. For each incoming packet Arctic compares two subfields of header bits with two reference values. Based on these comparisons Arctic selects two bits from the packet header (or a constant and one bit from the header, or two constants). The value of these two bits determines the appropriate output port for the packet.

6 Test and Control System

The test and control system (TCS) provides a complete set of maintenance features. The TCS can be used to thoroughly test the chip. It is used to configure the chip and to control normal operation. It provides error detection and limited error handling.

A host/diagnostic processor (DP) is used to control an Arctic network. The DP controls each Arctic through the Arctic's TCS. The DP accesses an Arctic's TCS through that Arctic's JTAG port.

6.1 Test

Arctic provides more support for in-circuit chip verification than previous router chips. The TCS can be used to place Arctic in a special *low-level-test* mode. While in this mode, Arctic has a single clock domain and the TCS can be used to access scan rings that contain almost all of the chip's state elements. A test vector can be applied through the scan rings. The starting state is scanned in, the system clock is cycled, the resulting system state is scanned out, and the results are checked by the DP. This scan facility can be used to run in-circuit verification tests that have been generated by an automatic test pattern generation program. Such tests should provide a high level of stuck-at fault coverage.

The TCS can also be used to access boundary scan rings that contain all the chip inputs and outputs. These rings can be used to run any desired sequence of test packets through Arctic. In addition these rings can be used to load and and read test patterns from the packet buffers.

The statistics memory has a built-in-self-test circuit. The TCS is used to initiate the test and to read the results.

6.2   Configuration

Arctic's configuration information is primarily composed of routing configuration but it also includes some error handling configuration and some flow control configuration. The TCS is used to scan in this information in *configuration* mode.

6.3   Normal Operation

During normal packet routing operation, the TCS is used to monitor the operation of the chip, detect errors, provide some error handling, and count packet flow statistics.

Errors. The design of Arctic assumes that Arctic's links are very reliable, but Arctic has extensive circuitry for detecting link errors should they occur. Each packet contains a 16 bit CRC field. Arctic checks the CRC of each incoming packet. An idle pattern is sent on a link whenever packets are not being sent and the receiving Arctic checks for this idle pattern. Arctic checks that all incoming frame and flow control signals are correctly encoded. Lastly, Arctic checks that each incoming clock is not disconnected by checking that the clock is toggling. A two bit counter is used for each possible link error for each link. The TCS can be used to access or clear the error counters. In addition, a special error pin is also provided. The pin is asserted if any error occurs.

The DP can make network modifications in response to a static error. While normal packet routing is occurring, the DP can issue commands through an Arctic's TCS to enable or disable a port, block an output port, or invoke flush on an output port. When the DP determines that an error has occurred, it can read the error counters of the Arctics and determine the faulty link or the faulty router. The DP can then disable the input ports connected to the unusable link(s) and invoke flush on the output ports connected to the unusable link(s). Flush causes those output ports to discard all packets sent to them. In *T the DP can also instruct the processing elements to update their route generation tables so that no new packet is routed over an unusable link(s). Thus Arctic's features allow the DP to provide some error handling. Of course this scheme causes packets to be flushed and data to be potentially lost. However it is possible for the processing elements to use an end-to-end acknowledgment/retry protocol on top of the packet transport layer provided by the Arctic network and such a protocol can avoid the loss of data at the cost of additional messaging complexity.

Statistics. Arctic records various statistics about the flow of packets out of each of its output ports. These include the number of packets transmitted, the number of priority packets transmitted, and a special statistic for use in fat tree networks. The fat tree statistic indicates either the number of packets output on the port that came from above this router or the number that came from below this router, depending on the configuration of the output. A 36 bit count is kept of each statistic. The TCS can be used to access or clear the statistics counters.

7 Conclusion

Arctic is a high bandwidth packet routing chip. It provides a more comprehensive set of features for implementing a staged network than previous router chips. The routing circuitry can support a wide variety of staged networks and is particularly well suited for fat tree networks. The buffer management scheme provides high utilization of network links. The ports can be directly connected to long PC traces that cross clock domain boundaries. Thorough error detection and statistics gathering are provided. The novel scan and test facilities make Arctic testable both in a tester and in circuit. Arctic has all the capabilities required for use in a commercial multiprocessor such as *T.

Acknowledgments

I would like to thank Greg Papadopoulos, Bob Greiner, and Chris Joerg for many of the concepts used in Arctic. I would like to thank Jack Costanza, Richard Davis, Tom Durgavich, Doug Faust, and Ralph Tiberio for concepts and design work. I would like to thank Yuval Koren, and Elth Ogston for testing the design. I would like to thank Mike Beckerle, Ed Greenwood, Jamey Hicks, and John Morris for reviewing the design. Finally I would like to thank Satoshi Asari, Steve Chamberlin, Thomas Deng, Eric Heit, Tom Klemas, Jimmy Kwon, Wing Chi Leung, and Gowri Rao for their contributions.

References

1. B. S. Ang, Arvind, and D. Chiou. StarT the Next Generation: Integrating Global Caches and Dataflow Architecture. CSG Memo 354, Computation Structures Group, LCS, MIT, February 1994.
2. W. J. Dally. Virtual Channel Flow Control. In *Proceedings of the 17th International Symposium on Computer Architecture*, May 1990.
3. Information Sciences Institute, University of Southern California, Marina del Rey, Calif. *Transmission Control Protocol, DARPA Internet Program, Protocol Specification*, September 1981. RFC: 793.
4. C. F. Joerg. Design and Implementation of a Packet Switched Routing Chip. TR 482, Laboratory for Computer Science, MIT, Cambridge, Mass., 1990.
5. C. F. Joerg and G. A. Boughton. The Monsoon Interconnection Network. In *Proceedings of the 1991 IEEE International Conference on Computer Design*, October 1991.
6. C. E. Leiserson. Fat Trees: Universal Networks for Hardware-Efficient Supercomputing. In *Proceedings of the 1985 IEEE International Conference on Parallel Processing*, August 1985.
7. R. S. Nikhil, G. M. Papadopoulos, and Arvind. *T: A Multithreaded Massively Parallel Architecture. In *Proceedings of the 19th International Symposium on Computer Architecture*, May 1992.
8. G.M. Papadopoulos, G.A. Boughton, R. Greiner, and M.J. Beckerle. *T: Integrated Building Blocks for Parallel Computing. In *Proceedings of Supercomputing '93*, November 1993.

9. Y. Tamir and H. C. Chi. Symmetric Crossbar Arbiters for VLSI Communication Switches. *IEEE Transactions on Parallel and Distributed Systems*, 4(1), January 1993.

10. Y. Tamir and G. L. Frazier. High-Performance Multi-Queue Buffers for VLSI Communication Switches. In *Proceedings of the 15th International Symposium on Computer Architecture*, 1988.

Springer-Verlag
and the Environment

We at Springer-Verlag firmly believe that an international science publisher has a special obligation to the environment, and our corporate policies consistently reflect this conviction.

We also expect our business partners – paper mills, printers, packaging manufacturers, etc. – to commit themselves to using environmentally friendly materials and production processes.

The paper in this book is made from low- or no-chlorine pulp and is acid free, in conformance with international standards for paper permanency.

Lecture Notes in Computer Science

For information about Vols. 1–774
please contact your bookseller or Springer-Verlag